THE CAMBRIDGE COMPANIC

THE SCOTTISH E1

D0583770

The Cambridge Companion to the Scottish Enlightenment offers a philosophical perspective on an eighteenth-century movement that has been profoundly influential on western culture. A distinguished team of contributors examines the writings of David Hume, Adam Smith, Thomas Reid, Adam Ferguson, Colin MacLaurin and other Scottish thinkers, in fields including philosophy, natural theology, economics, anthropology, natural science and law. In addition, the contributors relate the Scottish Enlightenment to its historical context and assess its impact and legacy in Europe, America and beyond. The result is a comprehensive and accessible volume that illuminates the richness, the intellectual variety and the underlying unity of this important movement. It will be of interest to a wide range of readers in philosophy, theology, literature and the history of ideas.

OTHER VOLUMES IN THE SERIES OF CAMBRIDGE COMPANIONS

AQUINAS   *Edited by* NORMAN KRETZMANN *and* ELEONORE STUMP

HANNAH ARENDT   *Edited by* DANA VILLA

ARISTOTLE   *Edited by* JONATHAN BARNES

AUGUSTINE   *Edited by* ELEONORE STUMP *and*
   NORMAN KRETZMANN

BACON   *Edited by* MARKKU PELTONEN

SIMONE DE BEAUVOIR   *Edited by* CLAUDIA CARD

DESCARTES   *Edited by* JOHN COTTINGHAM

EARLY GREEK PHILOSOPHY   *Edited by* A. A. LONG

FEMINISM IN PHILOSOPHY   *Edited by* MIRANDA FRICKER *and*
   JENNIFER HORNSBY

FOUCAULT   *Edited by* GARY GUTTING

FREGE   *Edited by* TOM RICKETTS

FREUD   *Edited by* JEROME NEU

GALILEO   *Edited by* PETER MACHAMER

GERMAN IDEALISM   *Edited by* KARL AMERIKS

HABERMAS   *Edited by* STEPHEN K. WHITE

HEGEL   *Edited by* FREDERICK BEISER

HEIDEGGER   *Edited by* CHARLES GUIGNON

HOBBES   *Edited by* TOM SORELL

HUME   *Edited by* DAVID FATE NORTON

HUSSERL   *Edited by* BARRY SMITH *and* DAVID WOODRUFF SMITH

WILLIAM JAMES   *Edited by* RUTH ANNA PUTNAM

KANT   *Edited by* PAUL GUYER

KIERKEGAARD   *Edited by* ALASTAIR HANNAY *and*
   GORDON MARINO

LEIBNIZ   *Edited by* NICHOLAS JOLLEY

LEVINAS   *Edited by* SIMON CRITCHLEY *and* ROBERT BERNASCONI

LOCKE   *Edited by* VERE CHAPPELL

MALEBRANCHE   *Edited by* STEVEN NADLER

MARX   *Edited by* TERRELL CARVER

MILL   *Edited by* JOHN SKORUPSKI

NEWTON   *Edited by* I. BERNARD COHEN *and*
   GEORGE E. SMITH

NIETZSCHE   *Edited by* BERND MAGNUS *and* KATHLEEN HIGGINS

OCKHAM   *Edited by* PAUL VINCENT SPADE

PLATO   *Edited by* RICHARD KRAUT

PLOTINUS   *Edited by* LLOYD P. GERSON

RAWLS   *Edited by* SAMUEL FREEMAN

ROUSSEAU   *Edited by* PATRICK RILEY

SARTRE   *Edited by* CHRISTINA HOWELLS

SCHOPENHAUER   *Edited by* CHRISTOPHER JANAWAY

THE SCOTTISH ENLIGHTENMENT   *Edited by*
   ALEXANDER BROADIE

SPINOZA   *Edited by* DON GARRETT

WITTGENSTEIN   *Edited by* HANS SLUGA *and* DAVID STERN

The Cambridge Companion to

THE SCOTTISH ENLIGHTENMENT

Edited by

Alexander Broadie
University of Glasgow

CAMBRIDGE
UNIVERSITY PRESS

PUBLISHED BY THE PRESS SYNDICATE OF THE UNIVERSITY OF CAMBRIDGE
The Pitt Building, Trumpington Street, Cambridge CB2 IRP,
United Kingdom

CAMBRIDGE UNIVERSITY PRESS
The Edinburgh Building, Cambridge, CB2 2RU, UK
40 West 20th Street, New York, NY 10011-4211, USA
477 Williamstown Road, Port Melbourne, VIC 3207, Australia
Ruiz de Alarcón 13, 28014 Madrid, Spain
Dock House, The Waterfront, Cape Town 8001, South Africa

http://www.cambridge.org

First published 2003
Reprinted 2005

Printed in the United Kingdom at the University Press, Cambridge

Typeface Trump Medieval 10/13 pt   *System* LATEX 2$_\varepsilon$ [TB]

A catalogue record for this book is available from the British Library

Library of Congress Cataloging in Publication data

The Cambridge companion to the Scottish Enlightenment / edited by
Alexander Broadie.
       p.   cm.   (Cambridge companions to philosophy)

Includes bibliographical references and index.
ISBN 0-521-80273-3   ISBN 0-521-00323-7 (pbk.)

1. Philosophy, Scottish – 18th century.   2. Enlightenment – Scotland.
3. Scotland – Intellectual life.   1. Broadie, Alexander   11. Series.
B 1402. E 55 C 36   2002
001′.09411′09033 – dc21   2002067261

ISBN 0 521 80273 3 hardback
ISBN 0 521 00323 7 paperback

CONTENTS

List of contributors   *page* vii

Acknowledgements   xi

Chronology of events relating to the Scottish Enlightenment   xii

Introduction
ALEXANDER BROADIE   I

1   The contexts of the Scottish Enlightenment
ROGER EMERSON   9

2   Religion and rational theology
M. A. STEWART   31

3   The human mind and its powers
ALEXANDER BROADIE   60

4   Anthropology: the 'original' of human nature
AARON GARRETT   79

5   Science in the Scottish Enlightenment
PAUL WOOD   94

6   Scepticism and common sense
HEINER F. KLEMME   117

7   Moral sense and the foundations of morals
LUIGI TURCO   136

8   The political theory of the Scottish Enlightenment
FANIA OZ-SALZBERGER   157

v

9   Economic theory
    ANDREW S. SKINNER   178

10 Natural jurisprudence and the theory of justice
    KNUD HAAKONSSEN   205

11 Legal theory
    JOHN W. CAIRNS   222

12 Sociality and socialisation
    CHRISTOPHER J. BERRY   243

13 Historiography
    MURRAY G. H. PITTOCK   258

14 Art and aesthetic theory
    ALEXANDER BROADIE   280

15 The impact on Europe
    MICHEL MALHERBE   298

16 The impact on America: Scottish philosophy and
    the American founding
    SAMUEL FLEISCHACKER   316

17 The nineteenth-century aftermath
    GORDON GRAHAM   338

    Select bibliography   351
    Index   359

CONTRIBUTORS

CHRISTOPHER J. BERRY is Professor of Political Theory at the University of Glasgow. He is the author of *Social Theory of the Scottish Enlightenment* (1997), *The Idea of Luxury: a Conceptual and Historical Investigation* (1994) and *Hume, Hegel and Human Nature* (1982). He has also published many articles on the Scottish Enlightenment, including a contribution to *The Cambridge Companion to Adam Smith* (forthcoming). He is currently working on a philosophical anthropology of politics with Hume as his vade mecum.

ALEXANDER BROADIE is Professor of Logic and Rhetoric at the University of Glasgow and a Fellow of the Royal Society of Edinburgh. He has published a dozen books, most of them in the field of Scottish philosophy, and is currently working on two further books, *Thomas Reid on Logic, Rhetoric and the Fine Arts* and *A History of Scottish Philosophy*, both to be published by Edinburgh University Press. He has contributed chapters to two forthcoming volumes, *The Cambridge Companion to Adam Smith* and *The Cambridge Companion to Thomas Reid*.

JOHN W. CAIRNS is Professor of Legal History at the University of Edinburgh. His main area of interest is the relationship between the legal profession, legal practice and legal theory in the eighteenth century. He is also particularly interested in natural law and slavery in that period. His publications include an edited volume on the history of the jury (2002) and another on the general history of Scots law (forthcoming).

ROGER EMERSON was until recently Professor of History at the University of Western Ontario. He is the author of *Professors, Patronage and Politics: the Aberdeen Universities in the Eighteenth Century* (1992) and of numerous articles on the Scottish Enlightenment. He is also an Associate Editor of the *Oxford Encyclopedia of the Enlightenment*, where his remit includes most of the articles dealing with Scotland.

SAMUEL FLEISCHACKER is Associate Professor of Philosophy at the University of Illinois in Chicago. He is the author of *Integrity and Moral Relativism* (1992), *The Ethics of Culture* (1994), *A Third Concept of Liberty: Judgment and Freedom in Kant and Adam Smith* (1999), and various articles on Kant, Smith and issues in moral and political philosophy. He is currently working on a philosophical companion to the *Wealth of Nations*.

AARON GARRETT is Assistant Professor of Philosophy at Boston University. He is the author of the chapter 'Human nature' in the forthcoming *Cambridge History of Eighteenth-Century Philosophy*, and, among other books, is editor of Francis Hutcheson's *Essay on the Nature and Conduct of the Passions* (2002). In addition to his work on the Scottish Enlightenment he has published on Spinoza, Locke, race and philosophy and the origins of animal rights.

GORDON GRAHAM is Regius Professor of Moral Philosophy at the University of Aberdeen, Convenor of The Reid Project, a major research initiative in Scottish philosophy, and a Fellow of the Royal Society of Edinburgh. He is the author of twelve books and over 60 papers, including essays, reviews and encyclopedia articles on eighteenth- and nineteenth-century Scottish philosophy.

KNUD HAAKONSSEN, Professor of Philosophy at Boston University, is General Editor of the Edinburgh Edition of Thomas Reid (Edinburgh University Press) and of *The Works and Correspondence of Francis Hutcheson* (Liberty Press). His books include *The Science of a Legislator: The Natural Jurisprudence of David Hume and Adam Smith* (1981) and *Natural Law and Moral Philosophy: from Grotius to the Scottish Enlightenment* (1996). He is editor of Thomas Reid's *Practical Ethics* (1990), of Adam Smith's *The Theory of Moral*

Sentiments (2002) and of *The Cambridge Companion to Adam Smith* (forthcoming).

HEINER F. KLEMME teaches philosophy at the Otto-von-Guericke-Universität Magdeburg. He is author of *Kants Philosophie des Subjekts* (1996), and editor of *Die Schule Immanuel Kants* (1994), *The Reception of the Scottish Enlightenment in Germany*, 7 vols. (2000), Kant's *Zum ewigen Frieden* (1992) and his *Kritik der Urteilskraft* (2001). He is co-editor of *Aufklärung und Interpretation* (1999), *The Reception of British Aesthetics in Germany*, 7 vols. (2001), and other works.

MICHEL MALHERBE, Emeritus Professor of Philosophy at the University of Nantes, is the author of *La philosophie empiriste de David Hume*, 2nd edn (1984), and has published a French translation of Hume's *Dialogues concerning Natural Religion* (1987). His many articles on eighteenth-century Scottish philosophy include 'Reid et la possibilité d'une philosophie du sens commun' and 'Hume and the art of dialogue'.

FANIA OZ-SALZBERGER is Senior Lecturer in History at the University of Haifa and council member of the Israel Democracy Institute. She was a Fellow of Wolfson College, Oxford, and of the Wissenschaftskolleg zu Berlin. Her publications include *Translating the Enlightenment: Scottish Civic Discourse in Eighteenth-Century Germany* (1995), an edition of Adam Ferguson's *Essay on the History of Civil Society* (1995), and articles on the European Enlightenment.

MURRAY PITTOCK is Professor in Literature at the University of Strathclyde and President of the Scottish Committee of Professors of English. A Fellow of the English Association and of the Royal Historical Society, he has published widely on historiography and the construction of history in books such as *The Myth of the Jacobite Clans* (1995) and *Inventing and Resisting Britain* (1997).

ANDREW SKINNER is Adam Smith Emeritus Professor of Economics at the University of Glasgow. He is a Fellow both of the British Academy and of the Royal Society of Edinburgh. Among many publications he has produced an edition of Sir James Steuart's *Principles of Political Oeconomy* (1966) and co-edited Adam Smith's *The Wealth of Nations* (1976). He has also published *A System of Social Science: Papers Relating to Adam Smith*, 2nd edn (1996).

M. A. STEWART is Honorary Research Professor in the History of Philosophy at the Universities of Lancaster and Aberdeen, and is Senior Research Fellow of Harris Manchester College, Oxford. He edited *Studies in the Philosophy of the Scottish Enlightenment* (1990), co-edited *Hume and Hume's Connexions* (1994), and has published also on Locke and on philosophy in the dissenting tradition.

LUIGI TURCO is Professor of the History of Philosophy at the University of Bologna. His research has mainly focused on the Scottish Enlightenment. He has published an annotated Italian translation of Hutcheson's *On the Nature and Conduct of the Passions*, and is author of *Dal sistema al senso comune: studi sul newtonismo e gli illuministi britannici* (1974) and *Lo scetticismo morale di David Hume* (1984).

PAUL WOOD is a member of the Department of History and Director of the Humanities Centre at the University of Victoria, British Columbia. He has written widely on the universities and on the natural and human sciences in the Scottish Enlightenment. His books include *The Aberdeen Enlightenment: the Arts Curriculum in the Eighteenth Century* (1993), and two edited volumes, *Reid on the Animate Creation* (1995) and *The Correspondence of Thomas Reid* (forthcoming), both in the Edinburgh Edition of Thomas Reid. He is currently working on a biography of Reid for Edinburgh University Press.

ACKNOWLEDGEMENTS

This is a wide-ranging *Companion* and my search for advice has been correspondingly wide ranging. Knud Haakonssen, M. A. Stewart and Paul Wood provided inestimable advice and I thank them warmly.

I am also deeply indebted to Patricia S. Martin for her unstinting help with the preparation of the typescript.

Hilary Gaskin, as philosophy editor at Cambridge University Press, has been involved in the project from its inception, and throughout has provided invaluable guidance. I am grateful to her.

Alexander Broadie
Glasgow

CHRONOLOGY OF EVENTS RELATING TO THE SCOTTISH ENLIGHTENMENT

1681	Viscount Stair's *The Institutions of the Laws of Scotland* (rev. edn 1691)
	Royal College of Physicians chartered by Charles II
1684–1758	Allan Ramsay (poet)
1685–9	Reign of James VII and II
1687	Sir Isaac Newton's *Mathematical Principles of Natural Philosophy* (the *Principia*)
1689	William and Mary ascended the throne
1689	Advocates' Library opened
1690	John Locke's *Essay Concerning Human Understanding*
1694–1746	Francis Hutcheson
1695–1768	John Erskine of Carnock
1696–1782	Henry Home, raised to the Bench as Lord Kames in 1752
1698–1746	Colin MacLaurin
1698–1748	George Turnbull
1702–14	Reign of Queen Anne
1704	Death of John Locke
	Sir Isaac Newton's *Opticks*
1707	Treaty of Union of England and Scotland
1710–96	Thomas Reid
1710	Bishop Berkeley's *Principles of Human Knowledge*
	Hutcheson matriculated at Glasgow
1710–90	William Cullen
1711–76	David Hume
1711	Lord Shaftesbury's *Characteristicks of Men, Manners, Opinions, Times*

	First year of Joseph Addison and Richard Steel's *Spectator*
1713–84	Allan Ramsay (painter)
1713–80	Sir James Steuart
1714–27	Reign of George I
1714	Bernard Mandeville's *Fable of the Bees*
1715	Jacobite Rising
1718	Carmichael's commentary on Pufendorf's *De officio hominis et civis*
1718–1800	Hugh Blair
1719–96	George Campbell
1721–93	William Robertson
1721–71	Tobias Smollett
1722	Reid enters Marischal College, Aberdeen
1723–90	Adam Smith
1723–1816	Adam Ferguson
1723	Hume enters Edinburgh University
1725	Hutcheson's *An Inquiry into the Original of our Ideas of Beauty and Virtue*
	MacLaurin elected Professor of Mathematics at Edinburgh
1725–6	Hutcheson's *Reflections upon Laughter* and *Remarks upon the Fable of the Bees*
1726–97	James Hutton
1728	Hutcheson's *Essay on the Nature and Conduct of the Passions, with Illustrations on the Moral Sense*
1729	Death of Gershom Carmichael, Professor of Moral Philosophy at Glasgow
	Hutcheson appointed Professor at Glasgow, becoming Professor of Moral Philosophy at Glasgow in 1730
1728–99	Joseph Black
1735–1801	John Millar
1736–1819	James Watt
1736/8–96	James Macpherson
1737	Foundation of Philosophical Society of Edinburgh
1739–40	Hume's *A Treatise of Human Nature*
1739–1805	John Robison

1740   George Turnbull's *Treatise on Ancient Painting* and
              Principles of Moral and Christian Philosophy
1740–95   William Smellie
1740–95   James Boswell
1743–86   Gilbert Stuart
1745–46   Jacobite Rising under Charles Edward Stuart
1747   William Cullen appointed Professor of Chemistry at
              Glasgow
1748   Hume's *Philosophical Essays Concerning Human
              Understanding* (later titled *An Enquiry Concerning
              Human Understanding*)
              Colin MacLaurin's *Account of Sir Isaac Newton's
              Philosophical Discoveries*
              Reid's 'Essay on quantity' in *Philosophical
              Transactions of the Royal Society of London*
              Charles-Louis Montesquieu's *L'Esprit des Lois*
1749   First volume of comte de Buffon's *Histoire Naturelle*
1750–74   Robert Fergusson
1751   Adam Smith appointed Professor of Logic and
              Rhetoric at Glasgow, becoming Professor of Moral
              Philosophy at Glasgow in 1752
              Reid appointed regent at King's College, Aberdeen
              Hume's *An Enquiry Concerning the Principles of
              Morals*
1752–7   Hume Keeper of the Advocates' Library, Edinburgh
1752   Foundation of Glasgow Literary Society
1753–1828   Dugald Stewart
1754–62   Hume's *History of England*
1754–1835   Sir John Sinclair
1754   Foundation of Select Society
1755   Hutcheson's *A System of Moral Philosophy*
1757   Hume's *The Natural History of Religion*
1758   Founding of the Aberdeen Philosophical Society, the
              'Wise Club'
1759   Adam Smith's *The Theory of Moral Sentiments*
              William Robertson's *History of Scotland*
1759–96   Robert Burns

1761	John Millar appointed Professor of Civil Law at Glasgow
	Jean-Jacques Rousseau's *Du Contrat social*
1762	George Campbell's *Dissertation on Miracles*
	Hugh Blair appointed first Regius Professor of Rhetoric and Belles Lettres at Edinburgh
1764	Thomas Reid's *Inquiry into the Human Mind on the Principles of Common Sense*
	Reid appointed Professor of Moral Philosophy at Glasgow
	Adam Ferguson appointed Professor of Pneumatics and Moral Philosophy at Edinburgh
1767	Adam Ferguson's *An Essay on the History of Civil Society*
	Sir James Steuart's *Principles of Political Oeconomy*
1768–71	First edition of *Encyclopaedia Britannica*, edited by William Smellie
1771	John Millar's *The Origin of the Distinction of Ranks* (republished with extensive revision in 1779)
1771–1832	Sir Walter Scott
1773	*An Institute of the Law of Scotland* by John Erskine of Carnock
1774	Lord Kames's *Sketches of the History of Man*
1776	Adam Smith's *The Wealth of Nations*
	George Campbell's *Philosophy of Rhetoric*
	American Declaration of Independence
1779	Hume's *Dialogues Concerning Natural Religion*
1780	James Dunbar's *Essays on the History of Mankind*
1781	Immanuel Kant's *Critique of Pure Reason*
1783	Founding of The Royal Society of Edinburgh
1785	Reid's *Essays on the Intellectual Powers of Man*
	Dugald Stewart appointed Professor of Moral Philosophy at Edinburgh
1787	The 'Kilmarnock' edition of Robert Burns
1788	Reid's *Essays on the Active Powers of the Human Mind*
	Immanuel Kant's *Critique of Practical Reason*

1789   French Revolution
1790   William Smellie's *Philosophy of Natural History,*
            vol. 1; vol. 2, 1799
1791–99   John Sinclair's *Statistical Account of Scotland*
1792   Adam Ferguson's *Principles of Moral and Political*
            Science
1795   James Hutton's *Theory of the Earth with Proofs and*
            Illustrations
            Adam Smith's *Essays on Philosophical Subjects*

Introduction

The Scottish Enlightenment, a remarkable intellectual flourish that lasted for much of the eighteenth century, was an event of great importance for western culture. During it scientific, economic, philosophical and other advances were made which had an immediate impact in Europe, America and beyond, and the impact is still felt. The seminal writings of the time are discussed by scholars who return to them in search of insights that can then be put to work in ongoing debates. Hence, though there is an antiquarian interest in the Scottish Enlightenment, interest in it is by no means solely antiquarian, as witness the numerous references we find to Hume, Smith, Reid and other Enlightenment thinkers in present-day discussions of contemporary issues. In this book the historical circumstances of the Scottish Enlightenment will be described; and thereafter attention is focused on the leading ideas, without however losing sight of the fact that the Scottish Enlightenment is a historical event located in a set of historical circumstances that were essential to the movement's birth and growth. Attention is also focused on the highly social nature of the movement. The writers were held together by bonds of friendship; they argued and debated with each other, and created many clubs and societies designed to facilitate discussion. This aspect of the Scottish Enlightenment is a crucial feature of it, and will be duly noted in the following pages. But these historical and social considerations would hardly hold our attention if it were not for the brilliant ideas that were the products of all this high-level clubbing. In the end, it is because of what they said, not because of whom they talked to, that Hume, Smith, Millar, Black, Hutton and others matter to us. And since the Scottish Enlightenment is essentially about ideas this book is in large measure an investigation of those ideas.

The authors in question are numerous. Among the leading protagonists of the Scottish Enlightenment were Francis Hutcheson, David Hume, Adam Smith, Thomas Reid, Henry Home (Lord Kames), Dugald Stewart, Adam Ferguson, John Millar, William Robertson, Hugh Blair, Colin Maclaurin, James Watt, Joseph Black and James Hutton. Among the fields to which major contributions were made are philosophy, natural theology, economics, social science, law, historiography, linguistics, mathematics, chemistry, engineering and geology. Although this might seem a very disparate set of fields, within the Scottish Enlightenment the unity of the set was emphasised, and the principle of unity was itself a matter of philosophical discussion. In this volume the range of fields is on display, and attention is also given to the unity of the overall movement.

Nevertheless the very existence of the Scottish Enlightenment has been questioned, and even among those who do not question its reality there has been considerable dispute about its nature. Its existence has been disputed on the grounds that the Enlightenment was an international movement with a distinctly international character, and that in the countries which participated in the movement the Enlightenment did not take on a national character, from which it would follow that though Scots participated they did not do so in such a way as to produce a distinctly Scottish Enlightenment. Nevertheless, the Enlightenment in Scotland was distinctively Scottish, and this is surely to be expected if the matter is considered in terms of the large structures that define us. A Scot writing on politics, economics, social structures, education, law or religion will think in terms of the politics, economics, society, education, law or religious dimension of his country, and it is impossible for his thought not to be affected by these distinctive features of his national context. The point is not that the Scottish models contribute irresistibly to the agenda from which Scottish thinkers work, though those models surely will be on their agenda. It is rather that the thinkers write as Scots, who have therefore lived in, worked with, and in large measure been formed by those institutions. Since there is demonstrably something distinctively Scottish about the large institutions – the Kirk, the legal system and the universities – which inform the experience that supports and motivates the thinkers' reflections, there will also be something distinctively Scottish about those reflections upon the concepts which the institutions embody, and upon the values of the institutions. The Scottish dimension of the reflections is particularly to be expected in view of the fact that most of the major figures of the Scottish Enlightenment were leading actors within the great institutions – they were professors, lawyers or preachers, and so were naturally likely to reflect deeply on the institutions they were helping by their activities to sustain.

The answer to the second of the two questions mentioned earlier, that concerning the nature of the Scottish Enlightenment, is of practical importance for this book. For of course the answer must affect the contents, both as regards which fields are to be included and as regards the relative weight that should be assigned to each of them. Something must therefore be said about this matter. The term 'Scottish Enlightenment' was coined in 1900 by William Robert Scott, who spoke of Francis Hutcheson as 'the prototype of the Scottish Enlightenment, that is, the diffusion of philosophic ideas in Scotland and the encouragement of speculative tastes among the men of culture of the generation following his own'.[1] But though Scott's coinage is in common use his account of it has been supplanted. Among the many alternative accounts three in particular have real strength. They may, perhaps tendentiously, be labelled the political economic, the scientific and the inclusive. This ordering is due to the order in which the classic statement of each position was first put into the public domain. The earliest of these was by Hugh Trevor-Roper (Lord Dacre), who defined the Scottish Enlightenment in terms of 'the social mechanism of progress', and subsequently, and apparently without changing his position, defined it in terms of the development of the discipline of political economy.[2] In this he has been followed by John Robertson, who has however taken the analysis further, arguing that the three central disciplines of the Scottish Enlightenment are moral philosophy, historiography and political economy, and that the most important of these for the Scottish Enlightenment's grand project of the analysis and advocacy of progress in society is political economy.[3] In this book several of the chapters, most conspicuously those by Luigi Turco, Murray Pittock and Andrew Skinner, focus upon the fields that Trevor-Roper and John Robertson have identified as central, while other chapters, by Christopher Berry, Aaron Garrett and Fania Oz-Salzberger, have focused on social scientific fields closely cognate with those high-lighted by Trevor-Roper and Robertson.

But there is reason to pause before assenting to the view of Trevor-Roper and Robertson. For if what is truly important about the analysis and advocacy of progress in society is that such activities might actually lead to such progress, then it is arguable that science is crucially important to the Scottish Enlightenment, perhaps more important than were moral philosophy, historiography and political economy. It is not merely that the hugely successful scientific enterprise of the Scottish Enlightenment, led by thinkers and doers such as William Cullen, James Watt and Joseph Black, was driven by the perceived need to better the material conditions of the country (which at the beginning of the eighteenth century were in desperate need of improvement), but that scientific ways of thinking – the deployment of scientific methodology and scientific concepts and categories – were at work across the whole range of intellectual disciplines. Science was even deployed, on all sides, in debates on the existence and nature of God. This view concerning the scientific nature of the Scottish Enlightenment is represented in this book in several chapters, especially those by Roger Emerson and Paul Wood, while other chapters, such as those by M. A. Stewart and A. Broadie, emphasise the centrality of science in debates in seemingly non-scientific fields.

These two positions, privileging in the first case the social sciences and in the second case the natural sciences (such as physics, chemistry, medicine and botany), seem mutually incompatible though each is supported by substantive arguments. A third way, seeking to rescue the valuable insights of each position, has been developed. It seeks inclusivity by focusing on the culture of the enlightened ones of Scotland, the so-called 'literati', those 'Scottish men of letters who placed a high premium on polite learning as well as on humane and humanitarian values, such as cosmopolitanism, religious toleration, sociable conviviality, and moral and economic improvement'.[4] Richard Sher, who formulated this cultural definition,[5] sees as one of its chief virtues the fact that it accommodates the insight that science and medicine were activities integral to the Scottish Enlightenment, while at the same time not privileging those activities at the expense of the no less integral investigations into ethics, history and political economy.

I have reported these three hard-defended positions not in order to adjudicate, but because it is necessary to justify the range of topics covered in this book. I have chosen to be inclusive because one feature of the debates conducted in eighteenth-century Scotland is the fact that they were conducted by thinkers who were, each of them, able to draw on a wide range of disciplines and who did in fact use their wide-ranging knowledge in the course of developing their positions, and attacking alternatives. For example, philosophers working on questions regarding both the means by which we come to form beliefs and also the reliability of powers through which we acquire beliefs, commonly deployed ideas concerning scientific methodology, concepts in physics and even advanced mathematics. (Heiner Klemme's chapter gives some examples of this.) This illustrates the fact that although it is of course possible to distinguish different disciplines or fields investigated during the Scottish Enlightenment, no attempt was made in practice to keep the separate disciplines in their separate boxes. A holistic approach to intellectual problems was characteristic of the literati, and I believe that an account of the Scottish Enlightenment should take due account of the formidably wide range of intellectual disciplines which were enriched by the Scottish thinkers of the eighteenth century.

It is noteworthy that most of the leading contributors to the Scottish Enlightenment lived in the three university cities of Glasgow, Edinburgh and Aberdeen, cities in which there was also a rich extra-academic life, thus giving the professors opportunities, grasped with enthusiasm, to exchange ideas with lively minded people who, as agents and not just as spectators, had well-informed insights into people and institutions. As one instance of this we might note Adam Smith, moral philosophy professor at Glasgow, who engaged often with the local merchants then trading across the world, and especially with America. Smith's *Wealth of Nations* was a product of many things, amongst which was Smith's close contact with the merchant class of Glasgow. Contact between town and gown was facilitated by the numerous societies and clubs, such as the Wise Club in Aberdeen, the Literary Society in Glasgow and the Select Society in Edinburgh.

Eighteenth-century Scotland was wide open to ideas from elsewhere. The Enlightenment was a Republic of Letters, a multinational company dealing in ideas, in which people put their ideas into the public domain to be criticised and improved, or criticised and sunk. Within this market place Scotland contributed a great deal, and was also the beneficiary of ideas which it then took up and tranformed into something appropriate to the Scottish context, as happened, for example, in the case of Scots who took up ideas of Grotius and Pufendorf, and developed those same ideas in characteristic ways. Chapters hereafter by Knud Haakonssen and John Cairns make clear Scottish indebtedness in this area, as does Andrew Skinner's chapter in dealing with Adam Smith's relation to French thinkers, particularly the physiocrats. Scottish openness to ideas from elsewhere can be illustrated across the board, as can the Scottish contribution to debates in the international Republic of Letters – thus we find that David Hume and Adam Smith were two of the most influential members of the wider Enlightenment movement.

The diffusion of the Scottish Enlightenment is an important topic both because it indicates the importance of the movement for western culture and also because it enables us to explain the direction of progress in the many countries that were beneficiaries of this Scottish invisible export. The Scottish Enlightenment might be considered Scotland's chief export to America. From the early mid-eighteenth century, Scots educated by Francis Hutcheson, Thomas Reid and others voyaged to North America where they taught in and helped to run colleges which in due course became great universities. The students of these immigrants, as Samuel Fleischacker demonstrates in chapter sixteen, thus came to receive an education in the leading ideas of the major Scottish thinkers of the period, and the 'Scottish philosophy' became widely diffused through the American education system. And in Continental Europe the influence of the Scottish thinkers, especially those of the common sense school, was no less great, as Michel Malherbe shows.

There is disagreement on the question when the Scottish Enlightenment ended, but most answers place its conclusion in the late eighteenth or early nineteenth century. Nevertheless the Scottish school of common sense philosophy flourished at least into the middle of the nineteenth century. Thereafter what happened is not so easily stated, largely because the philosophical scene in Scotland in the nineteenth century has hardly been documented. In the final chapter Gordon Graham traces the nineteenth-century story in terms of what he sees as the unravelling of the great philosophical project that had animated the eighteenth century.

While philosophy is only one of the many fields discussed in this book, philosophy had a central place in the Scottish Enlightenment, informing debates in all areas, and its centrality is properly represented here in the fact that the perspective of the book is throughout a philosophical perspective broadly conceived.

NOTES

1 William Robert Scott, *Francis Hutcheson: his Life, Teaching and Position in the History of Philosophy* (Cambridge: Cambridge University Press, 1900), 265.

2 H. Trevor-Roper, 'The Scottish Enlightenment', *Studies on Voltaire and the Eighteenth Century* 58 (1967), 1635–58; Trevor-Roper, 'The Scottish Enlightenment', *Blackwood's Magazine* 322 (1977), 371–88.

3 John Robertson, 'The Scottish Contribution to the Enlightenment', in Paul Wood, ed., *The Scottish Enlightenment: Essays in Reinterpretation* (Rochester: Rochester University Press, 2000), 37–62.

4 Richard B. Sher, 'Science and Medicine in the Scottish Enlightenment', in Wood, *Scottish Enlightenment*, 104.

5 Ibid., 99–156; also Sher, *Church and University in the Scottish Enlightenment: the Moderate Literati of Edinburgh* (Edinburgh: Edinburgh University Press, 1985), 3–14, for an early implicit statement of the position.

1 The contexts of the Scottish Enlightenment

I

There is no single context for the Scottish Enlightenment but there are several which were important. Let us start with the most basic, Scotland's geography, which made Scots poor but which also endowed them with the means of improvement and posed questions which the enlightened studied and sought to answer.

Of Scotland's 30,000 square miles less than 10 per cent was arable land in the eighteenth century. Somewhat more was comprised of grazing land of varying quality (more or less 13 per cent) and perhaps 3 per cent made up forest which was cuttable; perhaps a bit more was usable in some fashion.[1] The possible uses of this land were determined by altitude, by the kinds of soils, and by the micro-climates, of which Scotland has many.[2] Scotland was and would remain a poor country. Agricultural improvement, to produce both more food and the materials for industries (such as wool), was a concern which was recognised in the seventeenth century and grew in importance throughout the eighteenth century.

Physical geography informed the country's prospects in other ways. Scotland has long coastlines and Scots were an ocean-going people, but the river systems they possessed were not as useful for inland navigation as were those in England or France because of the short distances to the fall lines. Scottish waterfalls might power industry along the Water of Leith near Edinburgh and at New Lanark, but they did not generally become the sources for power in the early industrial revolution since the fall lines were often not located near enough to raw materials or to population centres. The solution to these problems for the Scots was the steam engine, coal and better transport, but these developments had to wait until the first quarter of the nineteenth century. Fully exploited, they would largely benefit people in the middle of the country, those in or near Glasgow and Edinburgh. While not determining Scottish prospects, geography limited improvements while focusing attention upon what Scots needed to know to best utilise and improve their resources for agriculture and industry. Scots became chemists in order that they might find better fertilisers, bleaches and dyes for their fabrics, and geologists as they sought to find their mineral wealth. At the same time, they had to consider the social and political-economic changes required for improvements.

The land and the resource base limited the population which the country could carry. Despite emigration, the population rose from about 1,100,000 in 1700 to 1,625,000 in 1801 (c. 50 per cent).[3] People were distributed around the edges of the country, along the river valleys and in low-lying fertile regions where the best lands lay. In 1700, somewhat over a third lived in the Highlands and Islands. By 1800 the percentage was much less. By 1765, although many Highlanders were still monolingual in Gaelic, about 75 per cent of the whole population spoke a Scots of some description.[4] Perhaps 50 per cent lived in the central part of the country with the rest in the Borders and outlying areas. Scotland was a culturally diverse land because of its geography.

The land carried more people in the eighteenth century than it had before partly because of declining standards of consumption, but also owing to increased efficiency in land use and to changes in the structure of markets.[5] Still, there was a precarious balance; Malthusian thinning occurred in the 1690s, perhaps in 1740 and was threatened in the 1780s. Demographic pressures on resources can be lessened by finding more resources, by using what exists more efficiently or with new technologies or by lowering the level of population. All four strategies characterised the Enlightenment period.

Scots had long moved around within their country and had travelled abroad to seek work, often as mercenary soldiers. Such migrants, all over Europe, usually came from the poorest areas – in Scotland, the Highlands and Borders. Skilled migrants tended to come from Lowland areas and from the towns, of which Scotland had a relatively large number.[6] Indeed, it was surprisingly urbanised[7] and the proportion of city dwellers grew rapidly in the eighteenth century. Moreover, within its burghs there were perhaps more schools than most Europeans enjoyed.[8] Scottish interest in education, particularly vocational education, rested on the fact that people, particularly men, had to leave to make a living. During the eighteenth century, 3,500 to 6,000 trained Scottish medical men left the country.[9] They were not the only educated men to do so. For the lower orders after 1707, the Empire provided opportunities in the army, navy and colonies. The export of people somewhat curbed population growth.

Scots had recognised by the 1680s that if the country were to prosper, men would need to be trained, the economy improved and science brought to bear on problems. Much of what the enlightened did only continued the plans and improvement schemes of men like Sir Robert Sibbald and his friends.[10] To reclaim land, find new mineral deposits, develop industries and new markets, to open fisheries and to increase trade were objectives not only of the late seventeenth century but throughout the Enlightenment. The enlightened continued to respond to constant underlying problems and sought the social changes which would allow meliorative changes.

II

Scotland had a complex religious-political-economic context which changed markedly between c. 1680 and 1800.

Scots were forced by worsening conditions towards the end of the seventeenth century to discuss the long list of causes for them.[11] Partly owing to wars, trade had been in a long decline.[12] Scotland was ceasing to be a viable state able to pay for its independence. Indeed, it could not be really independent while it was united to England through a common monarch. Religious tensions in the country were unresolved. In the 1690s all these problems were compounded by several years of famine and the costly failure of the effort to establish a Scots colony at Darien.

Between about 1690 and the Union of 1707, Scots discussed intensely their future as a nation. They debated the conditions under which economic growth might take place and considered both mercantilist and freer-trade solutions. The role of banks and the state in this process was canvassed. What was needed was more investment, more efficient industries[13] and larger markets. It was clear to many by 1707 that the solution to Scottish economic woes was closer union with England and access to the English and imperial markets in which Scots were already successful interlopers.[14] Economics and politics went together, as they continued to do in the works of eighteenth-century Scottish social thinkers and political economists. The social theory of the Scottish Enlightenment was not just a set of ideas and practices principally imported from the south or from Holland and France; it had native roots in the country's problems and in the analyses and solutions proposed to deal with them by William Paterson, Sir Robert Sibbald, Andrew Fletcher of Saltoun and others. These would-be reformers, improvers and intellectuals were among those who began the processes of enlightenment, and there are clear links between their discussions and later writings and actions. The various schemes for a Council of Trade which John Law and others set out for Scotland between about 1690–1707 resonate still in the promotion by one of Law's sponsors, the 3rd Duke of Argyll, of the Board of Trustees for Arts, Fisheries and Manufactures, established in 1727, and in Argyll's banking schemes of 1728 and 1743. It is equally clear that this early literature was known to Hume and helped to shape his economic thought.[15]

If economic matters were one part of the political context, another concerned Scotland's relations with the English. What was needed was the settlement of long-standing political problems centring on power: who was to be king? What powers should he have? How should the state be constituted and run? What would, could, or should be Scotland's relation to England? Issues about the governance of Scotland were set out in a protracted debate involving the rights of the crown and of the estates in Parliament. Inseparable from these issues were questions about Scottish independence and about possible conditions of union with England. Scots explored many of the republican and civic humanist ideas held by men like Andrew Fletcher of Saltoun.[16] They also thought about the nature of their Highland and Lowland societies, of their state and its history, which seemed so different from that of the English. Freedom and its meaning, the sources of change, the limits which should be placed on power, the ways in which climate and manners created or influenced institutions, how those interacted – these were all themes which had been noticed by Scots between the appearance of Lord Stair's *Institutions of the Laws of Scotland* (1681) and the efforts to prepare a well-researched narrative history of Scotland on which Sibbald's friends laboured in the early decades of the eighteenth century. These discussions, like the activities they provoked, reflected the pride which Scots felt in their past and the shame with which they regarded their present. Shamed by their apparent backwardness, but patriotically resolved to improve their circumstances in every way, Scots intellectuals, entrepreneurs and some politicians resolved to better conditions in their country. Their concerns led to the incorporating Union with England in 1707 and later to social theories and theoretical histories.

The first step to the permanent resolution of these problems came with the less than glorious revolution of 1689. This ended the reign of James VII, brought William and Mary to the throne and settled the succession in Scotland, England and Ireland. However, 1689 also brought conflict and produced an exchange of exiles as Jacobites[17] went often to the places from which triumphant Whigs returned. Union with England finally came in 1707, when it was entered into largely for economic advantages which were not forthcoming until after about 1725.[18] But this was not the end of the story.

Attempts were made to end the Union in 1712; other discontents fuelled the rebellions of 1715 and 1745. Politically, Jacobitism remained significant for another generation.[19] Religious and anti-union feelings, economic and political discontents coalesced around loyalty to the former ruling family. This partly reflected the differences between Highland and Lowland societies, but repressed Scottish Episcopalians everywhere held the Hanoverian regime and its established church to be illegitimate. Those feelings were shared by many who did not take up arms. Such sentiments also impelled men to consider over a long period the profound differences between the society of the Gaelic-speaking Highlanders, which seemed to outsiders archaic and disorderly, and that of their Lowland cousins, which seemed much more modern and polite. After 1745 moves were made to solve the Highland problem by ousting many of its leading families from their land and repressing the outward signs of clanship. This was to go hand in hand with the introduction of new industries and better agriculture, of towns and fishing ports, and of more soldiers to police the area. These policies largely failed, but they set off changes leading in time to the Highland clearances, the last great forced enclosure movement in Britain.[20] The consequences for the Scottish Enlightenment were much theorising about society, social change and the nature of freedom.

The Union was an ongoing problem to the enlightened, who attempted to remain Scottish while assimilating aspects of English culture. For politicians, like the 3rd Duke of Argyll, this meant keeping as much of the old Scotland as one could, keeping Englishmen out of Scottish offices, and making the most of opportunities in Britain and the Empire. The melding of English administrative procedures in the collection of taxes and the management of affairs with Scottish ways, institutions and laws was never easy and was not fully accomplished until the time of Henry Dundas, who was nationally prominent by 1778. For others in the political classes, the Union entailed equality with the English when it came to opportunities and matters of honour, such as the acquisition of a militia to protect a country left relatively defenceless at the time of the Seven Years War. Scots never wanted to give up their Scottishness and were sensitive to English slights. They remained defensive about their society's accomplishments even while they tried to speak a more correct English and write Addisonian prose.[21] The enlightened felt these tensions and expressed their hopes by calling themselves 'North Britons'.

The Union also had religious consequences for Scots. The Kirk had been restored to the Presbyterians in 1690, but after 1707 it was clear that it could not continue its persecuting ways: Thomas Aikenhead, who was hanged for blasphemy in 1697, was the last to be so treated. By 1712, toleration of Episcopalians and others had been forced on Scots by English Tories and patronage rights had been returned to the gentry and the Crown. In the long run this made for a more docile church, but also one in which the men appointed to Church livings would become more moderate and enlightened in outlook as they came to resemble their patrons more than their pious parishioners. These clerics differed from those of an earlier ideal. By about 1730 the Kirk had begun to change, partly because Argathelian politicians[22] had saved the Glasgow Professor of Divinity, John Simson, from the efforts of evangelicals to discipline him for teaching his students that God was not only just but also loving, and for encouraging them to think for themselves. After the Simson case, the evangelicals were in retreat and would not be able to control the teaching of theology anywhere.[23] When the Moderate Party triumphed in the mid-1750s the Established Church, under the administration of men like Edinburgh University's Principal William Robertson, could and did become an agency for enlightened change, sponsoring Highland surveys and, in 1779, even toleration of Catholics. The costs were continual dissension in the Kirk and the draining away from it of the very orthodox and rigid who joined splinter groups which had begun to form in the late 1720s and 1730s.

After the Union, Scots were not forced to think of themselves as a subject people. Their laws, universities and Kirk, like their manners and customs, remained different. However, by the 1730s, men like Henry Home, later Lord Kames, were hoping for a convergence of Scottish law and institutions with those of the English. Manners changed as more and younger men decided they wished to be North Britons. English standards of farming and of living were now what many Scots sought to emulate. Even the divinity taught at Glasgow, Edinburgh, Aberdeen and St Andrews, between c. 1710 and 1760, approached the liberal standards of the English Latitudinarians and Dutch Arminians from whom it was sometimes borrowed. The Union mattered very much; few enlightened Scots ever condemned it.

III

Power and control in Scotland were exercised through patronage as much as through the formal mechanisms of the state or church. Scotland's patrons, its political class, were familiar with conditions in eighteenth-century Europe, where patronage formed an important context for Enlightenment. Everywhere patronage worked to give local élites much more power than highly centralised states wanted them to have, or would allow them when power could be gathered to a centre kept in touch with its regions through better communications and a more efficient use of force. One result of this was that the political regime imposed on Scots, particularly by Robert Walpole and the 3rd Duke of Argyll after about 1723, was one in which Scots were left largely to rule themselves – but with English supervision.[24]

Patrons were few in number because Scotland was governed by a very small class of landowners and merchants – perhaps 1,300 in 1700 and no more than double that number in 1800. This meant that when changes were perceived as good by those groups, they could come rapidly. Great men would be followed by those in their queues, which were long. Tenants and dependents were forced to accept the wishes of their patrons. Without the endorsement and sanction of patrons, little happened. The men who counted most between about 1690–1710 included Sibbald's many friends and patrons – members of the Hamilton family, the Duke of Roxburghe, the Marquises of Tweeddale, Atholl and Montrose, the Earl Marischal and Earl of Cromarty, lesser landlords and politicians and professional men like himself.[25] By the early 1700s, the names of John and Archibald Campbell, successively the 2nd and 3rd Dukes of Argyll, have to be added to this list. Archibald was particularly important because of his personal interests.

The 3rd Duke, Lord Islay until 1743, was a book collector and omnivorous reader, a competent amateur scientist, an improver and banker, a botanist and gardener and a moderate, tolerant and secular-minded lawyer who had little use for evangelicals in the Church. Handling first the political interests of his family and then those of the Walpolean government in Scotland, he was, with the exception of a period of about four years, the chief patron of the country from about 1723 until his death in 1761.[26] He filled Scottish institutions not only with his own nominees but with men of whom he approved, men who, as time went on, became increasingly like himself. Among those whom he and his friends helped to offices were law lords like the younger Andrew Fletcher of Saltoun, Charles Erskine and Henry Home; men of letters such as Francis Hutcheson and Adam Smith; clerics like William Wishart II, William Robertson, John Home, Adam Ferguson, William Wilkie and George Campbell; and medical men, like the founders of the Edinburgh medical school and such successors as William Cullen and Joseph Black.[27] Argyll also patronised artists like William Adam and Allan Ramsay, senior and junior, and scientists and businessmen like Alexander Wilson and James Hutton. If anyone was the father of the Scottish Enlightenment, the 3rd Duke of Argyll deserves the title, because he did more than any other person to open careers to men of talent who then institutionalised enlightened ideas.

When Argyll died, he was followed by his nephew the 3rd Earl of Bute,[28] a man of the same kidney, and he in turn was followed by a collection of men of liberal views and scientific interests. By 1778, patronage power had fallen into the hands of the political machine of Henry Dundas, who could himself be enlightened when he found it in his interest.[29] His close friends edited the influential periodicals *The Mirror* (1779) and *The Lounger* (1785). The success of the enlightened in Scotland derives, then, from their sponsorship by men who shared many of their views and had the power to impose their values and ideas on an often reluctant society.

IV

The wider world and its Republic of Letters provided another context for the Scottish Enlightenment. The traumatic crises of the late seventeenth century seemed to men in the Republic to be both complex and requiring action, whether they experienced these in Bordeaux, Edinburgh or elsewhere. What was needed were new methods and a determination to change. Such men, whether in London, Amsterdam, Paris or Oxford, helped to set the agenda for enlightened Scots. They wanted to survey and improve their countries. They saw renovated educational systems and the application of the sciences as keys to progress and change. They believed that a nation's past was worthy of study and presentation in modern narratives resting on critically researched sources. They were keen to create institutions, such as Royal Societies, and to use them in statist ways as development agencies. They were generally tolerant and worldly in attitude and eager to find the fruits of religion in good works. Scottish virtuosi in the late seventeenth century were part of this European world of virtuosi who communicated with one another, swapped seeds and information and who saw themselves as men who could restore some of Adam's original nature and make life better for all.

The signs of an outward-looking Scotland can be found in many places by the end of the seventeenth century. Work by Richard Simon was published in Edinburgh in 1685; some Scots were reading Pierre Bayle and Newton not long after.[30] Others were keenly interested in the medicine taught at Leiden or in English literature. The reading of Hume and of his friends around 1725 points to a familiarity with continental literature and thought.[31] Some Scots had been abroad as exiles; many others had been educated in Holland; still more had been on the increasingly popular grand tour which took them to Catholic as well as Protestant countries. Genteel Scottish professional men also had a long tradition of going abroad for their

educations in divinity, medicine and law, a tradition which continued in these fields until, respectively, the 1720s, 1730s and 1740s.
Many Scots were more familiar with Holland and France than with
England and knew Paris better than London. This changed over the
course of the century, but even at the end of the eighteenth century,
Scots were still very cosmopolitan. After about 1740 fewer studied outwith Scotland, and those who did usually went to London
or Paris for medical training, but more went on the grand tour and
more yet into the armed services. Their heritage, the Scottish present
and their travels made them interested in innovations, emulative
of other Europeans and not servile imitators of the English. Scots
looked to London and the English for fashions, politics, literature
and science, but we should never think of the Scottish Enlightenment as a set of ideas and practices principally imported from the
south. Philosophical, medical and scientific ideas came from France
and Holland as readily as from England; toleration and liberal theology were Dutch and Swiss as well as English; polite standards of
taste owed as much to the French as to Addison.[32]

Increasing numbers of Scots also explored the rest of the world.
They went to the Carolinas and to Delaware in the 1680s and
over the ensuing hundred years to most of North America and
the Carribean.[33] Africa[34] and the Far East opened to them after
1707. By the end of the century, India was absorbing many Scots.[35]
Scots read travel literature with great interest and contributed
important items to it: one thinks of Cadwallader Colden's *History
of the Five Nations* (1727, 2nd edn 1747), William Douglass on
New England (1756, 1757), and various accounts by soldiers of
Indians, both American[36] and South Asian.[37] The Scottish experience in Russia evoked a wonderful book, John Bell's *A Journey from
St Petersburg to Pekin, 1719–1722* (1763).[38] Later, James Bruce and
Mungo Park produced books on Africa at which readers wondered.
All of that fuelled the speculations of the conjectural historians and
the social theorists.

V

The institutional context for the expression of the Scottish
Enlightenment had almost completely come into being by the end
of the seventeenth century, and what had not, was there by about

1730. University reforms in Edinburgh, sponsored in the 1680s by James VII, came to little,[39] but between 1690 and 1720, new chairs were added in humanity (Edinburgh and Glasgow), Greek (Glasgow, Edinburgh), history (Edinburgh, Glasgow) and mathematics (Glasgow, King's College, Aberdeen). Regenting (the instruction of an arts student by one master for the boy's entire university career) was abolished: at Edinburgh in 1708, at Glasgow in 1727, twenty years later at St Andrews, in 1753 at Marischal College and at the end of the century at King's. Professional education was strengthened by the addition of chairs of oriental languages (Glasgow, Edinburgh), ecclesiastical history (Glasgow, Edinburgh, St Andrews), law (two at Edinburgh, one at Glasgow), botany (Edinburgh, Glasgow), medicine and chemistry (Edinburgh) and medicine (Glasgow).[40] More chairs in law and medicine had been demanded and would be created when the country could afford them, and when patrons were strong enough to push them through or found it in their interest to create them. The universities tended to expand as patrons struggled to control the colleges.

These changes recognised a need for professional education but also paid some attention to polite subjects. They had the further effect of making the universities less seminary-like in nature and more open to new ideas. Newtonianism came in the wake of mathematicians and doctors, while the study of man and society derived from the moralists and lawyers. The universities steadily added to their libraries[41] and instrument collections.[42] By 1730, the universities were mostly formed and had a new generation of more forward-looking teachers than those of the 1710s and 1720s.

As those developments took place, the thinkers and improvers – one should not separate them too sharply – became numerous enough to change the institutional mix in the country. Scots had had intellectual clubs since at least the 1680s, but the first club which may have made any real difference to the country (none of the others had lasted long) was the Honourable the Improvers in the Knowledge of Agriculture in Scotland (1723–1746). This association of around 300 landowners and intellectuals interested in agriculture and its dependent industries provided a forum for the discussion of economic changes in a society still overwhelmingly agrarian. What may have mattered as much as its discussions and occasional publications were the demonstrated benefits of what it argued for. These could be seen in the increased productivity of those estates which had begun to increase arable land through the introduction of more animals, better crop regimes, and the adoption of practices such as longer, restrictive leases.

The 1720s saw other important cultural initiatives. *The Caledonian Mercury* began publishing in 1720. Three years later the Edinburgh Assembly was revived, created to cater to the needs of upper-class youth and their parents.[43] The Musical Society, which had existed in some form since 1701, was 'formally constituted in 1728'.[44] A year earlier, in 1727, the Royal Bank of Scotland, an innovator in banking practices, was established. The Board of Trustees for Arts, Fisheries and Manufactures, the vehicle to which men like Lord Kames looked for the improvement of the economy, opened in 1728. In 1729 the Royal Infirmary was started in Edinburgh and in 1738 the foundation stone of a purpose-built hospital was laid. The Academy of St Luke, Edinburgh's first effort to create an art school, began teaching in 1729.[45] By 1731 Edinburgh had a Medical Society which produced the *Edinburgh Medical Essays* (1732–44) in six volumes. These announced to the world (in several editions) the importance of the Edinburgh Medical School, which can be said to date from 1726. The Medical Society soon ceased to function as a society, but it was followed by the Philosophical Society of Edinburgh (1737–83), which in turn became the Royal Society of Edinburgh (1783–). Many other adult and student societies followed, creating fora for the discussion of ideas and sometimes for action on them.[46] Some of these bodies also created significant libraries.[47] By 1737 Edinburgh had a theatre, although it did not get a proper building for some years. The city bustled as the most active centre of Enlightenment in Scotland.[48] What Edinburgh had was wanted elsewhere and was largely created, in some form, by the 1760s.

VI

Glasgow and Aberdeen provided other contexts for the Scottish Enlightenment. By around 1700 each had virtuosi who shared Sibbald's interests and had been in contact with him and others in Edinburgh and elsewhere. Despite some similarities, the three towns had differing enlightenments largely because they recruited their enlightened men from different bases and in differing numbers.

Aberdeen's came almost exclusively from the city's two small universities, King's College and Marischal College. The city's churches, its medical community and the area's gentry supplied a few others. At Glasgow, university men, merchants and lawyers were represented, along with some learned tradesmen. Such men were all present in Edinburgh but so, too, were others more peculiar to capital cities: military men, genteel judges, civil administrators and office holders. They were joined by noblemen and gentry who made the capital their resort and marriage market. This meant the development of differing interests, ideas and emphases in these diverse settings.

Aberdeen in 1700 was a port town of about 10,000 people; by mid-century it had grown to 22,000 and it would rise to 27,000 by the century's end. Until the mid-century, it had many members of the Scottish Episcopal Church who were sympathetic to Jacobitism. Men like the philosopher George Campbell had attended college with boys like George Hay, who was to become a Roman Catholic bishop in Scotland. Aberdeen lacked Glasgow's Presbyterian intolerance and had closer relations with the Baltic, France and London than did Glasgow. Aberdeen's enlightenment took a decisive turn around 1720 with the appearance at Marischal College of three young teachers – Colin Maclaurin, George Turnbull and Thomas Blackwell Jr.[49] Maclaurin arrived in 1717 to reinforce the Newtonian ideas which had been brought to the city ten years earlier by Professor Thomas Bower, MD; Maclaurin came with interests in Shaftesbury and modern philosophy. So too did Turnbull, who had been a member of Edinburgh's Rankenian Club and had corresponded with the deist John Toland. Turnbull believed that all knowledge and standards of taste and morality were based on experience; he later tried to demonstrate this claim in works on natural law, ancient art and education. Blackwell, the Marischal College professor of Greek, wrote important works on Homer, Greek mythology and Roman history and, like his colleagues, was impressed by Shaftesbury. Their most distinguished student was to be Thomas Reid, who, along with James Beattie and George Campbell,[50] would articulate the Scottish common sense philosophy partly in reaction to the immaterialism of George Berkeley and the more sceptical philosophy of David Hume, which they sought to refute in the interests of common sense and Christianity. Their philosophy was to become the distinctive

Scottish philosophical empiricism, and was taken by Reid to Glasgow, where he taught after 1764, and polished in Edinburgh by his protégés James Gregory and Dugald Stewart.[51]

By the 1750s, the Aberdeen enlightenment was best found in the Aberdeen 'Wise Club' or Philosophical Society (1758–73).[52] Its papers centred on the epistemic and moral topics made pressing by the sceptical writings of Hume, but they also show that the members were aware of and engaged with the works of many British and continental thinkers. Dr David Skene, the Club's best naturalist, supplied specimens to Linnaeus; a number of others learnedly debated the views of Buffon, organised observations of the Transit of Venus and discussed other scientific matters. There were discussions of genius, style, language, the characteristics of human nature and evidence. All these topics surfaced in the works they published. Later in the century, professors such as James Dunbar and Robert Hamilton made contributions to the study of society and political economy. Hamilton, a mathematician, and Patrick Copland, a natural philosopher, were useful to the burgh's manufacturers and businessmen, the first by doing the actuarial mathematics for the first of the city's insurance companies, the second as a consultant for manufacturers and the teacher of classes for artisans. Such men were concerned to be useful improvers, as is shown by the work of the Gordon's Mill Farming Club (1758–after 1765), to which several of them belonged.[53] This group listened to papers on agricultural experiments and discussed such things as leases and ploughs, roads and markets. Aberdonians, like the enlightened elsewhere, protested against slavery – James Beattie in lectures given from 1760 on – and some of them even favoured both the American and the French Revolutions. They also supported the Aberdeen Musical Society (1748–after 1800), which gave concerts in the town after 1753 and which could boast a local composer or two as well as a notable list of scores by Handel, Corelli, Gluck, Rameau and other Europeans. Aberdeen may have been small, but it had an enlightenment and it made lasting contributions through the philosophy of Thomas Reid and George Campbell, who also wrote a widely used rhetoric book and an ecclesiastical history which praised Gibbon.

Glasgow in 1700 had perhaps 12,000 people, a figure which had burgeoned to 80,000 by the end of the century.[54] This growth was attributable to the increase of trade and the industrial developments which occurred as the shippers tried to find cargoes to send out in ships which would bring back sugar, tobacco, cotton and other goods which were processed in the city. This was a merchants' town, but the merchants had little to do with the polite professors until near the end of the century, and what brought them together tended to be not polite literature but science, which was useful. By 1800 Glasgow had developed two enlightenments: one oriented to the university, the other to the concerns of godly utilitarians. The first was not unlike Edinburgh's and found a large place for the moralists and academic scientists.

The Edinburgh-like enlightenment of the Glaswegians is best seen in the work of the Glasgow Literary Society (1752–c. 1803). This club listened to papers in which the scientific ideas of Maupertuis, Buffon, Linnaeus, and d'Alembert were discussed. It heard others reporting novelties such as Black's discovery of latent heat, T. C. Hope's discovery of strontium, or John Anderson's essays on firearms and how to improve them. (He was later to send a cannon to the French Revolutionaries.) There were papers and debates on language, the faculties of the mind, criticism, politics, history, education and much else. Most of Thomas Reid's work after 1764 was read to the Society, as were works published by other professors. William Richardson read poems as well as discourses. As much attention seems to have been given to continental thinkers as to the English. Beccaria, Buffon, Condillac, Rousseau and Voltaire – all occasioned papers by men who, in many cases, had met one or more of them.

This amalgam of polite literature, philosophy and science characterised the enlightenment of the university men, but Glasgow's other, rather different, evangelical enlightenment was supported by Professor Anderson and some local professional men and merchants. These Calvinists were, like Locke, willing to tolerate all but Catholics and atheists, whose political allegiance was not thought to be assured because their oaths could not be trusted. This enlightenment was less Tory than that of the Literary Society and supported the American rebels and, initially, the French Revolutionaries. These men hoped for more freedom in Britain, along with better and cheaper government. They tended to think that freer trade was good so long as theirs was not hurt. They had interests in science and improvements and thought that good letters and learning should always be useful and support true religion. The best guide to their thinking is the published testament of John Anderson, which sought to establish in Glasgow another university which would provide more useful learning and train ministers for every denomination of Presbyterian worship in Scotland. This university was not created, but the University of Strathclyde is the successor to his foundation.[55] The views of Anderson and his friends were close to those of many in the American colonies, where Glaswegians found friends in men like John Witherspoon, an emigré who became President of what is now Princeton University and an American Founding Father.

Outside the larger towns there were few other centres of enlightenment. St Andrews University possessed some distinguished men, such as the historian Robert Watson and the liberal theologian George Hill, but the town seemed to have few others. Perth, by the 1780s, had a small group of local ministers and teachers gathered around the Morison Press. No other towns could claim an enlightenment. A few enlightened landowners, Sir James Steuart for one, worked from their estates, but most of the enlightened were associated with the largest towns, their club life and conviviality, their libraries and schools. The enlightenment everywhere was an urban movement and it was equally a movement dominated by men. In Scotland women shone only in the drawing room, at the keyboard and in the writing of poems and songs. They were in the background, and hardly formed any part of the intellectual gatherings, which were often in taverns. Also in that background, everywhere in Scotland, was natural and revealed religion. Like most of the enlightened in Britain, Scots were generally sincere Christians who found it virtually unthinkable that there might be no God requiring duties of us. David Hume, driven by the hatred of religious belief which informs most of what he wrote, profoundly differed in outlook from most of his contemporaries.

The contexts shaping the Scottish enlightenment differed from those elsewhere. Geography had made Scots poor, culturally diverse and unable to sustain an independent modern state. Poverty challenged men to pursue the sciences of nature, in order both to understand God's world and to improve their lives. Scots elaborated the sciences of man to understand and change social conditions both in Scotland and abroad. They did so mindful of the intellectual trends which influenced the European Republic of Letters, but also with eyes on local conditions. Union with England changed them, but so did the ideas they found elsewhere or which they produced at home. By 1800, they could boast of an Enlightenment to which belonged several of the century's best philosophers, its most accomplished political economist and many notable social thinkers, important scientists and medical men, even rhetoricians and theologians. Scottish artists had been among the best portrait painters and architects of the time, with the Adam brothers even having an international style named for them. Scots had written textbooks which were used not only in Britain but also in continental and American universities. Their literary accomplishments resonated among the readers of romantic literature. Those things formed parts of a single development which had engendered excitement in Scotland; excitement marked the larger and unique context of the Scottish Enlightenment.[56]

NOTES

1   William Ferguson estimated that only a quarter of the Scottish land area 'was fit for cultivation of even the least rewarding kind', Ferguson, *Scotland: 1689 to the Present* (Edinburgh and London: Oliver and Boyd, 1968), 71; see also J. T. Coppock, *An Agricultural Atlas of Scotland* (Edinburgh: John Donald, 1976); Ian D. Whyte, *Agriculture and Society in Seventeenth-Century Scotland* (Edinburgh: John Donald, 1979), 19–22; T. C. Smout, 'The Great Caledonian Forest', in Smout, ed., *Nature Contested: Environmental History in Scotland and Northern England since 1600* (Edinburgh: Edinburgh University Press, 2000).

2   Coppock, *Agricultural Atlas*, 9–22; Peter G. B. McNeill and Hector MacQueen, eds., *Atlas of Scottish History to 1707* (Edinburgh: Department of Geography, University of Edinburgh, 1996), 6–7, 14–22.

3   Ian D. Whyte, *Scotland Before the Industrial Revolution: an Economic and Social History, 1050–1750* (London and New York: Longman, 1995), 113.

4   Charles Withers, *Gaelic in Scotland, 1698 to 1981: the Geographical History of a Language* (Edinburgh: John Donald, 1984).

5   A. J. S. Gibson and T. C. Smout, 'Scottish Food and Scottish History, 1500–1800', in R. A. Houston and I. D. Whyte, eds., *Scottish Society, 1500–1800* (Cambridge: Cambridge University Press, 1989), 59–84; see also their *Prices, Food and Wages in Scotland, 1550–1780* (Cambridge: Cambridge University Press, 1995).

6 I. D. Whyte, 'Population Mobility in Early Modern Scotland', in Houston and Whyte, *Scottish Society*, 37–58.

7 Michael Lynch, 'Continuity and Change in Urban Society, 1500–1800', in Houston and Whyte, *Scottish Society*, 85–117; T. M. Devine, *The Scottish Nation* (New York: Viking, 1999), 106–7.

8 R. A. Houston, *Scottish Literacy and Scottish Identity: Illiteracy and Society in Scotland and Northern England, 1600–1800* (Cambridge: Cambridge University Press, 1985); Donald J. Withrington, 'Schooling, Literacy and Society', in T. M. Devine and Rosalind Mitchison, eds., *People and Society in Scotland*, vol. 1, *1760–1830* (Edinburgh: John Donald, 1979), 163–87; Whyte, *Scotland*, 175.

9 This figure comes from my unpublished study of medical men in eighteenth-century Scotland.

10 R. L. Emerson, 'Sir Robert Sibbald, Kt, The Royal Society of Scotland and the Origins of the Scottish Enlightenment', *Annals of Science* 45 (1988), 41–72; R. L. Emerson, 'Did the Scottish Enlightenment Emerge in an English Cultural Province?', *Lumen* 14 (1995), 1–24; R. L. Emerson, 'Scottish Cultural Change 1660–1710 and the Union of 1707', in John Robertson, ed., *A Union for Empire: Political Thought and the British Union of 1707* (Cambridge: Cambridge University Press, 1995), 121–44.

11 A convenient bibliography for part of this literature is *Anglo-Scottish Tracts, 1701–1714: a Descriptive Checklist*, compiled by W. R. and V. B. Mcleod, University of Kansas Publications, Library Series, 44 (Lawrence: University of Kansas, 1979).

12 T. C. Smout, *Scottish Trade on the Eve of the Union, 1660–1707* (Edinburgh: Oliver and Boyd, 1963); Christopher A. Whatley, *Scottish Society, 1707–1830: Beyond Jacobitism, Towards Industrialisation* (Manchester: Manchester University Press, 2000).

13 It has recently been argued that much more freedom was actually attained by the businessmen of Edinburgh and other burghs during the eighteenth century; this made for efficiency, R. A. Houston, *Social Change in the Age of Enlightenment: Edinburgh, 1660–1760* (Oxford: Oxford University Press, 1994); for a discussion of the social base from which the century started in the capital, see Helen Dingwall, *Late Seventeenth-Century Edinburgh: a Demographic Study* (Edinburgh: Edinburgh University Press, 1994).

14 T. M. Devine and Gordon Jackson, *Glasgow*, vol. 1, *Beginnings to 1830* (Manchester: Manchester University Press, 1995), 69–85.

15 See R. L. Emerson, M. A. Stewart and John Wright, *Hume* (Cambridge: Cambridge University Press, forthcoming), ch. 6.

16 See John Robertson, *The Scottish Enlightenment and the Militia Issue* (Edinburgh: John Donald, 1985).

17 These were the supporters of the ousted king, James, whose name in Latin is Jacobus.

18 T. C. Smout, 'Where had the Scottish Economy got to by 1776?', in Istvan Hont and Michael Ignatieff, eds., *Wealth and Virtue: the Shaping of Political Economy in the Scottish Enlightenment* (Cambridge: Cambridge University Press, 1983), 45–72, 46.

19 A convenient and readable source in the vast and dismal literature on the risings is Bruce Lenman, *The Jacobite Risings in Britain, 1689–1746* (London: Eyre and Methuen, 1980).

20 A. J. Youngson, *After the Forty-five: the Economic Impact on the Scottish Highlands* (Edinburgh: Edinburgh University Press, 1973); Eric Richards, *A History of the Highland Clearances: Agrarian Transformation and the Evictions, 1746–1886* (London: Croom Helm, 1982).

21 For the cost to Scottish literature in all this, see David Craig, *Scottish Literature and the Scottish People, 1680–1830* (London: Chatto and Windus, 1961); David Daiches, *The Paradox of Scottish Culture: the Eighteenth-Century Experience* (London: Oxford University Press, 1964), ch. 1.

22 The political faction of the Dukes of Argyll was called 'the Argathelians'.

23 For Simson, see Anne Skoczylas, *Mr Simson's Knotty Case: Divinity, Politics and Due Process in Early Eighteenth-Century Scotland* (Montreal: McGill-Queens University Press, 2001).

24 The best accounts of this are in John Stuart Shaw, *The Political History of Eighteenth-Century Scotland* (London and New York: Macmillan Press, 1999); and Eric G. J. Wehrli, 'Scottish Politics in the Age of Walpole' (Ph.D. diss., Edinburgh University, 1983).

25 Emerson, 'Sibbald'; passim.

26 R. L. Emerson, 'The Scientific Interests of Archibald Campbell, 1st Earl of Ilay and 3rd Duke of Argyll, 1682–1761', *Annals of Science* 59 (2002), 21–56; R. L. Emerson, 'The Library of the 3rd Duke of Argyll', forthcoming, *Bibliothek*, 2003.

27 R. L. Emerson, 'Medical Men, Politicians and the Medical Schools at Glasgow and Edinburgh, 1685–1803', in A. Doig et al., ed., *William Cullen and the Eighteenth-Century Medical World* (Edinburgh: Royal College of Physicians of Edinburgh, 1993), 186–215; R. L. Emerson, 'Politics and the Glasgow Professors, 1690–1800', in Andrew Hook and Richard B. Sher, eds., *The Glasgow Enlightenment* (East Linton:

Tuckwell Press, 1995), 21–39; R. L. Emerson, *Professors, Patronage and Politics: the Aberdeen Universities in the Eighteenth Century* (Aberdeen: Aberdeen University Press, 1992).

28 R. L. Emerson, 'Lord Bute and the Scottish Universities 1760–1792', in K. Schweizer, ed., *Lord Bute: Essays in Re-interpretation* (Leicester: Leicester University Press, 1988), 147–79.

29 See Michael Fry, *The Dundas Despotism* (Edinburgh: Edinburgh University Press, 1992).

30 The Scottish political discussions c. 1700 had a continental analogue in the discussions of French thinkers described by Lionel Rothkrug, *The Opposition to Louis XIV* (Princeton: Princeton University Press, 1965). One of Simon's works was published in Edinburgh in 1685; see H. G. Aldis, *A List of Books Printed in Scotland Before 1700*, reprinted with additions (Edinburgh: National Library of Scotland, 1970), item 2608.

31 Emerson, 'Scottish Cultural Change'; Emerson, 'Did the Scottish Enlightenment Emerge in an English Cultural Province?'

32 Emerson, 'Scottish Cultural Change'; Emerson, 'Did the Scottish Enlightenment Emerge in an English Cultural Province?'

33 See Norman Feiring, ed., *Scotland and the Americas, 1600–1800* (Providence: John Carter Brown Library, 1995); Ned Landsman, ed., *Nation and Province* (Cranbury, NJ: Associated University Presses, 2001); J. Ralph Randolph, *British Travelers Among the Southern Indians, 1660–1763* (Norman: University of Oklahoma Press, 1973).

34 David Hancock, *Citizens of the World: London Merchants and the Integration of the British Atlantic Community* (Cambridge: Cambridge University Press, 1995).

35 Michael Fry, *The Scottish Empire* (East Linton: Tuckwell Press, 2001).

36 R. L. Emerson, 'American Indians, Frenchmen and Scots Philosophers', *Studies in Eighteenth-Century Culture* 9 (1979), 211–36.

37 C. G. J. Bryant, 'Scots in India in the Eighteenth Century', *Scottish Historical Review* 64 (1985), 22–41.

38 Bell's book was reprinted by Edinburgh University Press in 1965; see also Anthony Cross, *By the Banks of the Neva: Chapters from the Lives and Careers of the British in Eighteenth-Century Russia* (Cambridge, Cambridge University Press, 1997); Cross cites numerous works by others who have written on Scots in Russia.

39 Hugh Ouston, 'York in Edinburgh', in John Dwyer, Roger Mason and Alex Murdoch, eds., *New Perspectives on the Politics and Culture of Early Modern Scotland* (Edinburgh: John Donald, 1982), 133–55; Ouston, 'Cultural Life from the Restoration to the Union', in *The History of Scottish Literature*, vol. II, ed. Andrew Hook (Aberdeen: Aberdeen University Press, 1987), 11–31.

40 Emerson, *Professors, Patronage and Politics*, 140–1.

41 See the wonderful but unused *Catalogus Librorum Bibliothecae Universitatis Glasguensis*; this catalogues the collection of Glasgow University from c. 1691–c. 1720, not only for 1691, as the manuscript says; Glasgow University Library, MS Gen. 1312.

42 For the story at Aberdeen and Glasgow see Paul B. Wood, *The Aberdeen Enlightenment: the Arts Curriculum in the Eighteenth Century* (Aberdeen: Aberdeen University Press, 1993), 14–18; and R. L. Emerson and P. B. Wood, 'Science and Enlightenment in Glasgow, 1690–1802', in Charles G. J. Withers and P. B. Wood, eds., *Science and Medicine in the Scottish Enlightenment* (East Linton: Tuckwell Press, 2002).

43 On Scottish dance and its venues see works by George Emmerson, especially *A Social History of Scottish Dance* (Montreal and London: McGill-Queens University Press, 1972).

44 David Johnson, *Music and Society in Lowland Scotland in the Eighteenth Century* (London: Oxford University Press, 1972), 34.

45 There is no adequate monograph on this institution, but see Alastair Smart, *Allan Ramsay, 1713–1784* (Edinburgh: Scottish National Portrait Gallery, 1992), 16; Alexander M. Kinghorn and Alexander Law, eds., *The Works of Allan Ramsay*, 6 vols., Scottish Text Society (Edinburgh: Blackwood, 1951–74), vol. IV, 30–1. The Academy closed in 1733.

46 See the Collectivities section of the *New Dictionary of National Biography*; and Peter Clark, *British Clubs and Societies, 1580–1800* (Oxford: Oxford University Press, 2000).

47 Antonia J. Bunch, *Hospital and Medical Libraries in Scotland* (Glasgow: Scottish Library Association, 1975).

48 R. L. Emerson, 'The Select Society of Edinburgh', and Richard B. Sher, 'The Poker Club', both in *New Dictionary of National Biography*, volume on *Collectivities*.

49 See Wood, *Aberdeen Enlightenment*; and Jennifer J. Carter and Joan H. Pittock, eds., *Aberdeen and the Enlightenment* (Aberdeen: Aberdeen University Press, 1987).

50 Jeffery Suderman, *Orthodoxy and Enlightenment: George Campbell in the Eighteenth Century* (Montreal: McGill-Queens University Press, 2001).

51 P. B. Wood, ' "The Fittest Man in the kingdom": Thomas Reid and the Glasgow Chair of Moral Philosophy', *Hume Studies* 23 (1997), 277–313.

52 H. Lewis Ulman, ed., *The Minutes of the Aberdeen Philosophical Society, 1758–1773* (Aberdeen: Aberdeen University Press, 1990).

53 J. H. Smith, *The Gordon's Mill Farming Club, 1758–1765*, Aberdeen University Studies 145 (Edinburgh and London: Oliver and Boyd, 1962).

54 Emerson and Wood, *Science and Enlightenment*.

55 There is no good book on Anderson, but see: P. B. Wood, 'Jolly Jack Phosphorus in the Venice of the North; or Who Was John Anderson?', in Hook and Sher, *Glasgow Enlightenment*, 111–32; and John Butt, *John Anderson's Legacy: the University of Strathclyde and its Antecedents, 1796–1996* (East Linton: Tuckwell Press, 1996).

56 The author is grateful to T. C. Smout, Ian Steele, Charles Withers and Paul Wood for aid in the preparation of this essay.

2   Religion and rational theology

INTRODUCTION

To a modern readership the leading, and most provocative, figure writing in the philosophy of religion in eighteenth-century Scotland was David Hume. To Scots contemporaries too he was no doubt the most provocative, but he was far from leading. They sought to minimise his impact and played down his significance, and in the short term they succeeded. This was less because they had other major players than because the main traditions of thought ranged against Hume could count on enough broad support within their respective spheres to counteract a challenge that was not seen at the time particularly to tax their wits. If posterity has been less sure that they were entitled to be so complacent, it is important to be clear where the strength of opinion at the time actually lay. Accordingly, this chapter falls into three parts. The first explores the state of the subject before Hume wrote, distinguishing between an orthodox tradition for which theology was the primary science that could dictate terms of reference to philosophy, and a new, largely imported (English and Dutch), tradition of 'rational' religion that subjected the whole framework of religious belief to the same rational critique as other forms of knowledge and belief. Within the universities, this was part of a recognised adjustment of interests between divinity and arts faculties, but outside academia it generated bitter conflicts between conservative and progressive parties in the Kirk. With the context established, the second part of the chapter will concern Hume, represented especially by two essays in his *Philosophical Essays* (later called *An Enquiry*) *concerning Human Understanding* (1748), his *Natural History of Religion* (1757), and his *Dialogues concerning Natural Religion* (first published in 1779 but known to some in manuscript from the 1750s). His *Treatise of Human Nature* (1739–40) was the seminal work that first presented his sceptical philosophy and its supporting psychology, and it had implications for religious as for any other belief; these implications were suppressed prior to publication, but were not lost on contemporaries who expected an analysis of the human mind to culminate as a matter of course in an account of the foundations of religious belief. The final part of the chapter will summarise the Scottish response to Hume (but not the more extensive English response)[1] in the debate over a rational theology. In his appraisal of arguments for the existence and attributes of God, and arguments about the credibility of ancient revelation, Hume's philosophy almost inevitably brought him into conflict with ministers of the Kirk.

THE EARLY EIGHTEENTH-CENTURY DEBATE

At the beginning of the century, Scotland was a largely Calvinist country, and had been for over a century, regardless of which protestant interest – presbyterian or episcopalian – had the ascendancy. Aberdeenshire was an exception, where an episcopalian tradition had been infiltrated on the one hand by the Arminianism of the seventeenth-century Cambridge Platonists and on the other hand by a strain of Flemish mysticism;[2] but episcopalianism was a weak force for much of the eighteenth century because of its suspected Jacobitism and the legal constraints it suffered as a result.[3] Catholic enclaves in the highlands and islands were another exception; their centres of learning were abroad and they had no influence on the movement of thought in Scotland.

Calvinism did not deny the possibility of natural religion in the sense of a potentiality in humankind to detect something of the existence and nature of God in the evidence of Creation and in the urgings of the human heart. The opening sentence of the Westminster Confession of 1648, whose teaching was authoritative for presbyterians, acknowledges that 'the Light of Nature, and the Works of Creation and Providence do so far manifest the Goodness, Wisdom, and Power of God, as to leave Men unexcusable', and biblical texts reinforce the message. But this is not a matter of collecting evidence in propositional form, as premises for an inference. To the Confession's authors that would have been putting God rather than humanity on trial. Human nature is depraved and reason corrupt. Calvinist theologians inherited from Calvin a concept of *sensus divinitatis*, the idea that much as we have unmediated knowledge of the natural world by using our senses, so, even in our fallen state, we have the residue of a sense, a religious sense, by which we have an unmediated knowledge of things divine. From this perspective, the Book of the World and the Book of the Word are equally open to inspection, but the Word – the Bible – is the primary source for God's attributes.

The classic exponent of this standpoint at the dawn of the Enlightenment is Thomas Halyburton (1674–1712), minister of Ceres, and from 1710 briefly professor of divinity at St Andrews. As a student Halyburton had found the metaphysics and natural theology of the classroom disquieting. It catered to human vanity, offering prospects of knowledge, but served only to induce doubt.

My Disturbance was from Reasonings, and I thought to relieve my self by my own Reasonings. Nothing more, did I foolishly think, can be requisite to establish my Mind about this Truth, and for ever to quiet my Mind in a firm Assent to it, than to obtain Demonstrative Arguments for the Being of a GOD.

The arguments, however, brought only momentary assent. They exploited 'the Absurdity of the contrary Conclusion', but this purely intellectual technique gave no positive notions of deity and had no lasting practical effect.[4] He learnt to find such practical effect in 'hearing the Word', and came to construe the fruitless search for rational argument as the temptations of Satan. The temptations were renewed during two years as chaplain in an aristocratic household, where 'Persons smooth, sober, and who opposed the Truth with rational Arguments' challenged his confidence in scripture and providence.[5] This was the challenge of deism, a system founded solely on natural reason, which had begun to attract attention south of the Border.[6] Deists would embrace the existence and some of the attributes of deity, and often a humanitarian ethic, but held divergent opinions about the soul, immortality and a last judgement. Exploiting older sectarian battles, they tended to explain away naturalistically, often contemptuously, the supernaturalist claims made for competing revelations, and therefore lacked any doctrinal theology. Halyburton studied the deist and anti-deist literature, and again failed adequately to counter reason by reason. Eventually he found his 'outgate' in a spiritual conversion that left him permanently alienated from philosophy. He nevertheless did engage with the logic of those he opposed, and wrote to arrest the deist threat. Two significant works, *Natural Religion Insufficient and Revealed Necessary to Man's Happiness* and *An Essay concerning the Reason of Faith*, issued together, posthumously, in 1714, were reprinted throughout and beyond the Enlightenment period. The first is directed against Edward Herbert and Charles Blount and unnamed English pamphleteers of the late seventeenth century; in arguing that natural reason is inadequate to demonstrate the divine nature, human duties, the afterlife, and the conditions of salvation, Halyburton condemned the unwitting encouragement these writers received from a too philosophical approach to theology among English latitudinarian divines. He drew support from the English thinker John Locke to show the impossibility of faith without revelation. In *An Essay concerning the Reason of Faith*, however, he criticised Locke and the Amsterdam Huguenot Jean Le Clerc for subjecting the revealed Word to historical appraisal and undermining the certainty of faith. For Halyburton, the Bible speaks with a distinctive, consistent voice that shows it is no human artifact, and this is his only counter to Locke's challenge that without public signs claims to revelation are mere 'enthusiasm'. When, in the second and third decades of the century, John Simson (c. 1668–1740), professor of divinity at Glasgow, was thought by opponents to set human judgement over scripture, a new generation of critics developed a position similar to Halyburton's.[7]

Halyburton confronted deism privately among educated Scots. As a public phenomenon it is harder to document. The only Scottish deist identified by him in *Natural Religion Insufficient* is Thomas Aikenhead (1676–97), his former classmate before Halyburton transferred from Edinburgh University to St Andrews in 1693. In 1696 the General Assembly of the Kirk responded to 'credible' hearsay with an 'Act against the Atheistical Opinions of the Deists', and the Privy Council ordered the searching of Edinburgh bookshops for irreligious importations. This was the prelude to two blasphemy trials – of John Frazer and, fatally, of Aikenhead; both admitted imbibing ideas from Blount.[8] By the end of his life Halyburton was also aware of Archibald Pitcairne's anonymous *Epistola Archimedis* (c. 1706), and directed his inaugural lecture against it in 1711. Pitcairne (1652–1713), the leading Scots physician of the day, had no time for Calvinism. Pretending to the character of Archimedes, he accepted that the reducibility of natural philosophy to a mathematical system was proof of a unitary deity, but thought that only the common factor in different religions was likely to be true; their distinguishing doctrines were imposed on an ignorant populace by self-interested leaders and wonder-workers. After Pitcairne, William Dudgeon (1706–43) put out a series of tracts in the 1730s, most of them posthumously collected in his *Philosophical Works* (1765). Dudgeon was hostile to institutional religion and the sourness of the Calvinist ethic, but defended an ethical religion that he considered underlay all systems of belief, and justified it from the two commonest arguments for the being and attributes of deity – from the impossibility of the causal chain without a first cause or necessary being, and from signs of design in the natural world.[9] From the perfection of the necessary being and the goodness of the design, he argued the unreality of evil. Human nature is imperfect but open to correction and self-discipline, and if our obligations to God and humanity cannot be discharged within this life there must be another.[10] Another dissident tradition, however, involving young anti-Calvinists who had trained for the ministry at Edinburgh but bridled at confessions and catechisms in the early 1720s and wished the church to be less intrusive in politics and education – William Wishart the younger (1692–1753), George Turnbull (1698–1748) and Robert Wallace (1697–1771) – still defended revelation against the deists.[11]

   After Halyburton's death, some modification in the Calvinist hard line starts to show among orthodox writers. His friend William Wishart the elder (1660–1729), in *Theologia* (1716), continued to deny that the scriptures need appraisal: 'there are more clear Marks and Characters of a Deity stamped upon the holy Scriptures, than upon all the Works of Nature'. The written word, the 'external Instrumental Cause' by which we attain saving and practical knowledge of God, derives its efficacy directly from the divine spirit working 'by and with the Word in our Hearts'. At the same time, no one will reach this point who does not acknowledge God's existence, and here it *is* legitimate to invoke reason alongside potentially direct insight, to meet the waverer on his own ground. Wishart agreed with

Halyburton that the 'moral and transient assent' that reason elicits is not the 'saving fixed assent' required by religion. It is, however, a precondition: 'Unless we firmly believe that *God is*, how can we believe any Revelation from him?' Wishart accordingly summarises the first-cause and design arguments as if they are one and the same, and arguments from providence (the ability of non-rational nature to seek and attain its ends), universal consent, universal yearning and the fulfilment of prophecy. From these he proceeds to the divine attributes in seemingly random order. His evidence is an awkward amalgam of a priori principle, natural data, and biblical citation, but the intention is in part to show how the Bible gives credence to natural reason.[12] Archibald Campbell (1691–1756), a St Andrews theologian, considered the discrepancy between the fact (as he judged it) of early monotheism, the inadequacy of ancient theistic arguments, and the natural tendency of depraved minds to polytheism. He argued that monotheism must have been initially founded on angelic revelation, against the deist view that a rational basis for belief has always been available to natural reason. Campbell nevertheless believed that the explosion in scientific knowledge in the late seventeenth century had transformed the evidence of design, and that it was no longer realistic to maintain the permanent hopelessness of reason.[13] The influence of the Royal Society – whose very research was motivated by the design evidence – was starting to be felt.

This helps to explain a tendency, common among educated orthodox divines during the eighteenth century, to move to a middle ground on natural religion. Campbell's friend and teacher, Simson, suffered for holding out too strenuously and too early for the promise of demonstrative certainty in the exceptionally detailed formulation of the first-cause argument by the English divine, Samuel Clarke, at a time when others were still scandalised by Clarke's rationalising interpretation of the doctrine of the Trinity.[14] It is no accident, however, that Demea, Hume's orthodox stereotype in the *Dialogues*, defends the metaphysical certainty of the first-cause argument against the probabilism of the new 'rational' theologian. Most supporters of a rational theology embraced the methods and discoveries of the new science and sought to make natural religion respectable by providing an experimental foundation. Clarke, however, seemed to hold out the prospect of something better – the certainty of a formal demonstration – although probably only a few of those who supported or criticised his argument followed its subtlety. Despite its formal character, in which a carefully ordered sequence of propositions is derived by *reductio ad absurdum* through seemingly self-evident axioms, it starts from the same kind of empirical basis as any other version of the argument – the contingency that something now exists in Clarke's case; the fact of one's own existence in the formulations of Descartes and Locke; the existence of a chain of cause and effect in others. It is important to realise that arguments for the basis of theism were never arguments simply for the *existence* of God, as classroom caricatures of two and three centuries later portray them. They were about existence *and attributes*, and were traditionally directed not at atheists but at infidels. Something of a stated character – for Clarke, an independent or non-contingent being – was proved, and either from this character, or from the same evidence as proved the character, further attributes of this being were inferred. It is the ability to derive the attributes that shows if one has established theism or not; and the *way* they are derived – a priori or a posteriori – makes a difference to how one addresses the problem of evil. Clarke had a sharper sense of the issues here than many more popular writers, for while he believed that from the concept of 'one unchangeable and independent being' he could infer self-existence, eternity, infinity, omnipresence and unity, he required the empirical evidence of the created world before he could add intelligence, and from that go on to infer wisdom, liberty, power and moral perfection. Several Scots writers seem to have seen the significance of this distinction between a priori and a posteriori attributes, although they do not employ it consistently.[15] But this perhaps explains why, half consciously, the first-cause and design arguments are often presented together, as if mutually supportive, in textbooks and lectures of the period.

In the classroom, natural religion featured as a branch of pneumatology, the science of mind and spirit, in the study of moral philosophy; the analysis of divine and human nature and the relationship between them often provided a framework for conclusions about our obligations to God, self and humanity. Gershom Carmichael (1672–1729) at Glasgow published his *Synopsis Theologiae Naturalis* at the end of his life. He started, like Clarke, from the existence of something contingent and inferred the existence of an independent or necessary being; unlike Clarke, he judged that it must already be a being whose essence is to think, and the argument merges imperceptibly into one to explain the empirical fact that the system of dependent nature does not collapse.[16] He adds standard English and Dutch sources for the design data, and further evidence of cosmic intelligence from the existence of created intelligence in humans, and he criticises the arguments supplied by Descartes. His successor, the Ulster-Scot Francis Hutcheson (1694–1746), in *Synopsis Metaphysicae*[17] is again critical of Descartes. Part III of the *Synopsis* concerns the being, attributes, will and operations of God, and ends with the briefest comment on the support which miracles give to revelation. The argument for God's existence is a design argument, citing both celestial and terrestrial evidence, but concentrating on man and on the evidence of the life sciences. Hutcheson pushes the cosmological argument into a subordinate role and avoids the complexities of Clarke's formulation.[18] Both Carmichael and Hutcheson retain the traditional Reformed distinction between the incommunicable and communicable attributes: the former, like infinity and necessity, humans can neither share nor grasp; the latter, like knowledge and beneficence, are reflected but imperfectly understood in analogues in human nature.

The same distinction occurs in an Edinburgh student's notebook recording unidentified natural religion exercises from the early 1740s, which show the kind of argument circulating among students at the time.[19] 'A Scheme of Natural Religion' has an epistemological base, with a summary theory of evidence and probability. God's existence is proved from universal consent, design and providence – and the supposed evidence of 'testimony' for the recent origin of the world and the still more recent rise of arts and sciences. 'An Argument for the Christian Religion' makes the heroic claim, against deism, that Christianity is perfectly adapted to counter the ills induced by those who disregard its message of universal charity – an apparent variant on the design theme. We can also document George Turnbull's labours in natural religion in the graduation theses he published for his students at Marischal College, Aberdeen, in 1723 and 1726.[20] He commends the subtlety of the metaphysicians who have demonstrated the ultimate truth about causation and necessary being, but recommends those of ordinary talents to address the evidence uncovered by natural philosophy.

Independently of the curriculum, a number of Scots were writing their own books. Two exponents of the design argument who were practising scientists influenced Hume's portrayal of the experimental theologian, Cleanthes, in Parts II–III of the *Dialogues*. George Cheyne (1671–1743), an Aberdeenshire episcopalian who moved to England, attracted a wide following through his writings on nervous diseases and diet. His *Philosophical Principles of Religion, Natural and Revealed* (1715) had reached a fifth edition by 1736. It was an influential compendium of natural philosophy, and despite its Newtonian roots goes well beyond mathematical astronomy, drawing substantially on the life sciences. Hume borrowed Cheyne's picture of nature as 'this vast, if not infinite, *Machine* of the Universe... consisting of an infinite Number of lesser *Machines*, every one of which is adjusted by Weight and Measure'.[21] Cheyne's world view here is not mechanistic – a 'machine' is any contrivance or structure, but mechanism alone cannot explain animal nature or rationality; and whatever can explain them must be self-existent. He also argues the existence of rational beings on other planets from the evidence of design that is there to confront them.[22] Colin MacLaurin (1698–1746) also prepared a compendium of natural philosophy in his posthumous *Account of Sir Isaac Newton's Philosophical Discoveries* (1748), viewing the Newtonian system historically. A final chapter, 'Of the Supreme Author and Governor of the Universe, the True and Living God', again goes beyond the celestial data of Newton's telescopic world to consider living things, while using the poverty of present cosmological knowledge to argue for a future existence. Hume drew on MacLaurin's portrayal of the impatience of those for whom 'a manifest contrivance immediately suggests a contriver. It strikes us like a sensation; and artful reasonings against it may puzzle us, but it is without shaking our belief'.[23] MacLaurin's own 'reasoning' is more properly a first-cause argument, but he regularly appeals to the evidence of nature to give content to his character of the necessary being.

Others with less scientific expertise, like Hutcheson and Turnbull, would nevertheless have considered themselves experimentalists in their pneumatology. Besides his teaching materials, Hutcheson brought natural religion into the *Inquiry concerning Beauty, Order &c.* (1726) of his early Dublin period. This is misread if seen simply as an exercise in analysis: it is a study in the *metaphysics* of beauty. Hutcheson's theory of beauty, in terms of the relative proportions of uniformity and variety, takes him from the beauty of shapes and of mathematical proofs to the beauties of art and artifacts and of nature. Beauties in human creations lead us to admire their creators, and beauties in nature direct our minds not just to a superior intelligence, but to providential wisdom. What we find attractive in nature is found to serve the ends both of the agent and of the object, and is also beneficial to the well-ordering of human life.[24] The whole scheme of beauty therefore betokens purpose. This becomes the basis for a full-scale design argument in the work of Hutcheson's friend and fellow Ulster-Scot, John Abernethy (1680–1740). In *Discourses concerning the Being and Natural Perfections of God* (1740), Abernethy argued the existence of God from those features of nature that Hutcheson had identified as the determinants of beauty. Uniformity is inconsistent with chance, variety with necessity, and these features are traced through the 'frame' of the material world, the nature of animal and rational life, and the intelligent and moral nature of mankind. In a companion volume he carried further than Hutcheson the sublimation of the problem of evil within a thoroughly optimistic view of Creation.[25]

Turnbull's fullest exposition of natural religion is in the opening sections of his *Christian Philosophy* (1740), a sequel to *The Principles of Moral Philosophy* and later jointly marketed with it. He argues from the existence of derived power to the existence of underived, unlimited and independent power; and from the nature of the ordered world to a unitary, benevolent and moral agent. But Turnbull is also significant for raising philosophical issues about the foundations of belief in revelation. Questions about the validation of historical, including biblical, testimony had been raised in the previous century in the Port-Royal *Logic* and by Locke, and explored at length by Edward Stillingfleet and other English theologians.[26] They got short shrift from Halyburton, but neither Calvinist nor anti-Calvinist in Scotland saw historical validation as the major problem, until the work of Hume. Turnbull, in his *Philosophical Inquiry* (1731), took the gospel narratives as history, and used the *fact* of miracles to show how they confirmed the powers to which their workers testified. Jesus's teaching about a future state was open to 'experimental proof' in this life from miracles that were 'natural proper samples' of the power and knowledge they confirmed, to raise the dead and promote long-term well-being and happiness.

Although the first-cause argument, with or without Clarke's sophisticated elaboration, was more important to the Scottish debate than readers of Hume have supposed, few Scots were inclined to compete with Clarke's formulation. The one exception is the expatriate Andrew Michael Ramsay (1686–1743), whose two-volume *Philosophical Principles of Natural and Revealed Religion*, written in France, was published in Glasgow in 1748. Ostensibly directed, like Clarke's, against Spinoza's work, it has the same kind of axiomatic framework, but Ramsay is obsessed with mystical triads, including an a priori proof of the Trinity, that try the reader's patience. He claims by this means to solve a problem other proofs cannot solve, of how God can already be said to have moral (other-directed) qualities prior to the Creation: 'the eternal, permanent, consubstantial idea God has of himself, produces necessarily in him an infinite, eternal, immutable love' (proposition 12). Considerable historical creativity goes into demonstrating that a non-deistic Christianity is as old as the Creation. Thus, Adam and Noah as conscientious patriarchs *must* have realised the need to preserve sound religion for posteriority: Adam would have educated his offspring, and Noah would have committed all to writing, on a water-resistant surface. After this, one can almost face with equanimity Andrew Baxter's prolonged weaving of a first-mover version of the cosmological argument in and out of his *Enquiry into the Nature of the Human Soul* (1733). But he abandoned this in favour of the design argument in his later educational work, *Matho* (1740).

HUME ON RELIGION

Hume had drafted 'some Reasonings concerning Miracles' before December 1737 for possible inclusion in the *Treatise*,[27] and had composed some sections for either the *Treatise* or a lost work, detailing objections to 'the System of Theism'.[28] In the end, he seems to have published nothing on these subjects until the first *Enquiry*. There Hume confronts the rational grounds for believing in reported miracles (Section x) and the proper limits of natural religion (Section xi). The juxtaposition is an admission that there are two sides to the Judeo-Christian tradition, and that the foundations of doctrine are just as significant as belief in God. But not all believers did, or do now, consider that doctrine derives its validation from miracles – Halyburton and other evangelicals argued that the biblical miracles rarely attended doctrinal pronouncements and that they served other purposes, like rekindling a wavering faith or enforcing a sense of dependency. Nor did, or do, they all consider that the evidence underlying belief in God is of the form of premises for an argument. Those who did adopt these positions had felt the influence, at first or second hand, of writers like Stillingfleet, Boyle and Locke; but those writers often attached more weight than Hume acknowledges to the purported place of prophecy in history. Prophecy was a subject tailor-made for a Humean critique, but he dismissed it in the last paragraph of Section x as nothing more than another purported miracle, as if the issue were one of the credibility not of prophecy, but of *reports* of prophecy.[29]

The belief which Hume investigates is the belief that miracles were historically necessary to validate a revelation as 'the foundation of a system of religion'. The notion of a system is important. Miracles were not proofs of divinity in general; rather, for those already disposed to believe, they confirmed a specific historical dispensation such as Judaism or Christianity. Hume does not consider how we would handle a putative miracle in our present experience. He draws on the seventeenth-century tradition about probability and testimony and the quasi-legal criteria of sound evidence developed in that tradition. Applying the criteria – the number of witnesses, their expertise, their disinterestedness, the consistency and circumstances of their reports, and an even-handed application of the same criteria to contrary testimony – he finds all historical reports of miracles unsafe, and thus, by implication, the biblical reports: the sources were unsophisticated, superstitious, uncorroborated and untested, and the documentation comes after private interest and other defects of human nature have intervened. This appears to be meeting the proponents of miracles on their own ground – the assessment of the a posteriori evidence – and Hume does this in Part ii of his discussion, effectively repeating standard moves, and with much of the same dismissive contempt, that one finds in the deist literature.

Hume's own contribution is an a priori argument in Part i that shows why the contempt is justified: the defenders of miracles have not begun to grasp the magnitude of the task confronting them. The kind of logic that had been sketched in the Port-Royal *Logic* and developed by Locke in his *Essay* was a logic that worked for ordinary cases of human testimony, but appeared to go into reverse where the testimony, though human, pertained to divine action. The normal method was to consider the antecedent likelihood of an event of the kind described, according to whether events of that kind occur consistently, inconsistently or never in our experience and in the recorded experience of others. We come closest to certainty in respect of those matters that appear to be part of the uniform course of nature, which we attribute to steady and regular causes, and we rarely demur when something of a kind that has any tendency to occur is reported. The importance of the particular evidence from testimony is inversely proportional to the strength of the general evidence from common experience, and where testimony conflicts with experience the credentials of the witnesses become crucial in the 'proportioning' of assent.[30] Since Locke believed that 'where such supernatural Events are suitable to ends aim'd at by him, who has the Power to change the course of Nature, there, under such Circumstances, they may be the fitter to procure Belief, by how much the more they are beyond, or contrary to ordinary Observation', he effectively set up Hume's problem for him. Can there be witnesses so credible that they outweigh the incredibility of the event?

Hume's definition of miracle as 'a transgression of a law of nature by a particular volition of the Deity, or by the interposition of some invisible agent' (*Enquiry*, Sect. x, Part 1, note) takes the possibility of supernatural intervention as given, though what Hume gives in one section he may take away in another. There is nothing here that entails that miracles do not or cannot happen, or that the concept is incoherent. The problem is epistemological.[31] We need all the evidence of experience, including history, that nature follows a given uniform course as proof that the regularity is a law, but must pit against that a piece of evidence that on at least one occasion the course was not followed. The evidence needed to establish the natural uniformity transgressed by a miracle thus gets in the way of evidence that will establish the supernatural transgression. That the inconsistency is epistemological, not logical, is shown by the essay 'Of Suicide'. 'Every action, every motion of a man innovates in the order of some parts of matter, and diverts, from their ordinary course, the general laws of motion.' A law of nature describes not a blanket uniformity, but the course that nature takes if 'particular volition' does not intervene; in God's case, however, 'if general laws be ever broke by particular volitions of the deity, 'tis after a manner which entirely escapes human observation'.[32] But if this is a problem for the believer, there is a problem too for Hume, who employs past testimony to establish the laws of nature and must therefore filter the historical evidence, which cannot be done without begging the question.[33] What he does is to assume, *per impossibile*, the law of nature proved by actual observation, then mount against it the testimony in favour of a hypothetical counterexample. The case for the counter-example would be established where the weight of the witnesses exceeded the evidence for the uniformity, and even then only in proportion to the excess on the side of the witnesses. He concludes that the acceptance of a revelation must be due to a faith that 'subverts all the principles' of the understanding.

Plainly, in no realistic case will the witnesses outnumber the instantiations of the law of nature, so the believer appears to be in a bind; but it is a different bind from the one Hume sets up. No believer seriously envisaged the quantitative contest required by Hume's theory of belief: it is always a contest between quantity (the regular course of nature) and quality (the contrary witnesses), and that is where the sceptic should be addressing the disparity. Hume does indeed impugn the quality; but by portraying the central issue as a narrowly quantitative one he does not explain how we *can* recognise freaks of nature, and what the eighteenth century called 'monsters'. In casting about to explain the exception we do not abandon the uniformity – a point he concedes near the end of the section in discussing a hypothetical failure of the sun to rise.

In considering the arguments of natural religion in Section xi,[34] Hume makes two points. Assuming for argument's sake that the evidence of nature warrants belief in a being exercising some degree of design and other attributes, he argues through an *alter ego* that the degree should be proportional to the effect; data derived from 'the present scene of things, which is so full of ill and disorder' cannot be inflated as they pass through the argument, to imply a 'superlative intelligence and benevolence'. This is fair criticism if the only consideration is the empirical design data, but overlooks that the 'inflation' commonly derived from a different source: the argument for the attributes of a first cause or necessary being. His other criticism concerns the uniqueness of the universe, as assumed by those who seek a unique cause. Hume seems to doubt both whether the cause of the universe is entirely dissimilar to all other causes known to us, and whether we could reason about it if it were, causal reasoning being dependent on our ability to subsume things under types or species. This seems only to require what the design theorist will readily grant, although the pursuit of similarities may drive him to a less than edifying picture of his deity.

In Section x Hume challenged the foundations of the belief in revelation without directly considering the existence and attributes of the deity; he now raised questions about the latter independently of the evidence of revelation. Clearly, two independently weak arguments cannot make a strong one, and Hume is entitled to target them singly as the readiest way to expose their weakness. But were they ever meant to be independent? That is, at best, a deist agenda, and when handled sceptically, it leaves the two pillars of belief so individually weakened that neither can effectively come to the other's support. But the believing Jew or Christian who considers the totality of the evidence would see the metaphor differently, and liken Hume to someone trying to test the pillars and arches of a bridge in isolation from each other. This fragmentation has parallels elsewhere. Hume considers the powers of reason in isolation from the senses, and the powers of the senses in isolation from reason; each singly leads to scepticism, first with regard to reason, then with regard to the senses (*Treatise*, 1.iv.1–2). But sense and reason, and feeling or sentiment also, are all parts of our make-up, and Hume shows how with the combination we can make sense of the world; if we do not exactly reconcile the elements, at least we keep them in a kind of constructive tension. The beliefs he rescues are fundamental beliefs upon which thought, action, communications and social relations depend: the mechanisms of the mind compensate for the deficiencies of reason and experience with regard to the external world, the self, causality and the uniformity of nature. These associations of ideas are the foundation of 'common life', the sphere within which, once the foundation is laid, causal reasoning can be effective because it relates to recurrent experience. Religion, however, projects us beyond our regular orbit for effective reasoning, as Hume indicates both in *Enquiry* xi and in the *Dialogues*,[35] and it opens up legitimate questions about our ability to understand what lies beyond. In this context scepticism is not the incoherent position it would be in common life.

This raises the so-called 'problem' of the *Dialogues*, where in Part XII Hume seems to permit the sceptic, Philo, to relent, and to present a compromise in which a religious outlook is built upon the ruins of scepticism (*DNR* 116). He would then seem to side with Cleanthes, who earlier tried to make a virtue of the logical weaknesses exposed by Philo, by self-consciously emphasising the 'irregularity' of the argument (57), that is, its power to carry more conviction than its logic justifies. Some have used this to argue that Hume, regardless of the logic of his position, finds some residual religious belief as inescapable as the beliefs of common life.[36] But Philo's compromise has no content, and the believer is not going to accept that the dispute between theism and atheism is purely verbal (118–19, cf. 121 note). The real message of the *Dialogues* remains a substantive one. All parties to the debate accept the existence in principle of a 'first cause', that is, a point where explanation would run out (43–4), but Hume's consistent position is that the ultimate principles in any subject of enquiry are unknown. Calling the first cause 'God' is a concession to convention, but when his characters agree that the attributes, not the existence, of such a being are the issue, this is not irony. Hume barely alludes to the quantities of design data that constitute the mass of the evidence for other thinkers. That is because the 'adapting of means to ends, throughout all nature' is never disputed. The question is what hangs on it, and one issue stands out. Experience reveals many 'springs and principles' in nature, and different kinds of order, none being an adequate model for all of nature; it cannot prove the ultimate priority of ordering mind over ordered matter, because the essence of both is unknown, and the possibility has to remain that the ultimate principles of nature are internal to the system, not external to it. Hume issues an important challenge to the metaphysics that had prevailed from Descartes to Clarke and Cheyne – the a priori demonstration that the properties of matter logically preclude the power of thought, which is therefore external. But he does not adequately address it at the point where it comes into their system – in the context of a debate on the causal principle, the nature of efficient causation, and the limitlessness of an independent being, which in Part IX of the *Dialogues* Hume misrepresents.[37]

In challenging the basis of belief in miracles, Hume did not expect to eradicate the belief, and when he exposed the logical weakness of 'philosophical' theism he did not expect to eradicate religious attitudes. His Calvinist upbringing had taught him to believe in deep irrationalities in human nature. *The Natural History of Religion* explores some of these. It is an important second prong to his critique of religious belief, but it is addressing a new target – the non-rational instead of the rational believer – and calls for different tools. It provides a none-too-favourable exposé of the psychology of the belief that underlies popular and institutional religion, which arises and prospers in Hume's view chiefly by stimulating the negative passions. His 1741 essay 'Of Superstition and Enthusiasm', identifying the two extremes of popular religion, laid the groundwork. Hume's argument in the *Natural History* is under-documented historically, but is consistent with familiar stereotypes of the fall of man and of sectarian corruption. Unsophisticated people do not understand the normal processes of causation; they are terrified by untoward events, posit unknown agents, magnify their powers, and seek appeasement. Those who are inclined to authority take on the role of mediators and come to be surrogates for the powers themselves, usurping control of people's lives. A situation born of ignorance, hope and fear becomes one of servitude, corrupting society, morality and the human spirit in equal measure, and the effect is particularly insidious when philosophy itself becomes an accessory to this social control. Even if Hume is right about the psychology of popular belief, however, his analysis cannot of itself show that there is no legitimate object for the popular fears, any more than his critique of rational religion could show that there is no legitimate object for the attempted proofs. This is the sceptic's dilemma, and commentators disagree on whether the place-marker left by Hume's rare references to a potentially 'true religion' or 'genuine theism'[38] are anything more than a recognition of the need for an ethical society. Since, however, beliefs that could not be justified appealed to something deep in human nature, it was important that they should be beneficial rather than harmful to society; and in the *History of England* (1754–62), despite a regularly unsympathetic portrayal of the motivation of religious leaders, and of religion's role as a source of social evils, Hume supports the view that 'there must be an ecclesiastical order, and a public establishment of religion in every civilized community' (*History* III.134–5) to avoid factional fighting. He commends a somewhat unhistorical idealisation of the English Reformation as non-fanatical, suggesting that the Anglican reformers under the eye of the monarch carried the people with them by slow, piecemeal change, retaining much that was familiar in both ceremonial and doctrine (iv.119–20). But though controlled public management can avert the turbulence that uncontrolled religion fosters, the Stuarts learnt that it can only do so by avoiding persecution and practising toleration (vi.165–6). A well-regulated civil religion is thus part of the cement of society. There is a subtext here intended to back the Moderate interest in the Scottish church.

AFTER HUME

Scepticism is a philosophy that questions and, if necessary, suspends judgement; it avoids dogmatism, including negative dogmatism. So it should not be surprising that Hume could be on social terms with liberal clerics, and yet it is doubtful if many of them understood him. Little was known or understood about philosophical scepticism in eighteenth-century Scotland. The religious and philosophical debates of post-Reformation Europe, in which sceptical techniques had been a significant weapon,[39] were largely played out and forgotten; the negative assessment of human knowledge that once motivated pioneers of the Royal Society[40] had lost its edge. Hume's searching critique of our faculties and our fundamental beliefs addressed questions few were inclined to ask, with a subtlety few could fathom. He seemed full of contradictions, and contradiction was the unbeliever's tool. Well-educated Edinburgh ministers vetoed Hume's candidacy for a philosophy chair in 1745 when he was seen as undermining the grounds of religious belief;[41] others futilely contemplated excommunicating him in the 1750s from a church he did not attend. By the 1760s, the clerical literati of Aberdeen took a more detached view: Hume's challenge to religion challenged *all* belief, and if one could establish a sound general theory of knowledge, religion would recover its place. Frequently under fire was Hume's account of causation. His analysis of our experience of causality was read as a dissolution of causality itself, and his inability to demonstrate the principle of universal causation seemed like a denial of the whole causal order and a reduction of the world to chance.

An important transitional figure is Hume's early friend and mentor, the lawyer Henry Home, Lord Kames (1696–1782). An idiosyncratic thinker, he sought to reconcile orthodox belief with a scientific world view, including the perfect uniformity of nature, but critics thought they saw too much of Hume in his system. His *Essays on the Principles of Morality and Natural Religion* (1751) was significantly revised in 1758. Drawing on some of the same psychological foundations as Hume and sharing much the same scepticism with regard to demonstrative reason, Kames nevertheless thought he had found in our native resources of 'sense and feeling' the answer to most of Hume's sceptical dilemmas, with regard both to common life and to religion. They include a sense of power or cause, and in some cases of design, and experience teaches us when we are beyond the range of human design. Divine design, being established, then provides a framework to understand the faculties by which it was discovered; it is invoked to counteract appearances that seem to run counter to scientific knowledge and to generate scepticism, by showing their planned usefulness. One such 'deceptive' appearance is that of human liberty, if considered as something more than the 'moral necessity' whereby people consistently act in conformity with their 'motives'. Both this and Kames's wider natural theology were attacked by an uncomprehending George Anderson (c. 1677–1756) in *An Estimate of the Profit and Loss of Religion* (1753), a work that occasionally also targets 'Esquire' Hume's *Enquiries*. Many of Anderson's philosophical views, and some of his criticisms of Kames and Hume, are repeated in *A Remonstrance against Lord Viscount Bolingbroke's Philosophical Religion* (1756).[42] An interesting reversal of the conservative stereotype, Anderson defended reason against the new 'sensitive' philosophy both in ethics and in metaphysics. He had developed a broad sympathy for the natural theology of English thinkers like Cudworth, Clarke and Wollaston. He supported Clarke on the inertness of matter and the demonstrability of a necessary being, although in *Remonstrance*, section VI, he confused Clarke's argument with the ontological argument of Descartes, failing to see the anomaly in defending the latter on causal principles. Anderson defended the argument from universal consent, answering standard objections, but he discounted the design argument, as demonstrating nothing but 'skill' and 'power'. If wisdom and goodness cannot be proved a priori, we are at a loss. Order and symmetry in nature tell us nothing of the 'ultimate end and use' of the parts of creation (*Remonstrance* 89); we therefore have no a posteriori basis for inferring the divine attributes. Anderson was less confident of an a priori ethic, while sharing Clarke's view that ethical principles are timeless principles of 'eternal fitness'. Anderson rejected any ethic that was not founded in the law of a lawgiver, which he discovered only in revelation.

Kames's views stimulated the 'common sense' reaction to Hume, the chief exponents of which – Thomas Reid (1710–96), George Campbell (1719–96) and Alexander Gerard (1728–95) – had been mutual allies from early in their careers. By the 1760s they had developed a common front against Hume on miracles. Campbell's *Dissertation on Miracles* (1762) offers no stronger a defence of biblical history than Gerard's *Dissertations on Subjects relating to the Genius and the Evidences of Christianity* (1766), and the latter's defence, being less *ad hominem*, raises deeper theoretical issues than Campbell's riposte to Hume's often slapdash use of sources. Both support the orthodox position that monotheism originated in revelation rather than reason, but Gerard renovates Turnbull's theory of 'proper samples' and makes much of the distinction between evidence and argument. 'Evidence perceived is the immediate cause of belief; reasoning is but one mean of bringing men to perceive the evidence' (*Dissertations* 43). Both Campbell and Gerard develop the same theory of evidence and testimony that Reid was enunciating in his logic lectures in the same period, lectures whose main substance was of longer standing and predates any interest in Hume's *Enquiry*.[43] Campbell's work was not then unique, but he had the greatest impact of the three, popularising the thesis that testimony is 'a natural and original influence on belief', moderated rather than proved by experience. The burden of proof lies with someone who wants to contest rather than accept a testimony (*Dissertation* 15–16), and then the weight of contrary testimony on the particular occasion is more significant than the extraordinary nature of the event attested (19). A witness to a disaster does not lose credibility from the fact that no such disaster has occurred before, but only from a proven record of unreliability (21–8); unreliability cannot, however, be established by opposing putative testimony to the experienced course of nature since, on the contrary, our knowledge of the latter embodies testimony (38).

The common sense response to Hume on natural religion is less clear from published works, but apparently none of them before Dugald Stewart (1753–1828) considered that the *Dialogues* merited an answer.[44] James Oswald (1703–93), in his earlier *Appeal to Common Sense in Behalf of Religion* (1766), accepted Hume's critique of reason so completely as to credit unexamined 'common sense' with the solution to every problem in philosophy, but he was never part of the Aberdeen philosophical circle.[45] He is no more significant in this connection than James Beattie (1735–1803), whose condemnation of the religious implications of Hume's philosophy in *An Essay on the Nature and Immutability of Truth* (1770) is unsubstantiated bombast.[46] Reid, in Essay VI of *Essays on the Intellectual Powers of Man* (1785), tried to show what followed on common sense principles and simple logic from the recognition of signs of design in the world. But his lectures show that he reached that recognition by the traditional induction from empirical data; he conceded, moreover, that even if we grant the signs of intelligent causes across nature, the evidence does not show there is just one such cause, or that its intelligence reaches perfection. He gets those results from the proof of a necessary being. Reid too, then, belongs to the tradition that runs the cosmological and design arguments in tandem; so does Gerard.[47] So up to a point does Campbell's successor, the Dutch-trained William Laurence Brown (1755–1830), but Brown was prepared for different individuals to find conviction in different proofs and cautioned against leaving religion entirely to reason. He drew widely on eighteenth-century natural theology, including English and Irish dissenters, and had the benefit of William Paley's *Natural Theology* (1802), the highly successful English riposte to Hume. 'That Philosophy [Hume's], as far as it relates to *Religion*, and Morals, has been exposed, as utterly false, by men of the most distinguished talents', so Brown could safely ignore it. Hume's writings 'are, now, very seldom perused, and will soon be forgotten'.[48] The Secessionist preacher John Ballantyne (1778–1830) was perhaps the only Scot of his day who had sufficient grasp of Hume's arguments to realise that Paley's rebuttal had loopholes, but his perceptive appraisal appeared only posthumously.[49]

In other pedagogic contexts, we have outlines of Adam Ferguson's (1723–1816) pneumatology lectures at Edinburgh. The existence of God is founded on universal assent, on the same design data as had been standard since the seventeenth century, and particularly on the appearances of providence operating as a kind of divine language, in which the signs are natural and the interpretation instinctive.[50] In deriving the attributes Ferguson emphasises inducements to morality embodied in the design. For Ferguson's successor, Dugald Stewart, we have the actual substance of his lectures on natural religion, firmly embedded in his theory of duty in Book III of *The Active and Moral Powers* (1828). He reserved judgement on Clarke's cosmological argument, beyond saying that Clarke's handling of space and time helped in understanding the concept of necessary existence. Stewart put his faith in universal consent and in the design argument, which he represented as a simple exercise of the reasoning powers from two 'first principles', that 'everything which begins to exist must have a cause' and that 'a combination of means conspiring to a particular end implies intelligence'. He shows more sympathy for Hume than earlier common sense writers, and judges much of Beattie's critique 'extremely frivolous'. He considers Hume's analysis of causal power incomplete rather than pernicious and shows how common sense principles can reconcile it to natural religion (III. ii. 1). But he thinks it unnecessary to proliferate the usual design data, except so far as a representative section proves the unity, wisdom and goodness of the designer. Stewart is thus another who believes that the problem of evil is resolvable within the framework of an a posteriori argument (III. ii. 2, III. iii. 1). But he is unusual among Hume's critics in agreeing that monotheism is a philosophical conception and that polytheism is our natural primitive condition (III.ii.3).

It is worth noting what happened to the evangelical John Witherspoon (1723–94) after he emigrated to Princeton in 1768 and had to present moral philosophy to arts students. He taught Clarke's demonstration and the design argument: 'There is, perhaps, at bottom no difference between these ways of reasoning, because they must in some degree, rest upon a common principle, viz. that every thing that exists must have a cause. This... must itself be taken for an original sentiment of nature, or' – hedging his bets – 'an impression necessarily made upon us, from all that we see and are conversant with'. He nevertheless warns against Hume, 'who seems to have industriously endeavoured to shake the certainty of our belief upon cause and effect' and other matters. The common sense writers have answered these 'metaphysical subtleties'. More distinctive is Witherspoon's use of the distinction between natural and moral attributes – a classification popularised by Clarke and adopted by Hume, but less common in the eighteenth century than in later philosophy of religion.[51]

Finally, acknowledgement should be made of a more substantial pedagogic aid: George Gleig's contributions to the third edition of the *Encyclopaedia Britannica* (1788–97). Gleig (1753–1840), the future primus of the Scottish Episcopal Church, prepared the massive essay 'Metaphysics', of which Part III, chapter VI, is 'Of the Being and Attributes of God'. He also wrote 'Theology', half of which is devoted to natural theology, including 'the duties and sanctions of natural religion'; and almost certainly also 'Miracles'. Gleig's argument for God's existence is an original version of the argument for a necessary being. He devotes particular attention to the impossibility of an infinite series, the kind of necessity involved in a necessary being, and the singleness of a necessary being. He springs a surprise in his discussion on singleness: for all we know there could be other necessary beings with other domains. But one is both necessary and sufficient to explain *our* existence, so no other can have meaning for *us*. Like Clarke (whom he criticises on detail), Gleig derives some of the attributes a priori, some a posteriori; unity was an a priori attribute for Clarke but is a posteriori for Gleig, inferred from the integrated nature of the natural system. Gleig is another who employs the distinction between natural and moral attributes, but unlike Clarke he thinks the moral attributes derivable a priori. Throughout this discussion there is no mention of Hume, but Hume is unmistakably a presence in the article on miracles. Gleig argues from examples that we discover empirically 'the established constitution and course of things' and can distinguish things simply extraordinary ('miraculous' cures) from things truly contrary to the course of nature (as would be the resurrection of someone dead and decayed). Only the last, he reasons, are impossible without deity, who will intervene only on occasions of great moment for humankind as a whole, 'the principal creature in this world'. In particular, miracles, including prophecy, are the essential evidence when 'a religion, or any religious truth, is to be revealed from heaven'. Gleig endorses Campbell's criticisms of Hume but goes further, calculating that the falsehood of the apostles' testimony 'would have been a deviation from the laws of nature less probable in itself' (Hume's 'greater miracle') than the miracles recorded in the Gospels, thus vindicating the Gospel record. This argument recurs in another Scots theologian, George Cook (1772–1845), later professor of moral philosophy at St Andrews. Cook additionally sharpens the common sense response of those for whom the biblical record is convincing, arguing that Hume sets a 'doubtful conclusion' about an unexampled event against 'a *law* of our constitution, an inclination to assent to unexceptionable testimony, a law ... instituted by the Supreme Being, and discovered by experience, although experience does not, as Mr Hume supposes, create it'.[52]

In the 1750s, Scots who opposed Hume saw his work as an affront, though they would have considered it a threat too, if he had held a university post. By 1762, however, he is described as 'so well known for the incredible mischief he has done to this age, by his loose and sceptical writings'.[53] Beattie in 1770 claimed that 'many, to my certain knowledge' had adopted Hume's 'tenets' though they did not understand 'the grounds of them'. 'His philosophy hath done great harm. Its admirers, I know, are very numerous; but I have not yet met with one person, who both admired and understood it.'[54] By 1805 a vocal minority of ministers, following James Finlayson, professor of logic at Edinburgh, persuaded themselves, but few others, that anyone who endorsed Hume's account of causation in a treatise on heat was an atheist and unfit to profess mathematics;[55] and in 1816 William Laurence Brown looked back to a time when Hume's philosophy 'which did so much mischief to the young and volatile' was 'in high fashion in Scotland. To sneer at Religion was deemed to be *genteel*.'[56] It was, however, sneering at Hume that was deemed genteel. Perhaps he did have closet supporters – Adam Smith up to a point, and certainly William Cullen – among intellectuals who were as capable as he was of reading and thinking for themselves. But no evidence has been found that he ever had a popular following, among Scottish youth or any other part of the community. On matters pertaining to religion, he was a voice in the wilderness.

NOTES

1   For the English and Irish responses see Isabel Rivers, 'Responses to Hume on Religion by Anglicans and Dissenters', *Journal of Ecclesiastical History* 52 (2001), 675–95.

2 Platonism came through the English thinkers, Henry More, John
   Smith and Ralph Cudworth; mysticism from the heretical writings
   of Antoinette Bourignon. Those showing this influence included the
   Aberdeen brothers George and James Garden (the latter lost his divinity
   chair at King's College in 1697) and several political figures.

3 William Walker, *Life of the Rt Rev. George Gleig* (Edinburgh: Douglas,
   1878).

4 *Memoirs of the Life of the Rev. Thomas Halyburton* (1714), II.iv.13,
   14. It is particularly the first-cause argument that invokes *reductio ad
   absurdum*.

5 Ibid., III.i.6.

6 See Leslie Stephen, *History of English Thought in the Eighteenth
   Century*, 3rd edn (London: Murray, 1902); R. M. Burns, *The Great
   Debate on Miracles* (London: Associated University Presses, 1981).

7 James Hog, *A Letter to a Gentleman concerning the Interest of Reason in Religion* (1716), 16–17; John McLaren, *The New Scheme of
   Doctrine contained in the Answers of Mr John Simson* (1717), ch. 12;
   Alexander Moncrieff, *Remarks on Professor Simson's First Libel and
   his Censure Considered* (1729), 43–59. On Simson see Anne Skoczylas,
   Mr Simson's Knotty Case (Montreal: McGill-Queen's University Press,
   2001).

8 Michael Hunter, ' "Aikenhead the Atheist" ', in Michael Hunter and
   David Wootton, eds., *Atheism from the Reformation to the Enlightenment* (Oxford: Clarendon Press, 1992), ch. 8. What Frazer and Aikenhead
   really believed cannot be established with any certainty. Halyburton
   discusses Aikenhead in *Natural Religion Insufficient, and Reveal'd
   Necessary to Man's Happiness in his Present State* (1714), 119–20.

9 These have been commonly called, since Kant, the 'teleological' and
   'cosmological' arguments, though strictly each is a *class* of arguments.
   The 'ontological' argument of Descartes and Leibniz is of no significance for Scottish, or indeed British, thought in the eighteenth
   century.

10 See *The State of the Moral World Considered* (anon., 1732), a work
   that was half-heartedly investigated by the Presbytery of Chirnside,
   and prompted Andrew Baxter's first publication, *Some Reflections on
   a Late Pamphlet* (1732). Both shared enough of Samuel Clarke's metaphysics to derive their natural theology from him; Dudgeon, however,
   was both a necessitarian and an immaterialist, and faced opposition on
   both fronts.

11 Turnbull's *Philosophical Inquiry concerning the Connection between
   the Doctrines and Miracles of Jesus Christ* (1726, 1732, 1739) was written in anticipation of a work by Anthony Collins, and his *Christianity
   neither False nor Useless, tho' not as Old as the Creation* (1732) was

directed against Matthew Tindal, as was Wallace's *The Regard Due to Divine Revelation, and to Pretences to it, Considered* (1731). Dudgeon responded to Wallace, and Wallace to Dudgeon.

12 William Wishart, *Theologia* (1716), discourse 11.

13 Archibald Campbell, *The Necessity of Revelation* (1739).

14 Simson's support for Clarke's *Demonstration of the Being and Attributes of God* (1705) is shown in correspondence with Campbell held in the National Archives of Scotland. Clarke had, however, denied any biblical basis for the doctrine of the Athanasian creed that God is three coequal, coeternal, consubstantial persons, and offered an 'Arian' reading that gave priority and pre-eminence to God as Father in his *Scripture-Doctrine of the Trinity* (1712). Simson eventually, and perhaps reluctantly, dissociated himself from the latter work.

15 It is found even in Dudgeon (*Philosophical Works*, 181), in a work that would be targeted by Campbell.

16 Given this Newtonian twist to the argument, it is interesting that Colin MacLaurin was Carmichael's student.

17 An unauthorised version, *Metaphysicae synopsis*, was published in 1742; Hutcheson made hasty revisions for an authorised edition dated 1744.

18 Hutcheson in his youth had challenged Clarke in correspondence, as had another Scottish thinker, Henry Home, and the future Scots antiquary Walter Bowman. I owe information on the last to Alessandro Lattanzi, who has found correspondence from Clarke to Bowman in the Biblioteca Nazionale, Florence.

19 Notebook of R. Brown, Edinburgh University Library, MS Gen. 74D.

20 Thomas Reid attended the latter class. See Turnbull, *De pulcherrima mundi cum materialis tum rationalis constitutione* (1726).

21 Cheyne, *Philosophical Principles*, 5th edn (1736), 2. Cf. Hume, *Principal Writings on Religion including 'Dialogues Concerning Natural Religion' and 'The Natural History of Religion'* (hereinafter *DNR* and *NHR*), ed. J. C. A. Gaskin (Oxford: Oxford University Press, 1993), 45.

22 An argument renewed a century later by the popular evangelical writer Thomas Dick (1774–1857).

23 MacLaurin, *Account*, 381; Hume, *DNR* 56.

24 Hutcheson does not hold that utility is the *source* of the beauty – a position George Berkeley seems to argue, against Hutcheson, in *Alciphron*, III.9.

25 *Discourses concerning the Perfections of God* (1742), sermon III.

26 Antoine Arnauld and Pierre Nicole, *Logic, or The Art of Thinking*, trans. J. V. Buroker (Cambridge: Cambridge University Press, 1996), Part IV, chs. 12–14; John Locke, *An Essay Concerning Human*

Understanding, ed. P. H. Nidditch (Oxford: Clarendon Press, 1975), iv.xv–xvi; Stillingfleet, *Origines Sacrae* (1661), Book 11.

27 *Letters of David Hume*, ed. J. Y. T. Greig, 2 vols. (Oxford: Clarendon Press, 1932), 1.24. The material belonged in the context of Hume's discussion of probability and the psychology of belief.

28 A surviving fragment on the problem of evil – a problem that for Hume was a permanent impediment to the detection of moral purpose in nature – foreshadows the position of Philo in the *Dialogues*: M. A. Stewart, 'An Early Fragment on Evil', in M. A. Stewart and J. P. Wright, eds., *Hume and Hume's Connexions* (Edinburgh: Edinburgh University Press, 1994), 160–70.

29 The English theologian A. A. Sykes had characterised prophecy as miraculous in *A Brief Discourse concerning the Credibility of Miracles and Revelation* (1742), 36, 43.

30 Locke, *Essay*, iv.xvi.6–8; cf. 13.

31 Antony Flew, *Hume's Philosophy of Belief* (London: Routledge, 1961), ch. 8. None of Flew's other writings on the subject are of the same standard.

32 David Hume, *Essays Moral, Political and Literary*, ed. Eugene F. Miller (Indianapolis: Liberty Fund, 1985), 581–2.

33 A significant critique of Hume's argument about miracles is provided by J. Houston, *Reported Miracles* (Cambridge: Cambridge University Press, 1994). Other recent studies have been stridently critical of Hume, but to less effect.

34 The section was first called 'The Practical Consequences of Natural Religion', to argue that there are none. Hume retitled it 'Of a Particular Providence and of a Future State', with another negative purpose, to show that natural religion cannot handle these topics; but many believers would have agreed, and entrusted them to revelation.

35 Hume, *DNR*, 36–7. Cf. *Enquiry Concerning Human Understanding*, Section v, Part 1; Section vii, Part 1; Section viii, Part 11, in David Hume, *Enquiries Concerning Human Understanding and Concerning the Principles of Morals*, ed. L. A. Selby-Bigge, 3rd edn, rev. P. H. Nidditch (Oxford: Clarendon Press, 1975). In *NHR*, 136–7, Hume will argue that the ordinary mind does not naturally have the synoptic view of nature that is the precondition for theism.

36 The shortest exposition of this view remains the best: R. J. Butler, 'Natural Belief and the Enigma of Hume', *Archiv für Geschichte der Philosophie* 42 (1960), 73–100.

37 His most serious misrepresentation is in the suggestion, '*External causes* there are supposed to be none' (*DNR* 91). An external cause is precisely what the argument is about. He also fails to see that the

necessity attributed to the necessary being is a necessity relative to the
contingency of the world, not the necessity of a *proposition* regardless of
any premises from which it is derived. He does however recognise that
the argument is intended to prove God's infinite character and unity
(*DNR* 90).

38 E.g. *Essays*, 73, 577–9; *NHR* 134; *DNR* 42, 121, 124, 126; Hume, *History
of England*, 6 vols. (Indianapolis: Liberty Classics, 1983–85), III.135.

39 Richard H. Popkin, *The History of Scepticism from Erasmus to
Descartes* (Assen: Van Gorcum, 1960).

40 For example, Joseph Glanvill, *Scepsis Scientifica* (1665) and other works.

41 The accusations are discussed in *A Letter from a Gentleman to his
Friend in Edinburgh* (1745).

42 In 1755–6 efforts were made in the General Assembly to excommunicate Kames and Hume, prompting a flurry of anonymous pamphlets
on their alleged views, but no philosophical debate. Anderson himself
submitted to the presbytery of Edinburgh a 'petition and complaint'
against the printer and publishers of Kames's *Essays* and published a
paper detailing ostensibly offensive passages, *The Complaint Made to
the Presbytery of Edinburgh Verified* (1756).

43 M. A. Stewart, 'Rational Religion and Common Sense', in J. Houston,
ed., *Thomas Reid: Context and Significance* (Edinburgh: Scottish Academic Press, 2003). On Campbell, see also Jeffrey Suderman, *Orthodoxy
and Enlightenment* (Montreal: McGill-Queen's University Press, 2001).

44 Reid in his 1780 lectures (n. 47, below) mentioned it only once in
a critique that still addressed the *Enquiry*; Beattie in correspondence
considered it contained nothing new. John Ogilvie (1733–1814), an
Aberdeenshire minister, commented on it briefly in a work against
English deism, *An Inquiry into the Causes of the Infidelity and Scepticism of the Times* (1783), sect. II. Stewart discussed Hume's characterisation of Philo in *The Philosophy of the Active and Moral Powers of
Man* (1828), Book III, ch. 2.

45 M. A. Stewart, 'Oswald, James', *Routledge Encyclopedia of Philosophy*,
10 vols. (London: Routledge, 1998), VII.168–70.

46 James Beattie, *An Essay on the Nature and Immutability of Truth,
in Opposition to Sophistry and Scepticism* (1770). In *Evidences of the
Christian Religion* (1786) Beattie is less polemical, but dismisses Hume
on miracles as an irrelevance: 'I need not quit the tract of my argument, for the sake of a paradox, so contrary to the natural dictates of
rationality', 61.

47 Reid, *Essays on the Intellectual Powers of Man* eds. Derek R. Brookes
and Knud Haakonssen (Edinburgh: Edinburgh University Press, 2002),
Essay VI,chs. 5–6; Reid, *Lectures on Natural Theology 1780*, ed. Elmer

Duncan (Washington: University Press of America, 1981); Alexander and Gilbert Gerard, *A Compendious View of the Evidences of Natural and Revealed Religion* (1828).

48 William Laurence Brown, *An Essay on the Existence of a Supreme Creator* (1816), xxxix, 174n. Cf. Ian Clark, 'The Leslie Controversy, 1805', *Records of the Scottish Church History Society* 14 (1963), 179–97, at 191–4.

49 John Ballantyne, 'On the Being of a God', in John Brown, ed., *Theological Tracts*, 3 vols. (Edinburgh: Fullarton, 1853–4), II.37–53. The most novel Scottish reading of the *Dialogues* is by the episcopalian Robert Morehead (1778–1842), *Dialogues on Natural and Revealed Religion* (Edinburgh: Oliver and Boyd, 1830). Morehead sees Cleanthes as a shifty deist and regards Philo's philosophy as the sounder basis on which eventually to found belief in revelation.

50 Adam Ferguson, *Analysis of Pneumatics and Moral Philosophy* (1766), 26; Ferguson, *Institutes of Moral Philosophy*, 3rd edn (1785), pt. III.

51 John Witherspoon, *Lectures on Moral Philosophy*, ed. Jack Scott (London: Associated University Presses, 1982), lectures VI–VII. Quotations from 96.

52 *An Illustration of the General Evidence Establishing the Reality of Christ's Resurrection*, 2nd edn (1826), 57–9n. Emphasis added.

53 Patrick Nisbett, *A Seasonable Address to the Citizens of Glasgow*, 24n.

54 Beattie, *Essay on Truth*, 8, 12.

55 Clark, 'The Leslie Controversy'.

56 Brown, *Existence of a Supreme Creator*, xxxviii.

3   The human mind and its powers

INTRODUCTION

Scottish Enlightenment discussions of the human mind and its powers developed from areas of investigation that on the face of it could hardly have been more disparate. Among them were angelology and scientific methodology. I shall comment on perceived relations between these various fields and shall then discuss some of the salient features of the studies on the mind and its powers. I shall pay particular attention to the fact that philosophers writing on the human mind saw themselves as natural scientists in exactly the sense in which physicists, botanists and physiologists were natural scientists. For they were all investigators of the natural world, a world which includes not only bodies, human and otherwise, but also human minds, and they all sought to work within the methodological constraints that characterise good natural science.

PNEUMATOLOGY AND NATURAL SCIENCE

Under the heading 'pneumatology', theologians had for centuries written on the nature of spirits, divine, angelic and human. It was, however, common for such writings to focus on angels, the good ones and the bad. In the Scottish universities through the seventeenth and into the eighteenth century angels slipped down, and in some cases off, the agenda of pneumatological studies as the focus shifted to humans, and pneumatology was transformed into the systematic study, particularly the philosophical study, of the human mind because that is the kind of mind into which we have the most insight.

Thomas Reid (1710–96), who lectured on pneumatology at King's College, Aberdeen from 1752 to 1764, describes the subject as 'the branch [of philosophy] which treats of the nature and operations of minds',[1] and adds that though we are in no position to say how many varieties of mind there may be in the universe, we do at least have certain knowledge of three, the brute animal, the human and the divine. Of these, Reid attends almost entirely to the human mind in the development of his pneumatology.

In this respect he follows George Turnbull (1698–1748), his teacher at Marischal College, Aberdeen. Turnbull's discussion on the mind and its powers in *The Principles of Moral and Christian Philosophy*[2] is in a sense the product of a religious consciousness, for he held that nature and nature's laws exist by divine will, and that a scientific investigation of nature can lead us to the discovery of the divine purpose for which things, including human minds, were created. As regards the human mind we can learn that it is a belief-forming mechanism whose purpose is to enable us to grasp truths. That is, such faculties as sense perception, memory and consciousness not only by their nature enable us to form beliefs, but also are reliable in the sense that they can be relied on to produce beliefs which are true.

Evidently, therefore, Turnbull thought that a scientific account of nature that was not placed in systematic relation to certain theological positions missed much of the point of doing the science. He was not alone in this. His colleague Colin Maclaurin (1698–1746), professor of mathematics first at Marischal College, Aberdeen, and then at Edinburgh, declared:

But natural philosophy is subservient to purposes of a higher kind, and is chiefly to be valued as it lays a sure foundation for natural religion and moral philosophy; by leading us, in a satisfactory manner, to the knowledge of the Author and Governor of the universe. To study nature is to search into his workmanship; every new discovery opens to us a new part of his scheme.[3]

Hence the better the science the better it serves the interest of theology, by giving us a truer insight into the created order and therefore into the mind of the creator. But if scientific study of the physical world can yield up knowledge of God, then scientific study of the human mind can be no less effective at yielding up such knowledge, and perhaps would be even more effective, as enabling us to extrapolate from a scientifically grounded understanding of the nature of the human mind to the nature of God's.

As regards the scientific nature of the study of mind, Turnbull is clear about it in general terms. An enquiry into 'the parts and proportions of the human mind, and their mutual relation and dependency...is an enquiry into a real part of nature, which must be carried on in the same way with our researches into our own bodily contexture, or into any other, whether vegetable or animal fabrick'.[4] Some flesh is put on these bones when he declares elsewhere that

every Enquiry about the Constitution of the human Mind, is as much a question of Fact or natural History, as Enquiries about Objects of Sense are: It must therefore be managed and carried on in the same way of Experiment; and in the one case as well as in the other, nothing ought to be admitted as Fact, till it is clearly found to be such from unexceptionable Experience and Observation.[5]

The empirical science of natural history, to which Turnbull here refers, focuses on the composition of substances and also on the processes or changes proper to them. In this sense during the Scottish Enlightenment the study of the mind came under the heading of 'natural history', since not only were the various powers of the mind and their interrelations investigated empirically, but attempts were made to trace the development of the mind as it passes through its natural span.

THE NEWTON OF THE MORAL SCIENCES

From the earliest years of the Scottish Enlightenment, therefore, the human mind was seen as located in nature, and as no less available for empirical scientific study than are other phenomena that are part of nature. Though Hume's *Treatise of Human Nature* (1739–40)[6] was groundbreaking in many ways, it was not groundbreaking in respect of the intention signalled in its subtitle – 'being an attempt to introduce the experimental method of reasoning into moral subjects' – for the first volume of Turnbull's *Principles of Moral and Christian Philosophy*, based on lectures Turnbull delivered during the middle years of the 1720s, more than a dozen years before the publication of the *Treatise*, could with no less propriety have had the same subtitle as the *Treatise*. Nor did Hume think of himself as the first to apply the experimental method of reasoning to moral subjects, though he did see himself as applying the method with particular rigour and as being able, in consequence, to go further than, for example, Locke, Shaftesbury, Mandeville, Hutcheson and Butler, whom he saw as likewise respecting the need for a properly scientific approach.

The famous description of Hume as 'the Newton of the moral sciences' should not be allowed to mask the fact that most of his contemporaries and near-contemporaries who wrote on mental philosophy saw themselves as Newtonians. Reid declared of Newton: 'His *regulae philosophandi* are maxims of common sense, and are practised every day in common life; and he who philosophizes by other rules, either concerning the material system or concerning the mind, mistakes his aim.'[7] Hume was rare, not in being a Newtonian, but in the extent to which he saw himself as accomplishing for the moral sciences what Newton had accomplished for the physical.

As regards what makes the Humean science of man a science, Hume tells us that it is 'impossible to form any notion of its [the mind's] powers and qualities otherwise than from careful and exact experiments, and the observation of those particular effects, which result from its different circumstances and situations . . . we cannot go beyond experience' (*Treatise*, xxi). The reference to 'experiments' should be handled lightly. Hume is not referring to acts similar to the experiments carried out in laboratories by modern cognitive psychologists experimenting on human beings. Instead he means little, if anything, more than 'observations', including introspective observations.

Hume's 'observations' are extensive. They have to be because he is constructing a science and therefore aims to reach some propositions that make a universal claim, one about the nature and workings of the mind of every person. In that case it is better if his propositions are grounded on many observations, and the more the better since additional observations tend to confirm (or disconfirm) hypotheses. Also, the wider the range of observations the better. Observations in widely separated places and at widely separated times are more helpful to the construction of a science of mind than are observations which are clustered around the here and now. Historical studies are therefore especially important to Hume, as a means of extending our powers of observation by seeing not only present human acts here through our own eyes, but also distantly past acts through the eyes of the distantly past eyewitnesses.

Hume writes of history: 'These records of wars, intrigues, factions, and revolutions, are so many collections of experiments, by which the politician or moral philosopher fixes the principles of his science, in the same manner as the physician or natural philosopher becomes acquainted with the nature of plants, minerals, and other external objects, by the experiments which he forms concerning them.'[8] That Hume refers to records of wars, intrigues, and so on, as 'so many collections of experiments' demonstrates that by 'experiment' he means little more than 'observation'.

The historical approach to the compilation of data contributory to a science of the mind essentially requires a third-person perspective, the scientist as a spectator of another person's acts. Hume also speaks of the need for a first-person perspective, that is, introspective observation, 'spectating one's own mind'. Hume tends however to privilege the third-person case, as witness his discussion of human freedom. He notes that when we act we *feel* free and thereby have evidence of our freedom gleaned by introspective examination, but that 'a spectator can commonly infer our actions from our motives and character; and even when he cannot, he concludes in general, that he might, were he perfectly acquainted with every circumstance of our situation and temper, and the most secret springs of our complexion and disposition'.[9] Hume sides with the spectator's judgement as against the agent's. The reason for this is Hume's belief that within the field of human liberty the spectator's judgement about the mind of a third person is more properly scientific, for he is judging in light of a much wider and richer database than is the agent, who instead relies chiefly on an immediate feeling of liberty, and who fails to deploy the array of evidence concerning past regularities in his behaviour. Indeed, unlike the spectator the agent may even have failed to notice the regularities in his own behaviour and so his belief is grounded in nothing more than his immediate feeling. When that one feeling is weighed in the scientific balance against a large batch of observational reports of past regularities, it is clear that the wise man, proportioning his belief to the evidence, would support the spectator's judgement.

Nevertheless Hume does not totally disregard the evidence yielded by introspection, though he advises caution. Suppose I want to know the feelings and thoughts I would have if in a given situation.

If I then place myself in that situation with a view to attending to my feelings and thoughts I will, by that very act of attention combined with the motive for that attention, affect my thoughts and feelings, and hence the results are distorted. In short the experiment is bad science. As Hume says: "tis evident this reflection and premeditation would so disturb the operation of my natural principles, as must render it impossible to form any just conclusion from the phaenomenon.'[10] Two points are in order here, the first emphasised by Thomas Reid, the second by Reid and Hume. First, most kinds of mental act are by their nature directed away from the mind and the acts in which it is engaged. Engrossed in the objects of the mental acts, we almost never attend to the mental acts themselves.[11] So, for example, we have thousands of memories, but perhaps have never tried to focus on the act itself of remembering through which we have immediate insight into past events. This is because it is the past events that matter to us, and not at all the act of remembering by which we gain access to them. So we know much more about the past than about the mental acts by means of which we gain access to it.

The second point is that introspection has a natural tendency to annihilate the mental act we are trying to introspect. Where the act is directed to an object then the object sustains the act, as for example an act of memory is sustained by the event being remembered, so that my act of memory is destroyed if my attention shifts from what I am remembering to, say, a flying saucer hovering overhead. Consequently the act that we are trying to introspect also disappears, and introspection has worked against itself.[12] What is required, according to Reid, is the development of our power of reflection. Reflection is more than mere consciousness. We can be conscious that we are remembering something even though we are not reflecting upon the recollective act, because in being conscious of something we may be barely noticing it, whereas in reflecting on something we are focused upon it and scrutinising it. Without such scrutiny, of which, in Reid's view, few of us are capable,[13] we can never have a distinct notion of the powers of the mind. Plainly mere consciousness of a mental act does not necessarily involve scrutiny of the act of which we are conscious.[14]

Despite such reservations, which were common currency, concerning introspection as a scientific tool for delivering up truths about the mind, Hume acknowledges in his practice the need to rely on it for establishing certain facts. Salient amongst these are the facts that we have ideas, and that our ideas tend to associate in accordance with certain principles. I shall now consider his teaching on ideas, and shall then turn to the principles of association.

THE THEORY OF IDEAS

Although Hume has a good deal to say about perception he does not have what we would now call a theory of perception, a theory about how external objects so affect the mind that we have sensory perceptions. Such a theory starts on the outside, with the external objects, and works inward to explain the mind's reaction to those objects. Hume cannot comfortably make such a move, since for him the metaphysical status of external objects is problematic. Instead he starts on the inside and proceeds to an explanation of how, starting with certain items in our mind, we come by our beliefs about the external world: 'All the perceptions of the human mind resolve themselves into two distinct kinds, which I shall call IMPRESSIONS and IDEAS.'[15] Impressions are those perceptions that have greater liveliness or vivacity, and these include 'all our sensations, passions and emotions, as they make their first appearance in the soul'. Ideas, on the other hand, are 'the faint images of these in thinking and reasoning'. Hume's belief that it was not necessary for him to employ many words explaining this distinction was over-optimistic. But the broad picture is clear enough, for we know the distinction between looking at something and later remembering what it looked like, or feeling a pain and later recalling what we felt. In each of these two pairs of perceptions something is first really present to us and is then re-presented, that is, is presented again, but this time only in our mind. In each pair the first perception is an impression and the second an idea.

Ideas, whether complex – that is, composed of several ideas in relation – or simple, form the content of acts of memory and of imagination, which differ, we are told, in two respects, the first being that ideas of memory are more lively and strong than those of imagination, and the second being that 'the imagination is not restrain'd to the same order and form with the original impressions; while the memory is in a manner ty'd down in that respect, without any power of variation'.[16] Here I want to focus on Hume's teaching on the imagination, a mental power that is worked harder than any other in his system, and to attend in particular to 'the liberty of the imagination to transpose and change its ideas'.[17] Even though we cannot, according to Hume, have a simple idea which does not resemble an antecedent corresponding simple impression, we can conjoin ideas to form a complex idea of something of which we have not previously had a unitary impression.[18] In making these new imaginative associations we are only giving assistance to something that is in any case happening, namely that ideas are associating with each other. It is only because the situation in our mind is by nature dynamic – with ideas on the move because the imagination is by nature an associative power – that we can by an act of will make a contribution to this ideational swirl by affecting the direction of change.

But even when the will is not engaged the associative process will proceed on its way. Hume knows this by introspection and, again by introspection, he discovered the three associative principles of resemblance, contiguity and causation. He here applies the 'experimental method of reasoning' to moral subjects; that is, he is doing empirical science on the basis of his observation that ideas come together in the imagination not randomly, but in an orderly fashion.

There is a Newtonianism at work in Hume's account not just in respect of the methodology deployed but also in respect of the content of the scientific doctrine. The law of gravity concerns the attraction of particles: every particle of matter in the universe attracts every other particle with a force which varies directly as the product of their mass and inversely as the square of the distance between them. For Hume simple ideas are analogues of Newtonian particles – as particles attract each other, so also do ideas. There is, therefore, in the human mind an analogue of the law of gravity. There are differences, of course, but the analogy is there, and is recognised by Hume, and might well have shaped his thinking on this matter: 'Here is a kind of ATTRACTION, which in the mental world will be found to have as extraordinary effects as in the natural, and to shew itself in as many and as various forms.'[19] As the law of gravity is universal in the natural world, so also there are some 'universal principles' by which the imagination is guided and which 'render it, in some measure, uniform with itself in all times and places'.[20] Since each principle of association is 'a gentle force which commonly prevails', what is at issue here with respect to principles of movement of ideas in our minds is only an analogy of gravity in the physical universe, for gravity always, and not merely 'commonly', prevails according to the Newtonian picture.

Philosophers of the Scottish Enlightenment had already put the concept of a natural principle of association of ideas to use. Francis Hutcheson ascribed a central role to association in the course of his discussions of disagreement in matters of ethics and of taste.[21] George Turnbull also, in his lectures at Marischal College in the 1720s, deployed the doctrine of association of ideas in a significant way. Turnbull's first move is to make clear what he means by the phrase 'association of ideas'. Whenever we think of a peach we imagine something of a particular shape, colour, and so on. But this complex idea is not a product of an associative act, because the qualities corresponding to these simple ideas really do by nature co-exist in the object. If certain qualities naturally belong to an object then the idea of one of those qualities is not *associated* with the idea of the object, because it is too late for such an association to occur. To have an idea of the object is thereby already to have an idea of the object's constituent qualities. On the other hand, if the object has always been presented to us in pleasant circumstances so that we have always been in a happy frame of mind when we have met with the object, then when the object is next presented to us it brings to mind the pleasure we had felt on previous occasions. By this means an association has been established between the idea of the object and the idea of our pleasure. The pleasure is not a component or constituent of the object, but by the repeated conjunction of the two things, the object and the pleasure, an association of ideas has been formed linking the object and the pleasure. The idea of the pleasure is, as Turnbull puts the point, 'added by the mind itself'.[22] The mind has to do the work, because the associated idea, the idea of pleasure, is not given as part of the idea of the object with which the idea of pleasure is associated.

Turnbull has a good deal to say about the importance of principles of association for our practical lives: 'what indeed is the whole of our labour in regulating the passions, in correcting, informing, or directing them; but an endeavour to render our passions suitable and proportioned to the nature of things as they are in themselves distinguished from all wrong associations?'[23] In respect also of sensory perception the law of association is essential if we are to learn to perceive the world in a characteristically human way, for it is only by the establishment of associations between the data of sight and touch that we learn to judge magnitude and distance on the basis of sight. Furthermore it is on the basis of associations established by repetitions that we learn to connect causes with their effects, and effects with their causes. Turnbull is therefore able to conclude that without the power to associate ideas, 'we would plainly continue to be in old age, as great novices to the world as we are in our infancy; as incapable to foresee, and consequently as incapable to direct our conduct'.[24]

Other philosophers also, from the earlier years of the Scottish Enlightenment, could be cited on the subject of association. Hence by the time Hume wrote the *Treatise* the topic was recognised as of major importance in the wider area of the scientific investigation of the mind. What is perhaps distinctive about Hume's treatment of the association of ideas is his rhetoric, the explicit comparison with particles in Newtonian space, as if the mind is a kind of mental space in which association occurs when mental particles gravitate to each other in a principled way. The Newtonian rhetoric needs watching, however, for Hume also deploys an alternative metaphor: 'what we call a *mind*, is nothing but a heap or collection of different perceptions, united together by certain relations, and suppos'd, tho' falsely, to be endow'd with a perfect simplicity and identity'.[25] Hume does indeed appear to reject this doctrine, for he declares: 'The mind is a kind of theatre, where several perceptions successively make their appearance; pass, re-pass, glide away, and mingle in an infinite variety of postures and situations.'[26] This metaphor is suggestive of a Newtonian conception of space as the place of particles in motion, but Hume immediately withdraws the metaphor: 'The comparison of the theatre must not mislead us. They are the successive perceptions only, that constitute the mind; nor have we the most distant notion of the place, where these scenes are represented, or of the materials, of which it is compos'd.'[27] The experimental method of reasoning is being deployed here. Hume has no impression, nor therefore an idea, of a mind unless mind is nothing more than perceptions in mutual relation. His experience cannot take him beyond impressions and ideas to something which is neither an impression nor an idea but is instead that to which impressions and ideas belong or in which they inhere. Perceptions must therefore be what mind is; it is not some perception or other, but the bundle.

REID'S ACCOUNT OF THE MIND

Hume's account of *mind* duly came under attack from the direction of common sense. Reid affirms: 'By the mind of a man, we understand that in him which thinks, remembers, reasons, wills.'[28] Later he makes it clear that he is not ducking the issue: 'Again, if it should be asked, What is mind? It is that which thinks. I ask not what it does, or what its operations are, but what it is. To this I can find no answer; our notion of mind being not direct, but relative to its operations.'[29] We are conscious of the operations of mind. But why should we add 'of mind'? Surely what we are conscious of are the operations themselves, and if we are not conscious of the mind engaged in these operations then by what right do we refer the operations to a mind? Indeed if we are not conscious of a mind then what do we mean by the term? We presumably mean something by it since if we know we are not conscious of it we must know enough about the mind to know that none of the things we are conscious of is a mind.

In an early manuscript (dated 22 October 1748) Reid expressed ignorance on the question of what the mind is: 'When my thoughts and Ideas and passions change what it is that continues and is called the Mind I know not. I seem to have no Idea of it and yet am under an invincible Necessity of believing there is some such thing.'[30] There are obscurities in this passage, and in others quoted earlier, but it is plain that Reid's expression of ignorance is not unqualified, for he has in fact formed a concept of mind, that is, a concept of 'that which thinks, remembers, reasons, wills'. He has been able to do this though he is not directly conscious of his mind, nor knows what it is about his mind as a result of which it is able to perform such acts as thinking, remembering, reasoning and willing.

It is necessary to emphasise Reid's use of the phrase 'not direct, but relative' in the passage cited above. We know our mental acts directly, for we are conscious of them and consciousness gives us direct or unmediated knowledge of its object. But other things can be known only indirectly or in a mediated fashion, and Reid holds that knowledge of mind is relative, being relative to knowledge of its acts.[31]

Reid, who regards our languages, especially their syntax, as a route to philosophical truth, finds ample support in linguistic usage for his doctrine that our minds are agents. He writes:

There are certain common opinions of mankind, upon which the structure and grammar of all languages are founded. While these opinions are common to all men, there will be a great similarity in all languages that are to be found on the face of the earth. Such a similarity there really is; for we find in all languages the same parts of speech, the distinction of nouns and verbs, the distinction of nouns into adjective and substantive, of verbs into active and passive ... This similarity of structure in all languages, shews an uniformity among men in those opinions upon which the structure of language is founded.[32]

For example: 'In all languages, we find active verbs which denote some action or operation; and it is a fundamental rule in the grammar of all languages, that such a verb supposes a person – that is, in other words, that every action must have an agent.'[33] Since we normally refer to the mind with the aid of the active voice of the verb, as when we say that we think, remember, imagine, suppose, wonder and so on, the implication is that we operate with a conception of the mind as an agent, something whose nature is to perform acts. For Reid, investigation of language was part of the battery of means we employ in the course of a properly scientific investigation of mind.

The fact that for Reid mind can be investigated scientifically should not be permitted to mask the fact that he believed mind to be as different from matter as any two things in the created order can be. In short he held that mind is essentially active and matter passive. It is only because material things, such as groves, seas and winds, were once thought of as containing a principle of activity, namely the spirits that inhabited them, that the verbs employed to speak about such material things were employed in the active voice.[34] The awesome range of scientific methodology could not, for Reid, be demonstrated more definitively than by showing that it is no less applicable to mind than to matter.

REID, DUGALD STEWART AND MENTAL ACTS

In a lecture note dated 6 February 1765, Reid affirms that 'as far as Reasoning is used in Pneumatology it must commonly be of the Inductive kind.'[35] He hereby signals his belief that the study of mind must be in large measure empirical and scientific. Thirty years later he was still firm in this belief, as we learn from an interesting manuscript, composed c. 1790, in which he has critical things to say about doctrines concerning memory that were formulated by his former student Dugald Stewart.[36] The latter discusses memory in relation to acts of attention. Stewart believes that our attention span is more limited than we realise, and that our failure to realise its limitations is due to the fact that our memory is working harder for us than we suppose it to be. On this account we can attend to only one thing at a time, and when we appear to attend to several things at once this appearance is due to the speed at which the mind works. Thus, while it might seem that a person with a good musical ear can attend simultaneously to several parts of a piece of music, what is actually happening is that the mind is continually redirecting its attention from one part to another and doing so with such speed that the redirections are imperceptibly fast.[37] Likewise, with respect to vision, according to Stewart, though the mind seems able take in a geometric figure all at once, it does not in fact do so. Instead it attends successively to the various points in the figure but performs these acts of attention so fast that, as Stewart puts it, 'the effect, with respect to us, is the same as if the perceptions were instantaneous'.[38] Since in each of these cases we are dealing with a succession of acts, and are not taking in several things simultaneously, there must be a series of acts of memory, even if these are so fast that we do not notice that they occur.

Stewart's willingness to countenance the occurrence of mental acts of which we are not conscious is also evident in his explanation of the fact that we can recognise the truth of a theorem instantaneously even though we cannot state immediately what our conviction is based on. The explanation, in short, is that there is 'an intellectual process, which, as soon as it is finished, vanishes almost entirely from the memory'.[39] Plainly, therefore, Stewart sets considerable store by his hypothesis that we have recollections of which we are unconscious, or at least which are irretrievably lost by the time we come to give an acount of our mental acts or processes.

But Reid will have none of this, because he thinks Stewart is doing bad empirical science – he is positing hypotheses under the guise of presenting facts. Reid finds a target for this criticism early on in Stewart's *Elements*, where the latter discusses the case of a person who is in a room in which a clock strikes though he is unable to say a moment later whether he heard the chimes. Stewart thinks that sensation and perception occurred and that due to inattention there was, a moment later, no recollection of these acts. Reid wants to know how Stewart knows this. Reid thinks it probable that the sound makes an impression on the ear, but argues that, for the occurrence of a sensory perception, at least two further things must be in place, first an auditory sensation and secondly a belief in the occurrence of the physical sound. And if we have no recollection of sound, then how are we to decide whether we heard it or not? 'If therefore one Man says, that in this Case we had both the Sensation & Perception but were not conscious of them; another that we had both with Consciousness, but without any degree of Memory; a third that we had the sensation without the perception; & a fourth that we had neither; I think they all grope in the dark, and I would not trust much to conclusions built upon any of these Hypotheses.'[40]

This response by Reid is formally the same as his response to all Stewart's examples of mental acts of which we are unaware: 'Every thing in this Discourse that I dissent from is grounded upon the Hypothesis of hidden trains of thinking of which we have no Remembrance next Moment upon the most attentive Reflection. This after considering all you have said seems to me a Hypothesis which admits neither of proof nor of refutation. And I wish you to be much upon your guard against Hypotheses.'[41]

Yet Reid also, no less than Stewart, posits mental events or mental acts of which we are unconscious. He holds that a perceptual act has three parts, a sensation, a conception of a quality in the thing that causes the sensation, and a belief in the existence both of the conceived quality and of the thing that has the quality.[42] Of these three elements the sensation functions purely as a natural sign of the quality that we conceive. We do not naturally attend to it, and most of us go through life not knowing of the existence of visual sensations, as opposed to our perceptions of visible objects. But although we get by without noticing them we can train ourselves to notice them, by persistent reflection, inner scrutiny, over a long period of time. Herein lies the difference between Reidian sensations and the fast mental processes which Stewart posits. We can access Reidian sensations, and bring them under scrutiny, but we cannot bring under scrutiny the processes that Stewart posits. In the one case there is good empirical evidence available, to the few if not the many, and hence Reid's philosophy of perception is not based on a mere hypothesis; and in the other case Stewart lacks good empirical evidence for the occurrence of unconscious rapid mental acts, and instead he hypothesises them, nothing more.

Reid's deployment of Newton's scientific methodology was as extensive as that of any philosopher of the eighteenth century, and it was guided by a profound grasp of Newton's scientific work. Arguably Reid's grasp of Newtonian methodology was more profound than Hume's, and if indeed it was then a likely explanation for this would be that Reid, in contrast to Hume, had spent many years in close study of Newton's scientific writings, and in working intensively in the mathematical and natural sciences.

A COMMON SENSE APPROACH TO POWER

Reid uses the term 'power' in at least two senses, one general and the other more specific. First the general sense. Any operation implies a power to perform such an operation. As he affirms: 'to suppose any thing to operate, which has no power to operate, is manifestly absurd'.[43] The mind has many powers, some of which are part of the original constitution of the mind, such as the power to imagine, to remember, to conceive, to judge. As with the power of sight or hearing, we can be taught to make these other powers more effective, but if we lack one totally we cannot be taught to acquire it. This is to be contrasted with powers, of the kind Reid terms 'habits', that we can acquire by use, exercise or study, such as the power to speak Latin. Those powers of the mind which are not habits but are instead part of the original constitution of the mind are termed 'faculties' by Reid.[44]

Any power, whether a faculty or a habit, is known indirectly, in the sense indicated earlier when we were considering our knowledge of the existence of our own minds. That is, our powers are known only in virtue of their relations to other things which are known directly. In particular, we know a power only through our knowledge of the acts which constitute the exercise of the power. Power is therefore not an object of consciousness, for such objects, for example our acts of mind, are, unlike powers, known directly. It is true that we can reason our way from the existence of an act to the existence of a power to perform that act, but this does not imply that we are after all conscious of powers of mind, for reason is a different faculty from consciousness.

I turn now to the more specific sense of 'power'. In this latter sense, 'power' is the central concept in Reid's *Essays on the Active Powers*.[45] Traditionally a distinction has been made between active and passive power, for example the power to heat something and the power to be heated. Reid however rejects this kind of language. He thinks that the sun's heating a stone is not an exercise of power because the sun is wholly unable to do anything whatsoever about it. It heats the stone by necessity, and its inability to refrain from doing what it does is a form of powerlessness, not of power. Reid develops a concept of freedom or liberty in light of these considerations. Beings that are able to do and also to refrain from doing what they do have active power, and it is such beings, and such only, that are free. As to what it is about a being that enables it to be free, Reid focuses on two powers, those of intellect and will. As regards will, Reid affirms: 'Every man is conscious of a power to determine, in things which he conceives to depend on his determination. To this power we give the name of *Will*.'[46] The exercise of such a power cannot proceed without a corresponding exercise of intellect, for we cannot will without willing to do something, and we must therefore have a concept of the 'something'. Since the formation of concepts is an act of intellect, for this reason, if no other, will cannot operate without intellect.[47] Intellect proposes and the will disposes.

It follows from this analysis that there is no active power in dead matter; but we human beings have active power, and centrally what it permits us to do is to pause between alternative lines of action and then to perform one and not the other, though in that very circumstance we could instead have performed the one that we did not choose. The act that is performed has, therefore, contingent existence, in the sense that had the agent so willed he could instead have performed the other act to which he was open. According to this account the cause of the act is neither a desire that the agent has, nor any other of his motives; it is instead the agent himself, exercising active power and therefore free not to do whatever he does and whatever the strength of his motive.

This power does not lift us human beings out of the natural realm, but it does give us a special place in it, in so far as we have an openness to contraries that appears not to be a feature of the nature of other things around us. From a Reidian perspective this last point implies that even though we are free beings we are not any the less appropriate objects of empirical scientific investigation than are all the other things that we meet with in the natural order. And it is just such an empirical investigation of human agency that we find in the *Essays on the Active Powers*. Reid's conception of philosophy is thus identical to Hume's. It would be a pity if this identity of conception were masked by the fact that they reached very different conclusions on so many other matters.

NOTES

1   Thomas Reid, *Essays on the Intellectual Powers* (hereinafter *IP*), text edited by Derek Brookes; annotations by Derek Brookes and Knud Haakonssen; introduction by Knud Haakonssen (Edinburgh: Edinburgh University Press, 2002), Preface 12.

2   George Turnbull, *The Principles of Moral and Christian Philosophy* (London, 1740). It was originally conceived as two separate books, the first entitled *The Principles of Moral Philosophy*, and the second entitled *Christian Philosophy*. The London publisher evidently thought that the sales prospects of the second book would be improved if it was tacked on to the first book, and declared to stand to the first book as volume two to volume one of a unitary work, *The Principles of Moral and Christian Philosophy*. The publisher seems to have thought of this late in the day, since the second volume has two title pages, one with the title only of the second book, and the other with the title *The Principles of Moral and Christian Philosophy. In Two Volumes*. The first book however, *The Principles of Moral Philosophy*, gives no indication that it is volume one. It was published fourteen years after Reid ceased to be his pupil. But Turnbull tells us that the book is 'the substance of several pneumatological discourses (as they are called in the School language) read above a dozen years ago to students of Moral Philosophy, by way of preparative to a course of lectures, on the rights and duties of mankind' (1.i). It is therefore safe to assume that Reid was familiar with Turnbull's ideas and had attended the lectures in which they were expounded. For helpful discussion of Turnbull's career see M. A. Stewart, 'George Turnbull and Educational Reform', in Jennifer J. Carter and Joan H. Pittock, eds., *Aberdeen and the Enlightenment* (Aberdeen: Aberdeen University Press, 1987), 95–103.

3   Colin Maclaurin, *An Account of Sir Isaac Newton's Philosophical Discoveries* (London, 1748), 3.

4 Turnbull, *Moral and Christian Philosophy*, 1.i.

5 George Turnbull, *A Treatise on Ancient Painting* (London, 1740), x.

6 David Hume, *A Treatise of Human Nature*, ed. L. A. Selby-Bigge, 2nd edn, rev. P. H. Nidditch (Oxford: Clarendon Press, 1978). (Hereinafter *Treatise*.)

7 Thomas Reid, *An Inquiry into the Human Mind on the Principles of Common Sense*, ed. Derek R. Brookes (Edinburgh: Edinburgh University Press, 1997), 12.

8 *Enquiry Concerning Human Understanding* (hereinafter *EHU*), in David Hume, *Enquiries Concerning Human Understanding and Concerning the Principles of Morals*, ed. L. A. Selby-Bigge, 3rd edn, rev. P. H. Nidditch (Oxford: Clarendon Press, 1975), 83–4.

9 *Treatise*, 408–9.

10 Ibid., xxiii.

11 *IP*, 1.vi, 60–61.

12 Ibid., 61.

13 '[T]he candid and discerning Few, who are capable of attending to the operations of their own minds', Reid, *Inquiry*, 3.

14 *IP*, 1.v, 58.

15 *Treatise*, 1.

16 Ibid., 9.

17 Ibid., 10.

18 In *Treatise*, 5–6 Hume famously allows that a person can have a simple idea of a shade of blue, even though he had not previously had an impression of that same shade. The literature on the 'missing shade of blue' is extensive.

19 *Treatise*, 12–13. For discussion of the doctrine of association of ideas in the Scottish Enlightenment see A. Broadie, 'The Association of Ideas: Thomas Reid's Context', *Reid Studies*, 5:2 (2002), 31–53.

20 Ibid., 10.

21 See ch. 14 of this volume.

22 Turnbull, *Moral and Christian Philosophy*, 1:85.

23 Ibid., 1.88.

24 Ibid., 1.90.

25 *Treatise*, 207.

26 Ibid., 253.

27 Ibid., 253.

28 *IP*, 1.i, 20.

29 *Essays on the Active Powers* (hereinafter *AP*), in *The Works of Thomas Reid*, ed. Sir William Hamilton, 6th edn, 2 vols. (1863; reprint, Bristol: Thoemmes, 1999), 513B.

30 Aberdeen University Library MS 2131/6/I/18: 2. See *Inquiry*, 317.

31 *AP*, 513A–515A.

32 *IP*, 1.i, 36.
33 Ibid., 1.ii, 44.
34 *AP*, 515B–517A.
35 Aberdeen University Library MS 2131/4/1/9, fol.1 recto, entitled 'Of Inductive Reasoning'. My *Thomas Reid on Logic, Rhetoric and the Fine Arts* (Edinburgh: Edinburgh University Press, forthcoming) will contain an edited version of this manuscript.
36 For helpful discussion of aspects of this manuscript see Daniel N. Robinson, 'Thomas Reid's Critique of Dugald Stewart', *Journal of the History of Philosophy* 3 (1989), 405–22.
37 Dugald Stewart, *Elements of the Philosophy of the Human Mind* (London: William Tegg, 1867), 70.
38 Ibid.
39 Ibid., 67.
40 Aberdeen University Library MS 2131/3/11/3: 3, in Paul B. Wood, ed., *The Correspondence of Thomas Reid* (Edinburgh: Edinburgh University Press, 2002), Letter 115.
41 Aberdeen University Library MS 2131/3/11/3: 6.
42 *IP*, II.xvi, 193–200.
43 Ibid., 1.i, 21.
44 Ibid.
45 See also Thomas Reid, 'Of Power', ed. J. Haldane, *Philosophical Quarterly* 51 (2001), 1–12.
46 *AP*, 530A–B.
47 For discussion of this relation see A. Broadie, 'The Scotist Thomas Reid', *American Catholic Philosophical Quarterly* 74 (2000), 385–407.

4 Anthropology: the 'original' of human nature

THE NATURAL HISTORY OF MAN

In a number of thinkers of the Scottish Enlightenment[1] – David Hume, Adam Ferguson, Adam Smith, and others less well known – the philosophical analysis of human nature and the 'empirical' analysis of human societies, human history and the natural world merged in a distinctive synthesis that led to the rise of the human and social sciences. This was not the only eighteenth-century mixture of philosophy with history and anthropology; some equally famous fusions are Gibbon's 'philosophical history' (which was influenced by Hume and Smith), Montesquieu's *Spirit of the Laws* and Rousseau's *Discours sur l'origine et les fondements de l'inégalité parmi les hommes* (both of which were influences on the later Scottish Enlightenment). Yet the combination brewed in Aberdeen, Edinburgh and Glasgow, though akin in important ways to these works, was also quite distinctive.

One aspect of the manner in which Scottish authors analysed human nature has come to be called 'conjectural history'. Dugald Stewart coined the term 'conjectural history' to describe the methodology adopted by Adam Smith in 'Considerations concerning the First Formation of Languages' and by Hume in the *Natural History of Religion*.[2] Conjectural history responded to a basic problem:

Whence...the different forms which civilized society has assumed in different ages of the world? On most of these subjects very little information is to be expected from history...A few insulated facts may perhaps be collected from the casual observations of travellers, who have viewed the arrangements of rude nations; but nothing, it is evident, can be obtained in this way, which approaches to a regular and connected detail of human

79

improvement . . . In such inquiries, the detached facts which travels and voyages afford us, may frequently serve as land-marks to our speculations; and sometimes our conclusions *a priori*, may tend to confirm the credibility of facts, which, on a superficial view, appeared to be doubtful or incredible.[3]

Some of the best-known Scottish intellectuals did not approve of a priori history, and in fact 'strong' conjectural history was not common even in the works of Smith and Hume. Adam Ferguson, and following him William Robertson, criticised 'conjectures' that moved from observations about our present state to inferences about what rude man must have been like.[4] Yet Ferguson did not reject historical speculation as such but rather the unwarranted conjectures found in Rousseau's *Discours sur l'inegalité*, since although we have limited access to man in his rude state it was important to know *something* about this state and not just give way to fancy, as Rousseau did. We ought instead to base our judgements on warranted claims about man's unequal development and first-hand reports of less developed societies in places remote from Europe. Consequently, Ferguson drew on works such as Lafitau's *Mœurs des sauvages ameriquains comparées aux mœurs des premiers temps* (1724) and Buffon's *Histoire naturelle* (1749–88) that provided information about men in rude climes and a comparative model on which to build. He also drew on ancient histories such as Tacitus' *Germania* (as did the contentious Gilbert Stuart in *A View of Society in Europe* (1778)) as credible accounts of man's early state.

Smith's student (and Hume's admirer) John Millar provided one of the best statements of the underlying assumptions of many of the Scottish theorists. In *The Origin of the Distinction of Ranks*, Millar made a case that 'the common improvements which gradually arise in the state of society' lead to the transformation in 'the manners, the laws, and the government of a people'.[5] For Millar these changes were almost entirely positive, the emancipation of social inferiors, women, slaves and children from their barbarous conditions in rude times through the emergence of liberal societies and governments. In the 'Preface' he remarked:

When illiterate men, ignorant of the writings of each other, and who, unless upon religious subjects, had no speculative systems to warp their opinions, have, in distant ages and countries, described the manners of people in similar circumstances, the reader has an opportunity of comparing their several descriptions, and from their agreement or disagreement is enabled to ascertain the credit that is due to them.[6]

A comparative historical method can establish regularities in temporally and geographically discontinuous accounts offered by different peoples in remote times and places, and use these regularities to collect general characterisations of a given epoch or state. This was not to serve as a base for a priori conjectures. Ferguson would probably have accepted Millar's description despite the fact that the particularities of the history as well as the politics it warranted (civic republicanism versus classical liberalism) were quite different. But both Millar and Ferguson agreed – like Lafitau, Montesquieu and others before them – that a general picture of man in his rude state could be accessed by comparisons of travel narratives, histories and other sorts of information, and that the comparison was predicated on man's unequal development. And even Ferguson, who was wary of separating 'man' from particular 'men', emphasised certain consistent passions in rude societies, like the praiseworthiness of fortitude,[7] despite the variations wrought by climate. A paradigmatic example of this sort of analysis of man's initial state was Robertson's *History of America* with its description of the many commingled features of the savage state – the passionate tempers of savages and their lack of capacity for abstraction, their love of equality and community (as in Tacitus' *Germania*), listlessness and fortitude under torture, the unequal status of women, etc.[8]

This could even be independent of a progressive theory of history. Although the best-known Scottish historically based philosophical arguments about human nature offer a series of progressive stages of development, each superior in some specifiable economic, political or cultural particulars to the prior stages from which they developed, this was not mandatory. Ferguson strongly criticised the excesses of Hume's arguments on behalf of commercial society, and emphasised the importance of civic virtue that flourished and decayed in different times and places without a strictly specifiable *telos*. Criticisms can also be found in Lord Kames, William Smellie and John Gregory, among others. Even the historical arguments of Hume, Smith and Millar are not completely linear.

Lord Monboddo, though, makes for a particularly striking example. Monboddo, an unabashed admirer of the ancients, argued in two repetitive works of six lengthy volumes each – *The Origin and Progress of Languages* and *Antient Metaphysics* – that modern philosophy and culture were at best derivative of and at worst destructive of the ancient wisdom derived from the Greeks and Egyptians. Yet, when Monboddo analysed human nature, like Millar and Ferguson he presented a stadial theory built on the works of ancient and modern historians, travel narratives, natural scientific works and observations (some first hand) of 'wild children' and orang-utans who were representatives of man in his 'rudest' pre-societal state, alongside metaphysical considerations on man's eternal essence. Each source when properly analysed could be seen to display different features of the historical stages through which humans had passed.[9] Thus male orang-utans – whom Monboddo considered, like Rousseau, to be not animals but wild humans – were swifter than Achilles and thus were examples of a historical stage of man prior to the Trojan War. Female orang-utans exhibited great modesty, showing the proper mores and sentiments of the earliest stages of society. The Wild Girl of Songi provided an example of an even earlier stage than either Peter the Wild Boy or the socialised if pre-linguistic orang-utan tribes. And so on. So, despite Monboddo's disdain for the corrupting influence of the 'experimental philosophy' and his arguments for eternal neo-Platonic universals, he was also an 'experimental' philosopher, although quite 'conjectural' in Stewart's sense. Monboddo makes clear the enormous range of what could be considered fodder for such a theory, including the natural world as well as 'living experiments' like Peter the Wild Boy (whom he studied first hand). Granted civilisation has been on a slide since the Egyptians, but the means for investigating it are all around us in the empirical survey of the uneven development of man and the interconnection of stages in a stadial history.

There were many ways of delineating the stages. In Adam Smith, who would appear to be the clearest case, although the four stages of society are famously delineated in terms of the need to alter the means of subsistence due to population pressure, as Smith develops them they are overlaid with many other considerations including religion, science and culture.[10] Millar's *Origin* makes for an even more striking case, as his four stages at first appear to be delineated economically but come to be differentiated more in terms of forms of political authority. Dunbar argued for a three-stage theory built around the emerging intellectual capacities of man. In Ferguson's *Essay* many variables are intertwined in the discussion due to the complexity of contemporary civil society. All assumed some cross cultural and trans-historical needs and functions that allowed for the comparison of various historical stages, and all assumed an initial state.

In the remainder of this chapter, I will consider a few of the ways Scottish philosophers accessed and characterised the initial state, the original of human nature. I will first discuss some background assumptions about the 'human frame', and then consider the ways in which historical and observational evidence was used by Scottish philosophers to try to understand human nature.

THE 'HUMAN FRAME' AND THE HISTORY OF SENTIMENT

The Scottish thinkers I have mentioned had a wide range of intellectual influences, from philosophers such as Montesquieu and Rousseau to natural lawyers such as Barbeyrac and Pufendorf to speculative historians such as Lafitau and Charlevoix. Two British progenitors were also centrally important: Bernard Mandeville and Lord Shaftesbury. Mandeville and Shaftesbury agreed little on the content of the human frame[11] – a defence of Shaftesbury from Mandeville's harsh criticisms in 'A Search into the Nature of Society'[12] was the ostensible motive for the first major work of the Scottish Enlightenment, Hutcheson's *Inquiry into the Original of our Ideas of Beauty and Virtue* (1725). But both agreed that the frame was composed of passions that were the basis of our relations with others, our mores, our conventions and our morality: to understand the frame one must understand the mores, and vice-versa.

Hutcheson and Hume construed this in very different ways[13] and against different background assumptions about human nature. In Hutcheson's case a teleological Christianised Stoicism meant that our frames were created to harmonise with other humans – and even animals, as I will discuss shortly – in various social institutions made providentially to maximise human happiness. Yet, although Hutcheson's influential emphasis on benevolent sentiments was *contra* Mandeville, he was in substantial agreement with Mandeville on the motivating character of the passions and their central place in human life. In Hutcheson's work this was closely wedded to a natural-law theory derived from Pufendorf and Barbeyrac, which delineated the various social and familial duties and offices of man in thriving moral communities. In Hume's case a combination of Epicurean naturalism and scepticism led to the argument that humans create and organise their mores, institutions and morals; and 'providence' is just the end result of the historical process of individuals seeking their interest and aiding those for whom they have benevolent sentiments.

This difference in Hutcheson's and Hume's respective attitudes toward the economy of the passions can be seen in the manner in which the philosophers considered animals. Hutcheson was the first consistent British theorist of animal rights. He considered animals, within a natural-law scheme, as falling between property and servants, and emphasised that man's superiority entailed duties to inferiors. Domestic animals and humans form providentially guided associations that are structured by the needs of the superiors. As all such associations aspire towards happiness, animals as associates too have a 'right' to happiness and 'a right that no useless pain or misery should be inflicted on them'.[14]

Although few took up Hutcheson's theory of animal rights,[15] his providentialism – as well as Shaftesbury's and Butler's – in considering the animal world had a different legacy. If the animal system reflects the ends of nature and the fitness of these ends, and if man is the perfection and goal of nature, then we can learn something about man by looking at the animal system and the 'animal oeconomy'. John Gregory's *A Comparative View of the State and Faculties of Man with those of the Animal World* (1765) argued, in a way deeply influenced by Rousseau, that human artifice had alienated us from our instinctual capacities, and in order to understand instinct we could – by analogy – investigate animal nature. Thus in the *Comparative View* conjectural history as a natural history of man is pursued, quite literally. Gregory believed that by examining human and animal physiology one can access human instinct, which lies behind and beyond human history.

Gregory's method had some surface similarities with Hume, although the analogy he proposed, as well as the critique of luxury and the elevation of 'natural man', is thoroughly un-Humean – as is Gregory's philosophy in general. For Hume, unlike Hutcheson, although animals may merit our benevolent temper, they cannot extract our benevolence as a right, since they are incapable of artifice and of the human institutions like obligation, promises and justice which are built on such artifice. Consequently there is no obligation between men and brutes. For Hume animals functioned not as a mark of the richness of providence and our pre-existent teleological duties but rather as a sceptical razor. As we share our passions with animals, any philosophical explanation of human passions that is too complex or baroque to apply equally to animal passions can be ruled out. Thus, although the consanguinity of animal and human passion cannot be the basis of a moral duty, it does check excessive speculation and human pride and thus functions much like an account of man in his 'rude state'. If you think your pride makes you special just look at the pride of the peacock.[16]

Despite their differences Hutcheson, Gregory and Hume agreed that the analysis of our passions and sentiments and their social, natural historical and human historical manifestations provided access to the basic stuff of human nature, Hume with a far more Mandevillean slant than Hutcheson and Gregory.[17] Even Thomas Reid, who would seem to be completely at odds with historical accounts of man in his criticisms of Humean and Lockean empiricism, shares some of this picture.[18] Reid implicitly accepted the Hutchesonian argument that the manner in which the passions manifested themselves in different times and places tells us something about human nature and its providential purpose. He also accepted that the human passionate frame was essential to human nature, and could not be dispensed with. In certain ways he also has much in common with Ferguson.

If, for Hume, animals provided a sceptical check on our tendency towards wild conjecture and a bulwark against our corruption by metaphysical schemes, he had to look elsewhere for a way to evaluate and delineate historical stages, as well as the differences between the ancients and the moderns. His influential essay 'Of the Origin and Progress of the Arts and Sciences' (1742) was the first major Scottish presentation of a theory of historical stages in tandem with an empirical analysis of human nature. He argued that there were fundamental, natural differences between the sexes, and these differences anchored powerful affections between men and women. Since men had strong passions for women, who were weaker by nature and of more polite temper, men created a variety of different social and political institutions that provided an artificial corrective to natural differences. But the artificial correctives – political protections in marriage, chivalry, the culture of politeness and the consequent rise of the arts, etc. – were predicated on men's natural desire for women, arising from the natural differences between them. The treatment of women is thus a basic index of historical progress: 'the ancient Muscovites wedded their wives with a whip instead of a ring' and ancient Greek men had absolute dominion over women, whereas in civilised nations men defer to women. In both cases men have natural authority but in modern societies it expresses itself not as physical violence but in general rules and social mores.

For Hume a constant set of passions taking different forms under differing social and historical forces is a basic key to the character of the stages of human history. Furthermore it can be used to judge the progressive character of diverse times and cultures. This points to another interesting aspect of the Scots' discussions of human nature: that although it is assumed by many that human nature is in some sense uniform, it is also assumed that there are fundamental disuniformities between different sorts of humans – men and women (as well as the races of men which I will discuss below). The difference between men and women is taken as the 'motor' of the arts for Hume, and as having far reaching positive political effects, notably the tempering of modern absolutist monarchy making it far less coercive in character than ancient despotism. This line was taken up both by Millar and Smith:

Of all our passions, it should seem that those which unite the sexes are most easily affected by the peculiar circumstances in which we are placed, and most liable to be influenced by the power of habit and education. Upon this account they exhibit the most wonderful variety of appearances, and, in different ages and countries, have produced the greatest diversity of manners and customs.[19]

The constancy of this passion allows it to be a consistent transhistorical unit of analysis and a reliable metric of progress revealing the drastic differences in authority in successive historical eras. Ferguson similarly analysed the progress of the passion, but within a framework derived from Montesquieu that in opposition to the Hume–Smith–Millar line emphasised the impact of climate on the passions between the sexes.[20] Part of what culture tempers, though perhaps never entirely, is the dominion of climate over the passions.

There were numerous others who considered this passion and its history. William Alexander wrote a history of women,[21] and the relations between women and men figured, at least tangentially, in most of the Scottish arguments being considered here. Kames and Gregory in particular were deeply influenced by Rousseau's *Emile* and viewed the sentimental differences between men and women as far more dramatically and constitutively different than even Hume and Millar did.[22]

Sometimes the use of animals to get at the original of man and the passions between men and women were mixed together, as was the case in Monboddo's discussions of orang-utan mores. William Smellie, printer, editor of the first edition of the *Encyclopaedia Britannica*, translator of Buffon and author of the *Philosophy of Natural History* claimed, following Buffon's arguments against domestication in *Histoire naturelle*, that love is generally destroyed by human institutions and artificial distinctions between the ranks. These distinctions draw beautiful women to marry 'puny', wealthy men leading to 'debilitated races' and 'universal degeneration'.[23] One can see how natural monogamy falls into artificial polygamy by looking towards the animal world: '[t]he dunghill cock and hen, in a natural state, pair...[i]n a domestic state, however, the cock is a jealous tyrant, and the hen a prostitute'.[24]

The analogy between the animal world and humans was also important in discussions of the 'races of man' which considered another issue of man's origins. Throughout the eighteenth century in France, Germany, England and Scotland there was a great deal of equivocation about the difference between race and national character.[25] 'Race' was generally used to discuss variations among populations due to climates, while 'national character' expressed cultural variations. It was not until the late eighteenth century that systematic theories of racial difference were developed based on human features independent of climate – skull types, skeletons, cranial nerves, etc. Buffon's 'Variété des espèces de l'homme' was the paradigm of an eighteenth-century climactic racial theory, and by far the most influential. Buffon claimed that just as all dogs belonged to one species and varied dramatically according to climate, so too did men. Despite their phenotypical differences and the relative merits of these differences they were all ultimately descended from the same stock.

The Hume–Smith–Millar strand of the Scottish Enlightenment emphasised 'moral causes' as against 'physical causes', arguing that human variation was not rooted in climate or terrain but rather in differences in *moeurs* and institutions that arose from human artifice and were transmitted via contagions of the passions.[26] Hume claimed, in an infamous footnote appended to the 1748 edition of 'Of National Character', that the non-white races are too amorphous and impoverished to exhibit sufficient regularities in their passions to serve as useful objects for the study of human nature. This was a fairly unusual position among Scottish Enlightenment intellectuals and was vocally criticised by Monboddo and James Beattie. Hume's idiosyncratic position on race was of course independent of the Hume–Smith–Millar economic (and in Smith's and Millar's cases political) argument against slavery. George Wallace, perhaps the most important eighteenth-century Scots legal critic of slavery, cited Hume's 'Of the Populousness of Ancient Nations' and its argument against slavery with approbation on this issue, unaware of or uninterested in the scandalous footnote.[27] For Hume the white race showed the greatest distinctness of character – witness the difference in mores between a Frenchman and an Englishman – and consequently the most developed moral causes. National character was thus an achievement of human populations cultivating moral causes, and the more society progressed the more character was diversified. Race was a failure to do so.

Most philosophers did not completely deny the explanatory value of physical causes – particularly Robertson and Ferguson and those who were influenced by them, such as James Dunbar and John Logan. To what degree, then, was climate the basis for racial difference and to what degree mores? Were the great variations in dogs considered by Buffon due solely to climate?[28] The most interesting and the oddest response is to be found in Lord Kames. Kames argued that dogs did not belong to one species but were a clustering of diverse species. If dogs were shown not to belong to one species then, by analogy, 'there are different species of men as well as of dogs: a mastiff differs not more from a spaniel, than a white man from a negro, or a Laplander from a Dane'.[29] In order to allow for this, Kames posited many Adams and Eves 'fitted by nature for different climates'.[30] All were human and made in the image of God. Their variations were due to divinely implanted qualities given to humans in order that they might successfully cope with their original climates. In this way the sort of theory of man's teleological nature found in Hutcheson and others was applied to the problem of racial diversity. Climate only altered racial groups when the progeny of an Adam and Eve suited to one region migrated to another region, resulting in degeneration as opposed to their original suitedness to a particular climate.

This diversity of species also meant a diversity of mores that was due not to climate but rather to inborn qualities for the good of each species. Kames saw the enormous variety of racial characters, in similar stages of society, as proof of the empirical falsity of most of the linear progressive or anti-progressive theories that took all men as having a similar sort of character at the simplest stages of society.[31] This went against the argument, made by Hume and most of the other historically based Scottish philosophers, that there was a uniform character of 'savage man'. If man was diverse in his first stage, the history of mankind was irremediably sketchy and conjectures had to proceed along very general lines. Progress was intermittent and complicated.[32]

CONCLUSION

The combination of the empirical analysis of the human passions and the argument for a series of empirical stages as arising from this analysis is particularly identified with Scottish Enlightenment thinkers, and took numerous forms. But there was a core commitment for many Scottish philosophers to examining man in his rude state and using a variety of sources to access the said state in order to anchor a historical account of human nature. The sources ranged from the 'living experiments' of wild children to anthropological information on the races of men. Similarly, the differences between men and women and humans and animals offered regularities for analysis of the ways in which passions and mores manifested themselves over the course of human history and dictated diverse and interrelated stages. When taken together they demonstrate the wide-ranging and extraordinarily creative character of Scottish anthropology. They also point towards its influence in the many naturalistic and historical studies of man: social psychology, the social sciences, cultural anthropology, the evolutionary study of human beings and the human sciences.[33]

NOTES

1   The idea of 'Scottish Enlightenment' goes back to the later eighteenth century. Gibbon famously extols Hume, Robertson and Smith as providing 'a strong ray of philosophic light [which] has broken from Scotland in our own times' (Edward Gibbon, *The Decline and Fall of the Roman Empire*, ed. David Womersley (London: Penguin, 1994), III.728 n. 69 [ch. 51]). For Gibbon this was an extraordinary consequence of the dissolution of the Roman empire, that Lowlanders so savage when encountered by the empire as to barely be included within its walls were now the strongest light of progress in Modern Europe. In the following I will primarily consider exceptional individuals – Hutcheson, Hume, Smith, Kames, Reid, Millar, Ferguson – although I will refer to some less-known writers – including John Gregory, Lord Monboddo, William Smellie, John Oswald, and James Dunbar. My approach is necessitated by the brevity of the chapter and by my primarily philosophical (as opposed to historical) emphasis. For a broader picture see Richard B. Sher, *Church and University in the Scottish Enlightenment* (Edinburgh: Edinburgh University Press, 1985), particularly on Robertson (whom I will only consider tangentially); Christopher Berry, *Social Theory of the Scottish Enlightenment* (Edinburgh: Edinburgh University Press, 1997) (with a current and useful biography), as well as the superb collection of primary sources in Richard B. Sher, ed., *Conjectural History and Anthropology in the Scottish Enlightenment*, 7 vols. (Bristol: Thoemmes Press, 1995).

2   Dugald Stewart, 'Account of the Life and Writings of Adam Smith, LL.D.', ed. Ian Simpson Ross, in Adam Smith, *Essays on Philosophical Subjects*, eds. W. P. D. Wightman and J. C. Bryce (Oxford: Clarendon Press, 1980), 293.

3   Ibid., 292–3.

4   Adam Ferguson, *An Essay on the History of Civil Society*, ed. Fania Oz-Salzberger (Cambridge: Cambridge University Press, 1995), 75 [II.1]; William Robertson, *The History of America*, in *The Works of William Robertson, D. D.*, ed. Dugald Stewart, 8 vols. (London, 1827), IV.254–5 [first published 1777]. On conjectural history and natural history, and also much of the discussion that follows, see P. B. Wood, 'The Natural History of Man in the Scottish Enlightenment', *History of Science* 28 (1990), 89–123.

5 John Millar, *The Origin of the Distinction of Ranks*, 3rd edn, in William C. Lehmann, ed., *John Millar of Glasgow* (Cambridge: Cambridge University Press, 1960), 173–332.

6 Ibid., 180.

7 Ferguson, *Essay*, 90 [11.2].

8 Robertson, *History of America*, ch. 4 passim.

9 See particularly James Burnet, Lord Monboddo, *Antient Metaphysics*, 6 vols. (Edinburgh, 1779–99), IV.1.ii.

10 See Knud Haakonssen, *The Science of a Legislator: the Natural Jurisprudence of David Hume and Adam Smith* (Cambridge: Cambridge University Press, 1981), ch. 8; Roger L. Emerson, 'Conjectural History and the Scottish Philosophers', *Historical Papers of the Canadian Historical Association* (1984), 63–90. For Smith's strongest statement of the four-stage theory see Adam Smith, *Lectures on Jurisprudence*, eds. R. L. Meek, D. D. Raphael and P. G. Stein (Indianapolis: Liberty Fund, 1982), 14–16.

11 Their influences were very different also, for Shaftesbury the Cambridge Platonists and Locke, for Mandeville Cartesian physiologists, Bayle, French, British and Dutch sceptics and Epicureans.

12 'A Search' was added to Mandeville's 1723 edition of the *Fable of the Bees*. Even though Mandeville had earlier begun publishing the materials making up the *Fable of the Bees*, it was via the much expanded 1723 edition that he had his impact on British letters. Hence although a younger contemporary of Shaftesbury he was a bogeyman for Hutcheson's generation.

13 Although Hutcheson was a central influence in Scottish letters and Hume an anomalous figure, Hume and Hutcheson each initiated an important, and distinct, line of influence in Scottish Enlightenment philosophy. On their differences, see James Moore, 'Hume and Hutcheson', in M. A. Stewart and John P. Wright, eds., *Hume and Hume's Connexions* (Edinburgh: Edinburgh University Press, 1994), 23–57.

14 See Francis Hutcheson, *A System of Moral Philosophy* (1755; reprint, Hildesheim: Georg Olms, 1969), 1.316.

15 Two interesting exceptions are Thomas Reid, see his *Practical Ethics*, ed. Knud Haakonssen (Princeton, NJ: Princeton University Press, 1990), 205; and the Jacobin John Oswald. In *The Cry of Nature; or, an appeal to Mercy and Justice, on behalf of the persecuted animals* (1791; reprinted in Aaron Garrett, ed., *Rights and Souls in the Eighteenth Century*, 6 vols. (Bristol: Thoemmes, 2000), v. 4) John Oswald merged together Rousseau and Monboddo to argue for a degenerative four-stage theory of man's cruelty to animals, destruction of nature and finally self-alienation. The stages were distinguished in terms of forms of

cruelty and authority. As he left Edinburgh at fifteen he is not really a member of the Scottish Enlightenment, although an important and neglected Scots thinker.

16   See particularly David Hume, *A Treatise of Human Nature*, ed. L. A. Selby-Bigge, 3rd edn, rev. P. H. Nidditch (Oxford: Clarendon Press, 1978), 1.iii.16 and 11.i.12.

17   Hume's essays of the 1740s are, along with the works of Montesquieu (who admired Hume) and Rousseau (who admired Hume and was influenced by him), key influences on the post-1745 generation. Hutcheson belongs to the prior generation and his discussions of history are cast within the neo-Pufendorfian framework dictated by his teaching duties.

18   See particularly Reid, *Practical Ethics*, 134.

19   Millar, *Origin of the Distinction of Ranks*, 183; see also Smith, *Lectures on Jurisprudence*, 133–75.

20   Ferguson, *Essay*, 111.1; see also James Dunbar, *Essays on the History of Mankind in Rude and Cultivated Ages*, 2nd edn (1781: reprint, intro. C. J. Berry, Bristol: Thoemmes Press, 1995), 296.

21   William Alexander, *The History of Women, from the Earliest Antiquity to the Present Time*, 2 vols. (London, 1779).

22   See Henry Home, Lord Kames, *Loose Hints upon Education, chiefly concerning the Culture of the Heart* (Edinburgh, 1781); and John Gregory's incredibly popular (particularly in America where it went through innumerable reprints) *A Father's Legacy to His Daughters* (London, 1774).

23   William Smellie, *The Philosophy of Natural History* (Edinburgh, 1790), 1.271–2.

24   Ibid., 278.

25   See Aaron Garrett, 'Human Nature', in Knud Haakonssen, ed., *Cambridge History of Eighteenth-Century Philosophy* (Cambridge: Cambridge University Press, forthcoming).

26   See 'Of National Character', in David Hume, *Political Essays*, ed. Knud Haakonssen (Cambridge: Cambridge University Press, 1994), 78–92; Adam Smith, *The Theory of Moral Sentiments*, eds. D. D. Raphael and A. L. Macfie (Oxford: Clarendon Press, 1976), v.1.4.ii.

27   George Wallace, *A System of the Principles of the Law of Scotland* (Edinburgh, 1760), 1.96. Slavery and race were often surprisingly independent issues in eighteenth-century Europe. This was in part due to the importance of 'antique servitude' in political discussions of slavery. For Smith, though, bigotry was intertwined with protectionism. The refusal to engage in transactions with others, reinforced by the 'monopolistic' institution of slavery was a font of racial bigotry.

28 This discussion was popularised through Smellie's translations of Buffon in 'Canis' in the first edition of the *Encyclopaedia Britannica* (Edinburgh, 1768). On race in the later editions of the *Encyclopaedia* see Silvia Sebastiani, 'Race as a Construction of the Other: "Native Americans" and "Negroes" in the Eighteenth-Century Editions of the *Encyclopaedia Britannica*', in Bo Stråth, ed., *Europe and the Other and Europe as the Other* (Brussels: Peter Lang, 2000), 195–228.

29 Henry Home, Lord Kames, *Sketches of the History of Man*, 4 vols. (1788; reprint, intro. John Valdimir Price, Bristol: Thoemmes, 1993), 1.20.

30 Ibid., 23.

31 Ibid., 44–5.

32 The non-linear theory of history offered by Kames in the *Sketches* is quite different from the stadial theory offered in the *Historical Law-Tracts*, 2 vols. (Edinburgh, 1776).

33 See Charles Darwin, and his *The Expression of the Emotions in Man and Animals* (London: John Murray, 1873).

5   Science in the Scottish Enlightenment

During the past thirty years the role of the natural sciences and medicine in the Scottish Enlightenment has been hotly debated. Elaborating on the interpretation of the Scottish Enlightenment advanced by Nicholas Phillipson, John Christie argued in a series of influential essays that the pursuit of natural knowledge was one of the 'major elements whose combination formed the culture of the Scottish Enlightenment'.[1] Stronger claims for the importance of science and medicine were subsequently made by Roger L. Emerson, who contended that if we are properly to understand the origins and defining characteristics of the Scottish Enlightenment then we must see the cultivation of natural knowledge as being central to enlightened culture in eighteenth-century Scotland.[2] On the other hand, following the lead of Hugh Trevor-Roper (Lord Dacre), John Robertson recently insisted that the Scottish Enlightenment should be defined in terms of a core of related enquiries in moral philosophy, history and political economy, and that the natural sciences and medicine were peripheral to the intellectual preoccupations of enlightened savants in Scotland and in the Atlantic world more generally.[3] Richard Sher likewise rejects Emerson's claims, and suggests that the Scottish Enlightenment can be more fruitfully defined in terms of the 'culture of the literati' which, for Sher, encompassed science and medicine but was not rooted in these fields.[4] While it would be inappropriate here to enter into the complexities of this debate, we should recognise that the points at issue are far from trivial because they raise serious questions not only about how we characterise the Enlightenment as an historical phenomenon but also about how we conceptualise the genesis of our own world. In answering these questions we are led to confront the problem of locating natural knowledge in the making of modernity and identifying the place of science in contemporary society, and our answers thus speak to our own views of both past and present.

In this chapter, I trace the growing prominence of science and medicine in Scotland during the long eighteenth century, that is, the period from roughly 1660 until 1815. In so doing, I align myself with scholars like Christie and Emerson who see natural knowledge as being a pivotal component of the intellectual culture of the Scottish Enlightenment. As I attempt to show in what follows, science and medicine played a conspicuous part in both the transformation of the curricula in Scottish academies and universities and in the formation of the public sphere in Scotland. The 'new science' born in the Scientific Revolution of the seventeenth century also provided methodological inspiration for the 'science of man' constructed in the Scottish Enlightenment, and posed a number of metaphysical and epistemological problems that puzzled Scottish savants during the course of the long eighteenth century. Furthermore, natural knowledge was used as a cultural resource in the ongoing religious disputes of the period, and occasioned periodic anxieties about atheism and irreligion which focused public attention on the broader meanings of the scientific enterprise. Lastly, the desire to improve Scottish society on the part not only of the landed classes but also of merchants and manufacturers was bound up with the perceived need to apply the knowledge and techniques of Scotland's men of science to practical ends. Science and medicine were central to, and in some cases the driving force behind, the intellectual changes encompassed by the term 'the Scottish Enlightenment', and hence were instrumental in shaping modernity in Scotland as elsewhere. The story narrated in this chapter is therefore of the broadest historical significance and consequently has implications for the stories told elsewhere in this book.

MATHEMATICAL PRACTITIONERS AND THE VIRTUOSI

Two figures, George Sinclair (d. 1696) and Sir Robert Sibbald (1641–1722), can be taken as representative of the generation that in the late seventeenth century laid the groundwork for the achievements of Scottish men of science during the Enlightenment. Sinclair was a regent at the University of Glasgow who was ousted in 1666 because of his loyalty to the Presbyterian cause, and reinstated following the Glorious Revolution before becoming professor of mathematics in 1691. The twists and turns of his career tell us much about the cultural changes then taking place in Scotland. Sinclair's contact with the Royal Society of London in 1662 via the expatriate Scot, Sir Robert Moray, exemplifies the new links being forged between savants in Scotland and England following the Restoration; such links became progressively stronger, so that by the early eighteenth century increasing numbers of Scottish medics and scientists were heading south in search of success.[5] Moreover, Sinclair's publications, including his best known work, *Satan's Invisible World Discovered* (1685), show that he was well versed in the writings of English authors such as Joseph Glanvill, and that he championed the form of experimental philosophy developed by Robert Boyle and members of the early Royal Society.

Moreover, Sinclair's career pattern exhibits all of the hallmarks of that of a mathematical practitioner. Historians of the Scientific Revolution have recently come to recognise the importance of the many individuals across Europe, such as Galileo, who taught mathematics either extramurally or in schools and universities and who applied their mathematical skills, inter alia, to constructing better scientific instruments or completing civil or military engineering schemes.[6] From the 1650s onwards, Sinclair lectured on mathematics at Glasgow and extramurally in Edinburgh and participated in various practical projects, including the improvement of both Scottish mining techniques and Edinburgh's water system. But he was not the only figure in Scotland to engage in this range of activities. Other mathematical practitioners plying their trade at this time included James Corss(e), David Gregory of Kinairdy and his brother James Gregory 1, the inventor of the reflecting telescope. All of these men sought to apply natural knowledge to some useful purpose. They were all in touch with the latest scientific developments in London and on the continent, and were partly responsible for the shift in the curricula of the Scottish universities away from Aristotelian natural philosophy, first to the system of Descartes in the 1660s and 1670s, and then to that of Newton at the turn of the eighteenth century.[7]

Lastly, Sinclair was apparently the first in Scotland to give public lectures on mathematics and natural philosophy. In November 1670 he was licensed by the Edinburgh Town Council to 'profess severall usefull sciences' in the burgh, including mechanics, pneumatics, hydrostatics, astronomy and the many branches of mathematics, using demonstration experiments performed with air pumps and other scientific apparatus.[8] Nothing else is known about these lectures, but even if they were short lived they were among the earliest of their kind in Europe, and they show that Sinclair sought to present natural knowledge and illustrate its uses in the newly emerging public sphere of late seventeenth-century Scotland.[9] The origins of extramural public instruction in the sciences in Scotland can therefore be traced back to Sinclair's efforts to market his knowledge and expertise in the 1670s, which mark the beginnings of the integration of natural knowledge into Scottish public culture.

Working alongside and sometimes in collaboration with the mathematical practitioners were Scottish virtuosi like Sir Robert Sibbald. Educated in Leiden as a physician and in Paris as a botanist, Sibbald had wide interests in natural philosophy, medicine, natural history, civil history, chorography and antiquarianism that were melded together not only by a Baconian view of the relations between the various branches of knowledge but also by a Baconian belief in the cultivation of learning for human benefit. More than any other figure of his generation, Sibbald helped to gain social legitimacy in Scotland for the pursuit of natural knowledge, not least because of his knighthood and his appointments as Geographer Royal and Physician to the King in 1682. Thanks to the efforts of Sibbald and his associates, a number of institutions fostering the natural sciences were established in Edinburgh.[10] In conjunction with his kinsman Robert Balfour and their mutual friend Patrick Murray of Livingstone, Sibbald helped to establish a physic garden in 1670 which later transmuted into the Edinburgh Botanical Garden, and the physic garden's first keeper, James Sutherland, was made professor of botany at the University of Edinburgh in 1695. Balfour and Sibbald also spearheaded the establishment of the Royal College of Physicians of Edinburgh in 1681 and, in 1685, Sibbald was appointed as a professor of medicine at the University by the Town Council, along with Drs James Halket and Archibald Pitcairne. Although this trio did little or no teaching, the move by the Council was nonetheless significant because it underlined the Council's desire to remodel the college along the lines of continental universities such as Leiden, where many Scottish medics went to study. Sibbald subsequently made an important contribution to the improvement of the facilities at the University of Edinburgh when, in 1697, he presented his substantial collection of natural history specimens, which were then combined with those bequeathed by Balfour to form a museum.

But Sibbald's improving vision was not focused exclusively on Edinburgh. Rather, he sought to advance the interests of the nation as a whole, largely through his attempts to compile a natural history of Scotland modelled on those produced earlier by English Baconians like Robert Plot. Using his extensive correspondence network (which also extended to virtuosi in England), Sibbald issued standardised questionnaires to his contacts in order to elicit information about the flora, fauna, topography, natural resources and people of Scotland which could then be used as the basis for economic improvement schemes and political policy making. Complementing these surveys were Sibbald's attempts to map Scotland using the skills of Martin Martin and the mathematical practitioner John Adair.[11] Unfortunately for Sibbald, and perhaps for the Scots more generally, much of this work bore little fruit. Apart from publishing his *Scotia Illustrata, sive Prodromus Historiae Naturalis* (1684), Sibbald did not produce the comprehensive catalogue of the nation he initially projected and thus failed to realise his Baconian dream of translating knowledge into power. Moreover, despite the success of a number of the virtuoso and medical clubs he belonged to in Edinburgh, his proposals to found a Royal Society of Scotland in the years 1698 to 1701 likewise came to naught.[12] Nevertheless, Sibbald's activities had a lasting impact. Through his correspondence network he managed to foster a sense of community among hitherto isolated individuals in Scotland, and he strengthened the links between Scottish virtuosi like Robert Wodrow and their counterparts in England. The Botanical Garden and the Royal College of Physicians in Edinburgh served as institutional foci for the advancement of medical and natural historical knowledge throughout the Enlightenment, and he thus contributed to the process through which the natural sciences and medicine became a constitutive part of the public sphere. Later naturalists were keenly aware of, and emulated, his work as a natural historian and patriotic improver. Hence Sibbald left a rich legacy to Scottish men of science of the eighteenth century.

NEWTONIANISM

In the period 1690 to 1720 the Scottish universities were transformed. Although there had been periodic rumblings of reform earlier in the seventeenth century, in 1690 a Parliamentary Commission of Visitation was struck to ensure that all those teaching in the Scottish universities were loyal to the new political regime, and to consider changes to the curricula and pedagogical practices of the colleges. In the end, little was accomplished apart from rooting out those who remained sympathetic to Episcopalianism and the Stuarts and establishing chairs of Greek in each of the universities. Still, the very fact that the Commission was formed at all acted as a stimulus for a public debate about the nature of higher education. Perhaps the most interesting contribution to this discussion is the anonymous 1704 pamphlet, *Proposals for the Reformation of Schools and Universities* (commonly attributed to Andrew Fletcher of Saltoun), which outlines an ideal curriculum for the universities in which mathematics and natural knowledge figured more prominently than they actually did in the classrooms of the Scottish universities at the turn of the eighteenth century. Whereas most students were given only rudimentary instruction in mathematics and a basic introduction to natural philosophy, the author of the *Proposals* recommended that during the initial four years of a six-year course they should be 'taught *Arithmetick, Geography* and *Chronology*, to greater Perfection, the first six, with the eleventh and twelfth Books of *Euclid*, the Elements of *Algebra*, [and] the Plain and Spherical *Trigonometry*', which would prepare them for their final two years which would be 'spent in Learning *mixt* Mathematicks, or *Natural* Philosophy, *viz.* The Laws of *Motion, Mechanicks, Hydrostaticks; Opticks, Astronomy, &c.* and *Experimental* Philosophy'.[13]

Although none of the universities or the Parliamentary Commission went as far as the author of the *Proposals* suggested in increasing the proportion of the curriculum given over to mathematics and the natural sciences, efforts were made to enhance teaching and research in these fields. Chairs in mathematics were either newly founded or re-established in St Andrews (1668), Edinburgh (1674), Glasgow (1691) and King's College Aberdeen (1703) to add to the professorship founded at Marischal College Aberdeen by the distinguished Scottish mathematician and astronomer Duncan Liddell in 1613.

Observatories were built at St Andrews (c. 1677), King's (1675) and Marischal (1694), while all of the universities enlarged their stock of scientific apparatus. New professorships in medicine were also created at Marischal College (1700), Glasgow (1713) and St Andrews (1722), as well as a chair in medicine and chemistry at Edinburgh (1713). In addition, Glasgow opened a physic garden in 1704 and appointed a local surgeon, John Marshall, to maintain it. Edinburgh, however, remained in the forefront of efforts to promote the study of medicine. Although the chairs established in 1685 amounted to little more than sinecures, the original hopes of the Town Council were finally realised by Provost George Drummond (1687–1766), who engineered the formation of the University's medical school in 1726. As Drummond intended, by the 1740s the school had displaced Leiden as the primary academic site in Europe for medical education which in turn transformed Edinburgh into one of the leading centres for the cultivation of natural knowledge in the Atlantic world.[14]

These institutional changes created new pedagogical and career opportunities which were exploited by a phalanx of disciples and associates of Isaac Newton, led initially by members of the Gregory family, who variously held the chairs of mathematics at St Andrews and Edinburgh almost continuously from the 1660s to the 1720s.[15] Among the Scottish professors of mathematics, only the ageing George Sinclair and his successor at Glasgow, Dr Robert Sinclair, remained outside Newton's orbit. But in 1711 Glasgow too became part of the Newtonian network with the election of Robert Simson to the mathematics chair. Prior to his appointment, Simson had gone to London for a year to improve his skills as a mathematician, and there he was befriended by the Newtonians William Jones, Humphrey Ditton and Edmond Halley.[16] Back in Glasgow, Simson took Newton's avowed preference for the geometry of the ancients as a point of departure, and devoted his scholarly life to the study and editing of Greek mathematical texts.[17] As a teacher, Simson trained a whole new generation of Newtonian men of science, including Matthew Stewart (Edinburgh Professor of Mathematics, 1747–75), William Traill (Professor of Mathematics at Marischal College, 1766–79), and John Robison (Glasgow Lecturer in Chemistry, 1766–70, and Edinburgh Professor of Natural Philosophy, 1773–1805).

Also linked to Glasgow was the greatest Scottish mathematician and natural philosopher of the eighteenth century, Colin Maclaurin (1698–1746). Maclaurin graduated from the University of Glasgow in 1713, defending a highly sophisticated thesis in which he expounded Newton's theory of gravitation and sketched out a research programme which involved the use of the concept of an attractive force operating on particles of matter to explain fermentation, crystallisation, precipitation, the behaviour of fluids, electricity and other natural phenomena, much as Newton had done in the Queries of the *Opticks*.[18] Following a period in which he briefly studied theology and acted as a tutor, the scientifically precocious Maclaurin was chosen as the Liddell Professor of Mathematics at Marischal College Aberdeen in 1717. At the time of his election, Marischal was just reopening after the disruption caused by the '15 and the ejection of all but one of the faculty by a Royal Commission of Visitation which purged the Scottish universities of suspected Jacobites. The Commission ensured that the colleges were all staffed by men who were loyal Presbyterians and Hanoverians like Maclaurin, and these new appointees typically proved to be enthusiastic spokesmen for the Newtonian system as well as promoters of the value of natural knowledge more generally.[19] Maclaurin and his new colleagues turned Marischal into a bastion of Newtonianism, but despite his success in Aberdeen, he was soon looking for greater rewards elsewhere and began to cultivate the friendship of Newton and other prominent members of the Royal Society. This finally bore fruit in 1725, when Maclaurin left Marischal to become assistant and successor to the ailing James Gregory II in Edinburgh.[20]

Maclaurin's career blossomed once he moved to Edinburgh. Each year he had an onerous teaching load: an introductory class on the basics of arithmetic, geometry and algebra, as well as surveying, fortification and geography; a second class on algebra, solid geometry, spherical trigonometry, conic sections, gunnery and 'the elements of Astronomy and Optics'; a senior class on fluxions, perspective, astronomy, optics, Newton's *Principia* and experimental philosophy; and 'sometimes a fourth, upon such of the abstruse parts of the science as are not explained in the former three', which was most likely a private course for his most advanced students.[21] Nonetheless he remained an extremely active man of science, publishing papers, textbooks and his *Treatise on Fluxions*, in which he answered the objections to Newton's fluxional calculus raised in George Berkeley's *The Analyst* (1734).[22] In 1737 Maclaurin was one of the founders of the Edinburgh Philosophical Society, which eventually became the Royal Society of Edinburgh in 1783, and he was a member of the Honourable the Society of Improvers in the Knowledge of Agriculture in Scotland, which was formed in 1723 with the aim of turning agricultural practice into a rational applied science.[23] He also collaborated with a network of astronomers across Scotland who made observations which were relayed via Edinburgh to the Royal Society in London (of which Maclaurin was a Fellow); to facilitate his work as an observational astronomer, he proposed to the Edinburgh Town Council that an observatory be built, but nothing came of the plan.[24] In addition, Maclaurin provided advice on various schemes involving the practical application of mathematics, and he and his students gave public lectures on experimental philosophy to the ladies and gentlemen of Edinburgh.[25] His life was, however, cut tragically short in June 1746, and it was left to his family to publish his magisterial *Account of Sir Isaac Newton's Philosophical Discoveries*, which ranks as one of the most adept popular expositions of Newtonian natural philosophy published in the Enlightenment. In sum, Maclaurin was arguably the most capable and energetic exponent of Newtonianism working in Scotland, if not in Britain, during the first half of the eighteenth century. He helped not only to consolidate the Newtonian hold on Scottish academe, but also to create public science in the Scottish Enlightenment.

Individual initiative and institutional factors, such as the creation of new teaching positions, thus conditioned the rise of Newtonianism in Scotland. But so too did changing cultural values and religion. In the late seventeenth century, the rejection of Aristotelianism and scholasticism within the universities led to a reconceptualisation of the norms and values associated with the pursuit of learning. Inspired by the writings of Sir Francis Bacon and a host of commentators, figures like the anonymous author of the *Proposals for the Reformation of Schools and Universities* called for an end to scholastic pedantry, dogmatism and disputatiousness in education and for the inculcation of polite and gentlemanly standards that would better equip students to engage in the affairs of the world around them. The author of the *Proposals* memorably remarked that 'the natural Tendency of our present Methods is to unfit a Scholar for a

Gentleman, and to render a Gentleman ashamed of being a Scholar. And, till we reconcile the Gentleman with the Scholar, it is impossible Learning should ever flourish'.[26] Natural knowledge and mathematics were increasingly presented as polite forms of learning and gentlemanly accomplishments, which meant that the study of the natural sciences could be seen as exemplifying the values now thought to be appropriate to academe. Newtonianism, in turn, benefited from this shift, because it too was construed as a branch of knowledge fit for a polite gentleman, as Locke had observed in *Some Thoughts concerning Education* (1693).[27]

Moreover, natural knowledge was also increasingly regarded as being genuinely *useful*. Utility was prized by educational reformers from the late seventeenth century onwards, although their notion of utility was somewhat broader than the simplistic view espoused by many pundits and politicians in our own day. In the Enlightenment, the concept of 'usefulness' encompassed both practical, economic benefit and a sense of utility related to the moral or intellectual improvement of the individual. One of the legacies of the Scientific Revolution of the seventeenth century was that natural philosophy was presented as being of practical benefit, and this theme was taken up by those who taught in the Scottish universities to justify offering new courses in natural or experimental philosophy, and acquiring more instrumental hardware.[28] From the beginning, Newtonianism was marketed as being useful in terms of economic improvement, and Scottish Newtonians like Maclaurin and the eminent mathematician James Stirling likewise presented their brand of natural philosophy as being applicable to mining and other forms of economic activity.[29] Men of science in Scotland, as elsewhere, played the improvement card, and in so doing enhanced the status of natural knowledge within both the universities and Scottish society more generally.

Moral utility was, however, equally important in conditioning the spread of Newtonianism in the early eighteenth century. Although the Scottish colleges were no longer regarded as mere seminaries for the training of clerics, they were still expected to instill their students with sound Christian principles. Thanks to the writings of Robert Boyle and the apologists for the early Royal Society, natural knowledge was widely thought to bolster religion because it served to illustrate God's providential governance of nature and consequently could be mobilised for the broader purposes of a university education. Beginning with the Boyle Sermons delivered by Richard Bentley in 1692, Newtonianism offered itself as the best defence of Christian belief, the heterodoxy of Newton and his closest disciples notwithstanding. In Scotland, the compatibility of Newton's natural philosophy with Christianity was urged by no less a figure than Colin Maclaurin, who affirmed that 'natural philosophy is subservient to purposes of a higher kind, and is chiefly to be valued as it lays a sure foundation for natural religion and moral philosophy'. In a revealing letter from 1714, Maclaurin said that he had wanted to establish the universality of the law of gravitation in his graduation thesis 'because it is of the greatest importance & use seeing it furnishes us with a most clear & mathematical proof of the existence of a god and his providence', and observed that ' 'tis a sort of impiety to have no regard to the course and frame of nature as indeed it is a piece of real worship to contemplate the great beautiful drama of nature, the admirable law by which the world's great Lord rules this his workmanship'. Similar sentiments informed his *Account of Sir Isaac Newton's Philosophical Discoveries*.[30] Hence Newtonianism, and natural knowledge more generally, were accorded a prominent role in both the academy and public culture because they could be used to consolidate religious belief, and even though tensions later appeared between the natural sciences and religion, for much of the Scottish Enlightenment natural knowledge was used to underwrite Christianity. Those searching for the inspiration behind the irreligion of David Hume must, therefore, pass over the natural sciences because he was a heterodox thinker in spite of, not because of, the Newtonian texts he read.[31]

This is not to say that Newtonianism was without its opponents. The Lord President of the Court of Session, Duncan Forbes, was a convert to the religious ideas of the Englishman John Hutchinson, who developed a system of natural philosophy in opposition to that of Newton, while Henry Home, Lord Kames, had a life-long aversion to Newtonian metaphysics, as did his fellow law lord, James Burnett, Lord Mondboddo, who was highly critical of Newton in his *Antient Metaphysics*.[32] Even the most dedicated of Newton's followers like Thomas Reid were aware that the great man was occasionally mistaken and that some natural phenomena could not be explained in terms of the attractive and repulsive powers associated with matter.[33] But it would not be an exaggeration to say that Newtonianism (in all of its many guises) provided the conceptual inspiration for much of the research carried out in mathematics and the natural sciences during the course of the eighteenth century, and that Newton's writings also had a profound impact on the development of the moral sciences in the period.

In mathematics, David Gregory, Colin Maclaurin and James Stirling were part of the research programme in Britain spawned by Newton's formulation of the fluxional calculus, while the work of Robert Simson and Matthew Stewart was inspired by Newton's preference for geometrical as opposed to algebraic analysis. In the past, historians have maintained that the 'mathematical Hellenism' of Simson and Stewart defined the style of enquiry cultivated by Scottish mathematicians in the eighteenth century. More recent scholarship, however, has indicated not only that Simson and Stewart were atypical in their avoidance of algebraic techniques, but also that there was a dynamic tension in Newton's own work between the ancient geometrical ideal and a recognition of the power of modern algebra which played itself out in the mathematical researches of Maclaurin and later figures like John Playfair.[34]

Closely related to mathematics were the allied fields of astronomy and optics which were likewise cultivated by Newton's Scottish disciples. We have seen that Maclaurin was a dedicated observational astronomer, and in the 1730s he, as well as James Stirling, sought to prove the validity of Newton's contested claim that the earth is an oblate spheriod.[35] Other prominent Newtonians who carried out astronomical investigations included the first Glasgow Professor of Practical Astronomy, Alexander Wilson, who won a gold medal from the Royal Danish Academy of Sciences and Letters for his detailed observations of sun spots, and who published, inter alia, a pamphlet in which he argued on the basis of Newton's theory of gravitation that the universe as whole must have a regular motion about a central point.[36] One problematic area, involving both astronomy and optics, that generated a considerable amount of research among the Scottish Newtonians in the second half of the eighteenth century was the aberration of light. Prompted by the theory of aberration advanced by the Astronomer Royal James Bradley, Thomas Melvill was led to consider the vexed issue of refractive dispersion, while the writings of Roger Joseph Boscovich subsequently led John Robison,

Reid and Wilson's son Patrick to see that the dispute between proponents of the undulatory and projectile theories of light could be resolved through the investigation of aberration. As adherents to Newton's projectile theory, they closely scrutinised the opposing view of Boscovich and succeeded in showing the flaws in his reasoning.[37] Robison also applied his formidable skills as a mathematician and experimentalist to the study of electricity, and perhaps as early as 1769 formulated the inverse-square law of electrical force that is otherwise credited to Coulomb.[38]

The protean nature of eighteenth-century Newtonianism is well illustrated by the research tradition in chemistry initiated in Scotland by William Cullen and Joseph Black, and carried forward by William Irvine and a host of other chemists based largely in Glasgow and Edinburgh.[39] Cullen and Black were concerned with the quantitative analysis of heat and other chemical phenomena, and can thus be seen as adopting a style of enquiry modelled on that championed by Newton. Yet they also took up another, more speculative strand of Newtonianism, namely the notion of an etherial medium, especially as formulated by the Dublin physician Bryan Robinson, who elaborated on Newton's ether Queries added to the 1717 edition of the *Opticks*.[40] These two aspects of the Newtonian legacy were then blended together with a third, the experimental study of 'air' based on the innovative experiments first undertaken by Stephen Hales, who (like Newton) assumed that the atmosphere is made up of various airs consisting of material particles possessing attractive and especially repulsive forces.[41] While the groundbreaking discoveries of Cullen and Black regarding fixed air and latent and specific heats were thus firmly rooted in Newtonianism, identifying the various Newtonian elements combined in Scottish chemistry highlights the complexities involved in defining the Newtonian tradition in the Enlightenment.

The use of Newton's ideas was, however, by no means restricted to mathematics and the physical sciences. In the 1690s, Archibald Pitcairne began a new phase of physiological theorising in Scotland by advancing a form of Newtonian iatromechanism, and he was soon joined by physicians like George Cheyne, who likewise mined Newton's writings for clues to explain the workings of the human body. By the 1740s, iatromechanism had fallen into disrepute, but Newton's works continued to serve as a resource for Robert Whytt,

William Cullen and other physiologists caught up in debates over the role of the soul in the functions of the body.[42] Their work was complemented by that of anatomists like the Monros, whose investigations of the nervous system similarly raised questions about the interactions of mind and matter. The relations between mind and body in turn posed problems regarding the notion of causality, and Scottish thinking about causation in the Enlightenment was also informed by the Newtonian legacy.[43] Indeed, it is arguable that the exchanges between Leibniz and Samuel Clarke over the philosophical foundations of Newtonian natural philosophy, first published in 1717, set many of the parameters for metaphysical debate in Scotland for the remainder of the century. Moreover, Newton's proclaimed nescience about the cause of gravity served to reinforce the message regarding the limits of human knowledge which Scots like David Hume and Thomas Reid derived from the writings of Locke. More importantly, Scottish moralists ostensibly modelled their methods of inquiry on those articulated by Newton. Maclaurin's colleague at Marischal College, George Turnbull (1698–1748), was the first to advocate in print that moral philosophers ought to adopt the Newtonian methodology employed by natural philosophers; his views were subsequently echoed by Hume, Reid and many others.[44] Yet some caution needs to be exercised when assessing the impact of 'moral Newtonianism' in eighteenth-century Scotland, for the Scots who constructed the 'science of man' also drew on an array of methodological models, including mathematics, anatomy and natural history.[45] Nevertheless, the Newtonian corpus shaped the pursuit of the human sciences in the Scottish Enlightenment to a far greater extent than is often recognised.

NATURAL KNOWLEDGE IN THE LATE SCOTTISH ENLIGHTENMENT: 1783–1805

The founding of the Royal Society of Edinburgh in 1783 marks a period of change in the cultivation of natural knowledge in Scotland, for in the late eighteenth century, the natural sciences were becoming increasingly specialised (and medicine professionalised), as can be seen in the growing independence of chemistry and botany. This meant that the Baconian map of learning, which had informed the activities of earlier generations of Scottish men of science, was no longer a reliable guide to the topography of human knowledge. With the emergence of the brave new world of the 'scientist', the era of the virtuoso was effectively at an end.[46] There were also signs of the dissolution of the Newtonian consensus of previous decades, most notably in the interest in continental analytical mathematics displayed by John Playfair and the growing awareness of the profound theoretical implications of the new system of chemistry developed at the hands of French chemists led by Lavoisier.[47] But amid the changes, some continuities stand out, not least in the continued collective commitment to agricultural improvement, which was finally given academic recognition with the establishment of a Chair of Agriculture at the University of Edinburgh in 1790.[48] The related field of natural history also remained of considerable interest to the Scots, due in part to its inclusion in the curricula of the universities and to the creation of a Regius Chair of Natural History at Edinburgh in 1767. During the eighteenth century, Scottish natural historians not only worked to the agenda earlier established by Sibbald, but also responded to the initiatives of the two major naturalists of the European Enlightenment, Buffon and Linnaeus, and to the discovery of the puzzling reproductive properties of the fresh water polyp by the Genevan naturalist Abraham Trembley. Moreover, Scottish natural historians made significant contributions to debates in the science of man, as can be seen in William Smellie's *The Philosophy of Natural History*.[49] Furthermore, natural history served as a fertile matrix for the birth of geology as a distinct science at the turn of the nineteenth century.

The earliest evidence we have for Scottish interest in the reconstruction of the history of the earth is a pamphlet published by the Aberdeen surgeon Matthew Mackaile in 1691 attacking Thomas Burnet's *Sacred Theory of the Earth*.[50] Descriptions of the earth were later a standard part of university natural history courses, and Buffon's cosmogony outlined in the first volume of his *Histoire naturelle* sparked off a debate amongst Scottish naturalists in the 1750s over the validity of his ideas.[51] But the 1780s saw an upsurge of publication and dispute, beginning with William Smellie's English translation of Buffon's *Histoire*, which apparently acted as a stimulus for the heterodox geological speculations of the Edinburgh medical student George Hoggart Toulmin (1754–1817), who in 1780 argued that both the earth and humankind had existed from eternity.[52] Shortly thereafter, the great Scottish natural historian James Hutton (1726–97) sketched his revolutionary theory of the earth before the Royal Society of Edinburgh, prior to publishing his vision of a world in which 'we find no vestige of a beginning, – no prospect of an end'.[53] Hutton's claim that the age of the earth cannot be known struck at the heart of the (sometimes uneasy) alliance between Genesis and geology that had been forged earlier in the century, and, in the shadow of the French Revolution, his avowed nescience was taken as a sign of covert religious unbelief. Hutton was, however, no atheist. He held firm to a deistic belief in a benevolent Creator who had allotted humankind a privileged moral status in the natural order. Nonetheless, the hostile reaction which Hutton's system elicited in some quarters showed that the relations between natural knowledge and Christianity were being renegotiated and were again a matter of serious public concern.

The fact that Hutton's theory was scrutinised in such a public manner also tells us something about the wider place of natural knowledge in Scottish culture at the end of the Enlightenment. During the course of the eighteenth century, mathematics and the natural sciences figured ever more prominently in the curricula of the academies and universities, and, through the efforts of professors such as John Anderson in Glasgow, university classrooms were opened up to increasing numbers of artisans and towns-people who wanted to study chemistry and natural philosophy. Joseph Black eventually lectured to some 200 in his chemistry course at Edinburgh, while his successor, Thomas Charles Hope, occasionally addressed over 500 auditors. Within the academic setting, therefore, natural knowledge was conveyed to an audience far in excess numerically of what it was in 1700, and this was also true outside academe, where many of the clubs and societies formed in the eighteenth century promoted the discussion of the natural sciences, as did the courses of itinerant lecturers and the publication of books, newspapers and periodicals.[54] Furthermore, instruments such as the barometer were more widely available, which meant that subjects like meteorology became a gentlemanly avocation along with the compilation of a natural history cabinet. More importantly, natural knowledge also began to circulate among women, who had been part of the audience for the natural sciences in Scotland since at least the 1740s. In the 1790s, John Anderson came to recognise that academic courses in natural philosophy ought to be targeted at women, and when his educational brainchild, Anderson's Institution (now the University of Strathclyde), first opened in 1796, a large number of women attended the lectures of the first Professor of Natural Philosophy, Dr Thomas Garnett.[55] By the end of the Scottish Enlightenment, then, natural knowledge had truly become public knowledge, with all of the costs and benefits that this transformation entailed.

NOTES

The author wishes to thank Roger Emerson and Carol Gibson-Wood for the comments on an earlier version of this chapter.

1   Nicholas Phillipson, 'Culture and Society in the Eighteenth-Century Province: the Case of Edinburgh and the Scottish Enlightenment', in Lawrence Stone, ed., *The University in Society*, 2 vols. (Princeton: Princeton University Press, 1974), II.407–48; John R. R. Christie, 'The Origins and Development of the Scottish Scientific Community, 1680–1760', *History of Science* 12 (1974), 122–41; 'The Rise and Fall of Scottish Science', in Maurice Crosland, ed., *The Emergence of Science in Western Europe* (London: Macmillan, 1975), 111–26; 'The Culture of Science in Eighteenth-Century Scotland', in Andrew Hook, ed., *The History of Scottish Literature*, Volume 2: *1660–1800* (Aberdeen: Aberdeen University Press, 1987), 291–304 (the quotation is taken from 294).

2   Roger L. Emerson, 'Science and the Origins and Concerns of the Scottish Enlightenment', *History of Science* 26 (1988), 333–66.

3   Hugh Trevor-Roper, 'The Scottish Enlightenment', *Studies on Voltaire and the Eighteenth Century* 58 (1967), 1635–58; Trevor-Roper, 'The Scottish Enlightenment', *Blackwood's Magazine* 322 (1977), 371–88; John Robertson, 'The Scottish Contribution to the Enlightenment', in Paul Wood, ed., *The Scottish Enlightenment: Essays in Reinterpretation* (Rochester, NY: University of Rochester Press, 2000), 37–62.

4   Richard B. Sher, 'Science and Medicine in the Scottish Enlightenment: the Lessons of Book History', in Wood, *Scottish Enlightenment*, 99–156.

5   Thomas Birch, *The History of the Royal Society of London for Improving of Natural Knowledge from its First Rise*, 4 vols. (London: A. Millar, 1756–7), I.105.

6   John Henry, *The Scientific Revolution and the Origins of Modern Science* (Basingstoke: Macmillan, 1997), ch. 2 and the references cited there.

7   John L. Russell, 'Cosmological Teaching in the Seventeenth-Century Scottish Universities', *Journal for the History of Astronomy* 5 (1974), 122–32, 145–54; Christine M. King (Shepherd), 'Philosophy and Science in the Arts Curriculum of the Scottish Universities in the Seventeenth Century', (Unpublished PhD thesis, University of Edinburgh, 1974).

8   Marguerite Wood, ed., *Extracts from the Records of the Burgh of Edinburgh, 1665 to 1680* (Edinburgh and London: Oliver and Boyd, 1950), 92–3.

9   On natural knowledge and the public sphere in Scotland see Paul Wood, 'Science, the Universities and the Public Sphere in Eighteenth-Century Scotland', *History of Universities* 13 (1994), 99–135; Charles W. J. Withers, 'Towards a History of Geography in the Public Sphere', *History of Science* 36 (1998), 45–78.

10 That Sibbald's circle succeeded in establishing these institutions was largely due to the patronage of James VII; see Hugh Ouston, 'York in Edinburgh: James VII and the Patronage of Learning in Scotland, 1679–1688', in John Dwyer, Roger A. Mason and Alexander Murdoch, eds., *New Perspectives on the Politics and Culture of Early Modern Scotland* (Edinburgh: John Donald, 1980), 133–55.

11 Charles W. J. Withers, 'Geography, Science and National Identity in Early Modern Britain: the Case of Scotland and the Work of Sir Robert Sibbald (1641–1722)', *Annals of Science* 53 (1996), 29–73; Withers, 'Reporting, Mapping, Trusting: Making Geographical Knowledge in the Late Seventeenth Century', *Isis* 90 (1999), 497–521.

12 Roger L. Emerson, 'Sir Robert Sibbald, Kt, the Royal Society of Scotland and the Origins of the Scottish Enlightenment', *Annals of Science* 45 (1988), 41–72. The Royal College of Physicians grew out of one of Sibbald's clubs which began meeting in 1680.

13 Anon., *Proposals for the Reformation of Schools and Universities, in order to the better Education of Youth; humbly offered to the serious Consideration of the High Court of Parliament*, in *The Harleian Miscellany: Or, a Collection of Scarce, Curious, and Entertaining Pamphlets and Tracts*, 8 vols. (London: T. Osborne, 1744–6), 1.485–90, 489.

14 P. J. Anderson, ed., *Fasti Academiae Mariscallanae Aberdonensis: Selections from the Records of the Marischal College and University, 1593–1860*, 3 vols. (Aberdeen: New Spalding Club, 1889–98), 1.131–46, 381–3; R. G. W. Anderson and A. D. C. Simpson, eds., *The Early Years of the Edinburgh Medical School* (Edinburgh: Royal Scottish Museum, 1976); Christopher Lawrence, 'Ornate Physicians and Learned Artisans: Edinburgh Medical Men, 1726–1776', in W. F. Bynum and Roy Porter, eds., *William Hunter and the Eighteenth-Century Medical World*

(Cambridge: Cambridge University Press, 1985), 153–76; R. G. Cant, *The University of St Andrews: a Short History*, rev. edn (Edinburgh and London: Scottish Academic Press, 1970), 74–5, 88–9; James Coutts, *A History of the University of Glasgow: from its Foundation in 1451 to 1909* (Glasgow: James Maclehose and Sons, 1909), 170–1, 193, 195; Sir Alexander Grant, *The Story of the University of Edinburgh during its First Three Hundred Years*, 2 vols. (London: Longmans, Green and Co., 1884), I.296–7, II.293–6; Paul B. Wood, *The Aberdeen Enlightenment: the Arts Curriculum in the Eighteenth Century* (Aberdeen: Aberdeen University Press, 1993), 2, 14.

15   James Gregory I held the mathematics chairs in St Andrews (1668–74) and Edinburgh (1674–5). His nephew David occupied the Edinburgh chair (1683–92) before his election as the Savilian Professor of Astronomy at Oxford. David Gregory was succeeded by his younger brother James Gregory II, who had taught as a regent at St Andrews. The St Andrews chair of mathematics was occupied from 1709 to 1765 by Charles and then David Gregory III. On the role of the Gregory clan in the rise of Newtonianism in Britain see especially Anita Guerrini, 'The Tory Newtonians: Gregory, Pitcairne and their Circle', *Journal of British Studies* 25 (1986), 288–311.

16   William Traill, *Account of the Life and Writings of Robert Simson, MD Late Professor of Mathematics in the University of Glasgow* (Bath and London: G. and W. Nichol, 1812), 3.

17   On Newton's view of ancient mathematics see Richard S. Westfall, *Never at Rest: a Biography of Isaac Newton* (Cambridge: Cambridge University Press, 1980), 378–80, 423–4, 512–13, and Niccolò Guicciardini, *Reading the Principia: the Debate on Newton's Mathematical Methods for Natural Philosophy from 1687 to 1736* (Cambridge: Cambridge University Press, 1999), 28–32, 101–6. According to John Robison, it was apparently Edmond Halley who first introduced Simson to the geometrical works of the ancients; see Robison's entry on Simson in *Encyclopaedia Britannica*, 3rd edn, 18 vols. (Edinburgh: A. Bell and C. Macfarquhar, 1797), XVII.504–9, 506.

18   Colin Maclaurin, *De gravitate, aliisque viribus naturalibus* (Edinburgh: Robert Freebairn, 1713).

19   On the role of the regents in the rise of Newtonianism in Scotland see especially Christine M. Shepherd, 'Newtonianism in Scottish Universities in the Seventeenth Century', in R. H. Campbell and Andrew S. Skinner, eds., *The Origins and Nature of the Scottish Enlightenment* (Edinburgh: John Donald, 1982), 65–85.

20   Newton may have had a hand in Maclaurin's appointment; see Sir Isaac Newton to John Campbell, c. November 1728, in H. W. Turnbull,

J. F. Scott, A. Rupert Hall and Laura Tilling, eds., *The Correspondence of Isaac Newton*, 7 vols. (Cambridge: Cambridge University Press, 1959–77), VII.338; see also Newton to Maclaurin, 21 August 1728, VII.329.

21 'A Short Account of the University of *Edinburgh*, the Present Professors in It, and the Several Parts of Learning Taught by Them', *The Scots Magazine* 3 (1741), 371–4, 372; on Maclaurin's teaching see also Patrick Murdoch, 'An Account of the Life and Writings of the Author', in Colin Maclaurin, *An Account of Sir Isaac Newton's Philosophical Discoveries, in Four Books* (London: A. Millar et al., 1748), v, where Murdoch states that in his fourth class Maclaurin taught 'a system of fluxions, the doctrine of chances, and the rest of *Newton's Principia*'.

22 George Berkeley, *The Analyst: Or, A Discourse Addressed to an Infidel Mathematician*, in A. A. Luce and T. E. Jessop, eds., *The Works of George Berkeley, Bishop of Cloyne*, 8 vols. (London: Thomas Nelson and Sons, 1948–56), IV.65–102; Colin Maclaurin, *A Treatise on Fluxions: In Two Books*, 2 vols. (Edinburgh: T. W. and T. Ruddimans, 1742). For another response to Berkeley by a prominent Scottish Newtonian see John Stewart, *Sir Isaac Newton's Two Treatises of the Quadrature of Curves, and Analysis by Equations of an Infinite Number of Terms, Explained* (London: James Bettenham, 1745). Stewart was selected as Maclaurin's successor at Marischal College in 1727, and taught there until his death in 1766.

23 Roger Emerson, 'The Philosophical Society of Edinburgh, 1737–1747', *British Journal for the History of Science* 12 (1979), 154–91; Robert Maxwell, ed., *Select Transactions of the Honourable the Society of Improvers in the Knowledge of Agriculture in Scotland* (Edinburgh: Paton, Symmer et al., 1743), esp. xii–xiii.

24 D. J. Bryden, 'The Edinburgh Observatory, 1736–1811: a Story of Failure', *Annals of Science* 47 (1990), 445–74.

25 Colin Maclaurin to Sir John Clerk, 23 March 1742, and Maclaurin to Archibald Campbell, 21 February 1745, in Stella Mills, ed., *The Collected Letters of Colin Maclaurin* (Nantwich: Shiva Publishing, 1982), 87, 123–4; Judith V. Grabiner, ' "Some Disputes of Consequence": Maclaurin among the Molasses Barrels', *Social Studies of Science* 28 (1998), 139–68; 'Maclaurin and Newton: the Newtonian Style and the Authority of Mathematics', in Charles W. J. Withers and Paul Wood, eds., *Science and Medicine in the Scottish Enlightenment* (East Linton: Tuckwell Press, 2002), 143–71.

26 Anon., *Proposals*, I.487.

27 John Locke, *Some Thoughts concerning Education*, ed. John W. and Jean S. Yolton (Oxford: Clarendon Press, 1989), 246–9.

28 See for example the printed handbill, *Proposals for Setting on Foot a Compleat Course of Experimental Philosophy in the Marischal College of Aberdeen*, which is reproduced in Wood, *Aberdeen Enlightenment*, 17. Similar sets of proposals were issued by Thomas Bower at King's College (1709) and the universities of Glasgow (1710) and St Andrews (undated). All made the same claims about the usefulness of natural knowledge.

29 Larry Stewart, *The Rise of Public Science: Rhetoric, Technology and Natural Philosophy in Newtonian Britain, 1660–1750* (Cambridge: Cambridge University Press, 1992).

30 Colin Maclaurin to the Rev. Colin Campbell, 12 September 1714, in Mills, *Collected Letters of Maclaurin*, 159–61; Maclaurin, *Account*, 3, 377–92.

31 On Hume's engagement with the natural sciences see Michael Barfoot, 'Hume and the Culture of Science in the Early Eighteenth Century', in M. A. Stewart, ed., *Studies in the Philosophy of the Scottish Enlightenment* (Oxford: Clarendon Press, 1990), 151–90.

32 Albert J. Kuhn, 'Glory or Gravity: Hutchinson vs Newton', *Journal of the History of Ideas* 22 (1961), 303–22; C. B. Wilde, 'Hutchinsonianism, Natural Philosophy and Religious Controversy in Eighteenth-Century Britain', *History of Science* 18 (1980), 1–24; Ian Simpson Ross, *Lord Kames and the Scotland of his Day* (Oxford: Clarendon Press, 1972), 63–64, 174–5, 360–2; [James Burnett, Lord Monboddo], *Antient Metaphysics: Or, the Science of Universals*, 6 vols. (Edinburgh: T. Cadell and J. Balfour, 1779–99). The development of the Hutchinsonian movement in Scotland deserves further study.

33 Thomas Reid, *An Inquiry into the Human Mind, on the Principles of Common Sense*, ed. Derek R. Brookes (Edinburgh: Edinburgh University Press, 1997), 210–11.

34 The term 'mathematical Hellenism' comes from George Davie, *The Democratic Intellect: Scotland and her Universities in the Nineteenth Century*, paperback edn (Edinburgh: Edinburgh University Press, 1981), 112; see also Richard Olson, 'Scottish Philosophy and Mathematics, 1750–1830', *Journal of the History of Ideas* 32 (1971), 29–44. For an alternative view see Wood, *Aberdeen Enlightenment*, 91, and Niccolò Guicciardini, *The Development of Newtonian Calculus in Britain, 1700–1800* (Cambridge: Cambridge University Press, 1989).

35 Maclaurin, *Treatise on Fluxions*, II.522–66; Maclaurin, *Account*, 344–8; James Stirling, 'Of the Figure of the Earth, and the Variation of Gravity on the Surface', *Philosophical Transactions* 39 (1735–6), 98–105; Ian Tweddle, *James Stirling: 'This about series and such things'* (Edinburgh: Scottish Academic Press, 1988), 101–39.

36 Patrick Wilson, 'Biographical Account of Alexander Wilson, MD late Professor of Practical Astronomy in Glasgow', *Edinburgh Journal of Science* 10 (1829), 1–17; [Alexander and Patrick Wilson], *Thoughts on General Gravitation, and Views thence Arising as to the State of the Universe* (London: T. Cadell, 1777).

37 For an admirable survey of the work of Melvill and the other Scots see Geoffrey Cantor, *Optics after Newton: Theories of Light in Britain and Ireland, 1704–1840* (Manchester: Manchester University Press, 1983); see also Kurt Møller Pederson, 'Roger Joseph Boscovich and John Robison on Terrestrial Aberration', *Centaurus* 24 (1980), 335–45.

38 J. L. Heilbron, *Electricity in the Seventeenth and Eighteenth Centuries: a Study of Early Modern Physics* (Berkeley, Los Angeles and London: University of California Press, 1979), 465–8.

39 A. L. Donovan, *Philosophical Chemistry in the Scottish Enlightenment: the Doctrines of William Cullen and Joseph Black* (Edinburgh: Edinburgh University Press, 1975).

40 On Cullen as an ether theorist see J. R. R. Christie, 'Ether and the Science of Chemistry, 1740–1790', in G. N. Cantor and M. J. S. Hodge, eds., *Conceptions of Ether: Studies in the History of Ether Theories, 1740–1900* (Cambridge: Cambridge University Press, 1981), 85–110.

41 Stephen Hales, *Vegetable Staticks* (London: W. and J. Innys, 1727); Arthur Donovan, 'Pneumatic Chemistry and Newtonian Natural Philosophy in the Eighteenth Century: William Cullen and Joseph Black', *Isis* 67 (1976), 217–28.

42 Anita Guerrini, 'Archibald Pitcairne and Newtonian Medicine', *Medical History* 31 (1987), 70–83; Guerrini, *Obesity and Depression in the Enlightenment: the Life and Times of George Cheyne* (Norman, OK: University of Oklahoma Press, 2000); Akihito Suzuki, 'Psychiatry without Mind in the Eighteenth Century: the Case of British Iatromathematicians', *Archives Internationales d'Histoire des Sciences* 48 (1998), 119–46; John P. Wright, 'Materialism and the Life Soul in Eighteenth-Century Scottish Physiology', in Wood, *Scottish Enlightenment*, 177–97.

43 Michael Barfoot, 'James Gregory (1753–1821) and Scottish Scientific Metaphysics, 1750–1800', (unpublished PhD thesis, University of Edinburgh, 1983).

44 Paul Wood, 'Science and the Pursuit of Virtue in the Aberdeen Enlightenment', in Stewart, *Scottish Enlightenment*, 127–49.

45 Paul Wood, 'Science, Philosophy and the Mind', in Roy Porter, ed., *The Cambridge History of Science*, Volume 4: *The Eighteenth Century* (Cambridge: Cambridge University Press, 2002), 908–35.

46 For the suggestion that a 'second' scientific revolution occurred at the turn of the nineteenth century see Roger Hahn, *The Anatomy of a Scientific Institution: the Paris Academy of Sciences, 1666–1803* (Berkeley, Los Angeles and London: University of California Press, 1971), 275–6.

47 Guicciardini, *Newtonian Calculus*, 99–103; C. E. Perrin, 'A Reluctant Catalyst: Joseph Black and the Edinburgh Reception of Lavoisier's Chemistry', *Ambix* 29 (1982), 141–76.

48 Ian J. Fleming and Noel F. Robertson, *Britain's First Chair of Agriculture at the University of Edinburgh, 1790–1990* (Edinburgh: East of Scotland College of Agriculture, 1990).

49 Paul Wood, 'The Natural History of Man in the Scottish Enlightenment', *History of Science* 28 (1990), 89–123; William Smellie, *The Philosophy of Natural History*, 2 vols. (1790–9; reprinted with an introduction by Paul Wood, Bristol: Thoemmes Press, 2001).

50 Matthew Mackaile, *Terrae Prodromus Theoricus* (Aberdeen: George Mosman, 1691).

51 P. B. Wood, 'Buffon's Reception in Scotland: the Aberdeen Connection', *Annals of Science* 44 (1987), 160–90.

52 Stephen W. Brown, 'William Smellie and Natural History: Dissent and Dissemination', in Withers and Wood, *Science and Medicine in the Scottish Enlightenment*, 191–214; Roy Porter, 'George Hoggart Toulmin's Theory of Man and the Earth in the Light of the Development of British Geology', *Annals of Science* 35 (1978), 339–52; Porter, 'Philosophy and Politics of a Geologist: G. H. Toulmin (1754–1817)', *Journal of the History of Ideas* 39 (1978), 435–50.

53 James Hutton, 'Theory of the Earth; or an Investigation of the Laws Observable in the Composition, Dissolution and Restoration of Land upon the Globe', *Transactions of the Royal Society of Edinburgh* 1 (1788), 209–304, 304. The best introduction to Huttonian geology is now Dennis R. Dean, *James Hutton and the History of Geology* (Ithaca, NY, and London: Cornell University Press, 1992).

54 Withers, 'Geography in the Public Sphere'; John A. Cable, 'The Early History of Scottish Popular Science', *Studies in Adult Education* 4 (1972), 34–45; Sher, 'Science and Medicine in the Scottish Enlightenment'.

55 John Butt, *John Anderson's Legacy: the University of Strathclyde and its Antecedents, 1796–1996* (East Linton: Tuckwell Press, 1996), 22, 29.

6   Scepticism and common sense

INTRODUCTION

Scepticism has taken many forms in the history of European thought. Around the middle of the eighteenth century, there were four different versions that were especially significant, two of which were of ancient origin.[1] The *first* was Pyrrhonian scepticism. It was taken to claim that we have no evidence for any proposition, because any proposition may be contradicted by another proposition of equal probability. Pyrrhonism so understood leads to the suspense of judgement. The *second* form of scepticism derived from Academic scepticism. The members of the so-called 'New Academy' had argued against Pyrrhonism that scepticism cannot be founded on the claim that there are contradictory propositions of equal probability; rather, it is the result of the fact that we can never overcome deception with certainty. The threat of deception, however, did not exclude, for them, the possibility that some judgements are more probable than others: indeed, they thought that we could not live our lives without accepting at least some judgements as being warranted. *Thirdly*, in his *Meditations on First Philosophy* (1641) Descartes introduced the idea of methodological doubt as a means to overcome doubts and uncertainties. Descartes argued that knowledge of ourselves was the most fundamental kind of knowledge, and that only things we perceive as clearly and distinctly as the *cogito* ('I think, therefore I exist') can count as true knowledge. A *fourth* kind of scepticism is related to John Locke, who rejected much of Cartesian metaphysics and especially the concept of innate ideas that was inherent in it. Locke claimed that the faculties of our understanding are very limited indeed. We have intuitive or 'clear and certain Knowledge'[2] in geometry and arithmetic, but our thought concerning matters of fact amounts only to probabilities. Some of these probabilities 'border so near upon Certainty, that we make no doubt at all about them; but assent to them as firmly, and act, according to that Assent, as resolutely, as if they were infallibly demonstrated' (*Essay*, 655). They are absolutely sufficient for the conduct of our lives (*Essay*, 652). While Locke himself was certainly not a sceptic, he did reduce all empirical evidence to different degrees of probabilities. His theory of ideas and his concept of probability in particular thus prepared the way for a new version of scepticism, famously expressed in the first book of David Hume's *Treatise of Human Nature* (1739).[3]

Hume's scepticism itself had at least two aspects. Hume not only argued (like Locke) that the powers of our understanding are limited, and that we should, accordingly, be modest in our assertions, but he also threw doubt on all empirical evidence by arguing that we find manifest paradoxes and contradictions at the centre of our abstract as well as of our experimental reasoning. This sceptical conception of Hume's marks a turning point in the history of modern epistemology. His *Treatise* seems to have been written in the hope that experimental philosophy would contribute significantly to the science of man, but the argument of Book 1 of that work can actually be taken to prove that Pyrrhonism is at the heart of 'the most profound philosophy'.[4] This scepticism has always been considered one of the key features of his philosophy.[5]

The two most important reactions to Hume's scepticism were those by Thomas Reid and by Immanuel Kant. Kant considered scepticism philosophically important, but he never offered a direct refutation of Hume. In his *Critique of Pure Reason* (1781), he answered him indirectly by arguing that certain pure forms of intuition and thinking are necessary conditions of our knowledge about the world. For Reid, the very idea of paradoxes and contradictions was unattractive; and any philosophical system that allows them had to be wrong for him just because it allows them. The general strategy endorsed by Reid in his *An Inquiry into the Human Mind on the Principles of Common Sense* (1764), in the refutation of Hume, might be best described as a philosophical argument for the claim that at the foundation of our beliefs and knowledge about the world is a set of common sense principles. Scepticism is refuted neither by experience nor by reason but by some original principles of our constitution that make reason and experience possible. Reid's common sense theory was occasioned by David Hume's scepticism in the *Treatise*, and there can be no doubt that he regarded his own philosophy as the only alternative to Hume's scepticism.

Thomas Reid's own assessment of his relation to Hume has not always been accepted. Thomas Brown[6] argued relatively early that the two only emphasised different aspects of the same solution, and more recently Norman Kemp Smith[7] advanced a similar thesis. Following the lead of those who had argued that an exclusively sceptical reading of Hume overlooks his positive and naturalistic account of human knowledge, Kemp Smith claimed that he was really also a common sense philosopher.[8]

To be sure, Hume argued that human nature provides a way out of a total or Pyrrhonian scepticism. Because we share some instinctive principles with animals, Pyrrhonism may prove to be true in theory, but not in practice. It is this naturalism[9] that explains, for Kemp Smith, why Hume never publicly answered Reid and Beattie. While Kemp Smith's interpretation is controversial and cannot be accepted without important qualifications, one might concede that there are interesting similarities between the two Scottish doctrines.[10] Not only do they endorse a number of common sense convictions, they also advance different versions of naturalism.

In this chapter I will first provide a detailed account of Hume's exposition of the different meanings of scepticism in *An Enquiry concerning Human Understanding* (1748) (hereinafter *EHU*). Secondly, I will discuss some aspects of Hume's epistemological scepticism in the *Treatise* that cannot be found in the *Enquiry*. Thirdly, I will reconstruct the basic elements of Reid's critique of Hume's scepticism as well as Reid's concept of common sense, and finally I will compare significant aspects of Hume and Reid.

THE NATURE OF HUME'S SCEPTICISM

Hume discusses scepticism most explicitly in 'Of the Academical or Sceptical Philosophy', the final section of his *Enquiry*. He distinguishes in this context between one species of scepticism that is '*antecedent* to all study and philosophy' (*EHU* 149) and another species, '*consequent* to science and enquiry' (*EHU* 150). The first species is identical with the scepticism forwarded by Descartes. It seems to have two possible outcomes. If this sceptical method is taken to amount to a recommendation of universal doubt, then nothing will ever convince us of the truth of anything. Hume claims, however, that it is not possible for human beings ever to be in such a state. The sceptical method proves useful only if one takes it to mean that we should self-critically and impartially evaluate our thinking at all times.

The second species of scepticism is for Hume philosophically more interesting. Once we have tried to provide a secure foundation for our knowledge but have failed, scepticism about the possibility of philosophical justification seems only appropriate. Still, this kind of scepticism proves fruitful, if only because the 'paradoxical tenets' of the sceptics (*EHU* 150) excite our curiosity and lead us to examine their arguments more closely, even if we know that we will never solve them. For Hume not only metaphysics and theology are subject to this kind of scepticism, so also are the maxims of our daily lives.

What exactly, then, gives rise to this scepticism *consequent* to our studies? Hume starts with a discussion of scepticism with regard to the witness of our senses. Modern philosophy is among other things an attempt to show that while secondary qualities (such as colours, tastes, smells and sounds) exist only in the perceiving mind, primary qualities (such as shape, velocity and number) are properties of external objects. But arguments for the existence of external objects lead us to contradict ourselves. Our natural belief in the existence of external objects is contradicted by reason, since the 'slightest philosophy' shows us that nothing is ever present to our mind 'but an image or perception' (*EHU* 152). But our rational arguments, based on abstraction, are likewise unsound because the concept of abstraction is itself an absurd idea (*EHU* 154). On the other hand, if primary qualities are not properties of any external object, then an external object is nothing but an 'inexplicable *something*' (*EHU* 155). How this '*something*' could be the cause of our perception will be forever mysterious.

Hume argues that arguments, which undermine reasoning itself, are at the very centre of scepticism. As far as abstract reasoning is concerned, our sceptical doubts are mainly founded on our ideas of space and time. In the case of space, it is the concept of the infinite divisibility of extension, which 'shocks the clearest and most natural principles of human reason' (*EHU* 156). This concept is contrary to common sense, yet it rests on the clearest chain of reasoning. Here, we have a real contradiction in the concept of reason itself.

Hume argues that the result of such thinking is a total scepticism with regard to reason. This does not mean, however, that radical scepticism is victorious. We must also be sceptical about our scepticism, because we do not understand how first level scepticism – as we might call it – is itself possible. This scepticism 'arises from the paradoxical conclusions of geometry or the science of quantity' (*EHU* 158) but how any clear and distinct idea contradicts another clear and distinct idea is totally incomprehensible to us. Scepticism at the metalevel is the natural result of our ignorance in this regard.

A second type of scepticism about science concerns reasoning about matters of fact or existence, what Hume terms 'moral reasoning'. The objections to such reasoning are either popular or philosophical. The popular objections are for Hume weak and philosophically uninteresting. Pyrrhonians offer standard arguments, such as that human understanding has but narrow capacities, that our judgements concerning matters of fact vary in different situations and circumstances, and so on. If we took these objections seriously, however, we could no longer handle even the slightest affairs of our daily life (*EHU* 159).

The philosophical form of scepticism arises from our profound researches. All our testimony, which leads us beyond the immediate evidence of our sense and memory, rests, according to Hume, on causal judgements. As our idea of the relation between cause and effect is entirely based on the observation that two objects have been frequently conjoined, it is custom alone which makes us believe that they will also be conjoined together in the future. The sceptic therefore gains total victory because we have no a priori grounds or justifying reasons to believe that the future will resemble the past. But even the more profound reasonings of Pyrrhonism are only of speculative interest; they '*admit of no answer and produce no conviction*' (*EHU* 155n). As human beings, we lie under the necessity to judge, to breath, and to feel; nature gains victory over philosophical speculations (*EHU* 160).

As we have seen, Hume argues with regard to our first level scepticism in the abstract sciences that we should be sceptical about this scepticism itself. It is interesting to note that he does not likewise plead for second level scepticism with regard to Pyrrhonian scepticism concerning moral evidence. In the moral sciences we go beyond the immediate testimony of our senses and the mere comparison of ideas. Our reasonings concerning matters of fact are based on our experience and custom, and not on reason alone. Because custom can never afford a clear proof, we have reason to question the sustainability of all our judgements concerning matters of fact. The appropriate reaction to Pyrrhonism with regard to moral evidence, therefore, is provided by nature itself. As human beings, we must pay tribute to our nature and suspend our philosophical doubts.

Hume's insight into the function of nature in overcoming, although not refuting, Pyrrhonian scepticism with regard to our moral evidence leads him to a new concept of scepticism, which is the causal product of Pyrrhonism and natural instinct.[11] 'There is, indeed, a more *mitigated* scepticism or *academical* philosophy, which may be both durable and useful, and which may, in part, be the result of this Pyrrhonism, or *excessive* scepticism, when its undistinguished doubts are, in some measure, corrected by common sense and reflection' (*EHU* 161).

Hume distinguishes between two kinds of mitigated scepticism. The first species is directed towards dogmatic philosophers, who consider things from only one perspective. Because our natural capacities are very limited, we have to consider things from different perspectives and be cautious in our thinking. The second kind is more important, however. It consists in a lesson we can learn from the theoretical persuasiveness of Pyrrhonism: we should limit 'our enquiries to such subjects as are best adapted to the narrow capacity of human understanding' (*EHU* 162). Even if this is easier said than done, because our imagination takes delight in remote and extraordinary subjects, we should strive to confine our judgement 'to common life, and to such subjects as fall under daily practice and experience' (*EHU* 162).

Hume's discussion of scepticism has an objective and a subjective side. The objective side is constituted by the reasons we have to be epistemological sceptics. The subjective side consists in the reasons we have for engaging in philosophical reasoning. Nothing can free us from the desperate mood arising from our Pyrrhonian doubts except a 'strong power of natural instinct' (*EHU* 162). We prolong our philosophical studies because, first, they afford us immediate pleasure, and second, 'philosophical decisions are nothing but the reflections of common life, methodized and corrected'. Philosophers 'will never be tempted to go beyond common life, so long as they consider the imperfections of those faculties which they employ, their narrow reach, and their inaccurate operations'.[12] If we leave our philosophical armchairs, nature necessitates us, like everyone else, to believe in the existence of an external world. Pyrrhonism can even be of advantage because it frees us from those purely speculative enquiries, which admit of no answer and produce no conviction.

Scepticism, Hume claims, is also advantageous in the abstract sciences. The lesson we can learn from second level scepticism is similar to the lesson we learn from scepticism about moral evidence. We should confine our enquiries to those subjects which are best suited to the narrow capacities of our understanding. We can never go further in our enquiries and reflections than to observe the equality or inequality of quantity and number. No form of scepticism can make us believe that 'the cube root of 64 is equal to the half of 10' because this proposition 'can never be distinctly conceived' (*EHU* 164). But if we apply our thinking to the ideas of space and time, for instance, and introduce the concept of infinite divisibility, all certainty vanishes. Scepticism, in other words, is ineffective when directed at matters we conceive clearly and distinctly and without contradiction. In this context nature is not required for the formation of beliefs. Nature must supply this need only in the moral sciences, which lack strict demonstrations.

In the *Treatise* (hereinafter *T*), Hume does not mention the concept of 'mitigated' scepticism, nor does he refer to the ancient concept of 'Pyrrhonism'.[13] In 1739, 'moderate scepticism' (*T* 224, cf. *T* 272) is Hume's answer to 'total' or 'excessive' scepticism. It is a subject of dispute whether 'moderate scepticism' is identical to 'mitigated skepticism'. Although there is certainly no radical break in Hume's thinking about scepticism, there are some striking differences between 1739 and 1748. Hume did not argue in 1739, as he did in 1748, that we should confine our abstract and experimental arguments to subjects untouched by paradox and contradiction. Rather, 'moderate scepticism' seems to amount in 1739 to nothing more than the recommendation that we should at times change the perspective of the philosopher to that of a citizen of the common world.[14] As philosophers, our arguments undermine all evidence we may possess, but if we return to the common affairs of life, we will feel the impact of nature on us. Indeed, common sense and carelessness are the only remedies to the sceptical malady (*T* 218).

This change of perspective does not mean, however, that we can import common sense evidence into the moral sciences by restricting them to subjects free from contradictions. On the contrary, it only shows that there is a radical opposition of reason and sense (or feeling). This is the lesson Hume means to teach in *Treatise* iv.iv. We can learn it from the fundamental principle of modern philosophy, which is that primary qualities alone resemble external objects. For Hume this principle is altogether implausible, because it does not leave us with a satisfactory idea of solidity and matter. It may be true that in touching any object we seem to feel its solidity and independent existence, but this method of thinking is actually 'more popular than philosophical' (*T* 230). We seem to feel the independent existence of bodies, but our reasoning from cause and effect shows that qualities are nothing but perceptions. The result of this consideration is that our reason and the senses (or feeling) oppose each other directly, even if our doubts are not strong enough to cancel out our practical beliefs (*T* 238).

Hume's discussions of our knowledge with regard to 'our internal perception, and the nature of the mind' (*T* 232), and in the concluding pages of Book I (*T* I.iv.vii) are also of great interest for understanding his conception of scepticism in the *Treatise*. As regards the nature of our minds, Hume is willing to concede that though this subject involves infinite obscurities, our mind is not perplexed by such contradictions as it is by contradictions connected with thinking about the material world. Contradictions only arise on the false hypothesis of the immateriality of the soul (*T* 232). Although we have, therefore, no purely *cognitive* reason to hold a Cartesian concept of the substantiality of our soul, there might be a *sensitive* ground to assert the existence of a continuing self. Hume distinguishes between the problem of personal identity in thought and imagination on the one hand and 'our passions or [the] concern we take in ourselves' (*T* 253) on the other. He never questions personal identity on the basis of our passions.[15]

As Hume famously argues, there is no sensitive basis of personal identity based on thought and imagination, and the very concept of personal identity itself leads us into a 'manifest contradiction'

(*T* 251). The self is nothing but a bundle of perceptions. Personal identity is a fiction, based on our imagination (*T* 254). From the sceptical point of view, it is of special interest that Hume renounces his thesis, that this subject is free from contradictions, in an appendix to book three of the *Treatise* (1740). Looking again at his section on personal identity, Hume states, 'I find myself involv'd in such a labyrinth, that, I must confess, I neither know how to correct my former opinions, nor how to render them consistent' (*T* 633). The contradition arises because we subscribe to two different views, namely that we have no notion or idea of the self, distinct from all our particular perceptions on the one side, and our feeling of personal identity arising from our thought about the connections of our past perceptions. This connection is felt to be necessary. Hume writes: 'Most philosophers seem inclin'd to think, that personal identity *arises* from consciousness; and consciousness is nothing but a reflected thought or perception. The present philosophy, therefore, has so far a promising aspect' (*T* 635). But Hume sees himself as unable to provide any theory that would explain the principle, which unites all our distinctive perceptions. Such a theory is only possible on the assumption either that our perceptions are not distinct existences or that the mind can perceive some real connection between perceptions. Hume cannot renounce either of these principles, because they are the very centre of his empiricism. For this reason he declares the problem of personal identity as too difficult for his understanding, although it is not 'absolutely insuperable' in principle (*T* 636).

In the *Treatise* Hume did not claim that there is a contradiction between reason and sense, to be overcome by nature, nor does he plead for modesty in judgement or argue for a second level scepticism as he does in the *Enquiry*. But he seems to admit that his own theory of human understanding is defective[16] and that there is something profoundly problematic about the very basis of his philosophy, because he cannot account for our strong belief in personal identity on the basis of thought and imagination. One of the deep differences between Hume's conceptions of scepticism in the *Treatise* and the *Enquiry* is not that Hume has overcome these sceptical doubts of the *Treatise*, but that he is no longer willing to admit them in the *Enquiry*.

In the 'Conclusion' of Book 1, Hume rethinks the journey he has made into human understanding. It is perhaps his most personal piece of writing, in which he uses 'I' frequently. Looking at the results of his arguments, 'total scepticism' (*T* 268) seems to be the natural outcome. Hume finds contradictions, absurdities and confusion everywhere. If we rely on our imagination alone, illusions arise everywhere; if we rely instead on our understanding (our more established properties of the imagination), not even the lowest degree of evidence is left in philosophy and common life (cf. *T* 267–8). Hume is personally struck by philosophical or metaphysical scepticism and is willing to renounce even the slightest degree of probability.

Taking into account what Hume actually had argued in the preceding sections of the *Treatise*, he certainly overemphasises the sceptical implications of his philosophy. But there seems to be a reason why he does so. The stronger philosophical scepticism is, the stronger must be the means by which we are healed of our sceptical malady. It is nature itself which leads Hume back to common life: 'Most fortunately it happens, that since reason is incapable of dispelling these clouds, nature herself suffices to that purpose, and cures me of this philosophical melancholy and delirium, either by relaxing this bent of mind, or by some avocation, and lively impression of my senses, which obliterate all these chimeras' (*T* 269). Although philosophy is a valuable weapon in the fight against superstition, which can so easily arise from popular opinions and false philosophy (*T* 271–2), we do not have sound arguments that show why we should do philosophy any longer. Hume argues therefore that a genuine sceptic would even be sceptical about his scepticism (*T* 273). Indeed, he feels that he would be a 'loser in point of pleasure' if he gave up philosophy altogether; and he goes so far as to claim that 'this is the origin of my philosophy' (*T* 271).

In the *Treatise*, Hume's sceptical doubts about scepticism are not confined to scepticism with regard to the abstract sciences. Rather, moderate scepticism seems to be a form of life, or a stance for all those who, despite their first level scepticism, take a personal interest in philosophical speculations. A true sceptic achieves his aim, namely calmness or the ease of mind that the ancients called *ataraxia*, by being 'diffident' about his sceptical doubts. We not only should indulge our inclination to philosophy, we also 'shou'd yield to that propensity, which inclines us to be positive and certain in *particular points*' (*T* 273). Indeed, the sceptic, Hume argues, is likely to forget his scepticism and his modesty. We might suspend our judgements in many controversial subjects, but we cannot and should not suspend them in all matters, as classical Pyrrhonism suggested.

REID'S COMMON SENSE PHILOSOPHY AND HIS CRITIQUE OF SCEPTICISM

For Reid, Hume's *Treatise* marks the final step in the history of the 'ideal system' (Reid, *Inquiry*, 23), first defended in modern times by Descartes and then taken up and modified by Malebranche, Locke, and others. According to 'the Cartesian system' (*Inquiry*, 208), we do not know anything about objects except by ideas, which resemble them. This theory, Reid claims, leads directly to scepticism. The first step towards this scepticism was taken by Locke, who argued that only primary qualities resemble external objects, while secondary qualities are nothing but perceptions in the perceiving mind. Berkeley took the second step by claiming that there are no material objects existing independently of the perceiving mind. The final step was taken by Hume, who showed that we do not even have reasons to believe in our own existence. After reading the *Treatise*, Reid wrote, 'I see myself, and the whole frame of nature, shrink into fleeting ideas, which, like Epicurus's atoms, dance about in emptiness' (*Inquiry*, 22).

Reid does not question the validity and applicability of the arguments put forward by Berkeley and Hume (cf. *Inquiry*, 4, 19, 69, 217). On the contrary, he openly acknowledges that it was Hume who first convincingly worked out the true implications of the ideal system. The problem is that Hume never questioned the basic principles of the ideal system. Hence Reid takes the sceptical results of the *Treatise* as a sign of the system's fundamental mistake. He characterises the author of the *Treatise* as an absolute, if somewhat inconsequent, sceptic, and this because Hume did not question the basic principle that all our perceptions are either ideas or impressions (cf. *Inquiry*, 4, 71). Hume's attempt to limit his scepticism by natural principles of our mind and common sense is to no avail. Even moderate scepticism 'leaves no ground to believe any thing rather than its contrary' (*Inquiry*, 4). The lesson we must learn from Hume is that we should resist inventing systems altogether.

Reid does not altogether ignore Hume's endorsement of natural instincts and common sense, but to him, Hume's common sense is nothing but an expression of pyrrhonism. If sceptical principles were to take too strong a hold of him, this would have disastrous consequences. Hume did not realise that he could not live his scepticism even in solitude and that his philosophy is nothing but sophistry (cf. *Inquiry*, 20–1).

In Reid's view the contest and opposition between common sense and philosophy that is characteristic of modern philosophy should be given up altogether (cf. *Inquiry*, 68). The sceptics have undermined the authority of common sense through philosophy. Common sense, however, is in no need of philosophical hypotheses. The dictates of common sense are first principles of all thinking, and they cannot be proven to be true, nor do they need such a proof.[17] Therefore true philosophy 'has no other root but the principles of Common Sense; it grows out of them, and draws its nourishment from them: severed from this root, its honours wither, its sap is dried up, it dies and rots'.[18] The principles of common sense are the principles we take for granted in the common concerns of life because of the original constitution of our human nature (*Inquiry*, 32). Whereas the ideal system postulates that 'every object of thoughts must be an impression or idea' (*Inquiry*, 33), on the basis of the principles of common sense we can place our trust in the evidence of our senses and of our memory, both of which teach us that there is more to the world than just things in our mind.

While the province of common sense is to judge by means of self-evident principles, the province of reason is to draw conclusions from them, conclusions which themselves are not self-evident.[19] This does not mean, however, that we should not be cautious about what really are first principles (cf. *Essays on the Intellectual Powers*, 1.ii, 41, 46). Still, we cannot be as sceptical about them as we can be about our observations and arguments. Some of our presumed principles might be nothing but 'vulgar prejudice', (*Essays on the Intellectual Powers*, 1.ii, 41) some might hide their evidence; but at least some of them seem to be beyond any reasonable doubt. Reid counts among the latter the beliefs in our own existence, in the existence of material objects, and in the reliability of our faculties.[20] The only rational ground for scepticism about the first or original principles of human nature is that it might turn out upon further enquiry that these principles resolve into some more general principle of our constitution; they are true principles of our constitution, but they might not be original and truly 'first' principles (cf. *Inquiry*, 61).

The concept of 'suggestion' (*Inquiry*, 38) is of central importance to Reid's philosophy of mind. He claims that modern philosophers overlook it. There are some 'suggestions' which are original and natural, and others which are the result of experience and habit. Our sensations naturally, for instance, suggest the notion of present existences and the belief in what we perceive or feel; thoughts and sensations suggest the concept and belief in our own existence. On the other hand, it is only through experience that a certain sound suggests the belief that a coach is passing the street right now. We might be wrong with regard to the coach, but we cannot be mistaken in our belief that the perception of a tree amounts to a clear proof of its mind-independent existence.

Reid distinguishes between three different types of natural signs. The first class comprehends those signs 'whose connection with the thing signified is established by nature, but discovered only by experience' (*Inquiry*, 59). Natural signs of the second class are likewise established by nature, but discovered by principles which are natural to us. By such natural principles an infant is soothed by a smile and frightened by an angry face. The third class comprises those natural signs which suggest the existences of the things signified 'by a natural kind of magic, and at once give us a conception, and create a belief of it' (*Inquiry*, 60). The first class of signs are the 'foundation of true philosophy', the second of taste and the fine arts, and the third class 'is the foundation of common sense; a part of human nature which hath never been explained' (*Inquiry*, 61). It is therefore futile to hope, as Hume did, that our belief in the existence of external existences might be the result of habit and experience. That is to say, all natural signs of the first class are totally unsuitable to produce such a conviction. Basic beliefs suggested by the original constitution of our nature stand on their own.

SCEPTICISM AND COMMON SENSE

It is uncontroversial that Hume undermined the traditional concept of reason and true knowledge by arguing that all our judgements are based on belief. If belief is nothing but a peculiar feeling or sentiment produced by habit, there is no clear difference between reason, imagination, feeling and sense, or so Hume argues. Rather, even reason is based on imagination and feeling. If this is true, then the Cartesian project has lost its foundation, for then we cannot have any a priori knowledge of substances (body and mind), nor do we have any a priori guarantee that the general law of causality is true. 'Whatever *is* may *not be*. No negation of a fact can involve a contradiction' (*EHU* 164) is the battle cry of his empiricist philosophy. There might be, therefore, events in the world which are not even caused by anything. Hume never questioned the 'elements' (*T* 13) of his philosophy, nor did he ever have any sceptical reservations about his attack on traditional metaphysics.

It is also uncontroversial that Hume personally regarded himself as a sceptic. In a series of essays, he argued that there are four different kinds of philosophers:[21] the Epicurean, the Stoic, the Platonist and the Sceptic. It is clear where Hume's preferences lie. As sceptical philosophers, we must mistrust a priori arguments as well as any kind of dogmatic assertion. Our natural faculties are very limited and our arguments may exhibit manifest contradictions, but this does not mean that we should suspend all our judgements, as traditional Pyrrhonism claimed. On the contrary, suspending all judgement would result in self-destruction. Luckily, nature makes us reason on the basis of experience and custom.

Controversies have arisen over the nature of Hume's scepticism. Is his 'moderate', 'mitigated' or 'academic' scepticism to be viewed in opposition to the ancient form of Pyrrhonism, or did he misinterpret Pyrrhonism? Is his naturalism, a word he himself never used, part of his scepticism, or does it lead beyond epistemological scepticism? Is his naturalism an expression of common sense principles? There is no consensus on these issues.

Leaving aside the historical questions of whether Hume understood the ancient forms of scepticism correctly or whether he perhaps misrepresented them intentionally, some preliminary clarification of his epistemology might run as follows: (1) In terms of method, Hume is a descriptive naturalist, because he wanted to describe the workings of our faculties in belief formation.[22] (2) Hume is a normative naturalist, because he claims that we have good reasons to believe certain things (for instance, that the sun will rise again tomorrow). Good reasons are based on custom and habit. These

reasons may also be called justifying reasons because they are reasons in which we place our trust in doing science and in the common
affairs of life. (3) Where, however, justifying reasons are understood
as conceptual reasons, Hume is a sceptic. Conceptual reasons are
reasons we have independently of our believing anything because of
habit and custom. Descartes, Reid and Kant thought that we
have conceptual (or formal) reasons, while Hume clearly did not.
(4) Normative naturalism has not only a positive, but also a negative side. It shows (a) that Cartesian metaphysics is wrong, (b) that
we should be sceptical or modest about our causal judgements, and
(c) that some people hold unfounded or unreflective beliefs about
what is the case. Common sense, therefore, cannot stand on its own;
it needs the critical inspection of philosophy. (5) There are no justifying reasons within normative naturalism to overcome the contradictions and paradoxes inherent in our thinking. Because we cannot live
Pyrrhonian scepticism, nature ensures that in the common affairs of
our lives we disregard the contradictions and paradoxes. We are not
left with any choice in this matter if we are to avoid self-destruction.

It has been argued that Reid misrepresents Hume's position by
ignoring its positive and naturalistic elements. But though one might
admit that aspects of Reid's characterisation of Hume's philosophy
are exaggerated, his reading of Hume as a total sceptic makes perfect
sense. Because Hume did not accept that there are principles prior to
experience or reason, he must hold that ultimate justifying reasons
cannot be found. Reid on the other hand was not willing to accept
that Hume's normative naturalism is all we need in the sciences and
in the common affairs of life. He might have been willing to accept
Hume's second, more innocent, version of a scepticism antecedent
to study and sciences.

Reid's common sense philosophy also has a naturalistic outlook,[23]
but it is different in kind from Hume's. First, the original principles of our constitutions are not found with a method that can
be called descriptive naturalism. Rather, they are based on intu-
itions (*Essays on the Intellectual Powers*, 1.ii, 41). Secondly, Reid,
like Turnbull, is a 'providential naturalist':[24] he is of the opinion
that we can trust our faculties because we are God's creatures. But
this interpretation of Reid is not unproblematic either. Important as
'providential naturalism' is for Reid, it is not the normative basis
of his philosophy. If we accept the infallibility of first principles

because of the goodness of God, our common sense principles are either based on faith or they are based on a circular argument (because our knowledge of God is also based on first principles). With a fully developed 'providential naturalism', Reid would thus undermine common sense philosophy. At one point of his *Inquiry*, however, he claims that if God deceived us in the belief in first principles, there would be no remedy (*Inquiry* 72).

Reid and Hume 'shared a common philosophical culture'[25] and were engaged in what they took to be the 'anatomy' or 'geography' of the human mind. But there are decisive differences between them. Hume was a thoroughgoing empiricist, Reid was not.[26] For Hume, judgement is based on feeling; for Reid, we have knowledge about first principles that is based neither on feeling nor on demonstration. Hume's acute comment on a draft of Reid's *Inquiry* was that it 'leads us back to innate Ideas'.[27] But the most important difference between the two Scots is their personal stance towards philosophy. Hume was at the same time fascinated and disturbed by paradoxes, and philosophy was for him a means not only to advance our knowledge in the moral sciences, but also a personal expedient to ease his mind by suspending judgement on subtle and sublime subjects. Reid never seemed to be disturbed in this way. Being a preacher and practising Christian, he started his philosophical journey on firm ground, wanting only to show that scepticism is altogether absurd. Hume was surely aware of this side of Reid's philosophy. In the famous concluding passage of Hume's *Dialogues Concerning Natural Religion*, Philo ironically argues that a person 'seasoned with a just sense of the imperfections of natural reason, will fly to revealed truth', while the 'haughty dogmatist' erects a system of natural theology 'by the mere help of philosophy ... To be a philosophical sceptic is, in a man of letters, the first and most essential step towards being a sound, believing Christian'.[28]

The lesson we can learn from these discussions is that Hume's naturalism is 'fully compatible with his skepticism',[29] and that our arguments are on firm ground if, as Hume argues in the *Enquiry*, we restrict our science of man to the domain of common sense. 'Common sense', however, does not mean the same thing in Hume and in Reid. For Hume, our flight to common sense is the result of our ignorance about first principles; for Reid, common sense is nothing other than the domain of the original principles of our human nature; it is the fount of true philosophy.

NOTES

1 For detailed information on scepticism in the eighteenth century, see Richard H. Popkin, *The History of Scepticism from Erasmus to Descartes* (Berkeley, Los Angeles: University of California Press, 1979), and *The High Road to Pyrrhonism* (Indianapolis: Hackett, 1993).

2 John Locke, *An Essay concerning Human Understanding*, ed. Peter H. Nidditch (Oxford: Clarendon Press, 1975), 652.

3 David Hume, *A Treatise of Human Nature*, ed. L. A. Selby-Bigge, 3rd edn, rev. P. H. Nidditch (Oxford: Clarendon Press, 1978), Book I. Cf. Thomas Reid, *An Inquiry into the Human Mind on the Principles of Common Sense*, ed. Derek R. Brookes (Edinburgh: Edinburgh University Press, 1997), 31.

4 David Hume, *Enquiries Concerning Human Understanding and Concerning the Principles of Morals*, ed. L. A. Selby-Bigge, 3rd edn, rev. P. H. Nidditch (Oxford: Clarendon Press, 1975), 154.

5 On early and modern sceptical readings of Hume see David Fate Norton, *David Hume: Common-sense Moralist, Sceptical Metaphysician* (Princeton, NJ: Princeton University Press, 1982), 3–13.

6 Thomas Brown, *Observations on the Nature and Tendency of the Doctrine of Mr Hume Concerning the Relation of Cause and Effect*, 2nd edn (Edinburgh, 1806).

7 Norman Kemp Smith, 'The Naturalism of Hume', *Mind* 14 (1905), 149–73, 335–47, and *The Philosophy of David Hume: a Critical Study of its Origins and Central Doctrines* (London: Macmillan, 1941).

8 On this interpretation see Nicholas Capaldi, *David Hume: the Newtonian Philosopher* (Boston: G. K. Hall, 1975), 30–4; see also John Immerwahr, 'A Skeptic's Progress: Hume's Preferences for *Enquiry* I', in David Fate Norton, Nicholas Capaldi and Wade L. Robison, eds., *McGill Hume Studies* (San Diego: Austin Hill Press, 1979), 232–3. Nicholas Capaldi claims that the 'positive version of "scepticism" is Hume's dynamic, historical–evolutionary version of Kant's synthetic a priori' (Capaldi, 'The Dogmatic Slumber of Hume Scholarship', *Hume Studies* 18, no. 2 (1992)), 130.

9 Hume's so-called naturalism should not be confused with the claim that he was a sceptical realist. The sceptical realist interpretation of Hume holds that he acknowledges an eternal and inflexible standard of truth, which is, however, distorted by our knowledge being restricted to ideas and the connection between them. Ideas misrepresent reality. See John P. Wright, *The Sceptical Realism of David Hume* (Minneapolis: University of Minnesota Press, 1983), 4, 21; and Stephen Buckle, *Hume's Enlightenment Tract: the Unity and Purpose of 'An Enquiry concerning Human Understanding'* (Oxford: Clarendon Press, 2001).

10   See Norton, *David Hume*, 200–1.

11   See Robert J. Fogelin, *Hume's Skepticism in the 'Treatise of Human Nature'* (London: Routledge and Kegan Paul, 1985), 150.

12   *EHU* 162; see also Hume, *Dialogues concerning Natural Religion*, ed. Henry D. Aiken (New York: Hafner Press; London: Collier Macmillan, 1948), 9–10.

13   'Pyrrhonism' is first mentioned in Hume's *An Abstract* (1740), see *T* 657.

14   Terence Penelhum calls this the 'on-again-off-again policy' of the *Treatise*; see Penelhum, 'Hume's Skepticism and the *Dialogues*', in Norton, Capaldi and Robison, *McGill Hume Studies*, 260; see also Immerwahr, 'A Skeptic's Progress', Norton, Capaldi and Robison, *McGill Hume Studies*, 233–8.

15   Books II and III of the *Treatise*, therefore, do not answer Hume's sceptical doubts in *Treatise* I.iv; on an opposite view see Annette Baier, *A Progress of Sentiments: Reflections on Hume's Treatise* (Cambridge, MA: Harvard University Press, 1991), 141–2.

16   See Ira Singer, 'Nature Breaks Down: Hume's Problematic Naturalism in *Treatise* I.iv', *Hume Studies* 26, no. 2 (2000), 232–3.

17   A list of Reid's first principles is given in Daniel Schulthess, *Philosophie et sens commun chez Thomas Reid, 1710–1796* (Berne: Peter Lang, 1983), 53–65, and Keith Lehrer, *Thomas Reid* (London, New York: Routledge, 1989), 157–65. See also chapter two of Manfred Kuehn's, *Scottish Common Sense in Germany, 1768–1800: a Contribution to the History of Critical Philosophy* (Kingston, Montreal: McGill-Queen's University Press, 1987).

18   Reid, *Inquiry*, 19. On the relationship between philosophy and common sense in Reid see Nicholas Wolterstorff, *Thomas Reid and the Story of Epistemology* (Cambridge: Cambridge University Press, 2001), 246–9.

19   *Essays on the Intellectual Powers of Man*, ed. D. R. Brookes (Edinburgh: Edinburgh University Press, 2002), 433.

20   The special position of this principle among the first principles is stressed by Lehrer, *Thomas Reid*, 162–1, and Lehrer, 'Reid, Hume and Common Sense', *Reid Studies* 2, no. 1 (1998), 15–25.

21   See Hume, *Essays Moral, Political and Literary*, ed. Eugene F. Miller, rev. edn (Indianapolis: Liberty Fund, 1987), 138–80.

22   This is uncontroversial; see for instance Penelhum, 'Hume's Skepticism', 253–4; Barry Stroud, *Hume* (London: Routledge and Kegan Paul, 1977), 13; and Robert J. Fogelin, 'The Tendency of Hume's Skepticism', in Myles Burnyeat, ed., *The Skeptical Tradition* (Berkeley: University of California Press, 1983), 399. However, Hume did not apply this method to the problem of personal identity.

23 H. O. Mounce claims that both Hume and Reid are epistemological naturalists; see Mounce, *Hume's Naturalism* (London, New York: Routledge, 1999), 8.

24 See Norton, *David Hume*, 171.

25 P. B. Wood, 'Hume, Reid and the Science of the Mind', in M. A. Stewart and John P. Wright, eds., *Hume and Hume's Connexions* (Edinburgh: Edinburgh University Press, 1994), 134.

26 Wolterstorff, *Thomas Reid*, p. x.

27 P. B. Wood, 'David Hume on Thomas Reid's *An Inquiry into the Human Mind, On the Principles of Common Sense*: a New Letter to Hugh Blair from July 1762', *Mind* 95 (1986), 411–16, 416). The most recent discussion of this important letter is by Paul Stanistreet, 'Hume's True Philosophy and Reid's Common Sense', *Reid Studies* 4, no. 2 (2001), 55–69.

28 Hume, *Dialogues*, 94.

29 Terence Penelhum, *David Hume: an Introduction to His Philosophical System* (West Lafayette, IN: Purdue University Press, 1992), 18. Fogelin argues 'that Hume's naturalism and skepticism are mutually supportive' (Fogelin, *Hume's Skepticism*), 146.

7   Moral sense and the foundations of morals

HUTCHESON AND MORAL SENSE

Francis Hutcheson, David Hume and Adam Smith were the main Scottish participants in the British debate on the foundations of morals. Here their moral theories will be outlined as three rival systems, and then Thomas Reid's critical attitude towards their theories will be discussed.

Francis Hutcheson (1694–1746) was the first Scottish philosopher to approach the problem of the foundations of morals in an original way. His strategy was to construct a unitary doctrine drawing both on Lord Shaftesbury's teachings on the relation between natural affection and morality, and on Locke's new empirical epistemology. In response to Hobbes's theory that human nature is fundamentally selfish and anti-social, Shaftesbury had argued that God provided human nature with a number of generous forms of affection, from family affection to a love for mankind, that naturally predispose men to live together. Human beings are also provided with a natural capacity to feel attraction to these affections and a dislike for the contrary ones.[1] In Shaftesbury's works it is not clear whether moral distinctions derive from reason or sentiment,[2] an omission that Hutcheson was to remedy.

From Locke, Hutcheson took the doctrine that men lack innate ideas, and that they derive their complex ideas of things and actions from experience, compounding, enlarging and abstracting from simple original ideas.[3] According to Locke, man derives these original ideas from the action of bodies on the external senses, or from reflecting on the operations of his mind.[4] To this basic structure Hutcheson added new senses which produce simple ideas as the sense of beauty or the moral sense, conceiving these internal senses on analogy with the external senses. There are other parts of Locke's theory that are seminal for Hutcheson: Locke's doctrine that secondary qualities are only powers in external objects to produce certain ideas or sensations in us (e.g. tastes, smells, colours); his pervasive attention to pleasure and pain as feelings that accompany not only many sensible perceptions, but also most of our thoughts; and finally his observation that men are more motivated by the law of reputation than divine law or civil law.[5] Hutcheson compares the perceptions of the moral sense (as well of the sense of beauty) to our perception of secondary qualities;[6] he argues that God has given us the peculiar pleasure of moral sense to direct our actions; and he describes virtue as a quality that procures approbation towards the agent from the beholders.[7]

In his *Inquiry into the Original of our Ideas of Beauty and Virtue* Hutcheson distinguishes three kinds of good connected with three different kinds of pleasure. The feelings of pleasure connected with the ideas produced in us by external objects provide us with the first or original idea from which we construct our complex ideas of happiness or 'natural good'.[8] The feelings of pleasure connected with the ideas of objects that present uniformity with variety provide us with the idea of beauty. Finally, the feelings of pleasure connected with the ideas of human actions that reveal kind or benevolent intentions in the agent, that is the desire to procure happiness to others, provide us with the idea of moral good.[9]

'Interest or self-love' is the natural inclination to pursue the pleasures provided by external objects, or the means that is used to satisfy it.[10] A disinterested natural inclination directs men to appreciate beautiful objects of nature or art, the elegance of theorems in geometry, regularity and order in nature.[11] Benevolence drives us to seek the natural good or happiness of others. It is an 'instinct' that is 'antecedent to all reason from interest',[12] and is weaker than self-love.[13] However it is important to note that benevolence is also conceived as the common quality inherent in many affections or passions that motivate human actions. Fundamental to Hutcheson's moral philosophy is the doctrine that benevolence underpins every virtue. The cardinal virtues of temperance, courage, prudence and justice, which were supreme in the classical and Christian traditions, constituting the sum of all virtues, are approved by our moral sense only if practised in order to promote public good.[14]

Hutcheson stresses as well the disinterested character of our moral approbation. Moral sense is a kind of sense because, like external senses, it is independent of our will, is common to mankind and, above all, it is immediate, that is to say, its deliverances are not conclusions mediated by premises. In particular it is not mediated by considerations of personal advantage or harm. It is on account of this last feature that we are able to admire actions that took place in remote times and regions and even actions that are contrary to our own interests. Nor is it necessary to have the learning and the arguments of a Cumberland or a Pufendorf to appreciate virtues.[15]

However the analogy between the pleasures afforded by external objects and those afforded by moral sense has produced many problems of interpretation both in Hutcheson's time and in our own. The reference to pleasure seems to lay his doctrine open to the accusation that he is a hedonist. Perhaps the best interpretation is given by Hume when he says: 'We do not infer a character to be virtuous, because it pleases: But in feeling that it pleases after such a particular manner, we in effect feel that is virtuous.'[16] It is the particular character of the moral pleasure that makes us approve of benevolence, admire the moral agent and love him.[17]

As every man has a capacity to make moral distinctions, so the weighing of moral virtue is within the competence of every man. With the aid of a kind of moral algebra, Hutcheson seeks to show that the amount of public good produced by an action is directly proportional to the degree of benevolence and is inversely proportional to the natural abilities of the agent, that is to his mental endowments and external resources, from which Hutcheson concludes that moral excellence can be attained by any person, independently of his learning, power or riches.[18]

The concept of benevolence is not, however, always at the centre of Hutcheson's stage. He affirms that from the moral sense 'we derive our ideas of rights', including ideas pertaining to the doctrine of natural law.[19] The criterion he adopts, however, is not the quality approved by moral sense, that is benevolence, but public utility. It is not universal benevolence that induces us to work, but the strong ties of friendship and of natural affection for offspring.

Industriousness, from which, according to Hutcheson, nine-tenths of human resources derive, can be encouraged only by guaranteeing property rights.[20]

Hutcheson's *Inquiry* was almost immediately subjected to criticism as being religiously heterodox, and he subsequently clarified his doctrine in his *Essay on the Nature and Conduct of the Passions and Affections. With Illustrations on the Moral Sense* (1728). The broad thrust of the attack on him was to the effect that his conception of virtue seemed to be incompatible with religious piety, and that his moral sense appeared to reduce moral good to a mere sentiment of human nature. It will be instructive to consider the matter in some detail.

John Clarke (1687–1734), master of the Grammar School in Hull and author of a successful Latin grammar and many translations from the Latin, judged that the idea of a totally instinctive and disinterested benevolence contradicts the hypothesis of moral sense: should we not be induced by the pleasure of moral sense to be benevolent?[21] On the other hand, if moral sense makes us love virtuous people, their happiness or unhappiness becomes part of our own happiness or misery, and our benevolence is therefore not disinterested.[22] Joseph Butler's moral sermons of 1726 seem at first sight to come to Hutcheson's support on this matter. His concept of moral conscience has very similar functions to Hutcheson's moral sense.[23] Butler agrees with Shaftesbury and with Hutcheson that the gratification of sociable dispositions is essential to human nature.[24] However, Butler distinguishes between, on the one hand, a reasonable self-love, which under the direction of moral conscience establishes an individual's real interest, and, on the other hand, the particular passions.[25] In this way, he denies that the particular passions have moral value and also, in contrast to Hutcheson, largely rejects the idea of the spontaneity of virtue. In reply to John Clarke – and on the basis of Shaftesbury's authority – Hutcheson proposes a 'public sense' along with the moral sense. This is a 'Determination to be pleased with the Happiness of others and to be uneasy at their Misery', and it leads us to desire the happiness of all sensible creatures.[26] In reply to Butler – and drawing on Cicero and Malebranche – he distinguishes calm desires or pure affections, dictated by inner senses, from passions, that are always violent, produced by false associations of ideas.[27] He is not disposed, how-ever, to deny that generous passions have moral value, while he admits the role played by reason in curbing our passions.[28]

The intellectual relations between Hutcheson and Gilbert Burnet (1690–1726), son of the famous historian of the Church of England and chaplain to George I, is no less significant. Their public exchange of letters in 1725, together with the *Illustrations on the Moral Sense* that concluded it, is one of the most sophisticated and interest-ing episodes in the eighteenth-century debate on the foundations of morals. Burnet accepts benevolence as the ultimate end of action, and the pleasure of moral sense as a pleasure that accompanies the discovery of truth, but he is not willing to make moral sense the basis for moral distinctions. One can always ask, Burnet points out, whether benevolence or moral sense is reasonable: thus the judge-ment of morality rests ultimately on reason.[29] Hutcheson responds that Burnet reveals himself to be a disciple of Samuel Clarke and William Wollaston in his use of terms such as 'reasonable', 'right', 'fit', 'conformable to truth' and 'ought'.[30] These expressions have either a relative meaning or, if used in their absolute sense, a hidden evaluative meaning, and thus presuppose the very moral sense they are supposed to ground.

The disagreement between the two disputants is actually founded on a difference in the concept of reason that each deploys. Reason for Hutcheson is the neutral, formal one of the empirical tradition. Spec-ulative reason discovers the relations between things, while practical reason identifies the objects that are suitable for giving us pleasure and also the means required to obtain them. For any being lacking benevolence and moral sense it is, therefore, quite reasonable to pur-sue his own personal interest at the expense of others' happiness.[31] According to Burnet, on the other hand, speculative reason discovers the truth that the pleasure or happiness of twenty people is greater than the happiness of only one person. Practical reason reveals that I must prefer the happiness of twenty people to that of the single person, even when a benevolent inclination is lacking.[32] Hutcheson replies that twenty stones are more than just one, but that this does not drive us to accumulate stones if we have no desire to accumu-late them.[33] He uses the authority of Aristotle in support of the claim that it is pointless to ask oneself about the reasons for an ultimate end of action.[34] Thus benevolence is justified by, or based on, moral sense, while moral sense can find no further justification than can the sense of taste for distinguishing between sweet food and bitter food.[35]

In his *Illustrations* Hutcheson sums up the disagreement with Burnet, insisting on the absurdity of basing reciprocal obligations between rational beings on the relationships among things, as Samuel Clarke does.[36] He admits that reason can correct both the moral sense and the external senses, but just as it would be absurd to maintain that it is reason that permits us to perceive colours and extensions, so it is absurd to claim that it is reason that lets us perceive moral good.[37]

Hutcheson considered the *Essay on the Nature and Conduct of the Passions and Affections. With Illustrations on the Moral Sense* to be an integral part of his moral system. In due course he proposed corrected versions of his *Inquiry* and *Essay*, and also attempted to integrate them more into his *System of Moral Philosophy*, which was published posthumously. As Hume pointed out, he recognised, following Butler, the power that moral sense has over the various powers of the mind.[38] However, more explicitly than Butler and contrary to Shaftesbury's doctrine, Hutcheson maintained throughout that the object of moral sense, namely benevolence, cannot be subordinated to self-love.

HUME AND UTILITY

Hutcheson's *Inquiry into the Original of our Ideas of Beauty and Virtue* and his *Essay on the Passions* defend the reality of virtue against Bernard Mandeville's claim that it is an invention of legislators and politicians. Mandeville had argued that by exalting the excellence of virtue, politicians flatter men's pride and make them useful to society, while Hutcheson defended the claim that virtue is natural.[39] When Hume puts forward the main doctrine of Book II of his *Treatise of Human Nature* (*Of the Passions*), namely the double relations of ideas and impressions, he does not directly address this recent controversy between Hutcheson and Mandeville.[40] Nevertheless, his stance of scientific neutrality does not prevent him from making claims that become important for his own moral theory, which he develops later, in Book III of the *Treatise*. When he introduces pride and love as fundamental passions at the beginning of

Book II, he re-examines the principles that underlie the traditions of morals represented by the views of Hutcheson and Mandeville, namely the British Christian Neo-Platonist tradition on the one hand, and the French tradition on the other. On Hume's view the two have the same underlying problem: if Mandeville's 'pride' (or 'self-liking')[41] or Hutcheson's universal benevolence were instincts or the first principles of conduct, one's own self would be the cause of both of these passions. But the self (or the other's self) is not the cause, it is the object of pride and love, and since they have their opposites, humility and hatred, the cause must lie in some pleasant or unpleasant quality of the object that arouses them.[42]

The analysis of these four fundamental passions requires some explanation. Hume divides all our perceptions into impressions and ideas. The difference between them is a difference in force and vivacity, which is the same as the difference between feeling and thinking.[43] Impressions are either sensations, bodily pains, pleasures or passions. Passions are direct or indirect, that is they arise immediately from pains or pleasures, like desire, joy or fear, or require in addition the intervention of some ideas, as is the case with pride, love and their contraries.[44] Ideas tend to associate themselves in our imagination according to the relations of resemblance, contiguity in time and place and causality.[45] Impressions link to each other according as they are pleasant or painful. Indirect passions require a double association of ideas and impressions, and therefore they arise from a 'regular mechanism' of the mind.[46] For instance a beautiful house, if it is mine, arouses pride. Pride is a pleasant passion that directs our attention to our self. In this case the idea of property, which expresses the close and manifest tie that the house has with myself, is associated with the idea that we form of our self; the pleasure produced by its beauty naturally gives way to the pleasant passion of pride.[47] In order to understand Hume's mechanism for the generation of the four indirect passions one needs only to change the pleasant qualities of the cause into painful ones, or to substitute another person for oneself. One can also substitute other causes for that of the house: mental or bodily qualities or even an incidental physical resemblance with a famous person.[48]

Thus passions, as in the Cartesian tradition,[49] always contain an evaluative component and, in the case of the four passions mentioned, they also contain esteem or contempt for oneself or for the other. Though pride is a passion 'unattended with any desire', love is always followed by a desire for the happiness of the person loved. Because this relation between love and benevolence is part of the original constitution of the mind, Hume speaks of an instinct of benevolence, an instinct restricted to those we love.[50] Indeed, Hume reinforces the limited nature of our benevolence when he explains that 'relations of blood' and acquaintance in themselves suffice to arouse love and benevolence, whatever a person's qualities.[51]

Hume's account of our love of praise and our esteem of the rich and powerful further complicates the consideration of passions because by this account they require the intervention of the mechanism of sympathy. It is by that mechanism that through our observation of another person's action we come to have a passion of the same kind as the passion we believe the other to have.[52] As spectators, we can feel the passions of the agent and also those of the person affected by his action.[53] Sympathy will have a central role in the third book of the *Treatise*.

Passions direct our conduct by means of their regular mechanism, and Hume's determinism can be clearly seen in the famous thesis according to which 'reason is, and ought to be a slave of the passions'. Among other things, it implies that if, as Locke and Hutcheson claimed, reason cannot give rise to a passion, neither can it stop a passion, a claim which is opposed by Locke and Hutcheson.[54] On Hume's analysis the alleged combat between reason and passions is nothing but a struggle between calm and violent passions. Every passion, Hume held, in contradistinction to Hutcheson, can be calm or violent. Hume now adds that once a passion has become a settled principle of action it becomes imperceptible. So calm passions are not necessarily the weakest but, on the contrary, can be the strongest and dominate one's character. In this way, Hume substitutes Butler's theory of the ruling or hegemonic role of conscience with his own theory of the dominant passion.[55] Together with the theory of the four fundamental indirect passions it is a sound basis for justifying the variety of characters, virtues and moral feelings to be found in *Of Morals*, the third book of the *Treatise*.

It should be recalled that the third book of the *Treatise* was published twenty-one months after the first two.[56] Within a fortnight of the publication of the first two books, Hume already had doubts about their success and suggested a sad dilemma: that anyone who is accustomed to reflecting about abstract subjects is already totally prejudiced, and anyone who is not prejudiced has no knowledge of metaphysical subjects. He added that nobody would bother to read 'a book, that does not come recommended by some great name or authority'.[57] Twenty months later, the first part of Book III, *Of Morals*, included an ingenious strategy: in the first section Hume reconsidered the arguments proposed by Hutcheson against Clarke and Wollaston to show that moral distinctions are not derived from reason.[58] In the second section, he seems to accept the claim that moral sense has an instinctive immediacy and that moral sentiment has a peculiar quality that allows us to distinguish between moral good and evil.[59] Not surprisingly modern interpreters hear Hutcheson's voice in these doctrines.[60] Here Hume kills two birds with one stone: he presents himself as a disciple of Hutcheson, so that he may be taken seriously by the reader, and then holds his master responsible for making morals depend only on 'our sentiments of pleasure and uneasiness'.[61]

Once it had been established that moral distinctions depend only on feeling, the paths of Hutcheson and Hume separate. Far from deriving justice from moral sense, as Hutcheson seeks to do, Hume immediately points out that no interested or generous inclination will oblige me to pay back a debt.[62] A rational theory of morals, he had already warned,[63] must connect an inner disposition of the mind with a quality of the external world; on the basis of this consideration he proceeds to develop an account of the foundation of justice. The central thesis is that justice is an artificial virtue, one we embrace both because of a condition of the external world, namely the scarcity of goods and their easy transfer, and also because of a disposition of the mind, namely our limited benevolence, limited in that it is restricted principally to relations and acquaintances. If universal benevolence did exist, justice would become totally superfluous.[64] The security on which peace in society depends lies, therefore, in the invention of justice; self-interest underpins the natural obligation to respect the rules of justice, while 'sympathy *with public interest is the source of the* moral approbation, *which attends that virtue'*.[65]

In the third part of Book III, moral sense and sympathy come into conflict. Having ascertained that moral distinctions are based on the approval or disapproval of the observer, it must next be determined whether the distinctions are the immediate effect of a moral sense or the natural outcome of a reflection on utility and pleasure, for oneself or others, brought about by virtue.[66] Sympathy is basic to this evaluation. Through sympathy we participate in others' feelings, and it also permits us to have an impartial point of view, since we can consider the utility and pleasure given by virtues both to the person possessing them and to the person they affect.[67] And even though our sympathies can change, experience and conversation enable us to establish general rules and to create a stable, common language of moral praise and blame.[68]

While Hutcheson had held that benevolence underpins all the virtues, Hume ascribes an independent moral value to greatness of mind, to natural abilities and even to good manners, as Mandeville had done.[69] After a careful examination of all the virtues according to the four criteria of usefulness to self or others and agreeableness to self or others, Hume is hardly disposed to admit the existence of a moral sense that acts without prior reflection. In addition, he is not disposed to acknowledge any peculiarity in moral sentiment:[70] indeed, he underlines how variable our moral sentiments are, to the point of marvelling in the end that 'a convenient house, and a virtuous character, cause not the same feeling of approbation; even tho' the source of our approbation be the same, and flow from sympathy and an idea of their utility'.[71] However, this strangeness is common to our passions and sentiments, Hume remarks, since he had already explained that approbation or blame 'is nothing but a fainter and more imperceptible love or hatred'.[72] At the end of the *Treatise*, we understand that an original moral sense like that of Hutcheson and like the one proposed by Hume in the first part of Book III is entirely superfluous. Our sense of morality has become the product of history and society. Moreover, buried under the quality and number of artificial virtues and natural abilities, Hutcheson's benevolence is no longer the cement of society, but simply the virtue that makes a man 'an easy friend, a gentle master, an agreeable husband, or an indulgent father'. Above all, Hume recommends the search for knowledge and 'ability of every kind'.[73] It would be difficult to imagine any ethic that is more naturalistic or more open to the values of the Enlightenment.

When Hume reconsiders the controversy concerning the foundations of morals in the first section of his *Enquiry Concerning the Principles of Morals* he maintains, though provisionally, and in

Butler's somewhat Solomonic manner, the agreement of reason and sentiment in moral decisions.[74] Hume does not use the term 'moral sense' in the *Enquiry*, and the term 'sympathy' used in the *Treatise* now seems to coincide with the sense of humanity and even with Hutcheson's benevolence.[75] The truth is that Hume has learned from Hutcheson the art of warmly defending the cause of virtue and of putting forward his theses concretely, by means of examples, observations and clear-cut solutions. Moreover, he turns his own old strategy around: if the principle of sympathy was used in the *Treatise* to reveal the criteria of moral approbation, here the consideration of virtues according to the criteria of utility or pleasure for oneself or others proceeds alongside the defence of sympathy. The utility of justice and benevolence is approved of, in fact, because we sympathise with the interests of those who benefit from it.[76] As far as the virtues useful to the person possessing them are concerned, he maintains that the 'sentiments of morals' and the sense of humanity, that is to say sympathy, 'are originally the same' sentiment.[77] The egoistic theorist may well maintain, however mistakenly, that benevolence is praised because it is useful to the society to which he himself belongs, but he will never be able to turn into self-love 'the merit which we ascribe to the selfish virtues'.[78] Thus Hume's sense of humanity excludes the egoist far better than Hutcheson's moral sense does. In the first Appendix to the *Enquiry*, Hume's solution to the problem of the foundations of morals is disarmingly simple: '*Reason* instructs us in the several tendencies of actions, and *humanity* makes a distinction in favour of those which are useful and beneficial'.[79] However, for the sake of argument he considers what the situation would be if his position were false,[80] and the hypothesis prompts him to give five lengthy arguments, in which, once again, the expert will hear Hutcheson's voice.[81] As in the *Treatise* Hume makes Hutcheson responsible for confining moral good and evil to the 'internal frame and constitution of animals',[82] that is, to beings that have sentiments or feelings.

SMITH AND SYMPATHY

The immediate success of Adam Smith's *Theory of Moral Sentiments* (1759) is probably the fruit of the attention Smith paid in his earlier days to rhetoric and the popularisation of science. The *Theory of Moral Sentiments* is based on a single and familiar principle, that of sympathy. Smith manages to connect, in an apparently unified perspective, three successive and conflicting discussions of morals in Britain in the eighteenth century: the ethics of Samuel Clarke's 'fitness' or 'propriety', Hutcheson's benevolence and Butler's moral conscience.

Smith is also very close to Hume. But it should be noted that although Smith accepts many of Hume's doctrines, Smith's moral theory has a quite distinctive relation to the theories of the Ancients. As against Hume's obvious predilection for Epicurean doctrines, Smith prefers Stoic and Ciceronian ethics, in which respect he is rather close to Hutcheson and Butler. In the *Treatise* Hume had already shown that it is possible to sympathise with both the agent and the recipient of an action, and he warned that sympathetic participation is an imaginary, unreal process, in the sense that the information and the circumstances of the observer do not coincide with those of the protagonist of the action.[83] Smith takes these characteristics of sympathy from Hume, but he calls the sympathy for the person performing the action 'direct sympathy', and that for the person who is acted upon 'indirect'.[84] Sympathetic participation is raised by an illusion of the imagination, which leads us to feel passions that the agent does not feel and is even incapable of feeling: for example we can sympathise with a madman or a dead person.[85] Smith and Hume differ in one fundamental respect: for Hume the imaginary placing of the observer in another's situation means sharing the pleasures or advantages of the agent or the recipient of the action; for Smith, on the other hand, it means feeling, to a lesser degree, the passions of the agent or recipient of the action in order to carry out a comparison with the passions that they really display.[86] After offering a very sophisticated description of the phenomenon of sympathy Smith explains the pleasure of mutual sympathy. His eloquence succeeds in persuading us that it is equally enjoyable to share both pleasant and painful passions, although in the end it is not clear whether sympathising is a pleasure, a need or a duty.[87]

Smith explains that we hold passions to be appropriate when the passions of the protagonists of the action fully agree with those produced by sympathy, and that we must consider both the motive, or the cause arousing passion, and the end, or the effect produced by the passion.[88] He adds that not only does the spectator assume the guise of the agent, but the person carrying out the action also assumes the guise of the spectator. In this way Smith is able to reproduce the same catalogue of virtues presented by Hume, although he does not accept the latter's criterion of utility. The 'effort of the spectator to enter into the sentiments of the person principally concerned' is the foundation of 'amiable' or benevolent virtues, and the 'effort of the person principally concerned to bring down his emotions to what the spectator can go along with' is the foundation of the 'respectable' virtues, or the virtues that display greatness of mind.[89] It is interesting to make a comparison between Hume's and Smith's different accounts of the admiration for the virtue of greatness of mind. The more someone who inherits a great fortune seems indifferent to this, the happier we are for him, Hume remarks; conversely, the more someone bears a misfortune with dignity, the more pained we feel. According to Hume, we learn from experience the level of passion normally connected with a certain type of misfortune and we form a general rule; imagination, influenced by this general rule, makes us conceive of, or rather feel, a greater passion than that actually felt. 'The communicated passion of sympathy sometimes acquires strength from the weakness of the original.'[90] Hume presupposes greatness of mind in his explanation of sympathy, whereas Smith presupposes sympathy in his explanation of greatness of mind. Smith's magnanimous person, the person with the virtue of greatness of mind, is aware of the fact that we are not much inclined to sympathise with an unfortunate person, and hence attenuates his manifestation of the passion to the degree that the observers can sympathise with, and therefore approve of it.

The fact that it is not possible to feel equal sympathy with all passions leads Smith to a detailed classification of the passions as the basis for his explanation of many virtues. For example, temperance or fortitude are required because we are not very sympathetic towards physical pain. In the case of the unsocial passions of anger and resentment, self-command is particularly necessary, because the spectator is equally well-disposed towards both direct and indirect sympathy. In case of injury, the less we give vent to our anger while letting our true feelings of resentment be felt, the more we gain the esteem of the spectator.[91]

The recourse to sympathy to explain the 'merit' of virtue is less convincing. I approve of an action as benevolent, or I disapprove of it as unjust, if by means of indirect sympathy I am able to feel an appropriate gratitude or resentment. Yet it is evident that the real gratitude, or resentment, on the part of the recipient of the action in this case is quite irrelevant.[92] In fact, Smith uses the concepts of gratitude and resentment that are deployed in Butler's sermons to support his doctrine that benevolence and justice are virtues and to refute Hume's doctrine of utility, as well as Hume's doctrine of the artificiality of justice.[93]

The principle of sympathy and the dual role of agent and impartial spectator allow Smith to recover more easily the hegemony and dominance of Butler's conscience, and to resolve, at the same time, the problem of obligation. Following Hutcheson, Smith distinguishes the desire for praise from the desire to be worthy of praise.[94] If we are the natural judges of our behaviour, the desire to be worthy of praise is the foundation of the tribunal of our conscience.[95] The distinction is based on the difference between the amount of information possessed by the agent and by the spectator. As in Butler, conscience is capable of balancing egoistic and generous affections. In light of our capacity for self-deceit we need to construct general rules of conduct.[96] We frequently feel that we have to conform to these general rules, even when sentiments deriving from sympathetic participation are lacking. These general rules become sacred in the face of conscience, as if they were the divine commandments themselves.[97] Smith's attachment to Stoicism leads him to dedicate a whole section, in the 1790 edition, the last in his lifetime, to the virtue of self-command, a distant relation of the Stoics' apathy.

One great merit of Smith's *Theory* is that it provides a social justification for the emergence of moral values by means of a systematic exploration of the resources of the principle of sympathy. His rejection of Hume's criteria of what is useful and pleasing as the basis of morals is, however, equally evident in the fact that he systematically replaces them with the criterion of propriety. It is not the comfort of a house, the ease of wealth or the citizens' advantages derived from a sound political constitution that is the object of our approval and admiration, but rather the precise 'fitness' of the means that meet the aims for which an object has been conceived, that is to say the 'love of system'.[98] The Humean idea that it is the utility of virtue that makes virtue acceptable to the imagination derives from an abstract, philosophical consideration of human behaviour. It is only through the relations between the passions of the agent and those of the spectator in the concrete circumstances of life that the principle of sympathy and the criterion of propriety are of any worth.[99]

REID AND THE SENSE OF DUTY

Reid's attitude towards the eighteenth-century debate on the nature of virtue is well summarised in the following passage:

[T]he formal nature and essence of that virtue which is the object of moral approbation consists neither in a prudent prosecution of our private interest, nor in benevolent affections towards others, nor in qualities useful or agreeable to ourselves or to others, nor in sympathizing with the passions and affections of others, and in attuning our own conduct to the tone of other men's passions; but it consists in living in all good conscience – that is, in using the best means in our power to know our duty, and acting accordingly.[100]

No opinion about the doctrines of Hutcheson, Hume or Smith could be expressed in less flattering terms. In his *Oratio*, with which he took up his teaching post in Aberdeen in 1751, Reid fully espouses the doctrine of the Stoics, as expounded by Cicero in the *De Officiis*. He adds that all those, whether Ancients or Moderns, who asked themselves about the origins and nature of the virtues, used their subtleties to make what was clear and obvious obscure and confused, and he awards Butler first prize for the clarity of his ethics.[101] Reid's *Essays on the Active Powers of Man* (1788) confirm this opinion. He distinguishes here the 'system of morals' from the 'theory of morals', practical ethics from the foundations of ethics.[102] Through the course of history systems of morals have been quite reliable. A system of morals resembles a botanical system, in which classification facilitates the assimilation and recollection of all our duties. A theory of morals, on the other hand, is an account of our moral powers by which we distinguish the just from the unjust. This is a complicated matter and has little to do with knowledge of our duties.[103]

This is not to say that Reid was not interested in the foundations of ethics. In the early years of his teaching in Glasgow his view that the perception of external objects always implies a judgement had already paved the way for the doctrine that ethics has a rational basis.[104] His manuscripts and lecture notes prove that he

had read Hume's *Enquiry* and Smith's *Theory* carefully and with a
suspicious eye.[105] In the 1780 lectures he goes back to criticism of
Smith's *Theory*, which can be found in four earlier manuscripts.[106]
Reid recognised that Smith's system did not have Hume's 'licentious
tendency' and contained some excellent parts; however, he maintained that Smith tried to reduce sympathy to self-love, and moral
approbation to sympathy. The former is an unfounded criticism. The
only sympathy that Reid is willing to recognise is the involuntary,
contagious type, which results from love, affection and esteem for
people. As imagination, on Reid's account, is a voluntary power of
the mind, he views Smith's imaginary placing oneself in another's
shoes as a deliberate, egoistic act, which, 'while it lasts, puts an end
to our sympathy'.[107]

The second criticism is better founded: if the approval of conduct
depends on the observation of the agreement between another's passion and what we imagine we should feel in the same circumstances,
the term 'should' is ambiguous. It can mean both 'what we ought to
feel' and 'what we actually would feel'.[108] In the former case it is
presumed that we have a moral faculty that judges the rightness of
our feelings; in the second case moral approval is made to depend
on what we do, not on what we should do. The criticisms do not
end here, and many are addressed to Hume, but there would be little
point in mentioning them. It is more interesting to note that the
disagreement with Hume gives Reid an indication of how to continue his own line of thought. In order to demonstrate, for example, the artificiality of justice, Hume criticises a vicious circle: no
action can be virtuous unless it arises from a virtuous motive, so a
virtuous motive must precede the respect for virtue. The essence of
Reid's reply consists in distinguishing between the goodness of an
action, considered abstractly, and the moral goodness of the agent.
The moral goodness of the agent is the very 'regard to virtue' that
Hume condemns.[109]

Taking his concepts from Cicero, Reid maintains that when we
require that human behaviour should be rational, we are referring to
honesty and utility.[110] What is useful is identified with what is good
'upon the whole' for a rational being; what is honest is identified
with duty or with what one ought to do. Duty, or moral obligation,
is a simple and therefore indefinable notion. It is neither a quality
of the action, considered abstractly, nor of the agent considered
independently of the action, but is rather the relationship that ties

the agent to the action.[111] Man's rational actions are thus preceded by the judgement that this or that action is right or wrong. This sense of duty has the same capacity as has Butler's conscience to order our numerous powers and direct our behaviour.[112] However, Reid prefers to call it a moral sense because he wants to recover the analogy with external senses that Hutcheson propounded. Sight not only provides us with the sensations of colour, but also permits us to judge whether this is red or that is green. Analogously, 'by our moral faculty, we have both the original conceptions of right and wrong in conduct, of merit and demerit, and the original judgments that this conduct is right, that is wrong; that this character has worth, that demerit'.[113] In a well-known note that concludes his *Essays*, Reid points out that, while in the case of the outer senses, sensations precede judgement, in the case of moral perception, 'the feeling is the consequence of the judgment, and is regulated by it'.[114] Thus, in Reid's doctrine of perception, colour suggests a real physical quality, while it is evident that the sentiment the heart approves of comes afterwards and hence can suggest nothing. By saying that moral approbation includes moral judgement accompanied by esteem, benevolent affection and sympathy, Reid does not differ much from Gilbert Burnet. Esteem, with its consequent benevolence, is once again presented as a duty, whereas sympathy is merely a consequence of benevolent affections.[115]

There is no doubt that Reid's account of moral judgement is dramatically different from that of Hutcheson, Hume and Smith, and chiefly this is because of the role that Reid ascribes to moral judgement as against feeling in the moral dimension of our lives. Because of the attention devoted to Hutcheson, Hume and Smith, there is a tendency to associate the Scottish Enlightenment with the moral doctrine of sentimentalism. It is salutary to recall that the predominant philosophy in Enlightenment Scotland was that of common sense, and that those who subscribed to it regarded sentimentalism as a fatally flawed moral doctrine.

NOTES

1   Anthony Ashley Cooper, Third Earl of Shaftesbury, *An Inquiry Concerning Virtue or Merit*, in his *Characteristics of Men, Manners, Opinions, Times*, ed. John M. Robertson (Indianapolis: Bobbs-Merrill, 1964), 280, 251–5.

2 See Shaftesbury, *The Moralists*, in *Characteristics*, 144–53.

3 Francis Hutcheson, *An Inquiry into the Original of our Ideas of Beauty and Virtue* (London: J. Darby, 1725), 2–3.

4 John Locke, *An Essay Concerning Human Understanding*, ed. Peter H. Nidditch (Oxford: Clarendon Press, 1975), 119–22.

5 Ibid., especially pp. 134–5, 128–31, 353–7.

6 See Hutcheson, *Inquiry*, 13–14; and Hutcheson, *An Essay on the Nature and Conduct of the Passions and Affections. With Illustrations on the Moral Sense* (London: J. Darby and T. Browne, 1728), 281–3.

7 Ibid., 101, 123–4.

8 Ibid., 103.

9 Ibid., 15–16, 106, 123–4.

10 Ibid., 103.

11 Ibid., 10–14, 27–43, 43–6.

12 Ibid., 143.

13 Ibid., 148–9.

14 Ibid., 126–7.

15 See ibid., 110–15.

16 David Hume, *A Treatise of Human Nature*, ed. L. A. Selby-Bigge, 2nd edn, rev. P. H. Nidditch (Oxford: Clarendon Press, 1978), 471.

17 Hutcheson, ibid., 106–8.

18 See ibid., 168–70, 177–8.

19 Ibid., 256. Cf. also the title of the last section of the *Inquiry*.

20 Ibid., 262–4.

21 John Clarke, *The Foundation of Morality in Theory and Practice* (York: Thomas G., (1726)), 92–101.

22 Ibid., 51–6.

23 Joseph Butler, *Fifteen Sermons Preached at the Rolls Chapel*, ed. W. R. Matthews (London: G. Bell and Sons, 1964), 38–40, 53–8.

24 Ibid., 36–8, 167–74.

25 Ibid., xi, 33–8, 54–6, 67, 173–4, 197–8.

26 Hutcheson, *Essay*, 5; cf. Shaftesbury, *Characteristics*, I. 13, 69–74, 297–301.

27 Hutcheson, *Essay*, 27–32; cf. Cicero, *Tusculanae disputationes*, III.xi.24–5 and IV.vi.11–14; Nicolas Malebranche, *Recherche de la vérité*, v.iii, in *Oeuvres complètes de Malebranche*, ed. Geneviève Rodis–Lewis (Paris: J. Vrin, 1962), vol. II, 142–57.

28 See Hutcheson, *Essay*, 86–7, 165–8.

29 Francis Hutcheson, *Letters between the Late Mr Gilbert Burnet, and Mr Hutchinson, Concerning the True Foundation of Virtue or Moral Goodness Formerly Published in the London Journal* (London: W. Wilkins, 1735), 9–14.

30 Ibid., 18, 26; cf. Samuel Clarke, *A Discourse Concerning the Unchangeable Obligations of Natural Religion* (London: W. Botham, 1706), 45–8, 86–8; and William Wollaston, *The Religion of Nature Delineated* (London: Sam Palmer, 1724), 8, 12–13, 18.

31 Hutcheson, *Letters*, 18–19.

32 Ibid., 36.

33 Ibid., 52.

34 Ibid., 49–50.

35 Ibid., 53–4.

36 Hutcheson, *Essay*, 213–44, 247–9.

37 Ibid., 236–8.

38 Francis Hutcheson, *Philosophiae moralis institutio compendiaria* (Glasgow: R. and A. Foulis, 1742), 30; cf. J. Y. T. Greig, ed., *The Letters of David Hume*, 2 vols. (Oxford: Clarendon Press, 1932), I.47.

39 See Bernard Mandeville, *The Fable of the Bees: Or, Private Vices, Publick Benefits*, ed. F. B. Kaye, 2 vols. (Oxford: Clarendon Press, 1924), I.41–57.

40 Hume, *Treatise*, 295–7.

41 Mandeville, *Fable of the Bees*, II.129–30. Self-liking is not self-love, but rather Mandeville's translation of the French *amour-propre*, a predilection to be fond of, or devoted to, one's own self.

42 Hume, *Treatise*, 277–8, 328–9.

43 Ibid., 1–8.

44 Ibid., 275–6.

45 Ibid., 10–13.

46 Ibid., 282–4; cf. 'Dissertation on the Passions', in David Hume, *The Philosophical Works of David Hume*, eds. Thomas Hill Green and Thomas Hodge Grose, 4 vols. (London: Longmans, Green, 1882), IV.166.

47 Hume, *Treatise*, 285–90.

48 Ibid., 337, 304.

49 See René Descartes, *Les Passions de l'âme*, articles 27–9; Malebranche, *Recherche*, v.iii.

50 Hume, *Treatise*, 367–9.

51 Ibid., 351–5.

52 Ibid., 317–21, 358–61.

53 Ibid., 389, 602–3.

54 Ibid., 415; cf. Locke, *Essay*, 250–4, but cf. 263; Hutcheson, *Essay*, 217–18, but cf. 165–6.

55 Hume, *Treatise*, 413, 418–19; cf. 276. See also Greig, *Letters of David Hume*, I.47.

56 Cf. Hume, *Treatise*, 663. Vols. I and II c. 30 January 1739, and vol. III c. 30 October 1740.

57 Greig, *Letters of David Hume*, vol. 1, 27.

58 Hume, *Treatise*, 455–70.

59 Ibid., 471.

60 See Barry Stroud, *Hume* (1977; reprint, London: Routledge, 1995), 264; Vincent M. Hope, *Virtue by Consensus: the Moral Philosophy of Hutcheson, Hume, and Adam Smith* (Oxford: Clarendon Press, 1989), 53–4.

61 Hume, *Treatise*, 469; cf. Greig, *Letters of David Hume*, 1.40.

62 Hume, *Treatise*, 479–83.

63 Ibid., 464–5.

64 Ibid., 486–9, 494–5.

65 Ibid., 499–500.

66 Ibid., 589–90.

67 Ibid., 577–8, 581–2, 591.

68 Ibid., 580–3.

69 Ibid., 592–614.

70 Ibid., 607–8, 611–12.

71 Ibid., 617.

72 Ibid., 614.

73 Ibid., 606, 620.

74 David Hume, *Enquiries Concerning Human Understanding and Concerning the Principles of Morals*, ed. L. A. Selby-Bigge, 3rd edn, rev. P. H. Nidditch (Oxford: Clarendon Press, 1975), 170–3.

75 Ibid., passim; see esp. 231, 277, 281, 298, 303.

76 Ibid., 218.

77 Ibid., 235–6.

78 Ibid., 243.

79 Ibid., 286.

80 Ibid., 286–7.

81 See note 60 above.

82 Hume, *Enquiries*, 294.

83 Hume, *Treatise*, 370–1.

84 Adam Smith, *The Theory of Moral Sentiments*, eds. D. D. Raphael and A. L. Macfie (Oxford: Clarendon Press, 1976), 74.

85 Ibid., 12–13.

86 Ibid., 16–23.

87 Ibid., 13–16.

88 Ibid., 18.

89 Ibid., 22–3.

90 Hume, *Treatise*, 370–1.

91 Smith, *Theory of Moral Sentiments*, 27–43; see esp. 28–30, 36–8.

92 Ibid., 69–71.

93 Ibid., 75–8.

94 Ibid., 113–19.

95 Ibid., 134–56; see esp. paragraphs 1–3, 6, 25–6, 35–6.

96 Ibid., 156–61.

97 Ibid., 161–3.

98 Smith, *Theory of Moral Sentiments*, 179–87.

99 Ibid., 187–9.

100 Thomas Reid, *Essays on the Active Powers of Man*, in *The Works of Thomas Reid*, ed. Sir William Hamilton, 6th edn, 2 vols. (1863; reprint, Bristol: Thoemmes, 1999), 650B.

101 Thomas Reid, *The Philosophical Orations of Thomas Reid: Delivered at Graduation Ceremonies in King's College, Aberdeen, 1753, 1756, 1759, 1762*, ed. W. R. Humphries (Aberdeen: Aberdeen University Press, 1937), 13–14.

102 Reid, *Essays on the Active Powers*, 640–3.

103 Ibid., 642B.

104 See Thomas Reid, *Practical Ethics*, ed. Knud Haakonssen (Princeton: Princeton University Press, 1990), 16–17, 20, 25, 31–2.

105 Special Libraries and Archives, University of Aberdeen, Birkwood Collection, MSS 2131:3.1.23, on Hume's *Enquiry Concerning the Principles of Morals*, and III.i.26–28, VII.v.7, on Smith's *Theory of Moral Sentiments*.

106 Elmer H. Duncan and Robert M. Baird, 'Thomas Reid's Criticism of Adam Smith's *Theory of Moral Sentiments*', *Journal of the History of Ideas* 38 (1977), 509–22.

107 Ibid., 513–14.

108 Ibid., 515–16.

109 Reid, *Essays on the Active Powers*, 648–9; cf. Hume, *Treatise*, 478.

110 Reid, *Essays on the Active Powers*, 580–2.

111 Ibid., 588–9.

112 Ibid., 589–91.

113 Ibid., 590.

114 Ibid., 672B.

115 Ibid., 592–3.

8 The political theory of the Scottish Enlightenment

Scotland's singular voice within the polyphony of the European Enlightenment has attracted a great deal of debate. As historians attempt to weigh local varieties of Enlightenment, informed by disparate religious, political and cultural settings, against the transnational concerns and cosmopolitan aspirations of 'the' Enlightenment, Scotland posits a remarkable case in point. Scotland's European contexts have often been overlooked; by the same token, its distinct features can only be mapped against the contours of the European Enlightenment. David Hume, Adam Smith, William Robertson, John Millar and Adam Ferguson were subtle disciples of European intellectual traditions, and conversant with a range of Enlightenment cultures. At the same time, their writings convey a powerful sense of Scotland's incomparable position as a kingdom within the British union, set apart by its church and jurisprudence, and by its singular decision to trade sovereignty for empire. Nowhere is this apparent tension more pronounced than in the field of political theory.[1]

POLITICS AND THE SCOTS

Taken as a field of enquiry, politics is a conjuncture of mind-sets responding to contemporary political issues, critical perusals of intellectual traditions and cross-fermentation with other sciences.[2] The balance between these elements may differ according to era and culture; but eighteenth-century Scottish thinkers were able to draw vigorously on all three sources of inspiration. Their political thought was accordingly shaped by three sets of problems: Scotland's voluntary loss of sovereignty in an age when statehood and statecraft steadily gained importance; the need for a viable modern theory of politics amid clashing idioms of the good life and the good polity; and the tall order set by the natural sciences for standards of certainty, regularity and predictability in the study of human affairs.

Scotland's union of parliaments with England (1707) and its recognition of the Hanoverian succession embodied in the Act of Settlement (1701) did not only decide its political course for the century to come, but also determined the climate in which a new political theory was to emerge. Andrew Fletcher of Saltoun, who was the most distinct voice of scepticism in the Union debate, yet was perfectly willing to redraw Scotland's borders and regime within a new confederacy of European republics, bequeathed to the Scottish Enlightenment a complex legacy. Its effect lies less in the essence of his political suggestions than in their theoretical tenor and mood. Scotland's political future was to be determined against a new European horizon, where all traditional idioms of polity must be reworked to accommodate the rise of modern commerce and urban refinement. Consequently, the value of sovereignty could be weighted against justice, peace and prosperity.[3] If, as J. G. A. Pocock put it, in sixteenth- and seventeenth-century Scottish political discourse '"nation"and "monarchy"are organizing concepts',[4] then new organising concepts were urgently in demand. No classical model, not even the Machiavellian republicanism close to Fletcher's heart, could fully account for Scotland's position in a world of centralising commercial states and emerging metropolitan modernity.

Prior to the recasting of political idiom, however, it was important to state that political theorising itself had become requisite as never before. Scotland's place within the Union, its unique position as a willing terminator of its own sovereignty, suggested that its 'politics' must henceforth be conducted on a different level. Beyond the immediate wrestling with Jacobitism and loyalty, with the changing fortunes of Whiggism, with issues of patronage and representation, a new 'politics' was to be drawn on a more abstract scale. In one sense, what emerged was a distinctly modern cultural politics (as we would put it today), struggling to create a Scottish literature, theatre and philosophy distinct from the English and conversant with the European.[5] In another sense, a theory of politics was to be pulled like a delicate string out of the fabric of moral philosophy, and carefully woven to accommodate Scotland's distinctly modern rationale for its willingness to join England's empire.

Andrew Fletcher opened his *Discourse of Government with Relation to Militias* (1698) by saying that bad governments account for so much human misery that political ignorance is morally hard to condone as well as intellectually inexplicable. 'For though mankind take great care and pains to instruct themselves in other arts and sciences', he wrote, 'yet very few apply themselves to consider the nature of government, an enquiry so useful and necessary to both magistrate and people'.[6] Heralding Hume, Fletcher suggested that bad governments were able to lean on false pretences of their proponents and on self-delusion on the part of some of their subjects. From Fletcher onwards, the Scottish Enlightenment's engagement with politics was often played out as an exercise in verbal, conceptual and analytical clear-headedness. Politics, as Fletcher implied and Hume elaborated, was about *opinion*: about the ways people think and publicly work out their thoughts.

In one respect, eighteenth-century Scottish discourse did not have to reinvent its key concepts. It could draw on the idea of 'Britain' envisaged by seventeenth-century Scots since the Union of Crowns in 1603. As Pocock and several other historians have shown, '[t]he union of crowns diverted Scottish self-fashioning into a British context', complete with a 'discourse of Britain' to underpin the project of political and economic union.[7] Yet the concept of 'Britain' that became a political and juridical reality in 1707 was itself in need of a political theory to support it. The key to such a theory, as David Hume clearly spelled out, was not the 'vulgar' debate between Whigs and Tories on the legitimacy of the Glorious Revolution, the Act of Settlement and the recasting of England as a parliamentary monarchy. Nor was it the debate between eighteenth-century 'court' and 'country' factions over national debt and agrarian policy. Looming behind the British scene and its fleeting terminology of current affairs was the new European system of states, monarchic centralisation and the growth of modern manufacture, commerce, international trade and individual affluence. These grand-scale processes in European history were not merely a question of individual volition, ambition or virtue. They transcended dynastic quarrels and self-styling of regimes. Moreover, they could not be captured by the available models of governmental classification and political explanation.

Thus, the urgent need to create a new language of politics[8] was not merely an outcome of historical contingencies such as the Glorious Revolution and the Union of Parliaments; it came from a crisis in the Scottish perception of historical causality itself. Markets did not change because of kings, and social mores were not transformed by humanist rhetoric. Other forces were at work, forces unimagined by Aristotle, Epictetus or even Machiavelli. By the first third of the eighteenth century, these forces were ready for naming.

The rise of a new Scottish political philosophy owes important debts to Andrew Fletcher's wrestling with the Machiavellian idiom, and to the influential teachings of Francis Hutcheson, professor at Glasgow, who taught politics firmly – but distinctively – within the contours of moral philosophy. But it was David Hume who carried the Newtonian challenge, as he understood it, to its logical end: to remove politics, once and for all, off its feet of clay and provide it with scientific respectability. Hume's famous demand 'that politics may be reduced to a science'[9] was a polemic statement: it subjected historical and current political events to the organising hand of philosophy, imposed models of enquiry from the natural sciences upon human affairs, and also entailed that assertive choices be made from the available political idioms.

In his introduction to *A Treatise of Human Nature* (1739–40), Hume gave a misleadingly simple definition of political theory. '[P]olitics', he wrote, 'consider men as united in society, and dependent on each other'.[10] This is a brief but pregnant statement, suggesting that no pre-social condition (and hence no primeval contract) is relevant to politics as far as Hume was concerned. But even prior to Hume's contractarian reservations, it is noteworthy that Hume took the term 'politics' to mean political theory and not political practice. This (proper but partial) usage, in the *Treatise* and elsewhere in Hume's works, conveys his idea that only through rigorous philosophical treatment, through the purge of clear reasoning, can political practice be redeemed from the dimming inconsistencies and fuzzy thinking of everyday life.[11]

Accordingly, 'Politicians' in Hume's vocabulary are never statesmen, always philosophers (with Machiavelli so denoted only in the latter capacity).[12] By contrast, Adam Smith, in accordance with modern usage, shifted the word from would-be scientists to their exasperatingly shifty objects, 'that insidious and crafty animal, vulgarly called a statesman or politician, whose councils are directed by the momentary fluctuations of affairs'.[13] Vulgarity, for both Hume and Smith, went beyond the aesthetic dimension of common usage: it was, as Duncan Forbes has shown, a byword for conceptual fuzziness, for short-term unpredictability, for the weaknesses hindering actors and observers alike from approaching politics as a science.[14]

There is a deep connection, Hume asserted, between the rigour and consistency of thinking about politics, and the political realities that philosophy may help to understand, alter and improve. 'The sciences, which treat of general facts', he wrote, 'are politics, natural philosophy, physic, chemistry, &c. where the qualities, causes and effects of a whole species of objects are enquired into.'[15] Such science, fully up to Newtonian scratch, would harbour more than one 'universal axiom'.[16] In true empiricist vein, its facts could be collected from history and brought to scientific scrutiny: 'These records of wars, intrigues, factions, and revolutions, are so many collections of experiments, by which the politician or moral philosopher fixes the principles of his science, in the same manner as the physician or natural philosopher becomes acquainted with the nature of plants, minerals, and other external objects, by the experiments which he forms concerning them.'[17] But does political reality behave like the physical world? 'How could politics be a science,' Hume rhetorically asked, 'if laws and forms of government had not a uniform influence upon society?'[18]

Fortunately, they do. The perennial layers of human nature can furnish the politician with mineral-like consistency. Political regularities are decipherable. 'So great is the force of laws, and of particular forms of government, and so little dependence they have on the humours and tempers of men, that consequences almost as general and certain may sometimes be deduced from them, as any which the mathematical sciences afford us.'[19] Perhaps the keyword in this passage is the giveaway 'sometimes'. Hume knew that his science was still some steps away from mathematical constancy and astrophysical precision. His selective approach to history and to current political analysis suggests that Hume was aware of the vast tracts of fuzziness, of 'noise', of theory-resistant facts, stretching between the decipherable lines of meaningful political narrative. But this did not weaken his insistence on treating politics scientifically. Observation and analysis may take a while longer – Hume cheerfully granted 'that the world is still too young to fix many general truths in politics'[20] – but that was a matter of time alone. Upon the tripod of political practice, intellectual political traditions and the new sciences, the latter prevailed for Hume. It was Newtonian science that was to enforce ultimate sense and order on current affairs and on political legacies.

On the scientification of politics, as on other matters, Adam Ferguson was one of Hume's most adamant, if understated, adversaries. Ferguson noted that the very scholarliness of Hume's approach, his unapologetic *vita contemplativa*, is a phenomenon lamentably distinguishing the modern world from the ancient. 'It is peculiar to modern Europe, to rest so much of the human character on what may be learned in retirement, and from the information of books.'[21] In Ferguson's vocabulary, where politics was a lively practice as well as a scholarly pursuit, a man of action was no less entitled than a retiring scholar to be called a politician.[22]

The ancient classics of political thought, Ferguson argued, were created in the midst of an active political life. Set to motion by a *vita activa*, Cicero and the Stoics, as well as their Greek predecessors, produced texts that perforce shed much of their meaning in the reclusive calm of modern libraries. Politics, for modern men, has become an imagined practice and idle theory: '[W]e endeavour to derive from imagination and thought, what is in reality matter of experience and sentiment: and we endeavour, through the grammar of dead languages, and the channel of commentators, to arrive at the beauties of thought and elocution, which sprang from the animated spirit of society, and were taken from the living impressions of an active life'.[23] Echoing the rationale of the *Encyclopédie*, Ferguson therefore suggested that politics must *not* be reduced to a science, but, rather, enhanced to the level of a self-conscious and well-informed practice. 'Our attainments are frequently limited to the elements of every science, and seldom reach to that enlargement of ability and power which useful knowledge should give. Like mathematicians, who study the Elements of Euclid, but never think of mensuration, we read of societies, but do not propose to act with men: we repeat the language of politics, but feel not the spirit of nations: we attend to the formalities of a military discipline, but know not how to employ numbers of men to obtain any purpose by stratagem or force.'[24]

Thus, if Hume's politics is the theory of men socially united and mutually dependent, Ferguson suggested that these men should include, as in classical Rome, the political philosopher himself; and that theory, particularly the political, is not entitled to divorce action. If the mathematical certainty desired by Hume leaves the political philosopher 'feeling not the spirit of nations', then Ferguson forcefully questioned its desirability. But this activist critique of the 'noble science of politics' did not prevail. The last word, as far as the Scottish Enlightenment is concerned, was said by Ferguson's direct successor at the University of Edinburgh, Dugald Stewart, who developed the Humean paradigm for the use of nineteenth-century political scientists.

CANON AND SEGMENTS

The Scottish Enlightenment did not produce a shelf, or even half a shelf, of books dedicated to politics alone. Despite Hume's bid to reduce politics to a science, very few texts can be seen as specialist works in political theory. Hume's political essays clearly count, as well as Ferguson's *Principles of Moral and Political Science* (1792). More typically, however, a great deal of Scottish political theory is parcelled out – sometimes in designated chapters but more often in pregnant passages or lengthy excursions – within contributions to other fields of enquiry. Political theory surfaced in works on moral philosophy and the science of man;[25] on the history of nations[26] and universal history,[27] jurisprudence,[28] and political economy.[29] In some respects, this treatment of politics came from Scotland's unique intellectual climate. In other respects, its contexts are found in the history of European learning.

Aptly recognised (since Aristotle) as a specific area of knowledge, politics was nevertheless segmented and interwoven within other fields of enquiry for several sets of reasons. In the European universities of the early eighteenth century, politics was not yet an independent academic discipline; only during the second half of the century did the University of Göttingen begin to experiment with *Statistik* as an autonomous area of scholarship. In university teaching, politics was ancillary to moral philosophy, while the study of government remained firmly within the confines of jurisprudence. A different interweaving was part of the Enlightenment's philosophising drive (counter to the tradition of humanist 'erudition') to incorporate all aspects of human behaviour within the contours of philosophical history. Scottish authors were particularly prone to incorporate their political discussion into historical writings, be they in the form of 'national' or imperial histories, notably Hume's *History of England*, or in 'conjectural' histories of mankind, as in Millar. Ferguson and Robertson contributed to both genres.

Political economy was the most distinct Scottish alternative to Aristotelian politics as a high science of government. The ensuing admixture of jurisprudential and economic discourse with politics is explored elsewhere in this volume. The essential question, however, is whether the Scottish Enlightenment did not remove its theoretical onus away from political theory altogether. As one scholar recently put it, human improvement, economic advance, personal liberty and individual choice 'were not particularly political goals'.[30] Other historians view political economy as a creative extension of the traditional borders of politics.[31]

AVAILABLE IDIOMS AND PIVOTAL ISSUES

The debate on the scientification of politics, represented here by Hume and Ferguson, reflected a clash of political idioms and, deeper still, a philosophical disagreement about the mechanisms operating a stable polity and about the weight of human volition in political history. Man's social nature, the kernel of Hume's brief definition of politics, lay at the heart of Scottish political philosophy. Born into society, men have always shaped their political and cultural institutions according to their evolving expectations and needs, and were in turn shaped by these institutions. There was no pre-social state, no conscious moment of entering a social pact: Hume's withdrawal from the contractarian model associated with Hobbes and Locke, and his adoption of the natural lawyers' evolutionary, stadial account of economic and political change, set the stage for the Scottish Enlightenment almost as a whole.

Two major fault lines run across the Scottish discussion of man's sociability: the right balance between the social and unsocial elements of human nature, and the part-overlap and part-incongruity between society and polity. The first of these lines marked the limits of the civic, or Machiavellian, idiom of republican virtue and opened up new possibilities of accounting for non-virtuous, yet socially beneficial, behaviour. The second line involved a conscious expansion

of political theory beyond the core issues of government and constitution. What was common to both sets of problems was the need
to incorporate commerce, a factor unaccounted for by Machiavelli
and Hobbes, into political theory. Man's social nature was reassessed
against the rise of modern trade and manufacture, consumerism and
material refinement, as *the* distinctive attributes of modern states.
Here, Scotland's unique perspective as a post-sovereign member of
the British union, a state that traded independence for empire, proved
invaluable.[32]

In an important respect, the stage was set by a pre-Enlightenment
thinker, Andrew Fletcher of Saltoun, whose prominence in the
Union debate (1703–7) was based on a last-ditch attempt to
reconcile Machiavellian republicanism with modern statehood.[33]
Fletcher, like the English revolutionary James Harrington in the mid-
seventeenth century, drew directly on the great early moderniser
of classical republicanism, the Florentine Niccolò Machiavelli in
his *Discourses on the First Ten Books of Titus Livius* (completed
in 1519). This neo-republican tradition challenged monarchical
autocracy in its insistence on the participation of public-spirited,
property-owning citizens in the defence and government of their
country. In a mitigated form, more accurately labelled 'neo-Roman',
it hailed the civic alertness of a political nation offsetting any
absolutist aspirations of the English monarchs.[34] England's insularity vis-à-vis continental Europe was thus celebrated on two scales,
the geo-political and the constitutional.

Up to a point, the neo-republican idiom seemed better applicable to Scotland than the alternative anti-absolutist discourse, the
'old Whig' idea of an ancient constitution that posed a unique coun-
terbalance, gleaned from England's baronial past, against modern
continental-style monarchy. Scottish history was rich in feudal upheaval but unable to provide a tenable Magna Carta of its own. The
Scottish humanist and legal tradition, on the other hand, accommo-
dated Ciceronian and Stoic political rhetoric more easily. This set
of ideas proved especially relevant to Scotland on two occasions: the
debate preceding the Union of Parliaments in 1707, and the agitation
for a Scottish militia prior to the Union, and again in the second half
of the eighteenth century.

The vision of an independent classical polity run by propertied
citizen–soldiers clearly went against the tenor of Scotland's union

with England and its ensuing rise to commercial prominence. Hume, in particular, found the Machiavellian idiom wholly wrong for the state of post-Union Scotland. Machiavelli's crucial error, unforgivable even for an early sixteenth-century author once he could enjoy the excellent vantage point of Florence, is that he was blind to the stability and staying power of modern monarchies. Worse, Machiavelli and his contemporaries had ignored the political meaning of commerce.[35] Eighteenth-century neo-republicans, supporters of the 'Commonwealth' agenda, did not understand that neither civic virtue nor landed property could serve as the mainstays of a modern state. The social consequences of manufacture and commerce were public and private opulence on a new scale, complete with cultural refinement that allowed liberty to reside in large monarchies. Agrarian landholding was no longer the sole threshold leading into the political nation. Wealth made by commerce, and spent in sophisticated urban settings, introduced political interests far removed from those of the Ciceronian 'citizen' (cives) in his latter-day guise as an English or a Scottish country gentleman. These novelties, Hume asserted, were largely unintended outcomes of complex economic processes. They made the classical, polis-confined republican model all but obsolete.[36]

At stake was the appropriate use of history in the service of political philosophy. For Hume, Scottish political history could not underscore a viable philosophical analysis of modernity, because Scotland's baronial and monarchical past led nowhere; Scotland did not even have the kind of imagined 'ancient constitution' on which the English could draw a (false) justification for their genuine but quite novel constitutional achievement. If politics is gleaned from history, if 'history is public time', it was nevertheless English, not Scottish, political history that could furnish a truly theoretical understanding of what politics is about.[37]

Yet Scotland's 'Machiavellian moment' was more complex and more fertile than Hume's critique may suggest. Andrew Fletcher of Saltoun, the last true (and even so, not unqualified) standard bearer of Machiavellian virtù, was a formative voice for eighteenth-century Scottish political thought not primarily because of his civic commitment. Fletcher – in his later political essays – was one of the earliest thinkers to acknowledge the need to adapt the Machiavellian legacy for the new age of commerce and refinement. More poignantly,

Fletcher offered a political analysis of contemporary Scotland from a European perspective.[38]

Fletcher's vision of a European confederacy of city-states was not a viable legacy for the Scottish Enlightenment. His fear of a 'universal monarchy', the idea that one (probably Roman Catholic) ruler could come to govern vast tracts of Europe enjoying the dynastic luck of a Charles V, and wielding the arbitrary powers of an oriental despot, no longer haunted the Scottish Enlightenment. The Peace of Utrecht in 1714 left a political landscape in which states of varying sizes, monarchies as well as republics, enjoyed several decades of relative security. Forms of government, the crucial differentiating factors in classical political theory, were considerably less relevant than a general modern commitment to the rule of law and to the new dynamics of international trade. Fletcher's republicanism was thus overshadowed by a more prevailing insight of his: that Scotland's place within the British union subtly corresponded to the balancing factors within the European system of states.

Between the wars of the Spanish and the Austrian Succession, Scotland was able to share England's peaceful economic aggrandisement, revelling in the new conceptual environment of 'liberty' and 'security' vouchsafing 'justice'. It could also begin to envisage its new cultural politics as a distinct European province. Provided, that is, that the Jacobite challenge was promptly derailed. By the time Charles Edward Stuart arrived in Edinburgh for a brief and stormy sojourn in 1745, the Scottish Enlightenment, made from almost one Whig, lowland, and Presbyterian-moderate skin, was equipped with the theoretical tools to reject Jacobitism from a 'scientific' stance, brushing away the 'vulgarity' of more partisan interests. Jacobitism was the stuff of yesterday's politics (and of tomorrow's cultural-political imagination, but not yet). Not only was it closely identified with Catholic absolutism, evoking outdated fear of universal monarchy; it was contrary to the desirable course of modern Scottish history from both the Machiavellian perspective and the emerging philosophical Whig analysis. The failure of the Stuart cause was not just (or, rather, not interestingly) a question of dynastic legitimacy and military force. It was a victory of Hume's new politics of interest, a politics involving property and security, public opinion and justice. Scotland's full and wholehearted participation in the British state meant, for Hume, Smith and Robertson, membership in the most fortunate (but by no means anomalous) of modern European states, where strong institutions defend an ever-improving exchange of opinions and goods.

Adam Ferguson, the last 'neo-Roman' of eighteenth-century Scottish thought, an adamant Whig (but not fully a Lowlander), offered a partial correction of this analysis by overturning Fletcher's balance of concerns. His *Essay on the History of Civil Society* puts forward a theory of commercial modernity with classical-republican linchpins. Ferguson pointed at the moral loopholes of a politics devoid of virtuous civic alertness and over-dependent on the – essentially apolitical – ideas of 'unintended consequences' in economic and social processes and perennial constitutions of either the 'ancient' or the philosophical brand. There are no self-regulating mechanisms in politics, Ferguson argued. Even the Habeas Corpus Act, the vaunted patrimony of English freedom, 'requires a fabric no less than the whole political constitution of Great Britain, a spirit no less than the refractory and turbulent zeal of this fortunate people, to secure its effects'.[39] When a Scottish militia bill was presented to Parliament in the 1760s, Ferguson and his colleagues at the Edinburgh 'Poker Club' used a full republican artillery, inspired by Fletcher, to promote the bill, but in vain.[40]

On this point Ferguson's 'zeal' clashed head on with Hume's dreaded 'enthusiasm', a byword – as Hume developed it – for any irrational approach to politics, be it overridden by mysticism or by emotion. At stake was the role of impassioned human intervention in the institutionalised legal mechanism of the modern state. In Ferguson's view, constant civic alertness – the irreplaceability of citizens in the classical sense – is one Machiavellian insight that modern politics cannot leave off. Ferguson thus opposed Whiggism of both the 'vulgar' and the 'scientific' brands, to use Duncan Forbes's distinction. Britain could rely neither on the man-made clockwork of its political institutions, nor on the natural mechanism of self-regulating interests converging in the well-balanced commercial state. Nature and constitution were good but not enough; self-interest and professionalisation were historical explicatory factors but not political guarantors. All good states needed some degree of manual operation by keen amateurs.[41]

This Scottish Machiavellism was encumbered by an outdated moral philosophy. Echoing the Stoics, it regarded luxury and 'effeminacy', the mental corruption of the powerful, as the vices naturally threatening the simple and manly virtues of the active citizen-soldier. It was obliged to denounce 'corruption', in Stoic and Machiavellian vein, where a modern onlooker would find consumption and refinement conducive to commercial prosperity and political stability. Wealth, in the modern European state, could no longer be opposed to virtue; 'virtue' itself was being transformed into a civil, rather than civic, moral framework.[42]

Ferguson tried to push some modern conceptual demons back into their etymological bottles, summoning the 'polished' back to politics and reminding the 'civilised' of their civic origin. Yet the modern denotations of 'politeness' and 'civilisation' had new power of their own. Delicacy, sensibility, even luxury, were aspects of an advanced civil life which in some crucial ways surpassed the classical models. The traditional republican discourse had no answers for the new respectability of wealth and social refinement, which eighteenth-century Scots came to associate with the modern age. A choice had to be made: the civic values had to be radically adjusted to the new ethics of sociability, commerce and freedom under the law; or else new proof was required for their relevance to the modern state.

One mainspring for the Humean rejection of Machiavellian republicanism was the modern theory of Natural Law expounded in the works of Hugo Grotius and Samuel Pufendorf. Most effective was the latter's account of the emergence of property as a formative social institution, and his theory of economic progress from primitive communities to sophisticated commercial societies. The development of legal and political systems, Pufendorf suggested, was informed by patterns of production and trade. Technological advance and commercial exchange, these defining features of modern society, were to be taken on board any novel attempt to construct a political theory. It was from this starting point that Hume constructed his politics as the 'science of a legislator', positing justice, rather than forms of government or modes of participation and representation, as the modern politician's subject matter. In an important sense, Hume opted for law, not politics, as the idiom for modern government.[43]

The idea of the modern polity as a society resting on solid political institutions, freedom from governmental encroachment, and individual accumulation of wealth, acquired further coherence from another source. Bernard Mandeville's *Fable of the Bees* (1714) suggested an appealing type of historical causality, one which could explain why self-interested actions of private individuals, bent on

accumulating wealth, could amount to increasing comfort and liberty in the public sphere. Moreover, it provided a justification for
the replacement of political virtue with time-tested institutions.
Both the growth of these institutions and the beneficial outcome
of individual selfishness could be seen as the fruit of subtle historical mechanisms. Political and economic progress was grasped as an
accumulation of the unintended consequences of numerous human
actions: that, for a modern mind, was part of its beauty. It is therefore
no accident that all the major thinkers of the Scottish Enlightenment
drew a great deal of inspiration from Mandeville's metaphor.[44] The
question was, as Ferguson put it, to what extent could communities
of men be compared to beehives?[45]

Adam Smith's qualified understanding of the Mandevillian fable
was different from Ferguson's. In Smith's *Wealth of Nations*, spontaneous order stopped at the threshold of magistrates rather than
citizens. Smith retained a transformed Machiavellian commitment to wilful governmental intervention in human affairs where
education and security were concerned.[46] In the last account,
Hume's political theory too retained a powerful ingredient of human
volition. For Hume, the free and fermenting agent in politics was
neither the classical-republican citizen-soldier, nor the just magistrate, but the modern interlocutor in the public sphere, the purveyor
of 'opinion'. Politics is thus always more than the sum of unintended
consequences of historical processes. Its issues transcend the dichotomy of – in Humean terms – 'liberty and necessity'. Mandeville
had provided an insight, an explicatory device. But the decisive
positive theoretical context for the political thought of the Scottish
Enlightenment was provided by Charles-Louis de Secondat, Baron de
Montesquieu.

The direct impact of Montesquieu's *De l'Esprit des lois* (1748) on
his contemporaries Hume, Smith, Millar and Ferguson makes him
the single most important source of Scottish political innovation.[47]
Montesquieu offered the Scottish theorists three different, and very
useful, insights. In ascending order of importance, these were a
renovated taxonomy of governments bringing both democracy and
aristocracy under the rubric of 'republic', a powerful justification for
a modern type of political freedom in a large commercial state, and
a comparative geographic-cultural approach to political societies as
reflected by their laws.

Montesquieu's treatment of republican themes allowed Smith and Ferguson to feel at ease with the discreet, less-than-Machiavellian, republican residue of the British state.[48] Continental panegyrics to 'English freedom', such as Voltaire's and Montesquieu's and Lichtenberg's, were seldom taken at face value by informed denizens of the 'fortunate island' themselves, not least because neither Voltaire nor Montesquieu took the trouble to view the archipelago beyond the island. But Montesquieu condoned both the aristocratic element of the British constitution and its large-state viability, providing ammunition against Rousseau's small-state republican purism. Here was a theory of modern freedom inspired by England and geared for Britain: economic progress, social refinement and a well-balanced constitution could ultimately replace the freedom of the classical republic, whose chief resource was its virtuous citizen-soldiers. From a Scottish perspective, however, Montesquieu's *pièce de résistance* was the idea of *ésprit*, the anthropological-cultural analysis of politics. Here was a 'system of political knowledge', as Hume celebrated it, showing that 'the laws have, or ought to have, a constant reference to the constitution of governments, the climate, the religion, the commerce, the situation of each society'.[49] Montesquieu's Scottish disciples were quick to abandon his simplistic climatology and geographic determinism. Putting mores and manners before temperature and geology, they were now equipped with the tools for analysing modern European politics in the terms of a *histoire des mœurs*. William Robertson's 'View of the Progress of Society in Europe' (1769) and John Millar's *Origin of the Distinction of Ranks* (1771), along with Ferguson's *Essay*, are direct beneficiaries of 'the President' from Bordeaux.

Hume's corrective went further. In order for Montesquieu's method to be 'reconciled with true philosophy', the French author's theory of political right must be replaced by a politics of interest, where both sentiment and justice are accounted for. Justice does not correlate to social or political relations, but to interest.

Property is allowed to be dependent on civil laws; civil laws are allowed to have no other object, but the interest of society: this therefore must be allowed to be the sole foundation of property and justice. Not to mention, that our obligation itself to obey the magistrate and his laws is founded on nothing but the interests of society.[50]

Yet Montesquieu's historical and anthropological insight is crucial precisely because property, and all 'interest', can only be determined by 'recourse to statutes, customs, precedents, analogies, and a hundred other circumstances'.[51] Furthermore – and here Hume's corrective applied to the natural lawyers too – 'opinion', in modern commercial states with a degree of political freedom, is as important as property in determining interest.[52] The legal historian is thus the alter ego of Hume's 'politician', so long as the latter – a philosopher to boot – remains in control of the terminus of political theory: reminding legislators (and lawyers and historians) that 'the ultimate point' of all statutes and customs and precedents is 'the interest and happiness of human society'.[53]

CONCLUDING REMARKS

The creative use made by the Scottish thinkers of Montesquieu (and to a lesser extent of Turgot and Rousseau) was a conscious application of new European theory to the political contingencies of eighteenth-century Scotland, and to its particular intellectual climate. The effects of Hume, Smith and Ferguson – as political theorists – on contemporary European writers is a more complex and less-studied topic. The French and the German receptions of the major Scottish thinkers tended to subject their politics, often seen as pertaining to the 'fortunate accidents' of British political history and 'English liberty', to other aspects of their thought. Following the American and the French revolutions, Scottish political thought was often interpreted within the narrow confines of anti-Jacobinism and proto-conservatism.[54]

The American case projects a more variegated (and more amply researched) light on the political theory of the Scottish Enlightenment at its late eighteenth-century terminus.[55] Personal and intellectual contacts between Scots and Americans – with a particular input by Scots turned Americans such as John Witherspoon, the most famous mediator between the two Enlightenments – made the founding fathers of the United States better readers of Scottish politics than any of their European contemporaries.[56] The emphasis placed by Hume on the constitutional machinations of free governments in large states was taken up by James Madison and Alexander Hamilton as a major source of inspiration, along with Montesquieu, for designing the checks and balances of the American constitution and reworking, within a heavily institutionalised and legalised setting, what remained of 'the Machiavellian Moment'.[57] At the moment of truth in 1776, admittedly, John Witherspoon was obliged to work hard, and not quite successfully, to disperse American mistrust in the Scots; and neither the dying Hume, nor the very lively Ferguson, could accept the American upheaval as an apogee of their respective political teachings.[58] Yet the Scottish Enlightenment bequeathed to the new American republic much of what has remained usable of its political theory: the new collation of politics and the 'science of man', leading on to the nineteenth century's social sciences; the growing emphasis on constitutional machination as opposed to individual political intervention of the monarchic or the civic brand; and the signification of public opinion as a key to the new sociability of self-interested individuals in commercial modernity: not a revival of Machiavellian *virtù*, but yet a remainder of the *homo politicus* residing in the breast, as it were, of the *homo economicus* of the late eighteenth century.

NOTES

1   Three authoritative overviews, all counterbalancing Scotland's singularity with its European contexts, and between them reflecting the evolution of recent scholarship, are Hugh Trevor-Roper, 'The Scottish Enlightenment', *Studies on Voltaire and the Eighteenth Century* 58 (1967), 1635–58; Nicholas Phillipson, 'The Scottish Enlightenment', in Roy Porter and Mikulas Teich, eds., *The Enlightenment in National Context* (Cambridge: Cambridge University Press, 1981), 19–40; and John Robertson, 'The Scottish Enlightenment', *Rivista Storica Italiana* 108 (1996), 792–829.

2   Cf. the prologue, 'The Governing Science: Things Political and the Intellectual Historian', in Stefan Collini, Donald Winch and John Burrow, *That Noble Science of Politics: a Study in Nineteenth-Century Intellectual History* (Cambridge: Cambridge University Press, 1983), 3–21.

3   John Robertson, 'Introduction', in his edition of Andrew Fletcher, *Political Works* (Cambridge: Cambridge University Press, 1997); and his 'An Elusive Sovereignty: the Course of the Union Debate in Scotland 1698–1707', in John Robertson, ed., *A Union for Empire: Political Thought and the British Union of 1707* (Cambridge: Cambridge University Press, 1995), 198–227.

4 J. G. A. Pocock, 'Two Kingdoms and Three Histories? Political Thought in British Contexts', in Roger A. Mason, ed., *Scots and Britons: Scottish Political Thought and the Union of 1603* (Cambridge: Cambridge University Press, 1994), 294.

5 Phillipson, 'Scottish Enlightenment', 25–6; 'Introduction', in David Hume, *Political Essays*, ed. Knud Haakonssen (Cambridge: Cambridge University Press, 1994), xvi.

6 Fletcher, *Political Works*, 2.

7 Pocock, 'Two Kingdoms', 297, 311.

8 Phillipson, 'Scottish Enlightenment', 22.

9 David Hume, 'That Politics May be Reduced to a Science', first published in Hume, *Essays, Moral and Political* (Edinburgh, 1741), reprinted in Hume, *Political Essays*, 4–15.

10 David Hume, *A Treatise of Human Nature*, ed. L. A. Selby-Bigge, 2nd edn, rev. P. H. Nidditch (Oxford: Clarendon Press, 1978), xv.

11 Duncan Forbes set the agenda for studying Hume's 'scientific (or 'sceptical') Whiggism', as against 'what is best called vulgar Whiggism', in his *Hume's Philosophical Politics* (Cambridge: Cambridge University Press, 1975), esp. ch. 5.

12 David Hume, *Enquiries Concerning Human Understanding and Concerning the Principles of Morals*, ed. L. A. Selby-Bigge, 3rd edn, rev. P. H. Nidditch (Oxford: Clarendon Press, 1975), 173 and passim (hereinafter *EHU* and *EPM*); Hume, *Political Essays*, 9, 68, and passim.

13 Adam Smith, *An Inquiry into the Nature and Causes of the Wealth of Nations* [1776], eds. R. H. Campbell, A. S. Skinner and W. B. Todd, 2 vols. (Oxford: Clarendon Press, 1976), IV.ii.39.

14 Forbes, *Hume's Philosophical Politics*.

15 *EHU*, 165; cf. Haakonssen, 'Introduction'.

16 Hume, 'Politics Reduced', *Political Essays*, 7.

17 'Nor are the earth, water, and other elements, examined by ARISTOTLE, and HIPPOCRATES, more like to those which at present lie under our observation than the men described by POLYBIUS and TACITUS are to those who now govern the world', *EHU*, 84.

18 Ibid., 90.

19 Hume, 'Politics Reduced', *Political Essays*, 5; on the universal regularities of human actions and human nature cf. *EHU*, 83.

20 Hume, 'Of Civil Liberty', *Political Essays*, 51.

21 Adam Ferguson, *An Essay on the History of Civil Society*, ed. Fania Oz-Salzberger (Cambridge: Cambridge University Press, 1995), 33. Hume's own, self-conscious, progression from active to contemplative politician is analysed by Forbes, *Hume's Philosophical Politics*, 138–9.

22 Ferguson's *Essay* plays on both meanings of the word, hailing Montesquieu as a 'profound politician', (66) but also mentioning the active 'politician, whose spirit is the conduct of parties and factions'. (47)

23 Ibid., 34.

24 Ibid.

25 Hume's *Treatise of Human Nature* (1739–40), and *Enquiry concerning the Principles of Morals* (1751); Smith's *Theory of Moral Sentiments* (1759).

26 Hume's *History of England* (1754–62). Hume's retreat from the projected title, *History of Britain*, is a telling disclosure of his evolving political emphases; Robertson's *History of Scotland* (1759).

27 Ferguson's *Essay on the History of Civil Society* (1767); Robertson's 'View of the Progress of Society in Europe' (1769); Millar's *Origin of the Distinction of Ranks* (1771).

28 Smith's lectures on jurisprudence.

29 Smith's *Wealth of Nations* (1776), and James Steuart's *An Inquiry into The Principles of Political Oeconomy* (1767).

30 Robertson, 'Introduction', in Fletcher, *Political Works*, xxx.

31 Donald Winch, *Adam Smith's Politics: an Essay in Historiographic Revision* (Cambridge: Cambridge University Press, 1978), ch. 1.

32 Phillipson, 'Scottish Enlightenment'; John Robertson, 'The Scottish Enlightenment at the Limits of the Civic Tradition', in Istvan Hont and Michael Ignatieff, eds., *Wealth and Virtue: the Shaping of Political Economy in the Scottish Enlightenment* (Cambridge: Cambridge University Press, 1983), 137–78.

33 The classic exposition of English Machiavellism, with its (thereafter much debated) Scottish edge, is J. G. A. Pocock, *The Machiavellian Moment: Florentine Political Thought and the Atlantic Republican Tradition* (Princeton, NJ: Princeton University Press, 1975), chs. x–xiv; on Fletcher, see esp. 426–35; cf. Robertson, 'Introduction', in Fletcher, *Political Works*.

34 Quentin Skinner, *Liberty before Liberalism* (Cambridge: Cambridge University Press, 1998).

35 Hume, 'Of Civil Liberty', *Political Essays*, 51–2; cf. 'Politics Reduced to a Science', *Political Essays*, 10.

36 Forbes, *Hume's Philosophical Politics*, 160; Haakonssen, 'The Structure of Hume's Political Thought', in David Fate Norton, ed., *The Cambridge Companion to Hume* (Cambridge: Cambridge University Press, 1993), 182–221.

37 J. G. A. Pocock, *Virtue, Commerce and History: Essays on Political Thought and History, Chiefly in the Eighteenth Century* (Cambridge: Cambridge University Press, 1985), quote from 91; Colin Kidd,

Subverting Scotland's Past: Scottish Whig Historians and the Creation of Anglo-British Identity 1689-c. 1830 (Cambridge: Cambridge University Press, 1993).

38 Robertson, 'Introduction', in Fletcher, *Political Works*.

39 Ferguson, *Essay*, 160.

40 John Robertson, *The Scottish Enlightenment and the Militia Issue* (Edinburgh: John Donald, 1985).

41 Fania Oz-Salzberger, 'Introduction', in Ferguson, *Essay*.

42 See Hont and Ignatieff, *Wealth and Virtue*, especially the editors' Introduction.

43 Knud Haakonssen, *The Science of a Legislator: the Natural Jurisprudence of David Hume and Adam Smith* (Cambridge: Cambridge University Press, 1981); Robertson, *Scottish Enlightenment and the Militia Issue*.

44 Ronald Hamowy, *The Scottish Enlightenment and the Theory of Spontaneous Order* (Carbondale: Southern Illinois University Press, 1987).

45 Ferguson, *Essay*, 36–7, 173–4. The moral dimension of political society, where men cease to behave like bees, is set in blunt opposition to Mandeville's bees (and all other 'gregarious and political' animals) in Ferguson's *Principles of Moral and Political Science* (London, 1792), pt. I, 21–4.

46 Winch, *Adam Smith's Politics*; Knud Haakonssen, *Science of a Legislator*, ch. 4.

47 Montesquieu was 'illustrious' for Hume (*EPM*, 196–7). 'When I recollect what the President Montesquieu has written', Ferguson's famous tribute went, 'I am at a loss to tell, why I should treat of human affairs' (*Essay*, 66).

48 Richard B. Sher, 'From Troglodytes to Americans: Montesquieu and the Scottish Enlightenment on Liberty, Virtue and Commerce', in David Wootton, ed., *Republicanism, Liberty, and Commercial Society, 1649–1776* (Stanford: Stanford University Press, 1994), 368–402.

49 *EPM*, 196–7.

50 Ibid., 197, 197n.

51 Ibid., 197.

52 'Of the First Principles of Government', and 'Whether the British Government Inclines More to Absolute Monarchy or a Republic', in Hume, *Political Essays*, 16–19, 28–32; cf. Collini, Winch and Burrow, *Noble Science of Politics*, 18–19.

53 *EPM*, 198. On the further development of Hume's notion of 'opinion' by Dugald Stewart see Collini, Winch and Burrow, *Noble Science of Politics*, ch. 1.

54 Laurence L. Bongie, *David Hume: Prophet of the Counter-Revolution* (Oxford: Clarendon Press, 1965); Fania Oz-Salzberger, 'Die Schottische Aufklärung in Frankreich', in D. Brühlmeier, H. Holzhey and V. Mudroch, eds., *Schottische Aufklärung: 'A Hotbed of Genius'* (Berlin: Akademie, 1996), 107–22; Günter Gawlick and Lother Kreimendahl, *Hume in der deutschen Aufklärung* (Stuttgart-Bad Cannstatt: Frommann-holzboog, 1987); Fania Oz-Salzberger, *Translating the Enlightenment: Scottish Civic Discourse in Eighteenth-Century Germany* (Oxford: Clarendon Press, 1995).

55 A valuable collection of essays is in Richard B. Sher and Jeffrey T. Smitten, eds., *Scotland and America in the Age of the Enlightenment* (Edinburgh: Edinburgh University Press, 1990).

56 Thomas Jefferson and James Madison had Scottish-born mentors, and Benjamin Franklin made a famous visit to Scotland. See David Daiches, 'John Witherspoon, James Wilson and the Influence of Scottish Rhetoric on America', in John Dwyer and Richard B. Sher, eds., *Sociability and Society in Eighteenth-Century Scotland*, special issue of *Eighteenth-Century Life* n.s. 15 (1991), 163–180.

57 The vast literature on this subject is placed in a relevant context in Pocock's concluding chapter, 'The Americanization of Virtue', in his *Machiavellian Moment*.

58 J. G. A. Pocock, 'Hume and the American Revolution: the Dying Thoughts of a North Briton', in *Virtue, Commerce, and History*, 125–41.

9   Economic theory

INTRODUCTION

In 1954 A. L. Macfie gave a lecture to the revived Scottish Economic Society on the subject of the 'Scottish Tradition in Economic Thought',[1] which has produced a considerable debate.[2] While it seems doubtful that a *tradition* can be identified, there is ample evidence of a particular Scottish approach to the study of the social or moral sciences in the eighteenth century, which laid great stress on socio-economic aspects. In particular, Macfie noted the emphasis on the history of civil society, a procedure which has been neatly described by Donald Winch as involving 'the pursuit of the origins and development of civil society from rudeness to refinement by means of a form of history in which universal psychological principles and socio-economic circumstances played twin illuminating roles'.[3]

The impact of Montesquieu's *L'Esprit des lois* (1748) has been noted by numerous commentators. For example, Terence Hutchison has confirmed that 'the great significance of *L'Esprit des lois* for the development of political economy in the eighteenth century, and after, lay in its fundamental methodological approach, which is especially important in Scotland'.[4] A second major influence on Scottish writers at the time is represented by Isaac Newton, whose ideas were disseminated much earlier than was at one time supposed.[5] But later there was a significant attempt to make Newton's ideas more accessible, one notable contribution being Colin Maclaurin's *An Account of Sir Isaac Newton's Philosophical Discoveries*.[6] Maclaurin, latterly Professor of Mathematics in Edinburgh, and much admired by Newton, made three influential points.

First, Maclaurin accepted Newton's argument that we may 'infer from the structure of the visible world, that it is governed by one *Almighty and All wise Being*'.[7] Secondly, he drew attention to the issue of methodology: to the classic procedures of induction, deduction and verification.[8] Finally, he emphasised the Newtonian ideal – the comprehensive system of thought which was designed to explain complex phenomena – in his case the system of astrophysics. There were many contributors to the Scottish Enlightenment who shared the preoccupations and interests outlined above. Adam Ferguson, Henry Home, Lord Kames and John Millar are obvious examples. Moreover their writings are of interest to the student of political economy in that they show an interest in particular topics such as the analysis of the division of labour and, in the case of Kames, the theory of taxation. However, they tended to address specific topics: the treatment of political economy in a *systematic* way is now associated with Francis Hutcheson, David Hume, Sir James Steuart and, of course, Adam Smith.

The idea of system was important. As Smith noted: 'Systems in many respects resemble machines. A machine is a little system, created to perform, as well as to connect together, in reality, those different movements and effects which the artist has occasion for. A system is an imaginary machine invented to connect together in the fancy those different movements and effects which are already in reality performed.'[9]

The four men who contributed so much to the development of Scottish political economy in the period were interconnected. Hutcheson, Smith's teacher, is now known to have exerted a great influence on his lectures on economics.[10] Hume corresponded with Hutcheson, and it is well known that he was a close friend of both Sir James Steuart and of Adam Smith. While both Steuart and Smith were profoundly influenced by Hume's *Political Discourses* (1752),[11] they were to produce works on economics which were so different in perspective as to make dialogue between the men (and the texts) extremely complex.

DAVID HUME: ECONOMICS

Hume's *Discourses* contain nine essays on economic topics. They cover such subjects as money, the balance of trade, the rate of interest, public finance, taxation and population. As Rotwein has shown,[12] the essays are marked by a unity of purpose and of method. They also enable us to identify a number of particular interdependent themes.

The first theme is broadly methodological and arises from Hume's conviction 'that all the sciences have a relation, greater or less, to human nature, and that however wide any of them may seem to run from it, they still return back by one passage or another'. The study of human nature was thus to be based upon empirical evidence: as Hume himself made clear, the *Treatise of Human Nature* constituted an attempt to introduce the 'experimental method of reasoning into moral subjects'. The approach also allowed Hume to state a proposition which was profoundly influential in the eighteenth century, namely: 'It is universally acknowledged that there is a great uniformity among the actions of men, in all nations and ages, and that human nature remains still the same in its principles and operations.'

Among these 'constant principles' Hume included a desire for action, for liveliness and, of particular interest to the economist, avarice or the desire for gain; a constant principle of motion which allows the commentator to offer scientific generalisations at least in the sphere of political economy (*Essays*, 113).

A second major theme in the *Discourses* relates to Hume's employment of historical materials. From one point of view this perspective is straightforward, in the sense that the study of history is an 'invention' which 'extends our experience to all past ages, and to the most distant nations' (*Essays*, 556). But from the point of view of our understanding of economic phenomena, broadly defined, the picture which was to emerge from the 'economic writings' was in fact a complex one.

If Hume argued that the principles of human nature were constant, he also appreciated that the way in which they found expression would be profoundly affected by the socio-economic environment which might happen to exist, and also by habit, customs and manners. While this theme runs throughout the essays, perhaps two examples will suffice for the present purpose.

In the long essay 'Of the Populousness of Ancient Nations', a work which has scarcely received the attention it deserves, Hume addressed a proposition which had been advanced by both

Montesquieu and Robert Wallace, to the effect that population levels had been higher in ancient as compared with modern times. In deciding in favour of modern society, Hume drew attention to the use of slavery in the classical period as 'in general disadvantageous both to the happiness and populousness of mankind' (*Essays*, 396), pointing also to the incidence of military conflict and of political instability. But perhaps the most striking aspect of the argument is the attention given to the point that '[t]rade, manufactures, industry, were no where, in former ages, so flourishing as they are at present in Europe' (*Essays*, 416). Population is ultimately limited not just by political factors, but also by the food supply, and this in turn by the type of economic organisation prevailing. The same basic theme emerges in the essay 'Of Money', where Hume rejected the conventional wisdom that money can be regarded as wealth (*Essays*, 281) and stated the famous relationship between changes in the money supply and the general price level; a relationship which remained substantially unchallenged until the 1920s.

Less familiar is the point that Hume consistently contrasted the situation of a primitive economy with a more sophisticated version. It is, he argued, 'the proportion between the circulating money, and the commodities in the market, which determines the prices' (*Essays*, 291). In the primitive economy, 'we must consider that, in the first and more uncultivated ages of any state, ... men have little occasion for exchange, at least for money, which, by agreement, is the common measure of exchange'. But in the state of commerce, in contrast, 'coin enters into many more contracts, and by that means is much more employed'.

On the other hand, the changed form of economic organisation had given a greater scope to individual effort and must therefore massively increase the supply of commodities which are subject to exchange. Hume therefore concluded that although prices in Europe had risen since the discoveries in the West Indies and elsewhere, these prices were in fact much lower than the extent of the increase in the money supply might of itself suggest: 'And no other satisfactory reason can be given, why all prices have not risen to a much more exorbitant height, except that which is derived from a change of customs and manners' (*Essays*, 292).

The technique which we have just considered enables us to contrast and compare the operation of certain economic relationships in different institutional environments. But there was another dimension to Hume's historicism which, if loosely articulated, is none the less more explicitly dynamic in character. The theme of historical dynamics is addressed primarily in the essays 'Of Commerce' and 'Of Refinement in the Arts', where it is noted:

The bulk of every state may be divided into *husbandmen* and *manufacturers*. The former are employed in the culture of the land; the latter work up the materials furnished by the former, into all the commodities which are necessary or ornamental to human life. As soon as men quit their savage state, where they live chiefly by hunting and fishing, they must fall into these two classes; though the arts of agriculture employ *at first* the most numerous part of the society. (*Essays*, 256)

It was Hume's contention that there had been a gradual progression to a situation where the two main sectors of activity are fully interdependent, supported by merchants: 'one of the most useful races of men, who serve as agents between those parts of the state, that are wholly unacquainted, and are ignorant of each other's necessities' (*Essays*, 300).

The argument is rooted in Hume's deployment of a favourite thesis of the eighteenth century, namely that men have natural wants which gradually extend in a self-sustaining spiral. The tone is best expressed in the essay 'Of Refinement in the Arts', where Hume also contrasts the form of government found in 'rude and unpolished nations' with that likely to be associated with the modern state. In passages which are likely to have caught the attention of both Smith and Steuart, Hume observed that 'where luxury nourishes commerce and industry, the peasants, by a proper cultivation of the land, become rich and independent; while the tradesmen and merchants acquire a share of the property, and draw authority and consideration to that middling rank of men, who are the best and firmest basis of public liberty' (*Essays*, 277) – a development which may be expected further to encourage the rate of economic growth.

The final major theme in Hume's thought relates to the problem of international trade; a theme which, here as elsewhere, unfolds on a number of levels. To begin with, Hume drew attention to the general benefits of foreign trade. In the essay 'Of Commerce', for example, he made the point that if 'we consult history, we shall find, that, in most nations, foreign trade has preceded any refinement in home manufactures, and given birth to domestic luxury'. In the same context he drew attention to induced changes in taste and to the point that imitation leads domestic manufactures 'to emulate the foreign in their improvements'. Hume continued by noting that the encouragement of domestic industry would further enhance the opportunities for trade and economic growth.[13]

The second aspect of Hume's argument supports his repeated claim for freedom of trade on grounds that are essentially technical. Building upon the analysis in the essay 'Of Money', Hume examined the case of two or more economies with no unemployed resources with a view to demonstrating the futility of the mercantile preoccupation with a positive balance of trade. Against this, Hume contended, a net inflow of gold would inevitably raise prices in the domestic economy, while a loss of specie would reduce the general price level elsewhere – thus improving the competitive position in the latter case and reducing it in the former. In the essay 'Of the Balance of Trade', Hume concluded that 'money, in spite of the absurd jealousy of princes and states, has brought itself nearly to a level', just as 'all water, wherever it communicates, remains always at a level' (Essays, 312).[14]

The third dimension of Hume's treatment of foreign trade is much more complex. It is based upon the premise that countries have different characteristics and different rates of growth, and thus opens up a different and distinctive policy position compared with those so far considered. The argument effectively introduced what Hont has described as the 'rich country – poor country debate'. Hont has identified no fewer than twelve aspects of the argument.[15] But for the present purpose, we may approach the matter in a slightly different way.

While critical of Montesquieu's thesis regarding the role of physical factors, Hume was nonetheless conscious of the fact that different countries could have different factor endowments, and aware that climate could have some influence upon economic activity. But there is also a sense in which the rich country – poor country thesis reflects strands of thought which we have already identified in dealing with the comparative static and dynamic branches of Hume's argument. In this context it is worth recalling that the comparative static technique involves the comparison of different economic types, while the dynamic element draws attention to the importance of individual effort and to an accelerating rate of change as institutions and manners themselves change. On the one hand the reader is reminded of the phenomenon of a 'diversity of geniuses, climates and soil', while on the other attention is drawn to the point that the extent to which men apply 'art, care and industry' may vary in one society over time, and between different societies at a given point in time. Other factors which will affect the rate of growth and cause variations in rates of growth in different communities include the form of government and the degree to which public policies such as trade regulations, taxes and debt are deployed with intelligence. Hume illustrated this new phase of the problem by referring to the issue of regional imbalance (a concern which he shared with Josiah Tucker), citing the case of London and Yorkshire (*Essays*, 354). The regional dimension is just as relevant to the rich country – poor country debate as is the international, although it was upon the latter that Hume chose to place most emphasis.

Hume's treatment of the performance of the modern economy, especially in the context of the essays 'Of Money' and 'Of Interest', implies an increase in productivity which may give the developed economy an advantage in terms of the price of manufactures. He also recognised that an inflow of gold in the context of a growing economy need not generate adverse price effects. But Hume clearly felt that rich countries could lose their competitive edge, in noting that England feels 'some disadvantages in foreign trade by the high price of labour, which is in part the effect of the riches of their artisans, as well as of the plenty of money' (*Essays*, 265). It was thus recognised that advantages may be eroded, causing the loss in turn of particular industries, *unless care is taken to preserve them.*

Hume also seems to have felt that the tendency for the prices of labour and provisions to rise over time could lead to a *general* loss of markets and that this could involve a policy of protection to support employment levels, a situation which he contemplated with calm objectivity, noting that 'as foreign trade is not the most material circumstance, it is not to be put in competition with the happiness of so many millions' (*Essays*, 265).

Hume concluded, in the essay 'Of Money', 'There seems to be a happy concurrence of causes in human affairs, which checks the growth of trade and riches, and hinders them from being confined entirely to one people' (*Essays*, 283). The point was to be elaborated in correspondence with Lord Kames, and reflects an old preoccupation with the classical thesis of 'growth and decay'.

SIR JAMES STEUART

The major difference between Steuart and Hume is that the former attempted to offer a *systematic* treatment of political economy, linking the most interesting branches of modern policy, such as '*population, agriculture, trade, industry, money, coin, interest circulation, banks, exchange, public credit, and taxes*' (*PPO1* 1:7; *PPO2* 1:7).[16] As Paul Chamley has pointed out, Steuart's attempt to produce a systematic treatise shows that he sought to include economics in the body of organised science, and that as such it conforms to the design of the *Encyclopédie* as described by d'Alembert.[17]

In approaching the problems involved, Steuart chose to adopt the broadly historical perspective associated with David Hume. Steuart too had taken a hint from what the recent revolutions in the politics of Europe had indicated was the regular progress of mankind, from great simplicity to complicated refinement (*PPO1* 1:28; *PPO2* 1:34). The approach was to find expression in a number of areas which included sociology, politics and economics.

Steuart made use of a theory of stages, now recognised as a piece of apparatus which was central to the historical work of the Scottish School in particular. He cited, for example, the Tartars and Indians as relatively primitive socio-economic types of organisation, while concentrating primarily on the third and fourth stages – the stages of agriculture and commerce. In the former case, Steuart observed that those who lacked the means of subsistence could acquire it only through becoming dependent on those who owned it; in the latter, he noted that the situation was radically different in that all goods and services command a price. He concluded, in a passage of quite striking clarity:

I deduce the origin of the great subordination under the feudal government, from the necessary dependence of the lower classes for their subsistence. They consumed the produce of the land, as the price of their subordination, not as the reward of their industry in making it produce. (*PPO* 1:208; *PPO2* 1:257)

He continued, 'I deduce modern liberty from the independence of the same classes, by the introduction of industry, and circulation of an adequate equivalent for every service' (*PPO1* 1:209; *PPO2* 1:257). The change in the distribution of power which was reflected in the changing balance between proprietor and merchant led Steuart to the conclusion that 'industry must give wealth and wealth *will* give power'. As an earnest of this position, he drew attention, significantly in his Notes on Hume's *History*, to the reduced position of the Crown at the end of the reign of Elizabeth: a revolution which appears 'quite natural when we set before us the causes which occasioned it. Wealth must give power; and industry, in a country of luxury, will throw it into the hands of the commons' (*PPO1* 1:213n).

Against this background, it can be noted that the first economic problem to which Steuart addressed himself, following Hume, was that of population, where his stated purpose was 'not to inquire what numbers of people were found upon the earth at a certain time, but to examine the natural and rational causes of multiplication' (*PPO1* 1:31; *PPO2* 1:36). In so doing he stated that the 'fundamental principle' is 'generation; the next is food', from which it follows that where men live by gathering the spontaneous fruits of the soil (the North American Indian model), population levels must be determined by their extent.

Where some effort is applied to the cultivation of the soil (the agrarian stage), Steuart recognised that the output of food and therefore the level of population would grow. But here again he drew a distinction between cultivation for subsistence, which was typical of the feudal stage, and the application of industry to the soil as found in the modern situation.

The modern context was dominated by interdependent sectors of activity (manufacture, agriculture, trade) which in effect maximised the opportunities for economic growth and therefore the level of population. Hume and Steuart were well aware of a doctrine, later associated with J. B. Say, namely that it is products which open a demand for products. Steuart in particular noted that '*Agriculture among a free people will augment population, in proportion only as the necessitous are put in a situation to purchase subsistence with their labour*' (*PPO1* 1:40; *PPO2* 1:46).

The exchange economy

The preceding parts of Steuart's analyses imply a view as to the nature of the exchange economy. It is significant that Steuart made little use of the division of labour in the Smithian sense of the term (although he does cite the example of the pin (*PPO1* 1:158; *PPO2* 1:200). On the other hand, he gave a great deal of emphasis to the social division of labour, noting that 'we find the people distributed into two classes' – those engaged in agriculture and in manufactures (*PPO1* 1:43; *PPO2* 1:49).

The main theme is that of the interdependence of economic phenomena as a consequence of institutional structures and of the activity of individuals. As Steuart put it, no doubt following Hume, 'The principle of self-interest will serve as a general key to this inquiry; and it may, in one sense, be considered as the ruling principle of my subject, and may therefore be traced throughout the whole. This is the main spring' (*PPO1* 1:142; *PPO2* 1:182). This theme brought Steuart quite logically to the treatment of price and of the allocation of resources.

Having defined supply price in terms of the 'real expence' of making a product, with a 'small addition' for profit to the merchant or the manufacturer (*PPO1* 1:189; *PPO2* 1:235), Steuart noted that the process of price determination would be affected by competition *among and between* buyers and sellers. Steuart was thus able to offer a definition of *equilibrium*, but also a statement of a *stability* condition, in noting that '[i]n proportion therefore as the rising of prices can stop demand, or the sinking of prices can increase it, in the same proportion will competition prevent either the rise or the fall from being carried beyond a certain length' (*PPO1* 1:177; *PPO2* 1:221).

Steuart, in the same manner as Smith much later, would also appear to have been aware of the link between 'equilibrium' in a 'microeconomic' sense and macro-economic considerations. It was in this connection that he expanded his analysis to include a consideration of *aggregate demand and supply*, where the interaction of the latter variables would contribute to the determination of the general price level and of the level of employment.

It is also readily apparent that Steuart saw no reason to doubt the potential for economic development in the context of the *exchange* economy. Here, and for the first time in an *institutional* sense, 'wealth becomes *equably distributed*; for by *equably distributed* I do not mean, that every individual comes to have an *equal* share, but an equal chance, I may say a certainty, of becoming rich in proportion to his industry' (*PPO2* 11:131–2). Steuart also argued that the potential for economic growth was almost without limit or certain boundary in the current 'situation of every country in Europe' – and especially France, 'at present in her infancy as to improvement, although the advances she has made within a century excite the admiration of the world'. An equally dramatic confirmation of the general theme is to be found in the chapter on machines, which he considered to be 'of the greatest utility' in 'augmenting the produce or assisting the labour and ingenuity of man'.

The argument taken as a whole is not lacking in sophistication and can be regarded as taking us beyond Smith's *Lectures*. And yet, like Smith, it must be noted that Steuart did not clearly distinguish between factors of production (land, labour, capital) or categories of return (rent, wages, profit). Nor is there any evidence of a macroeconomic model of the kind which was developed by the French economists from the late 1750s. It is intriguing to think what effect the work of the French economists might have had on Steuart's *Principles* had he not felt obliged to quit Paris just prior to the first appearance of the new *Tableau*.

Economic policy

Yet Steuart's position was not without its subtlety. The modern economy, based upon interdependent sectors and upon a system where all goods and services command a price, could be described quite graphically as involving 'a general tacit contract, from which reciprocal and proportional services result universally between all those who compose it'. But later he noted, 'Whenever...anyone is found, upon whom nobody depends, and who depends upon everyone, as is the case with him who is willing to work for his bread, but who can find no employment, there is a breach of the contract and an abuse' (*PPO1* 1:88; *PPO2* 1:101). There is a real sense in which this sentiment brings the reader to the core of Steuart's problem; that of public policy, reflecting in large measure his understanding of the problems which he confronted in Europe, and in Scotland at the time of writing. In Steuart's view, the true purpose of political economy is to secure a certain fund of subsistence for all the inhabitants, to obviate every circumstance which may render it precarious; to provide every thing necessary for supplying the wants of the society, and to employ the inhabitants (supposing them to be freemen) in such a manner as naturally to create reciprocal relations and dependencies between them. (*PPO1* 1:17; *PPO2* 1:21)

As in the case of Smith, the justification for intervention is market failure, although Steuart's position with respect to the functions of the state in fact arises directly from the areas of analysis and policy with which he was primarily concerned.

Looking back over the arguments which we have reviewed, it is appropriate firstly to recall Steuart's interest in *pre*-modern societies and in the *emergence* of the exchange economy. Steuart's concern with society in a process of transition is reflected in his attempt to formulate policies designed to deal with the problems generated by *historical* developments; developments which had caused cities to expand, and feudal retainers to be dismissed. It is in this context that the statesman is invited to consider the employment of redundant nobles and of the 'multitudes of poor', together with the all-important issue of the means of communication (such as good roads). In a striking passage which reminds the reader of his remarkable range of experience, Steuart observed,

Pipure, blue bonnets, and oat meal, are known in Swabia, Auvergne, Limousin and Catalonia, as well as in Lochaber: numbers of idle, poor, useless hands, multitudes of children, whom I have found to be fed, nobody knows how, doing almost nothing at the age of fourteen…If you ask why they are not employed, their parents will tell you because commerce is not in the country: they talk of commerce as if it was a man, who comes to reside in some countries in order to feed the inhabitants. The truth is, it is not the fault of these poor people, but of those whose business it is to find out employment for them. (*PPO1* 1:108; *PPO2* 1:123–24)

Steuart's general interest in regional issues is also a marked feature of the *Principles* and was to find further expression in his *Considerations on the Interest of the County of Lanark in Scotland*, which was first published in 1769 under the name of Robert Frame. This short work was explicitly designed to illustrate general principles by reference to a particular case; namely that of the backward county in which Steuart resided. In particular he contended that the infant-industry argument which merchants had applied to the textiles of Paisley should be extended to agriculture.[18] He also advocated high and stable prices for agricultural products, while calling for a granary scheme which would in effect secure supplies and stabilise incomes at a level which could be consistent with improvement. Steuart, who was deeply conscious of the imperfections in the markets for grain, and who had witnessed the suffering in Spain in the late 1730s, advocated a managed market in his *Dissertation on the Policy of Grain: with a View to a Plan for Preventing the Scarcity or Exorbitant Prices in the Common Markets of England* (1759). In this important document Walter Eltis finds evidence to suggest that Steuart had anticipated the modern recommendations of the EC. The contrast with Smith's position could hardly be more marked.[19]

Steuart's position is also distinctive in that, following Hume, he emphasised that trade takes place not merely between regions, but also between economies whose economic conditions are likely to vary (*PPO1* 1:296; *PPO2* 11:21). The contrast with Smith is remarkable: as Friedrich List remarked, the former's 'book is a mere treatise on the question: How the economy of the individuals and of mankind would stand, if the human race were not separated into nations, but united by a general law and by an equal culture of mankind.'[20]

Steuart handled the large number of possible 'combinations' suggested by his thesis in developing Hume's treatment of the problems presented by trade between rich and poor countries with differential rates of growth.[21] It is also significant that he chose to develop the *policy* implications which were involved by elaborating upon the stages of trade which Mirabeau had identified: the stages of infant, foreign and inland trade, each with its own distinctive policy implications.

Infant Trade represents a situation where the economy requires protection in order to develop industries and infrastructures which will enable the country, at some stage, to compete effectively. It was this policy which attracted the attention of Alexander Hamilton, faced as he was with the problems likely to confront the infant American economy following the Peace of Paris in 1783.

In the case of *Foreign Trade*, where a given economy can compete, Steuart recommended freedom of trade and an unrestricted monetary policy. In the case of *inland trade*, where a mature economy has (temporarily) lost its competitive edge (Hume's case), protection of the level of employment becomes paramount as does a restrictive monetary policy.

But it is sometimes forgotten that Steuart's 'stages of trade' apply not only to national economies, but also to particular industries and regions within them. Indeed, it is fair to claim that the state of 'foreign trade' may be interpreted as involving a capacity to compete within the framework of a system of organised markets. The state of 'infant trade' may be restated to mean that active policies must be followed so that the necessary infrastructure is in place in order to ensure that markets are properly established, while 'industries' are sufficiently developed to enable a *capacity* to compete. In short, economic policy must always be related to *circumstances*.

Schumpeter's description of the work done by Ferdinando Galiani, whose *Della Moneta* (1751) was described by Hutchison as one of the 'peak achievements' of the period,[22] applied equally to Steuart (and Hume): 'one point about his thought must be emphasised... he was the one eighteenth century economist who... was completely free from the paralysing belief, that crept over the intellectual life of Europe, in practical principles that claim universal validity'.[23] The influence of Montesquieu is evident. But this line of thinking would be followed by Steuart, rather than Smith – fellow disciples though they were in respect of Hume.

ADAM SMITH

However relevant questions such as these may have been to the practical economist, they were not Smith's central concerns. As Hutchison has pointed out, 'from his observation and experience, both at home in Scotland, and during his travels in Europe – where he had studied economic problems more closely than any other English or Scottish economist of his time – Steuart had come to view policy from the standpoint of smaller and less advanced economies, and to develop his ideas regarding policy for infant trades'.[24]

Yet Smith was not unaware of many of Steuart's concerns. He readily acknowledged the benefit which he had received from his residence in a 'mercantile town [Glasgow] situated in an unimproved country' (*WN* III.iv.3). Earlier, in a letter to Lord Shelbourne, he had spoken of his admiration for the attempt (in Ireland) 'to introduce arts, industry and independency into a miserable country, which has hitherto been a stranger to them all. Nothing, I have often imagined, would give more pleasure to Sir William Petty, your Lordship's ever honoured ancestor, than to see his representative pursuing a Plan so suitable to his own Ideas which are generally equally wise and public spirited'.[25] Smith, who ignored Steuart in the *Wealth of Nations*, is said to have 'understood Sir James's system better from his conversation than from his volumes'.[26] Unfortunately, there is no record of a conversation which might have reflected credit upon both men.

Adam Smith resigned his chair in Glasgow in February 1764, by which time he was already in France. The visit, which took place between 1764 and 1766, was the result of his appointment as tutor to the young Duke of Buccleuch, an appointment which owed much to the statesman Charles Townshend. From the standpoint of the development of economic *theory*, the most interesting part of the story is the visit to Paris which took place between February and October of 1766. In this period Smith met many of the *philosophes*, but especially François Quesnay and the great Minister of Finance (yet to be), A. R. J. Turgot. Quesnay was the founder member of the 'Physiocratic School' of French Economists, whose original model of the *Tableau Economique* (1758) was undergoing a further revision, the *Analyse*, in this period. At the same time, Turgot was preparing his *Reflections on the Formation and Distribution of Riches*.

In due course, Smith was to recognise that the system, 'with all its imperfections, is, perhaps, the nearest approximation to the truth that has yet been published upon the subject of political oeconomy, and is upon that account well worth the consideration of every man who wishes to examine with attention the principles of that very important science' (*WN* iv.ix.38). The reason for this assessment may be found in the Physiocrats' definition of wealth, in their liberal attitude to trade policy, but above all else in the quality of the basic model. Quesnay's purpose was both practical and theoretical. As Meek has indicated, Quesnay announced his purpose in a letter to Mirabeau which accompanied the first edition of the *Tableau*: 'I have tried to construct a fundamental *Tableau* of the economic order for the purpose of displaying expenditure and products in a way which is easy to grasp. And for the purpose of forming a clear opinion about the organisation and disorganisation which the government can bring about.'[27] But the model in question sought to explore the inter-relationships between output, the generation of income, expenditure and consumption – or in Quesnay's words, a 'general system of expenditure, work, gain and consumption',[28] which would expose the point that 'the whole magic of a well ordered society is that each man works for others, while believing that he is working for himself'.[29] As Meek put it: 'In this circle of economic activity, production and consumption appeared as mutually interdependent variables, whose action and interaction in any economic period, proceeding according to certain socially determined laws, laid the basis of a repetition of the process in the next economic period'.[30]

The model which Quesnay (and Mirabeau) developed provided a 'picture' of an economic system with distinct sectors of activity (agriculture, manufacture, trade) and the appropriate socio-economic classes. Significantly, the model introduced the importance of both fixed and circulating *capital*, in the context of a model where all magnitudes are dated. Turgot went further in offering a distinction between factors of production (land, labour and capital) and categories of return (rent, wages and profit). Schumpeter described the basic model as marking 'the great breach' and went on to point out that only 'with the help of such an analysis was it possible for further knowledge of the economic life process of society to develop and were scholars enabled to survey all the general factors and their functions as well as all the elements which have to be considered in every economic problem'.[31] Elsewhere, Schumpeter noted that the model, so admired by Smith (*WN* IV:ix), represented the 'first method ever devised in order to convey an *explicit* conception of the nature of economic equilibrium'.[32]

That Smith benefited from his examination of the French system was quickly noted by Cannan. In referring to the theories of distribution and to the macro-economic dimensions, Cannan noted: 'When we find that there is no trace of these theories in the *Lectures*, and that in the meantime Adam Smith had been to France...it is difficult to understand, why we should be asked, without any evidence, to refrain from believing that he came under physiocratic influence after and not before or during his Glasgow period'. He added: 'Adam Smith, as his chapter on agricultural systems shows, did not appreciate the minutiae of the table very highly, but he certainly took these main ideas and adopted them as well as he could to his Glasgow theories'.[33] Smith's debts to the physiocratic model may be seen in the content of the analytical apparatus which was developed in the first two books of *WN*. In these books, Smith in effect transformed his earlier, sophisticated, analysis of the interdependence of economic phenomena in such a way as to permit him to create a system which was at once descriptive and analytical.

Smith: a model of conceptualised reality (the wealth of nations)

The concept of an economy involving a flow of goods and services and the appreciation of the importance of intersectoral dependencies were familiar in the eighteenth century. Such themes are dominant features of the work done, for example, by Sir James Steuart and David Hume. But what is distinctive about Smith's work, at least as compared with his *Scottish* contemporaries, is the emphasis given to the importance of *three distinct factors* of production (land, labour, capital) and to the three categories of return (rent, wages, profit) which correspond to them. What is distinctive to the modern eye is the way in which Smith deployed these concepts in providing an account of the flow of goods and services between the sectors involved and between the different socio-economic groups (proprietors of land, capitalists and wage-labour). The approach is also of interest in that Smith, following the lead of the French economists, worked in terms of period analysis – the year was typically chosen, so that the working of the economy is examined within a significant time dimension as well as over a series of time periods. Both versions of the argument emphasise the importance of capital, fixed and circulating.

Taking the economic system as a whole, Smith suggested that the *total stock of society* could be divided into three parts. There is, first, that part of the total stock which is reserved for immediate *consumption*, and which is held by all consumers (capitalists, labour and proprietors) reflecting purchases made in previous time periods. The characteristic feature of this part of the total stock is that it affords no revenue to its possessors, since it consists in the stock of 'food, cloaths, household furniture, etc., which have been purchased by their proper consumers, but which are not yet entirely consumed' (*WN* 11.i.12).

Secondly, there is that part of the total stock which may be described as '*fixed capital*' and which will be distributed between the various groups of society. This part of the stock, Smith suggested, is composed of the 'useful machines' purchased in preceding periods but currently held by the undertakers engaged in manufacture, the quantity of useful buildings and of 'improved land' in the possession of the 'capitalist' farmers and the proprietors, together with the 'acquired and useful abilities' of all the inhabitants (WN 11.i.13–17), that is, human capital.

Thirdly, there is that part of the *total* stock which may be described as '*circulating capital*', and which again has several components, these being:

1 The quantity of money necessary to carry on the process of circulation.
2 The stock of provisions and other agricultural products that are available for sale during the current period, but are still in the hands of either the farmers or merchants.
3 The stock of raw materials and work in process, held by merchants, undertakers, or those capitalists engaged in the agricultural sector (including mining).
4 The stock of manufactured goods (consumption and investment goods) created during the previous period, but which remain in the hands of undertakers and merchants at the beginning of the period examined. (WN 11.i.19 22)

The logic of the process can be best represented by separating the activities involved much in the manner of the physiocratic model with which Smith was familiar. Let us suppose that, at the beginning of the time period in question, the major capitalist groups possess the total net receipts earned from the sale of products in the previous period, and that the undertakers engaged in agriculture open by transmitting the total rent due to the proprietors of land for the current use of that factor. The income thus provided will enable the proprietors to make the necessary purchases of consumption (and investment) goods in the current period, thus contributing to reducing the stocks of such goods with which the undertakers and merchants began the period.

Secondly, let us assume that the undertakers engaged in both sectors, together with the merchant groups, transmit to wage-labour the content of the wages fund, thus providing this socio-economic class with an income that can be used in the current period. It is worth noting in this connection that the capitalist groups transmit a fund to wage-labour which formed a part of their *savings*, providing by this means an income that is available for current *consumption*.

Thirdly, the undertakers engaged in agriculture and manufactures will make purchases of consumption and investment goods from each other, through the medium of retail and wholesale merchants, thus generating a series of expenditures linking the two major sectors. Finally, the process of circulation may be seen to be completed by the purchases made by individual undertakers within their own sectors. Once again, these purchases will include consumption and investment goods, thus contributing still further to reducing the stocks of commodities that were available for sale when the period under examination began, and which formed part of the circulating capital of the society in question. Looked at in this way, the 'circular flow' could be seen to involve purchases that take goods from the circulating capital of society, which are in turn matched by a continuous process of *replacement* by virtue of current production of materials and finished goods – where both types of production require the use of the fixed and circulating capitals of individual entrepreneurs, while generating the income flows needed to purchase commodities (and services). Smith elaborated on the argument.

The expenditure of the consumers of particular commodities in effect replaces the outlays of those who retail them, just as the capital of the retailer replaces, together with its profits, that of the wholesale merchant from whom he purchases goods, thereby enabling him to continue in business (*WN* 11.v.9). In turn, the capital of the wholesale merchant replaces, together with their profits, the capitals of the farmers and manufacturers of whom he purchases the rude and manufactured products which he deals in, and thereby enables them to continue their respective trades (*WN* 11.v.10). At the same time, part of the capital of the master manufacturer is 'employed as a fixed capital in the instruments of his trade, and replaces, together with its profits, that of some other artificer of whom he purchases them. Part of his circulating capital is employed in purchasing materials, and replaces, with their profits, the capitals of the farmers and miners of whom he purchases them. But a great part of it is always, either annually or in a much shorter period, distributed among the different workmen whom he employs' (*WN* II.v.II). The farmers perform a similar function with regard to the manufacturing sector.

A conceptual analytical system: a modern analysis

The 'conceptual' *model* which Smith had in mind when writing the *Wealth of Nations* is instructive and also helps to illustrate the series of separate, but interrelated, problems which economists must address if they are to attain the end which Smith proposed, namely an understanding of the *full range* of problems which have to be encountered. Smith in fact addressed a series of areas of analysis which began with the problem of value, before proceeding to the discussion of the determinants of price, the allocation of resources between competing uses, and, finally, an analysis of the forces which determine the distribution of income in any one time period and over time.

The analysis offered in the first Book enabled Smith to proceed directly to the treatment of macro-economic issues and especially to a theory of growth, which provides one of the dominant features of the work as a whole.[34] The idea of a single all-embracing conceptual system whose parts should be mutually consistent is not an ideal which is so easily attainable in an age where the division of labour has significantly increased the quantity of science through specialisation. But Smith becomes even more informative when we map the content of the 'conceptual (analytical) system' against a model of the economy, which is essentially descriptive.

Perhaps the most significant feature of Smith's vision of the 'economic process', to use Blaug's phrase, lies in the fact that it has a significant time dimension. For example, in dealing with the problems of value in exchange, Smith, following Hutcheson, made due allowance for the fact that the process involves judgements with regard to the utility of the commodities to be received, and the disutility involved in creating the commodities to be exchanged. In the manner of his predecessors, Smith was aware of the distinction between utility (and disutility) anticipated and realised, and, therefore, of the process of adjustment which would take place through time. Jeffrey Young has recently emphasised that the process of exchange may itself be a source of pleasure (utility).[35]

In an argument which bears upon the analysis of the *Theory of Moral Sentiments*, Smith also noted that choices made by the

'rational' individual may be constrained by the reaction of the spectator of his conduct – a much more complex situation than that which
more modern approaches may suggest. Smith makes much of the
point in his discussion of Mandeville's 'licentious' doctrine that private vices are public benefits, in suggesting that the gratification of
desire is perfectly consistent with observance of the rules of propriety as defined by the 'spectator', i.e. by an external agency. In an interesting variant on this theme, Etzioni has noted the need to recognise 'at least two irreducible sources of valuation or utility; pleasure
and morality'. He added that modern utility theory 'does not recognise the distinct standing of morality as a major, distinct, source of
valuations and hence as an explanation of behaviour', before going on
to suggest that his own 'deontological multi-utility model' is closer
to Smith than other modern approaches.[36]

Smith's theory of price, which allows for a wide range of changes
in taste, is also distinctive in that it allows for competition among
and between buyers and sellers, while presenting the allocative
mechanism as one which involves simultaneous and interrelated
adjustments in both factor and commodity markets. As befits a
writer who was concerned to address the problems of change and
adjustment, Smith's position was also distinctive in that he was not
directly concerned with the problem of *equilibrium*. For him the
'natural' (supply) price was 'as it were, the central price, to which
the prices of all commodities are continually gravitating... whatever
may be the obstacles which hinder them from settling in this center
of repose and continuance, they are constantly tending towards it'
(*WN* I.vii.15).

The picture was further refined in the sense that Smith introduced
into this discussion the doctrine of net advantages (*WN* I.x.a.1). This
technical area is familiar to labour economists, but in Smith's case it
becomes even more interesting in the sense that it provides a further
link with the *TMS*, and with the discussion of constrained choice.
It was Smith's contention that men would only be prepared to em-
bark on professions which attracted the disapprobation of the spectator if they could be suitably compensated in terms of monetary
reward.[37]

But perhaps the most intriguing feature of the macro-economic
model is to be found in the way in which it was specified. As
noted earlier, Smith argued that incomes are generated as a result of

productive activity, thus making it possible for commodities to be withdrawn from the 'circulating' capital of society. As he pointed out, the consumption of goods withdrawn from the existing stock may be used up in the present period, or added to the stock reserved for immediate consumption, or used to replace more durable goods which had reached the end of their lives in the current period. In a similar manner, undertakers and merchants may add to their stock of materials, or to their holdings of fixed capital while replacing the plant which had reached the end of its operational life. It is equally obvious that undertakers and merchants may add to, or reduce, their *inventories* in ways which will reflect the changing patterns of demand for consumption and investment goods, and their past and current levels of production.

Smith's emphasis upon the point that different 'goods' have different life-cycles means that the pattern of purchase and replacement may vary continuously as the economy moves through different time periods, and in ways which reflect the various age profiles of particular products as well as the pattern of demand for them. If Smith's model of the 'circular flow' is to be seen as a spiral, rather than a circle, it soon becomes evident that this spiral is likely to expand (and *contract*) through time at variable rates.

It is perhaps this total vision of the complex working of the economy that led Mark Blaug to comment on Smith's sophisticated grasp of the economic process and to distinguish this from his contribution to particular areas of economic analysis.[38] Blaug noted:

In appraising Adam Smith, or any other economist, we ought always to remember that brilliance in handling purely economic concepts is a very different thing from a firm grasp of the essential logic of economic relationships. Superior technique does not imply superior insight and vice-versa. Judged by a standard of analytical competence, Smith is not the greatest of eighteenth-century economists. But for an acute insight into the nature of the economic process, it would be difficult to find Smith's equal.[39]

Joseph Schumpeter, not always a warm critic of Adam Smith, yet regarded the *Wealth of Nations* as 'the peak success of (the) period': 'though the *Wealth of Nations* contained no really novel ideas, and though it cannot rank with Newton's *Principia* or Darwin's *Origin* as an intellectual achievement, it is a great performance all the same and fully deserved its success'.[40] Writing from a different perspective, Macfie noted that 'the Scottish method was more concerned with giving a broad, well balanced comprehensive picture, seen from different points of view than with logical rigour'. The approach was not narrowly 'mathematical' at least in style.[41]

THE AFTERMATH

On the side of policy, the general impression left by the historical evidence is that by 1826 not only economists but a great many other influential public men were prepared to give assent and support to the system of natural liberty and the consequent doctrine of free trade set out by Adam Smith.[42]

Black recorded that the system of natural liberty attracted attention on the occasion of every anniversary. But a cautionary note was struck by Jacob Viner in 1926. Having reviewed Smith's treatment of the functions of the state in 'Adam Smith and Laissez Faire', a seminal article, Viner concluded: 'Adam Smith was not a doctrinaire of laissez faire. He saw a wide and elastic range of activity for government, and he was prepared to extend it even farther if government, by improving its standards of competence, honesty, and public spirit, showed itself entitled to wider responsibilities'.[43] But this sophisticated view, which is now quite general, does not qualify Lionel Robbins's point that Smith developed an important argument to the effect that economic freedom 'rested on a twofold basis: belief in the desirability of freedom of choice for the consumer and belief in the effectiveness, in meeting this choice, of freedom on the part of producers'.[44] Smith added a dynamic dimension to this theme in his discussion of the Corn Laws (WN IV.v.b). The thesis has proved to be enduringly attractive.

Analytically, the situation is also intriguing. Teichgraeber's research revealed that there 'is no evidence to show that many people exploited his arguments with great care before the first two decades of the nineteenth century'.[45] He concluded: 'It would seem at the time of his death that Smith was widely known and admired as the author of the *Wealth of Nations*. Yet it should be noted too that only a handful of his contemporaries had come to see his book as uniquely influential.'[46] Black has suggested that for Smith's early nineteenth-century successors, the *Wealth of Nations* was 'not so much a classical monument to be inspected, as a structure to be examined and improved where necessary'.[47] There were ambiguities in Smith's treatment of value, interest, rent and population theory. These ambiguities were reduced by the work of Ricardo, Malthus, James Mill and J. B. Say, making it possible to think of a classical system which was dominated by a short-run self-equilibrating mechanism and a long-run theory of growth. The new system was essentially mathematical in character.

Smith thus came to be regarded as the 'founding father' of a new discipline, an outcome which might have given him little pleasure, had he known it. If this was the perception of the early proponents of a classical system, the result was to prove unfortunate, not least because the history of the subject was seen to date from 1776. Donald Winch quotes an important passage from the French economist J. B. Say, a committed disciple, to the effect that 'whenever the Inquiry into the *Wealth of Nations* is perused with the attention it so well deserves, it will be perceived that until the epoch of its publication, the science of political economy did not exist'.[48]

This prevalent view caused problems. As Hutchison has argued, 'the losses and exclusions which ensued after 1776, with the subsequent transformation of the subject and the rise to dominance of the English classical orthodoxy were immense'.[49] Among these losses were many of the issues identified by Hume and Steuart. The use of the historical method in addressing theoretical issues was one such loss; another was the concern with unemployment and the model of primitive accumulation, while in addition the classical orthodoxy showed little interest in the problems presented by differential rates of growth or of underdeveloped economies.

Ironically, the conventional perception of Smith's own contribution also suffered as a result of the developing orthodoxy. Here attention may be drawn to Smith's concern with time; his concern with processes of adjustment rather than equilibrium states. Nor did Smith's vision of the 'circular flow' feature broadly in the new orthodoxy, with its complex focus on period analysis and on the fact that all commodities have different life-cycles.

More serious still was the fact that the classical orthodoxy made it possible to think of economics as quite separate and distinct from ethics and jurisprudence, thus obscuring Smith's true purpose. As Terence Hutchison noted, Adam Smith was unwittingly led by an Invisible Hand to promote an end that was no part of his intention, that of 'establishing political economy as a separate autonomous discipline'.[50]

NOTES

1   Subsequently reprinted in A. L. Macfie, *The Individual in Society* (London: Allen and Unwin, 1967).

2   D. Mair, 'Introduction', and S. C. Dow, 'The Scottish Political Economy Tradition', in D. Mair, ed., *The Scottish Contribution to Modern Economic Thought* (Aberdeen: Aberdeen University Press, 1990).

3   D. Winch, 'Nationalism and Cosmopolitanism in the Early Histories of Political Economy', in M. Albertone and A. Macoero, eds., *Political Economy and National Realities* (Turin: Fondazione Luigi Einaudi, 1994), 92.

4   T. W. Hutchison, *Before Adam Smith: the Emergence of Political Economy, 1662–1776* (Oxford: Blackwell, 1988), 224.

5   See C. Shepherd, 'Newtonianism in Scottish Universities in the Seventeenth Century', in R. H. Campbell and A. S. Skinner, eds., *The Origins and Nature of the Scottish Enlightenment* (Edinburgh: John Donald, 1982), 67.

6   Colin Maclaurin, *An Account of Sir Isaac Newton's Philosophical Discoveries*, 3rd edn (1775).

7   Ibid., 356.

8   Ibid., 9.

9   Adam Smith, *The History of Astronomy*, in Smith, *Essays on Philosophical Subjects*, eds. W. P. D. Wightman and J. C. Bryce (Oxford: Clarendon Press, 1980), IV.19.

10 See Adam Smith, *Lectures on Justice, Police, Revenue and Arms*, ed. E. Cannan (London: 1896); and W. R. Scott, *Francis Hutcheson: his Life, Teaching and Position in the History of Philosophy* (Cambridge: Cambridge University Press, 1900).

11 Included in David Hume, *Essays Moral, Political and Literary*, ed. Eugene F. Miller (Indianapolis: Liberty Fund, 1985).

12 E. Rotwein, ed., *David Hume: Writings on Economics* (Edinburgh: Edinburgh University Press, 1955).

13 Cf. Adam Smith, *An Inquiry into the Nature and Causes of the Wealth of Nations*, eds. R. H. Campbell, A. S. Skinner and W. B. Todd, 2 vols. (Oxford: Clarendon Press, 1976), III. (Hereinafter *WN*.)

14 Smith accepted the logic of this position in his *Lectures on Jurisprudence* rather than in his *Wealth of Nations*.

15 I. Hont, 'The Rich Country – Poor Country Debate in Scottish Political Economy', in I. Hont and M. Ignatieff, eds., *Wealth and Virtue: the*

Shaping of Political Economy in the Scottish Enlightenment
(Cambridge: Cambridge University Press, 1983), 274–5.

16 Sir James Steuart, *An Inquiry into the Principles of Political Oeconomy*,
ed. A. S. Skinner, 2 vols. (Edinburgh: Oliver and Boyd, 1966) (hereinafter
PPO1); also, Sir James Steuart, *An Inquiry into the Principles of Political Oeconomy*, eds. A. S. Skinner, K. Noboru and M. Hiroshi, 4 vols.
(London: Pickering and Chatto, 1998). (Hereinafter *PPO2*.)

17 P. Chamley, *Documents Relatifs à Sir James Steuart* (Paris: Librairie
Dalloz, 1965), 50.

18 Sir James Steuart, *Works, Political, Metaphysical and Chronological*,
6 vols. (London: 1805), v:308.

19 Walter Eltis, 'Sir James Steuart's Corporate State', in R. D. C. Black,
ed., *Ideas in Economics* (London: 1986), 44; cf. A. S. Skinner, *A System
of Social Science: Papers Relating to Adam Smith*, 2nd edn (Oxford:
Clarendon Press,1996), ch. 8.

20 K. P. Tribe, *Governing Economy: the Reformation of German Economic
Discourse, 1750–1840* (Cambridge: Cambridge University Press, 1988),
39.

21 Hont, 'Rich Country – Poor Country Debate'.

22 Hutchison, *Before Adam Smith*, 186.

23 J. A. Schumpeter, *A History of Economic Analysis* (London: Oxford
University Press, 1954), 293–4.

24 Hutchison, *Before Adam Smith*, 349.

25 Adam Smith, *The Correspondence of Adam Smith*, eds. E. S. Mossner
and I. S. Ross (Oxford: Clarendon Press, 1977), 32.

26 John Rae, *Life of Adam Smith* (1895; reprint, London: Macmillan, 1965),
63.

27 R. L. Meek, comp., *The Economics of Physiocracy: Essays and Translations* (London: Allen and Unwin, 1962), 108.

28 Ibid., 374.

29 Ibid., 70.

30 Ibid., 19.

31 Schumpeter, *History of Economic Analysis*, 43.

32 Ibid., 242.

33 Adam Smith, *The Wealth of Nations*, ed. E. Cannan, 2 vols. (London:
Methuen, 1904), 1.xxxi.

34 Cf. Skinner, *System of Social Science*, ch. 7.

35 Jeffrey T. Young, *Economics as a Moral Science: the Political Economy
of Adam Smith* (Cheltenham: Edward Elgar, 1997), 61.

36 A. Etzioni, *The Moral Dimension: Toward a New Economics* (London:
Collier Macmillan, 1988), 21–4.

37 Skinner, *System of Social Science*, 155.

38 Mark Blaug, *Economic Theory in Retrospect*, 4th edn (Cambridge: Cambridge University Press, 1985); cf. H. E. Jensen, 'Sources and Contours of Adam Smith's Conceptualized Reality in the *Wealth of Nations*', in J. C. Wood, ed., *Adam Smith: Critical Assessments*, 4 vols. (London: Croom Helm, 1984), 11.193–204; A. Jeck, 'The Macro-structure of Adam Smith's Theoretical System', *European Journal of the History of Economic Thought* 1, no. 3 (1994), 551–76; and K. R. Ranadive, 'The Wealth of Nations – the Vision and the Conceptualization', in Wood, *Adam Smith*, 11.244–70.

39 Blaug, *Economic Theory*, 57.

40 Schumpeter, *History of Economic Analysis*, 185.

41 Macfie, *Individual in Society*, 22–3.

42 R. D. C. Black, 'Smith's Contribution in Historical Perspective', in T. Wilson and A. S. Skinner, eds., *The Market and the State: Essays in Honour of Adam Smith* (Oxford: Clarendon Press, 1976), 47.

43 J. Viner, 'Adam Smith and Laissez Faire', in Wood, *Adam Smith*, 1.143–67, 164.

44 L. Robbins, *The Theory of Economic Policy in English Classical Political Economy* (London: Macmillan, 1952), 12.

45 R. Teichgraeber, 'Less Abused than I had Reason to Expect', *Historical Journal* 30 (1987), 339.

46 Ibid., 363.

47 Black, 'Smith's Contribution', 44.

48 Winch, 'Nationalism and Cosmopolitanism', 103.

49 Hutchison, *Before Adam Smith*, 370.

50 Ibid., 355.

10 Natural jurisprudence and the theory of justice

COMMON FEATURES

Natural jurisprudence in the Scottish Enlightenment was first of all a theory of justice. Understood in this way, there are at least a couple of characteristics which give Scottish natural jurisprudence a specific difference from other major schools of thought and lend it a certain coherence for a century or more. One of them is that justice was not seen as a particular state of affairs or condition of the world in general. Scottish justice is not directly a matter of the distribution of goods or relations between classes of people. Nor is justice a formal quality of law in the abstract, a criterion for whether a rule in some sense *really* is 'valid law'. To put it more directly, eighteenth-century Scottish natural jurisprudence is neither Platonic, Aristotelian, Thomistic, Kantian nor utilitarian. In several of its expressions, it does have features in common with the empirical and naturalistic sides of Aristotelianism and utilitarianism, but neither suffices to characterise it. The common feature of the various Scottish theories of natural jurisprudence is that justice is to be treated as a characteristic of the individual person. Of course, a society – or a world – consisting of people with this feature is *just*, but that quality derives from the individuals making up the collective, and in the same way the justice of just law is a matter of the character of the individuals who adhere to such law.[1]

In other words, for the Scottish theorists, justice was primarily a personal *virtue*.[2] By virtue they meant two things, the propensity to a certain type of behaviour, and the ability to appreciate the moral worth of such behaviour both in oneself and in others. The behavioural aspect of their theory was seen as – and sometimes

called – their practical ethics, while the concern with moral judgement was considered to be purely theoretical or 'metaphysical', a
part of the theory of the mind. Natural jurisprudence was that part
of practical ethics which dealt with the virtue of justice, and a central
task for this intellectual and academic discipline was to explain why
justice was distinguished from the rest of the virtues by being the
subject of the *institutions* of justice, namely adjudication, law and
legislation. For the second thing that is distinctive for the Scottish
theories of justice is the apparent paradox that their idea of justice as
a characteristic of the individual is intimately connected with their
social explanations of justice as an institutionalised practice.

DIVISIONS

As we have already seen, natural jurisprudence conceived as a theory
of justice must be seen as part of what the Scottish thinkers thought
of as a science of human nature or a moral science. While super-
ficially another common factor among them, this was in fact the
point at which their most fundamental division occurred – or, it is a
perspective from which the most important philosophical diversity
can be seen with particular clarity. The point is that 'science' (or
'philosophy'), both natural and moral, meant quite different things,
and it was theology that made the difference. While all the Scottish
thinkers saw themselves as 'Newtonians', concerned with the empirical demonstration of the regularities of the physical and the
moral realms, some of them – the large majority – took these regularities to be evidence of a divinely instituted order and purpose in
the world (thus following Newton himself and going a step further).
Stretching from Francis Hutcheson in the 1720s to Dugald Stewart
a century later, these people considered the sciences to have a moral
mission, namely to teach humanity the way in which individual
things and events, not least people's lives, had a role in the overall providence for God's creation.[3] However, outside of this mainstream of thought were a few thinkers, namely David Hume and
Adam Smith, who took a far more agnostic attitude to these matters
and for whom, accordingly, the morally prescriptive role of the sciences in general and of the moral sciences in particular was an issue
of a quite different order, as we will see.

THE MORAL SYSTEM

Central to the argument of the 'providentialists' in moral science was the idea of a moral *system*. They thought that humanity naturally forms an ordered moral community, not in the sense that such a community ever has been realised, but in the sense that it *would* be realised with the moral perfection of human nature in each individual and that it *will* be realised to the extent that we understand this possibility. A moral community is, at one and the same time, the natural goal and the natural motivation for people's moral development. The task of the science of morals is to explain this possibility and thus to encourage its realisation. This was one of the most important rationales for the pervasive practice of teaching moral philosophy, including natural jurisprudence, as the basis for all academic study. It was within the framework of this general concept of a moral order, an ideal system of humanity, that the Scots set about the empirical investigation of actual forms of order and system – societies and economies – and of how they arise from the activities of their component parts, namely individuals.

HUME'S AND SMITH'S DISSENT

This concern with empirical explanation was, of course, shared – in fact, led – by David Hume and Adam Smith, but neither of them endowed their scientific endeavours in morals with the kind of prescriptive task so characteristic of their contemporaries.[4] Both of them strongly criticised teleological explanations, and Hume was explicitly agnostic about a providential understanding of human life, while Smith made the (supposed) human susceptibility to providentialist thinking into a subject of explanation in its own right, thus side-stepping the question of its validity. For these two thinkers, therefore, any formation of human communities was not of morally prescriptive significance in its own right; moral community did not have transcendent, objective value; it was simply an empirical, historical fact. For thinkers such as Hutcheson the ultimate moral value of individual actions lay in their contribution to the perfection of the moral system of humanity (in the end of all moral beings); for Hume and Smith, no moral system could have such validating power. In fact, for the latter two men, actions, systems and moral judgements were empirical occurrences to be understood like all other parts of nature.

THE MORAL FACULTY

A central concern for all the Scottish thinkers in their 'Newtonian' endeavour was the moral faculties of the individual and on this topic, too, they put forward a variety of theories. From the point of view of the theory of the mind, the great dividing line was between those who saw the moral power in sensory terms and those who understood it as a power of judgement. For the former, such as Hutcheson,[5] Hume, and Smith, morality was a matter of a perceptive power which, in analogy with the external senses, stimulated the response of the sentiments and thus directed action. For the latter, notably Thomas Reid, James Oswald, James Beattie and Dugald Stewart, morality was a matter of judgement not inherently different from other forms of reasoning.[6] Several others – George Turnbull, Lord Kames, David Fordyce – tried to find compromise solutions in which sentiment and reason were balanced, though for most of them reason was the ultimate authority.[7] However, if we change the perspective from mental philosophy to natural jurisprudence, then Scottish moral theory can usefully be divided by a different criterion, namely whether the virtue of justice was an inherent part of human nature or whether it, somehow, was superadded to that nature.

MORALITY AS NATURE OR ARTIFICE

The question whether morality in general was natural or whether it was an artificial device invented to regulate man's passions and thus make social life possible was an ancient one raised with particular sharpness by the Epicureans. A similar question was made urgent by some strands of Reformation theology according to which fallen human nature was so depraved that it was incapable either of understanding or of following divine injunctions or of both. Accordingly, it was thought, humanity was left to invent its own political and juridical means of living in peace. In some major natural lawyers of the seventeenth century who were of great significance to the Scots, notably Thomas Hobbes and Samuel Pufendorf, such ideas were developed into a radically conventionalist view of morality, society and politics.[8] Furthermore, in the latter half of the seventeenth and in the early eighteenth centuries, neo-Epicureans, especially French, further accentuated the discussion of the foundation of morality by denying that morality had any hold in nature, a provocation that reached a high point in Bernard Mandeville's argument that all morality is a matter of vanity.

The reactions to these developments were many and varied. To mention just a few, within English moral thought in the seventeenth century the Cambridge Platonists, Benjamin Whichcote, Henry More and Ralph Cudworth, and the later ethical rationalists, Samuel Clarke and William Wollaston, were of particular importance; and within natural jurisprudence, there was a strong reassertion of basically scholastic ideas by Gottfried Wilhelm Leibniz and Christian Wolff. However, in our context an especially significant factor was a Christianised Stoicism which in Scotland was developed by Hutcheson.

NATURAL JUSTICE: HUTCHESON

Hutcheson took up, most directly from the English natural lawyer Richard Cumberland, the idea of a moral system which was outlined above and combined it with the notion of a native moral sense for which he found particular inspiration in Anthony Ashley Cooper, Lord Shaftesbury.[9] The basic argument was that human nature includes a moral sense which recognises benevolence as the core of moral action; further, that when the moral sense is enlightened and not distorted by selfish passions, a person's judgement and behaviour will tend to contribute to the overall happiness of society and humanity. In other words, harmony between the moral life of the individual and perfection of the moral community is a possibility and, hence, a moral, ultimately a religious, duty for humanity. In this scheme of things, justice was a support of or contributary to benevolence, and, accordingly, it was as much part of humanity's natural potential as the rest of morality. This combination of a theory of individual judgement with a theory of an overarching moral system was the framework for the whole of Hutcheson's thought from the early works on the moral sense to the late textbooks on natural jurisprudence and it was perhaps his most fundamental legacy to the moral philosophy of the later Enlightenment in Scotland.[10]

This idea of justice as a natural virtue, and as a fundamental part of the moral development of which man was naturally capable and to which he was providentially appointed, remained central to what I earlier called the mainstream of Scottish thought. It cut across the divisions over the 'metaphysical' concern with the specific character of the moral faculties of the mind which we indicated above. We thus find the same sort of argument concerning the natural character of justice in Kames and Reid as in Hutcheson and Turnbull.

NATURE AND ARTIFICE: HUME

It was a line of argument, however, which was severely challenged by Hume and, in his own way, by Smith. Basing his argument on what he considered empirical facts about human nature and its environment, Hume suggested that one part of morality was 'natural' to the species, another 'artificial'.[11] From the hand of nature, or considered in abstraction from social life, people exhibit a combination of benevolence towards those who are close to themselves and self-interested exclusion of those further removed. Hume details this basic thought in well-known analyses of the natural virtues and their limitations, the central point here being that these qualities are the foundation for small, close social groups, especially the family, but that they are incapable of supporting lasting society among people who are strangers to each other.

To this latter purpose, justice is needed – but justice is not part of our nature. A virtue such as benevolence is simply a sentiment that comes naturally to our mind when we are faced with particular individuals qua human beings who somehow touch us; it is natural in the sense that it is spontaneously shared with others in the same situation. Justice is an attitude which is always directed to objects that already presuppose a belief in the virtue of justice. Thus when I justly repay a loan, the justice of my action presupposes that loan repayment is a just form of behaviour; and the justice of such behaviour presupposes the justice of private property from which loans can be made; while the justice of private property presupposes the justice of dividing up the world between people at all. However, we can have no common notion of the justice of such division unless we already have agreed on it – in which case we have to have the notion before agreeing on it! In other words, while the objects of the natural virtues are natural persons, the objects of justice are human creations or artifices. But these cannot be of the sort that are brought into existence by deliberate human action for in that case they would be the result of virtuous – just – behaviour, thus creating the circle of argument indicated.

Justice is an 'artificial' virtue because its objects – typically property – must be brought into the world by human actions which do not have these objects as their intended object. It was the logic of this argument that led Hume to the most original contribution of all the Scots to the theory of justice, namely that the objects of justice as a virtue are the unintended creations of people. Humanity by luck, chance and necessity falls upon certain forms of behaviour, such as trusting strangers with one's goods. As such behaviour 'works' – i.e. serves the self-interest of most members of the group in question and thus the 'public interest' of the group as a whole – it becomes an observable pattern of behaviour. This will tend to be seen as a rule which can be the object of *common* sentiments of regard, moral sentiments. Not least, the failure of such behaviour on the part of individuals who break the rule can become the object of common displeasure and thus instil a sense of duty. In this way justice is superimposed upon human nature as a quality of character along with those issued to us by nature herself, such as benevolence or cleanliness.[12] However, justice is not superimposed by the scheming of reason; it has a firm anchor in nature, first, by being a practice that is necessary for the life of the species; secondly, by being a sentiment about such practices.

SMITH'S SYNTHESIS

Hume's denial that justice is a natural virtue on a par with the rest of morality was a serious provocation to the rest of the Scottish Enlightenment community and was one of the reasons why he was never allowed into a university.[13] In the case of Adam Smith, however, the provocation was not moral but intellectual. Continuing where Hume left off, Smith basically argued that not only justice, but the whole of morality supervened upon human nature in somewhat the manner that Hume argued for justice. One might say that Smith suggested that morality in general was 'artificial' – but that it was an artifice that, as it were, was 'natural' to humankind. In other words,

Smith tried to sidestep the controversy by showing that the old distinction between nature and artifice was spurious. At the core of Smith's intricate argument was the idea that people's personhood, their ability to be self-conscious agents vis-à-vis other persons and vis-à-vis their own past and future self, was something acquired in the social intercourse with others. As a consequence, it was impossible to conceive of a 'natural' person, a person in a pure state of nature such as that imagined by Rousseau. All our qualities as persons, including those we normally call moral, are derived from living socially with others.

This is one of the most important aspects of Smith's theory of spectatorship. The argument is that if the activity of a person is to be seen – by others and by the person herself – as belonging to that person in more than the sense of being physically caused by her, then the activity in question has to be seen from a standpoint that is common to both spectators and the person who is active. At least, there has to be awareness of an attempt to reach such a standpoint. Without a common perspective – or the will to get one – there can be no judgement of the activity as anything other than a causal event in time and space to which anyone may react subjectively or which may be explained in causal terms as a natural event. In order for the event to be an action of a person, it has to be seen as the sort of thing that is subject to common assessment by 'any' agent in a similar situation. The moral life of the species can be seen as the search for such common standpoints from which the propriety or suitability of actions to their situation can be judged.[14] Over time certain regularities can be discerned in this search and these are commonly specified in terms of the qualities of character that lie behind, that is in terms of the virtues, including justice.[15]

Although Smith boldly rejected the distinction between natural and artificial virtues which was the premise for Hume's theory of justice and for his profound differences with the rest of the moral thinkers of the Scottish Enlightenment, it is nevertheless the case that Smith in important ways was closer to Hume than to the rest in the theory of justice. For Hutcheson, just behaviour was an immediate expression of a natural sentiment; just as for Reid it was an effect of a common sense judgement. For Hume justice concerned three artificial extensions of the natural person, namely relations to things, other persons and events (property, promises and contracts) which were amoral in abstraction from conventional forms of behaviour. This, however, meant that justice was dependent upon general rules, as we have seen; consequently it was a virtue which was much more precise than the other virtues in its requirements of our behaviour. The good of another person, let alone of society at large, was a much vaguer notion than the idea of what is yours and what is mine because the latter is determined by the rules of the social group to which we belong.

This idea of the precision of justice was given a different, or at least a clearer, justification by Smith.[16] According to him the reason why individual questions of justice were open to clearer answers than individual questions of, say, benevolence, was not that the former were subject to general rules. The reason was, rather, that questions of justice were about injury and it was a matter of empirical fact about the human mind that it much more readily recognised what was injurious than what was beneficial to others. What was more, people tended to react with much greater strength against acts of injury than they did in favour of acts of benevolence; they were more willing to take action to suppress the former than to promote the latter. It was thus out of the general tendency of particular actions that general rules of justice, including punishment, arose and the precision of the latter derived from the certainty of the individual judgements. For this reason, Smith thought that the common law of England was more likely to achieve natural justice than the statute law of legislatures.[17]

JUSTICE AMONG THE VIRTUES

Against this background we can look again at the major dividing lines among the Scots concerning the status of justice among the virtues. The comparisons are at first confusing because *all* of the thinkers concerned maintained that justice was significantly different from the other virtues. As already mentioned, they all saw justice as the basis for law, which is to say as enforceable, and the reason for this was that 'mere' justice was the requirement for the minimal order that made society possible. In this Hume and Smith completely agreed; but behind the agreement were significant differences. For thinkers such as Hutcheson, Kames, Reid and Stewart, the special status of justice was a necessity arising from the less than satisfactory moral record of the species, a situation to be overcome. Through moral education humanity could and should be lifted to a stage where society did not rest on 'mere' justice but maintained a much richer common morality by political and legal means, as required by the greatest happiness or perfectibility of society and ultimately of the moral creation as a whole. In Hutcheson and Kames, the political implication was taken to be the promotion of an enlightened and civic-minded landed class, while Reid nourished a utopian vision of a moral commonwealth, a vision which Stewart turned into an historicist scheme of the march of the mind towards moral perfection.[18]

These lines of argument are entirely absent from Hume and Smith. For them civil society rested upon the enforcement of justice – the maintenance of the twelve judges, as Hume's hyperbole has it.[19] This is not to say that they did not agree that justice often was a less than admirable virtue, a purely negative virtue, as we have seen; one which we often may honour by sitting still and doing nothing, as Smith put it.[20] And in their ways Hume and Smith were as keen on a richer moral life as any of their contemporary compatriots. But they did not think that it was possible for people to discern a moral plot in the life of the human world that would justify a moral agenda for government. Governments might well have reasons for doing specific goods, such as promoting literacy, even on occasions when the good promoted was at the expense of justice, such as preventing starvation. But government could not have well-founded reasons for making people good.

THE QUESTION OF RIGHTS

It is an important feature of Scottish theories of justice in the Enlightenment that neither of the major lines of argument which were outlined above gives rights a fundamental role. This is despite the fact that modern natural jurisprudence was introduced into Scottish philosophy by a significant proponent of rights theory, namely Gershom Carmichael. In a major edition of Samuel Pufendorf's *De officio hominis et civis*, Carmichael, in notes and appendices, argued in the mode of Reformed scholastics in Holland and Switzerland that God with His brief to humanity, namely to seek the highest beatitude in the love of God through love of His creation, had issued man with the right to pursue this love in his own way, which meant first of all a right to take care of his own life and of that of people dependent upon him.[21]

Hutcheson's emphasis is quite different. For him the basic assumption is God's love of humanity which entails that people, in the image of God, will love each other. This is what he formulates in philosophical terms as the moral sense and the basic virtue of benevolence. In such a scheme, the idea of rights was of secondary importance.[22] Hutcheson certainly thought that people have a right to the virtuous behaviour of others; in the case of the positive virtues such as benevolence, the right was 'imperfect', that is to say, it could not justifiably be enforced; in contrast, the negative virtue of justice could be demanded as a matter of 'perfect' right, meaning that it was legally enforceable. However, in neither case was the right itself the ultimate justification of action. The claimed rights themselves rested upon the promotion of the highest good in situations where the moral sense of the agent had failed in virtuous behaviour, or in doing what was duty. Rights were a secondary device which was to be invoked in situations of moral malfunction and the moral ideal was to make them superfluous. Much the same can be said of the theories of Reid and Stewart. If morality is conceived as natural to humanity, then rights are either nothing but a different conceptualisation of virtue, or they are a demand for the restoration of virtue in cases of failure.

Hume found no use whatever for the concept of rights in his theory of justice. He did not explain why; nevertheless, it is possible to make a reasonable conjecture. Disregarding legal rights – rights in positive law – the concept of rights was commonly given a religious basis. In strong-rights theories such as in Carmichael and, more generally, in Calvinist resistance theory, the basic right of humanity, namely the right to free conscience, essentially meant God's voice in man. In weak-rights theories, such as that of Hutcheson's Christian Stoicism, rights were rather lowly means to the realisation of the divinely appointed happiness and perfection of the moral community. The former, strong-rights theory, was, to Hume's mind, nothing but a form of religious 'enthusiasm', while the latter, weak-rights theory, was tied up with the idea of a divine providence for humanity, an idea anathema to him.

It was left to Smith to rethink the matter of rights in light of his spectator theory of morals.[23] As we have seen, Smith stressed that justice was a 'negative' virtue, a virtue primarily of omission, namely omission of injury. The negative virtue of avoiding harm or injury was justice, which was the foundation of law and the subject of jurisprudence. The personal attributes and actions that are protected in each person when others show them justice, i.e. abstain from injuring them, are their rights. A right is a sphere of freedom to *be* or *do* or *have* something that the individual can maintain against all others because the spectatorial resentment of infringement of this sphere is so strong that it has been institutionalised in the form of the legal system. This was simply a different way of putting the idea of justice as something negative. The clarity and forcefulness with which we recognised and responded to injurious behaviour were the qualities that made rights special. Smith acknowledged that traditionally legal thinkers also talked of 'rights' to the performance of the positive virtues, but he clearly thought of this as less than perspicuous thinking.

As we saw above, Smith regarded moral personality as a product of socialisation; there was no room for the idea of a 'natural person'. Consequently injury and right would always be social concepts; there was no theoretically justified dividing line between natural rights and socially founded rights. The concepts of 'rights', 'injury' and 'personality' were linked. The moral imagination depends on social experience and hence varies from one stage of society to another. All consideration of our moral characteristics must therefore include the social setting; this applies not least to subjective claim-rights as a primary characteristic of humanity. Even so, certain minimal rights appear to be common to all social living. A social group is only viable if it, in general, recognises rights to physical, moral and some kind of social personality. These may accordingly be considered 'universal' and 'natural' rights in the sense that life without them would not be a recognisably *human* one. But it is important to appreciate that basic rights and, hence, justice in no other sense are necessary or have any special metaphysical status. They are as dependent upon the spectatorial recognition in social intercourse as are all other, 'positive', parts of morality. On this basic question, Smith is a completely consistent conventionalist.

JURISPRUDENCE AND HISTORY

The divisions which we have traced in Scottish natural jurisprudence in the Enlightenment may be pursued, finally, into the aspect of that intellectual culture which, perhaps, is most commonly known, namely its concern with history. The Scots took an historical view of, so to speak, all social and cultural phenomena but none was more important in the formulation of their historical view than law, as explained in John Cairns's chapter in this book. This raises the question of whether justice itself, as the moral foundation for law, also was subject to an historical view. While this was the case, it is complicated by the circumstance that there was more than one historical view. In the moral theories which built upon a providentialist idea of a moral community, or a moral system, as the goal of the moral life, history was basically a record of past attempts at moral perfection. But the moral perfection aimed at was a transcendence of history. In other words, morality in its pure form was above history.

In Hume and Smith, this was quite otherwise. Hume's theory of justice as a set of spontaneously emerging rule-bound practices for which people generate and internalise a regard was in its nature the framework for particular historical accounts. Even more radical in this regard, Smith's spectator theory made morality as a whole an historical phenomenon. The types of personality which were possible depended upon the available situations in which people could be spectators of each other and an important aspect of Smith's work was to create a rough typology of societies, namely the four stages theory, which indicated the major roles or forms of personality that were conceivable. The hunter could not see himself or his neighbour as a landowner, just as the nomad could not include in his notion of agency the control over paper money. From this it followed that rights and, hence, justice were temporal and historical phenomena. This historical perspective was developed in depth by Smith's greatest pupil, John Millar.[24]

Natural jurisprudence was first of all an academic subject in Enlightenment Scotland. It was taught extensively as a central part of the basic courses on moral philosophy. Overwhelmingly this was in a philosophical form which we here have sketched in terms of natural moral powers with the potential to be educated to serve the common good of society and humanity. As for Hume, he was debarred from teaching his theory of justice, or anything else. And Smith's empirical and historical analyses were close enough in content to those of the mainstream for it to be overlooked that, unlike them, he never provided any validating basis for the empirically and historically given practices of humanity. The common factor in all of the Scots was the concern with empirical studies of human nature and for this reason the courses in natural jurisprudence became the seedbeds for empirical social science and especially for political economy. This spectacular and often controversial crop has tended to obscure the ground from which it sprang, and the distinctiveness as well as the complexity of the theories of justice that were at the centre of Scottish natural jurisprudence have often been difficult to discern.

NOTES

1   The account of Scottish natural jurisprudence presented here is an extension of the interpretation in my *Natural Law and Moral Philosophy: from Grotius to the Scottish Enlightenment* (Cambridge: Cambridge University Press, 1996). For a survey with somewhat different emphases, see James Moore, in Mark Goldie and Robert Wokler, eds., *Cambridge History of Eighteenth-Century Political Thought* (Cambridge: Cambridge University Press, forthcoming). For an entirely different approach, see Alasdair MacIntyre, *Whose Justice? Which Rationality?* (Notre Dame, IN: University of Notre Dame Press, 1988), 260–80, 300–25.

2   For reasons that will become apparent, this does not mean that the Scottish doctrines meaningfully can be described as 'virtue ethics' in the contemporary sense.

3   Cf. David Fate Norton, *David Hume: Sceptical Metaphysician, Common-Sense Moralist* (Princeton, NJ: Princeton University Press, 1996).

4   The primary sources drawn on in the present essay are David Hume, *A Treatise of Human Nature: Being an Attempt to Introduce the Experimental Method into Moral Subjects* [1739–40], eds. David Fate Norton and Mary J. Norton (Oxford: Oxford University Press, 2000); and Adam Smith, *A Theory of Moral Sentiments* [1759, 6th edn 1790], ed. Knud Haakonssen (Cambridge: Cambridge University Press, 2002) (hereinafter *TMS*). Hume's *Enquiry Concerning the Principles of Morals* [1751] raises a number of special problems of interpretation which cannot be taken up here, but see James Moore, 'Utility and Humanity: the Quest for the *honestum* in Cicero, Hutcheson and Hume', *Utilitas* (forthcoming).

5   Hutcheson's innovative works in this regard are *An Inquiry into the Original of our Ideas of Beauty and Virtue; in Two Treatises: 1. Concerning Beauty, Order, Harmony, Design. 11. Concerning Moral Good*

and Evil [1725, 4th edn 1738], ed. Wolfgang Leidhold (Indianapolis, IN: Liberty Press, forthcoming); and *An Essay on the Nature and Conduct of the Passions and Affections, with Illustrations on the Moral Sense* [1728, 3rd edn 1742], ed. Aaron Garrett (Indianapolis: Liberty Press, 2002).

6 Thomas Reid, *Essays on the Active Powers of Man* [1788], ed. Knud Haakonssen (Edinburgh: Edinburgh University Press, forthcoming); James Oswald, *An Appeal to Common Sense in Behalf of Religion,* 2 vols. (Edinburgh, 1766–72); James Beattie, *An Essay on the Nature and Immutability of Truth in Opposition to Sophistry and Scepticism* (1770; reprint, intro. Roger J. Robinson, Bristol: Thoemmes Press, 1999); Beattie, *Elements of Moral Science,* 2 vols. (1790–3; reprint, intro. Roger J. Robinson, Bristol: Thoemmes Press 1999); Dugald Stewart, *Outlines of Moral Philosophy* [1793], in *The Collected Works of Dugald Stewart,* ed. Sir William Hamilton, 11 vols. (Edinburgh: Thomas Constable, 1854–60), vols. 2–4, 6–7; Stewart, *Philosophy of the Active and Moral Powers of Man,* 2 vols. [1828], in *Works,* vols. 6–7.

7 George Turnbull, *The Principles of Moral and Christian Philosophy,* 2 vols. [1740], ed. Alexander Broadie (Indianapolis, IN: Liberty Press, forthcoming); Henry Home, Lord Kames, *Essays on the Principles of Morality and Natural Religion* [1751, 3rd edn 1779], ed. Udo Thiel (Indianapolis, IN: Liberty Press, forthcoming); David Fordyce, *The Elements of Moral Philosophy In Three Books, With 'A Brief Account of the Nature, Progress and Origin of Philosophy'*, ed. Thomas Kennedy (Indianapolis, IN: Liberty Press, 2002).

8 Cf. Haakonssen, 'The Significance of Protestant Natural Law' in *Reading Autonomy,* eds. Natalie Brender and Larry Krasnoff (Cambridge: Cambridge University Press, forthcoming).

9 Concerning Cumberland, see his *De Legibus Naturae* [1672], trans. John Maxwell as *A Treatise of the Laws of Nature* [1727], ed. Jonathan Parkin (Indianapolis, IN: Liberty Press, forthcoming); cf. Knud Haakonssen, 'The Character and Obligation of Natural Law According to Richard Cumberland', in *English Philosophy in the Age of Locke,* ed. M. A. Stewart (Oxford: Oxford University Press, 2000), 29–47. Concerning Shaftesbury, see his *Characteristics of Men, Manners, Opinions, Times,* ed. Lawrence E. Klein (Cambridge: Cambridge University Press, 1999).

10 For the early works, see note 5 above. The late works are Francis Hutcheson, *Philosophiae moralis institutio compendiaria* [1742, 2nd edn 1745], with English translation *A Short Introduction to Moral Philosophy* [1747], ed. Luigi Turco (Indianapolis, IN: Liberty Press, forthcoming); Hutcheson, *A System of Moral Philosophy,* 2 vols. [1755],

ed. Knud Haakonssen (Indianapolis, IN: Liberty Press, forthcoming). The point made in the text is not meant to deny, of course, that if one sees Hutcheson's early and late works in their respective particular contexts, then one will find important differences between them; one can even find two (or more) 'systems'. For the latter, see a series of fine studies by James Moore, 'The Two Systems of Francis Hutcheson: on the Origins of the Scottish Enlightenment', in *Studies in the Philosophy of the Scottish Enlightenment*, ed. M. A. Stewart (Oxford: Clarendon Press, 1990), 37–59; Moore, 'Hume and Hutcheson', in *Hume and Hume's Connexions*, ed. M. A. Stewart and John P. Wright (Edinburgh: Edinburgh University Press, 1994), 23–57; Moore, 'Hutcheson's Theodicy: the Argument and the Contexts of *A System of Moral Philosophy*', in *The Scottish Enlightenment: Essays in Reinterpretation*, ed. Paul B. Wood (Rochester, NY: University of Rochester Press, 2000), 239–66.

11 See especially David Hume, *Treatise of Human Nature*, ed. L. A. Selby-Bigge, 2nd edn, rev. P. H. Nidditch (Oxford: Clarendon Press, 1978), III.ii.i–ii.

12 See ibid., III.iii, esp. section iv.

13 See Roger Emerson, 'The "Affair" at Edinburgh and the "Project" at Glasgow: the Politics of Hume's Attempts to Become a Professor', in *Hume and Hume's Connexions*, 1–22.

14 See Smith, *Theory of Moral Sentiments*, Parts I and III.

15 Ibid., Parts II and VI.

16 See ibid., II.ii and VII.iv. Concerning Smith's jurisprudence in general, see Haakonssen, *The Science of a Legislator: the Natural Jurisprudence of David Hume and Adam Smith* (Cambridge: Cambridge University Press, 1981), and David Lieberman, 'Smith on Natural Jurisprudence', in *The Cambridge Companion to Adam Smith*, ed. Knud Haakonssen (Cambridge: Cambridge University Press, forthcoming).

17 See John Cairns, ch. 11.

18 Francis Hutcheson, *Considerations on Patronage: Addressed to the Gentlemen of Scotland* (London 1735); Thomas Reid, *Practical Ethics; Being Lectures and Papers on Natural Religion, Self-Government, Natural Jurisprudence, and the Law of Nations*, ed. Knud Haakonssen (Princeton, NJ: Princeton University Press, 1990), 277–99. For Dugald Stewart, see the references in Haakonssen, *Natural Law and Moral Philosophy*, ch. 7.

19 Hume, 'Of the Origin of Government', in *Political Essays*, ed. Knud Haakonssen (Cambridge: Cambridge University Press, 1994), 20–3, 20.

20 Smith, *Theory of Moral Sentiments*, II.ii.1.10

21 See *Natural Rights on the Threshold of the Scottish Enlightenment: the Writings of Gershom Carmichael*, ed. James Moore and Michael

Silverthorne (Indianapolis, IN: Liberty Press, 2002). Cf. Moore and Silverthorne, 'Gershom Carmichael and the Natural Jurisprudence Tradition in Eighteenth-century Scotland', in *Wealth and Virtue: the Shaping of Political Economy in the Scottish Enlightenment*, eds. Istvan Hont and Michael Ignatieff (Cambridge: Cambridge University Press, 1983), 73–87.

22   Hutcheson, *Institutio/Short Introduction*, II, ch. 2; Hutcheson, *System*, II, ch. 3.

23   Adam Smith, *Lectures on Jurisprudence*, eds. R. L. Meek, D. D. Raphael and P. G. Stein (Oxford: Clarendon Press, 1978), (A) i. 9–26, (B) 5–11.

24   John Millar, *The Origin of the Distinction of Ranks, or An Inquiry into the Circumstances which give Rise to Influence and Authority in the Different Members of Society* [1770, 4th edn 1806], ed. Aaron Garrett (Indianapolis, IN: Liberty Press, forthcoming); Millar, *An Historical View of the English Government, from the Settlement of the Saxons in Britain to the Revolution in 1688*, 4 vols. [1787, 3rd edn 1803], ed. Mark Phillips (Indianapolis, IN: Liberty Press, forthcoming).

JOHN W. CAIRNS

11 Legal theory

Three features stand out in the legal theory of the Scottish Enlightenment: the engagement of the legal profession generally in such theorising; a strong interest in history and law, leading on to investigations of a proto-anthropological and proto-sociological nature; and the move away from an emphasis on legislation to one on development of the law through the formulation of new rules through the decision of specific cases. In all of these there was a complex interplay between legal theory and legal practice. Some of this was common to legal theorising in general in the period; some, however, was distinctive to the Scottish Enlightenment, arising not only out of the particular circumstances of the Scots lawyers themselves (particularly of the bar, the Faculty of Advocates), but also out of certain developments in ethics in Scotland.

To explore these features it is necessary to examine the development of thinking about law under the impact of the natural law tradition, focusing not so much on the natural law theories in detail, but rather on the institutionalisation among lawyers of an approach to law that valued natural law theorising in legal education and practice. This chapter will thus examine the intellectual culture that had arisen among Scots lawyers by 1700 and their education, showing how, through the eighteenth century, their training came to privilege learning in natural law in some form or another over an older legal humanism. It will then argue about the importance of legal theory in legal practice in Scotland, showing how the form of process in Scotland led to reliance on legal theory to develop the law. Finally, it will demonstrate how legal theorising led to a criticism of the current structure of the courts as inhibiting the just and efficient development of the law.

222

NATURAL LAW AND THE HISTORY OF SCOTS LAW

The years around 1600 were a turning point in Scots law.[1] The medieval era had seen the development of a common law, based around feudal land law, in many ways similar to early English common law.[2] One notable feature of the medieval Scottish legal system was, however, the lack of a central civil court and a very substantial devolution of royal justice to local lords. Alongside the secular courts with their inquests and juries developed a complex system of ecclesiastical courts, with an extensive jurisdiction, applying the universal Canon law of the church, found in the *Decretum Gratiani* of the twelfth century, and the later *Liber Extra, Sext, Extravagantes*, and other papal legislation (or decretals). Lower church courts also followed precedents of the Papal court, the Rota. These courts followed Romano-Canonical procedure, which originated in the Emperor Justinian's *Codex* of 534 AD and was further elaborated and refined in the Canonist legal texts and literature. The sources of Civil or Roman law, inherited by the Middle Ages from Justinian's Byzantium, were, as well as the *Codex*, the *Institutes*, the *Digest* or *Pandects* (the most important in this era with the *Codex*) and the *Novels*. With these was commonly associated a collection of Lombardic feudal laws known as the *Libri Feudorum*.[3]

The Civil laws were seen as supporting the Canon and were widely studied by churchmen.[4] This was so for Scotland. Indeed, details of the faculties of 230 Scottish students, all supported in study abroad by benefices, survive from before 1410: 200 ended with a degree in law. Such men generally returned home to take up the offices of the higher clergy.[5] The Civil and Canon laws (both the laws, the *utrumque ius* in Latin) were together seen to constitute a universal system of European 'common law', generally referred to by the Latin term '*ius commune*' (to distinguish it from the English common law), that was applicable failing suitable local law.[6]

Through the later Middle Ages, Scottish common law started to be influenced and enriched in practice by the Civil and Canon laws. This was because it was common that men skilled in the European 'common law' or *ius commune* not only advised secular judges but also aided individual litigants. Indeed, by 1500, it is clear that the lawyers acting in the secular courts and the ecclesiastical courts were becoming interchangeable, as trained Canonists practised in the local royal and franchise courts. At the same time, a central court, eventually known as the Session, developed in Scotland out of various expedients to deal with the legal business brought before the king's Council in the later fifteenth century. The lead in dealing with this legal business was taken by Canon lawyers on the Council, such as William Elphinstone, Bishop of Aberdeen, educated in Canon law in Paris and Civil law in Orléans. The Session, reconstituted as the College of Justice in 1532, adopted the Romano-Canonical procedure of the Church courts. A substantial proportion of its personnel were trained Canonists, while those admitted to plead before it were commonly university graduates in Civil and Canon law.[7]

By the 1540s, the most important book in practice before the Session was probably the commentary by Nicholas de Tudeschis (1389–1445) on the *Decretals*. This was primarily because of its authoritative analysis of Romano-Canonical procedure; Canon law, however, strongly influenced the Scottish action for recovery of possession of property, probably the most common action in Scots law at this period, as well as some other areas of the law. In practice before the Session, where Scots law was seen to consist of statutes and customs, the most important sources for decision-making were undoubtedly the texts of Canon and Civil law with their glosses and interpreters. The Civil and Canon laws, considered as the European 'common law', were what the court relied on automatically, failing 'native' material, or where they disliked an alleged custom.[8]

The significance of this cannot be overestimated. The law practised in Scotland's central court became imbued with Canonist notions of good faith and equity. For two generations, the potential direct applicability of Canon and Civil law was generally unquestioned in practice. Thus, in 1596, the Lords of Session issued an Act of Sederunt (an authoritative ruling on procedure) reinforcing the use of written pleadings called 'Informations', in which they promised to 'try quhat is prescryveit or decidet thairanent, als weill be the common law as be the municipall law or practick of this realme'.[9] The term 'common law' here means the European 'common law' – the Civil and Canon laws. This universal law was valuable in assessing the arguments of the parties.

The influence of Canonist principles meant that, in Scotland, law was seen as embodying a divine plan. This was to bear interesting fruit, first seen in the treatise, *Jus Feudale*, of Thomas Craig

(1538?–1608), the first work on Scots law to present a coherent account of Scots law related to political theory and philosophy.[10] Strongly influenced by the *De Republica* of Jean Bodin (1530–96), Craig, writing around 1600, argued that law-making was an attribute of sovereign power, so that only Popes and princes who acknowledged no superior could authoritatively legislate.[11] Craig had an essentially Thomist view (probably derived from his education in Paris) that human beings had an innate capacity to use their reason to know the equitable and the good and that exercise of this right reason allowed knowledge of natural law. This natural law was binding and 'neither the legislation of a kingdom, nor prescription of even the longest time, nor custom has force against this law'.[12] After natural law, the law of nations (in Latin, *ius gentium*) had to be followed. By this Craig meant not only the law that governed relations between nations, but also principles of law common to all or many nations. This meant that 'everything all nations observed ought to have force with us, no matter what the civil or municipal law'. In particular, the law of nations had to be observed in dealings with foreigners, even if contrary to a statute of the kingdom, while 'among citizens it would have authority unless some statute or specific law opposed it'.[13]

For Craig, therefore, it was no longer a simple matter of resolving difficult disputes by reference to the texts and literature of the European 'common law'. In cases of difficulty, recourse was first to be had to the natural law, then the laws common to all nations, then to Scottish statutes, and then to the custom of the courts. Civil law was relied on as a matter of fact, according to Craig, because there was so little written law in Scotland; he argued, however, according to his neo-Thomist approach, that 'we are bound by the Roman laws only in so far as they are congruent with the laws of nature and right reason'.[14] That is, Roman law was authoritative, not in itself, but only insofar as it represented right reason.[15] This approach potentially challenged traditional Scottish reliance on the Civil law; yet, this initially was not so. This was because:

There is surely no broader seedbed of natural equity, no more fertile field of articulated reasoning and arguments from those principles of nature than the books of the Roman jurists; from which ought to be drawn, as if from the very fountain, what is equitable and what inequitable by nature and what most agrees and what disagrees with right reason.[16]

So long as Civil law could be identified with right reason, the scope for reliance on it in legal argument was very great, especially since the law of nature (and to some extent that of nations) had a greater authority than municipal law.

Nonetheless, the change in attitude signified by Craig's justification for the use of Civil law marked the start of a re-evaluation of the role of Roman law. This encompassed not only the issue of its formal authority, but also its subjection to an historical and philological critique. At the same time, developments in discussions of sovereignty and politics led to a renewed emphasis on the older Scottish sources, with their publication by Sir John Skene in 1609, while there were also determined efforts to collect the statutes and the decisions of the courts.[17] This meant that, by 1700, Scotland was a country in which the current practice of Roman law (that is Roman law as used and relied on in contemporary legal systems) had become blended with Scottish source material to form what one might call the Roman-Scots law.[18] The results of this could be presented in works such as *Institutions of the Law of Scotland* in 1681 by James Dalrymple, Viscount Stair (1619–95) and *Laws and Customes of Scotland, in Matters Criminal* of 1678 by Sir George Mackenzie (1638?–91).[19] Both these works took account of the custom and decisions of the courts and Scottish statutes, while also attempting to rationalise the traditional habit of drawing on the Civil law in practice. They depicted the law as a coherent and logical whole integrated as a hierarchical series of norms, justified and made obligatory by a higher authority. In this, they were comparable to the other 'institutional' writings of this era, marking the creation of national laws in Europe.[20]

NATURAL LAW, LEGAL EDUCATION AND SCOTS LAW

From the initial development of universities in Europe, Scots had travelled abroad to study Civil and Canon law. Even when laymen in significant numbers started to study law from around 1500 onwards, the degrees they took were in Canon law and Civil law, while the education of judges and advocates in the European 'common law' was maintained after the Reformation.[21] For much of the seventeenth century, the preferred country for law students was still France, where there remained a relatively traditional curriculum of Civil law and Canon law leading to a licentiate in both the laws.[22] In the later seventeenth century, however, especially after the revocation of the Edict of Nantes in 1685 and William of Orange's accession to the throne, Scots turned in increasing numbers to the Dutch universities to study law, particularly to those of Utrecht and Leiden.[23]

This move to the Northern Netherlands was of profound importance. The Dutch universities were still at an intellectual peak in this period, with many of the most renowned professors of the era on their faculties; moreover, it was possible to follow a much freer and more innovative curriculum in law. This was because the traditional sequence and series of lectures had been supplemented or replaced by private classes (in Latin, *collegia privata*) given by the professors for a fee.[24] In these, for example, they might cover the whole *Digest* of Justinian teaching from a compendiary textbook. In such private classes, the professors also had scope to introduce new subjects, such as local law, and devote specialist classes to public law. Of particular interest were the laws of nature and nations. Not only did the new compendiary textbooks frequently emphasise those Roman texts that mentioned the laws of nature and nations, but specialist courses were developed based on the *De iure belli ac pacis libri tres* (*Three Books on the Law of War and Peace*) (1625) of Hugo Grotius (1583–1665) and the *De officio hominis et civis juxta legem naturalem libri duo* (*Two Books on the Duty of Man and Citizen according to the Law of Nature*) (1673) of Samuel Pufendorf (1632–94). It was common for Scots students to take such a private class on Grotius or Pufendorf, when offered. Thus, for many years, Ph. R. Vitriarius (1647–1720), Professor at Leiden, was the teacher in that University most favoured by Scots law students, despite a number of his colleagues being men more favoured by history. He taught a class on Grotius based on his own textbook, *Institutiones juris naturae et gentium... ad methodum Hugonis Grotii conscriptae* (*The Institutions of the Law of Nature and Nations...written according to the Method of Hugo Grotius*) (Leiden, 1692). Gerard Noodt (1647–1725), Vitriarius's more distinguished colleague, also taught a course on natural law that Scots attended.[25]

The interest in natural law reflected the seventeenth-century developments in Scots law. Stair's *Institutions*, for example, was heavily influenced by Grotian jurisprudence in placing Scots law in the framework of the law of nature and nations.[26] Stair wrote that

'[w]here our ancient law, statutes, and our recent customs and prac-
tiques are defective, recourse is had to equity, as the first and universal law, and to expediency, whereby laws are drawn in consequence
ad similes casus'.[27] Natural law – 'equity' – was obligatory, although
municipal laws could depart from it for good reason.[28] He also argued that the law of Scotland had an 'affinity' with the civil law
and that 'though it be not acknowledged as a law binding for its authority, yet [it was], as a rule, followed for its equity'.[29] Stair thus
considered civil law to have no special authority in itself; any authority it might have only derived from its embodiment of a rule of
natural law. The influence of Roman law in the *Institutions* was,
however, sufficiently obvious for it to have been perfectly plausible,
if inaccurate, for a contemporary to say of the work that it was
'a system of the civil law, intermixt with the law of Scotland'.[30]
Thus, Stair's *Institutions* was a typical institutional work of its era,
validating the use of the Civil law by reference to the law of nature
and nations.

Such reliance on natural law to justify Scottish reliance on Roman
law in legal practice had no immediate impact on thinking about
law in general at the beginning of the eighteenth century.[31] It essentially justified and explained what happened. Nonetheless, natural law was regarded as significant. The first chair in law to be
founded in Scotland after 1700 was that of Public Law and the Law
of Nature and Nations in Edinburgh in 1707, from which it was intended, as the title suggests, to expound Grotian natural law. While
there was undoubtedly a greater desire to have a chair in Roman law
founded (which followed swiftly in 1710, in any case), the establishment of this chair reflected the way in which the law of nature and
nations was seen as foundational to law and legal study.[32] It was
not only the lawyers who were interested in natural law. Gershom
Carmichael (1672–1729), who taught at Glasgow from 1694–1729,
relied on Pufendorf's textbook *De officio hominis et civis* as a teaching text for moral philosophy, producing an edition with an extensive commentary in 1718. While not an uncritical admirer of
Pufendorf, Carmichael recognised the significance of his identification of moral philosophy with natural jurisprudence. Carmichael
helped firmly establish the tradition of natural jurisprudence in the
Scottish universities.[33]

THE FORM OF PROCESS AND NATURAL LAW

By 1700, Romano-Canonical procedure had developed in Scotland into a largely written form of process. The Court of Session had for long been divided into an Inner and Outer House. The President and the Ordinary Lords sat together in the Inner House, deciding by vote on any issue before them. In turn, the Lords Ordinary would sit in the Outer House as Lord Ordinary of the Week, Lord Ordinary on the Bills, Lord Ordinary on Oaths and Witnesses, and Lord Ordinary on Concluded Causes. These were separate offices, but the Lord Ordinary of the Week would commonly also act as Lord Ordinary on the Bills (dealing with bills suspending the decrees of lower courts or advocating causes from them to the Session).[34]

The Ordinary of the Week dealt with the ordinary actions enrolled before him for that week on the basis of the pursuer's libel (or summons) and the defender's defences. The parties' counsel would debate the cause before him *viva voce* and he could dispose of the matter by interlocutor if it was unnecessary to take the evidence of witnesses. It was, however, common for the Lord Ordinary to require the parties to reduce their arguments to writing in the form of what were called Memorials if he considered there was a legal point of difficulty. He could also report any matters of difficulty to the Inner House for decision: this would generally require the production of written (printed) documents for the Inner House, embodying the parties' arguments. These were generally known as Informations. Where proof was necessary in a case because facts were in dispute, this would be taken by the Lord Ordinary on Oaths and Witnesses. Such proof could only be taken if the Ordinary of the Week had passed an act of litiscontestation; this act decided both issues of relevancy and which matters of fact required to be proved. The Ordinary on Oaths and Witnesses would either examine witnesses himself or order them to be examined on commission. Such evidence would be reduced to written form.[35] (Until 1686, the evidence had been taken by the judge in private and sealed up to be made available to the Court when it advised the cause; after 1686, the parties and their advocates could be present when witnesses were examined and could have access to the written depositions.)[36] Once witnesses had been examined, the process would pass to the Lord

Ordinary on Concluded Causes who would prepare an ultimately printed document, setting out the pleadings of the parties and the evidence of the witnesses, generally called a Statement of the Cause. This was the basis on which the Inner House would decide the case. It would also be accompanied by further Informations prepared by the counsel for the parties.[37] The extent of written pleading is what is significant here. The collections of such pleadings preserved indicate that citation of natural law was common. It was quite typical for advocates to argue from divine law, natural law and Roman law as well as presenting arguments drawn from Scottish municipal law.[38]

The Scottish criminal courts did not use Romano-Canonical procedure as such; but there the practice had also developed of an extensive legal argument over the relevancy of the libel in the indictment or criminal letters analogous to the legal argument in the process prior to litiscontestation in the Court of Session.[39] Before 1695, the advocates had commonly dictated their legal arguments to the clerk who entered them in the record in a rather formal debate. From 1695, the debate was to be *viva voce*, but the advocates had later to give in written Informations covering the material debated. This was obviously modelled on the growth of written pleading in the civil court.[40] Again one finds a similar return to first principles of Scots law in such Informations; this was so normal that the style given for an Information in a criminal case started off with the basis of the crime in the law of nature and the law of God, and also discussed the 'Laws of other Countries, particularly the Law of *England*' (that is, the law of nations), as well as Scottish authority.[41]

It is clear that Scots lawyers were interested in the law of nature and nations for practical as well as theoretical reasons. It is no surprise that, from the later seventeenth century, individual lawyers and institutional libraries started to collect the works of Grotius and Pufendorf and commentaries on them. New publications, such as an edition of Grotius by Jean Barbeyrac (1674–1744) and the translation of Pufendorf by Basil Kennet (1674–1715) with Barbeyrac's notes were advertised in the Edinburgh newspapers when they appeared. By the 1760s, so standard and normal had such knowledge become that the Faculty of Advocates advised all intending advocates to study the law of nature and nations, announcing they would examine them on it.[42] Natural law had become significant in the construction of arguments before the superior courts.

NATURAL LAW, MORAL SENSE, HISTORY AND LAW

In 1773, the *Institute of the Law of Scotland* of John Erskine (1695–1768), sometime Professor of Scots law in the University of Edinburgh, was posthumously published.[43] It provided a rationalist and voluntarist view of natural law ultimately deriving from the thinking of Pufendorf, though influenced by more modern authors. Erskine had been admitted as an advocate in 1719, perhaps after studies in Edinburgh and the Netherlands. His thinking was formed in that period and must have seemed very old-fashioned in 1773. This was because of developments in ethics in Scotland.

From the work of Francis Hutcheson (1694–1746), Carmichael's successor as Professor of Moral Philosophy in Glasgow, rationalist natural law theories in the tradition of Pufendorf had been progressively superseded in Scotland by versions of moral sense theory. A follower of the philosophy of Lord Shaftesbury (1671–1713), Hutcheson attempted to ground ethics in observation and study of the thinking and behaviour of human beings. He argued that humanity was able to judge of the rightness or wrongness of an action by virtue of a moral sense. In other words, the foundation of moral judgement was not in the reason, but in the senses, as morally beautiful actions gave pleasure.[44] Among lawyers, Henry Home, Lord Kames (1696–1782), a judge and prolific author, was the most noted follower of Hutcheson's rejection of ethical rationalism and espousal of a moral sense as the best explanation of how moral judgement was possible. He refined Hutcheson's views, however, as he disapproved of some of their (potentially utilitarian) consequences. Rather, he argued that the moral sense had two aspects, a sense of duty and a sense of propriety or fitness. Justice was derived from the sense of duty: many moral actions were right and fitting to be carried out, but could not be compelled, while just actions could be.[45] David Hume (1711–76), in his *Treatise of Human Nature* (1739–40), had provided the most radical version of moral-sense theory, mounting a devastating attack on ethical rationalism and natural law. He rejected the approach of Hutcheson to the virtue of justice, however, arguing that it was not derived from the moral sense, but was an 'artificial' virtue. By this he meant that it originated solely in social convention. This was not the natural lawyers' idea of a social contract; Hume thought that rules for the allocation of the scarce resources necessary for life developed out of customary practices on the basis of expediency and necessity. In his later *Enquiry Concerning the Principles of Morals* (1751), he stressed emphatically that the sole origin of justice was utility.[46]

The publication in 1748 by Charles de Secondat, Baron de Montesquieu (1689–1755), of his large and diffuse work, *L'Esprit des Lois* (*The Spirit of the Laws*), aroused considerable interest in Scotland. In the 1750s, in both France and Scotland, a theory that society developed through various stages of differing modes of subsistence was developed out of Montesquieu's insight that there were links between the laws of a nation and whether it lived by trade and navigation, or by cultivation of the soil, or by keeping flocks and herds or by hunting.[47] A seminal work here was Lord Kames's *Historical Law-Tracts* of 1758, in which he blended his version of moral-sense theory (developed partly in opposition to Hume's utilitarianism) with a theory of development derived and adapted from Montesquieu.[48] Kames's work carried a distinctly modernising message: Scots law required reform to make it a law suitable for a commercial nation.[49]

Kames's views, however, were part of a new approach to Scots law that had developed out of moral-sense theory. Prior to 1700, there had been a considerable desire for reform of Scots law in order to reduce it to a series of statutes. While the impulse to do this can be traced back to the later Middle Ages, in the last two decades of the seventeenth century it was twice proposed to establish commissions to produce digests of the statutes, decisions of the courts and practicks, and acts of sederunt (rules of procedure).[50] These were not essentially proposals to reform the *substance* of the law (although the later seventeenth century in fact saw a great deal of important law reform), but to render it in a statutory form. Sir George Mackenzie wrote in 1686 that 'our Statutes...be the chief Pillars of our Law'.[51]

Kames, however, stressed the importance of *courts*, rather than *legislatures*, in developing the law. He described them as possessing an equitable jurisdiction, whereby the judges, drawing on the moral sense, developed the law on the bases of justice and utility. His argument was, to put it somewhat simply, that historical development constantly turned duties of beneficence into duties of justice. The courts had to recognise this and develop the law accordingly.[52] In this Kames was in line with general thinking about law in this period in Scotland. In the *Theory of Moral Sentiments* (1759), Adam Smith (1723–90) presented a view that moral judgement was possible by our ability to judge the propriety and merit of the behaviour of others through the mechanisms of sympathy and the concept of the impartial spectator. He used these ideas to develop a notion of justice that did not rely on some special moral sense or that was derived from our 'reason', but arose from the confrontation of individuals with episodes that aroused our sense that an individual had been wronged and that the wronged person's sense of resentment was appropriate and ought to have an outlet in a due measure of punishment of the individual who committed the wrong.[53] On this basis, Smith developed an argument that the rules of justice generally arose from the moral sentiments. It is also obvious that he thought that the best way for such rules of justice to be transformed into laws was not through the intervention of legislation, but rather through the operation of precedent, with courts deciding such questions as and when they arose.[54]

Such an approach to law reform inevitably emphasised the need for adequately educated lawyers: philosopher lawyers, in a word. It is no surprise that Kames thus emphasised the need for suitable legal education. He argued that '[l]aw in particular only becomes a rational study when it is traced historically, from its first rudiments among savages, through successive changes, to its highest improvements in a civilized society.'[55] Such an approach allowed the law student to see the historical development of law with its close links to social changes. He concluded:

Were law taught as a rational science, its principles unfolded, and its connection with manners and politics, it would prove an enticing study to every person who has an appetite for knowledge. We might hope to see our lawyers soaring above their predecessors; and giving splendor to their country, by purifying and improving its laws.[56]

Smith's pupil and Kames's protégé, John Millar (1735–1801), Regius Professor of Civil Law in Glasgow, drew on this mode of thinking in his influential classes. The duties of his chair were defined as offering a course on Justinian's *Institutes* twice a year and one on Justinian's *Digest* once a year. Millar turned the second course on the *Institutes* into a course on Adam Smith's jurisprudence. It was described as a class 'in which [Millar] treated of such general principles of Law as pervade the codes of all nations, and have their origin in those sentiments of justice which are imprinted on the human heart'. His jurisprudence directed 'the enlightened Legislator...in the noble, but arduous, attempt, to purify and improve the laws of his country'. Moreover, that Millar's legal theory was historical in orientation prevented 'inconsiderate innovation, and indiscriminate reform', since it demonstrated that 'no institutions, however just in themselves, can be either expedient or permanent, if inconsistent with established ranks, manners, and opinions'.[57]

The new approach identified with Kames, Smith and Millar also emphasised the need for appropriately structured courts. Indeed a major theme running through Smith's lectures on jurisprudence to his class in Glasgow was the consideration of what made for successful courts (in the sense of courts that managed to inscribe into rules of law the needs of justice as identified by the moral sense or moral sentiments by responding appropriately to individual cases).[58] Much of Smith's account there can be read as a criticism of the contemporary Court of Session and its procedures. Judges were rendered irresponsible by the Romano-Canonical procedure of the Court and the spectatorial and sympathetic mechanisms on which his theory of justice was founded could not operate to produce just decisions of lasting value in the law.[59]

CONCLUSION

'Enlightenment' is an elusive and contested term. But one feature of the period and thinking associated with it is a desire to legislate to improve the lot of humankind: to promote its happiness. The work of the Englishman Jeremy Bentham (1748–1832) is an evident example.[60] In continental Europe one can point to projects such as the *Codex Theresianus juris civilis*, the legislative ambitions of Joseph II, and the work of Franz von Zeiler (1751–1828), just to take the example of the Austrian lands.[61] The standard general legal history for the modern period, admittedly with a German bias, Franz Wieacker's *History of Private Law in Europe*, states that, in law, the Enlightenment is marked by the translation of the modern 'law of reason' into the codification projects of the Enlightened absolutists of Prussia and Austria. Building on the seventeenth-century natural lawyers, such as Pufendorf and his school, the work of the legal philosopher Christian Wolff (1679–1754) is seen as providing the necessary theoretical underpinning for such legislative projects of codification.[62] Peter Stein has likewise commented: 'The rationalist natural law philosophy proclaimed that a complete set of laws could be stated simply and rationally, with existing complexities eliminated, and all that was needed to enact it was the will of the prince.'[63] In 1700, Scottish writers strongly valued legislation; Grotius and Pufendorf were the most important general thinkers about law; Scots law, legal procedure and legal education were generally comparable with those of much of continental Europe in the era of the contemporary usage in Roman law (the *usus modernus pandectarum*). Yet Scotland diverged in the eighteenth century; its Enlightenment did not lead to codification projects, but to piecemeal incremental reform of the law through the operation of the courts in elaborating law in their decisions.

In part, this failure to stay on the same path as Scots law's continental cousins to some extent reflected the political consequences of the Union with England of 1707; Scots looked more to London and intercourse with the Continent became less frequent. This is not entirely satisfactory as an explanation, however, since Scots did continue to study law in the Netherlands in reasonably substantial numbers until about 1750. The ending of this practice reflected not only the successful development of Scottish law schools, particularly at Edinburgh, in this period, but also indeed the refocusing of legal concern away from Roman law to natural law. A large part of the attraction of the Netherlands in the later seventeenth and early eighteenth centuries was that the Scots fully participated in the late humanistic culture found there based on study of the classics and the ancient world, including the historical and philological study of Roman law.[64] As such study became of less concern in the course of the eighteenth century, Dutch universities, starting in any case to enter on a decline, simply became much less interesting to the Scots. As Scots turned away from the Roman law, they did not move towards codification. Instead, the development of ethics through ideas of a moral sense focused on the significance of individual judgement in historical and social context in elaborating rights; systematic a priori reasoning was rejected. What such thinking did lead to, however, was an immense and progressive programme of legislative reform of the courts and their procedures in the early nineteenth century. This was necessary to allow the best law to emerge out of the competitive litigation of individuals seeking resolution of their individual disputes.[65]

NOTES

1   The following section of this chapter is based on John W. Cairns, 'Historical Introduction', in Kenneth Reid and Reinhard Zimmermann, eds., *A History of Scots Private Law* (Oxford: Oxford University Press, 2000), 1.14–184, at 15–142. Subsequent references will simply pinpoint specific sources cited in the text.
2   See W. David H. Sellar, 'The Common Law of Scotland and the Common Law of England', in R. R. Davies, ed., *The British Isles, 1100–1500: Comparisons, Contrasts and Connections* (Edinburgh: John Donald, 1988), 82–99; Hector L. MacQueen, *Common Law and Feudal Society in Medieval Scotland* (Edinburgh: Edinburgh University Press, 1993).
3   The nature of the texts in the Middle Ages differed somewhat from the modern editions, but that is not important here.
4   See, e.g., James A. Brundage, *Medieval Canon Law* (London: Longman, 1995), 44–70; R. H. Helmholz, *The Spirit of Classical Canon Law* (Athens: University of Georgia Press, 1996), 1–32.
5   D. E. R. Watt, 'University Graduates in Scottish Benefices before 1410', *Records of the Scottish Church History Society* 15 (1964), 77–88 at 79.
6   See, e.g., R. C. van Caenegem, *An Historical Introduction to Private Law* (Cambridge: Cambridge University Press, 1992), 45–85.
7   See, e.g., John W. Cairns, 'Advocates' Hats, Roman Law and Admission to the Bar, 1580–1812', *Journal of Legal History* 20, no. 2 (1999), 24–61.
8   These remarks are based on my study of Sinclair's *Practicks*, of which the best manuscript is Edinburgh University Library, MS La.III.388a. I have used the text prepared by Dr Athol Murray with notes by Professor Gero Dolezalek, available at http//www.uni-leipzig.de/~jurarom/Scotland. See generally A. L. Murray, 'Sinclair's Practicks', in Alan Harding, ed., *Law Making and Law Makers in British History* (London: Royal Historical Society, 1980), 90–104.
9   *The Acts of Sederunt of the Lords of Council and Session, from the 15th of January 1553, to the 11th of July 1790* (Edinburgh: Printed by Neill and Co. for E. Balfour, 1790), 26–7.
10 T. Craig, *Jus feudale tribus libris comprehensum*, 3rd edn, ed. James Baillie (Edinburgh: Thomas and Walter Ruddiman, 1732). All citations are to this edition, though texts have been compared with the first of

1655. Translations are my own, though I have generally compared them with the translation by Lord Clyde as *The Jus Feudale by Sir Thomas Craig of Riccarton with an Appendix containing the Books of the Feus* (Edinburgh: William Hodge, 1934).

11 Craig, *Jus feudale*, 1.i.8; 1.ii.3; 1.iii.6; 1.vi.7; 1.vii.3; 1.xii.6; 11.ii.2; 11.xiii.38; 111.v.16. There is, of course, an older debate here about the right to legislate: see Walter Ullmann, 'The Development of the Medieval Idea of Sovereignty', *English Historical Review* 64 (1949), 1–33.

12 Craig, *Jus feudale*, 1.viii.7. On the revival of Thomism and neo-Scholasticism in Paris as it affected legal thinking see, e.g., J. M. Kelly, *A Short History of Western Legal Theory* (Oxford: Clarendon Press, 1992), 141–4; Quentin Skinner, *The Foundations of Modern Political Thought* (Cambridge: Cambridge University Press, 1978), 135–73; James Gordley, *The Philosophical Origins of Modern Contract Doctrine* (Oxford: Oxford University Press, 1991), 69–71.

13 Craig, *Jus feudale*, 1.viii.8.

14 Ibid., 1.ii.14

15 Craig also stated (ibid., 1.iii.24; 1.viii.17) that, although Scotland had 'shaken off the papal yoke', nonetheless, when there was a conflict between Canon law and Civil law, the Canon law was preferred, especially in those areas under the jurisdiction of the Commissary Courts. In fact, the main significance of this was to favour Canonist equitable and good-faith principles in contract over the strict law approach of the Civilists.

16 Ibid., 1.ii.14

17 See, e.g., John W. Cairns, T. David Fergus and Hector L. MacQueen, 'Legal Humanism and the History of Scots Law: John Skene and Thomas Craig', in John MacQueen, ed., *Humanism in Renaissance Scotland* (Edinburgh: Edinburgh University Press, 1990), 48–74.

18 I initially called this the 'Roman-Scotch Law', using the alternative adjective because of its euphony with 'Roman-Dutch': see John W. Cairns, 'The Civil Law Tradition in Scottish Legal Thought', in David L. Carey Miller and Reinhard Zimmermann, eds., *The Civilian Tradition and Scots Law: Aberdeen Quincentenary Essays* (Berlin: Duncker and Humblot, 1997), 191–223 at 211. I have varied the adjective as some have seemed to see some extra significance in my use of the term 'Scotch'. On Roman law in current practice, more generally known by the Latin term *'usus modernus pandectarum'*, see e.g., Franz Wieacker, *A History of Private Law in Europe*, trans. by Tony Weir (Oxford: Clarendon Press, 1995), 159–95; Klaus Luig, 'Usus modernus', in Adalbert Erler and Ekkehard Kaufmann, eds., *Handwörterbuch zur deutschen Rechtsgeschichte* (Berlin: Erich Schmidt Verlag, 1971–98), vol. v, cols. 628–36.

19 James Dalrymple, Viscount Stair, *The Institutions of the Law of Scotland: Deduced from its Originals, and Collated with the Civil, Canon and Feudal Laws, and with the Customs of Neighbouring Nations* (Edinburgh: Heir of Andrew Anderson, 1681; 2nd edn Edinburgh: Heir of Andrew Anderson, 1693; new edn Edinburgh: Edinburgh University Press, 1981); Sir George Mackenzie, *The Laws and Customes of Scotland, In Matters Criminal. Wherein is to be seen how the Civil Law, and the Laws and Customs of other Nations do agree with, and supply ours* (Edinburgh: Thomas Brown, 1678).

20 Klaus Luig, 'The Institutes of National Law in the Seventeenth and Eighteenth Centuries', *Juridical Review* (1972), 193–226.

21 R. K. Hannay, *The College of Justice: Essays on the Institution and Development of the Court of Session* (Edinburgh: William Hodge, 1933), 145.

22 John Durkan, 'The French Connection in the Sixteenth and Early Seventeenth Centuries' in T. C. Smout, ed., *Scotland and Europe, 1250–1850* (Edinburgh: John Donald, 1986), 19–44; L. W. B. Brockliss, *French Higher Education in the Seventeenth and Eighteenth Centuries: a Cultural History* (Oxford: Clarendon Press, 1987), 277–330.

23 Robert Feenstra, 'Scottish-Dutch Legal Relations in the Seventeenth and Eighteenth Centuries', in *Legal Scholarship and Doctrines of Private Law, Thirteenth to Eighteenth Centuries* (Aldershot: Variorum Reprints, 1996), XVI at 36 (= Hilde de Ridder-Symoens and J. M. Fletcher, eds., *Academic Relations between the Low Countries and the British Isles, 1450–1700. Proceedings of the First Conference of Belgian, British and Dutch Historians of Universities held in Ghent, September 30-October 2, 1987* (Gent: Studia Historica Gandensia, 1987), 25–45); Kees van Strien and Margreet Ahsmann, 'Scottish Law Students in Leiden at the End of the Seventeenth Century. The Correspondence of John Clerk, 1694–1697', *Lias* 19 (1992), 271–330 and *Lias* 20 (1993), 1–65.

24 Margreet Ahsmann, 'Collegia publica et privata: eine Erscheinung deutscher Herkunft an den niederländischen juristen Fakultäten um 1600?', in Robert Feenstra and Chris Copppens, eds., *Die rechtswissenschaftlichen Beziehungen zwischen den Niederlanden und Deutschland in historischer Sicht* (Nijmegen: Gerard Noodt Institut, 1991), 1–20; Ahsmann, 'Teaching in Collegia: the Organization of *Disputationes* at Universities in the Netherlands and Germany during the Sixteenth and Seventeenth Centuries', in *Università in Europa* (Messina: Rubettino, 1995), 99–114.

25 See van Strien and Ahsmann, 'Scottish Law Students', 291–3; G. C. J. J. van den Bergh, *The Life and Work of Gerard Noodt (1647–1725):*

Dutch Legal Scholarship between Humanism and Enlightenment
(Oxford: Clarendon Press, 1988), 60, 131 n. 29, 283; C. J. H. Jansen, 'Over
de 18e eeuwse docenten Natuurecht aan Nederlandse Universiteiten en
de door hen gebruikte Leerboeken', *Tijdschrift voor Rechtsgeschiedenis* 55 (1987), 103–15; John W. Cairns, '"Importing our Lawyers from
Holland": Netherlands' Influences on Scots Law and Lawyers in the
Eighteenth Century', in Grant G. Simpson, ed., *Scotland and the Low
Countries, 1124–1994* (East Linton: Tuckwell Press, 1996), 136–53 at
136–9 and 144–6.

26   On Stair's views of natural law, see, e.g., A. H. Campbell, *The Struc-
     ture of Stair's Institutions: Being the twenty-first Lecture on the David
     Murray Foundation in the University of Glasgow delivered on 24
     February 1954* (Glasgow: Jackson, 1954); Neil MacCormick, 'Law, Obli-
     gation and Consent: Reflections on Stair and Locke', *Archiv für Rechts-
     und Sozial Philosophie* 65 (1979), 387–411; MacCormick, 'Stair's
     General Concepts. 2. Stair as Analytical Jurist', in D. M. Walker, ed.,
     Stair Tercentenary Studies (Edinburgh: Stair Society, vol. XXXIII, 1981),
     187–99; MacCormick, 'The Rational Discipline of Law', *Juridical Re-
     view* (1981), 146–60; P. G. Stein, 'Stair's General Concepts. 1. The
     Theory of Law', in Walker, *Stair Tercentenary Studies*, 181–7; J. D.
     Ford, 'Stair's Title "Of Liberty and Servitude"', in A. D. E. Lewis and
     D. J. Ibbetson, eds., *The Roman Law Tradition* (Cambridge: Cambridge
     University Press, 1994), 135–58. On Stair's use of Grotius, see W. M.
     Gordon, 'Stair, Grotius and the Sources of Stair's Institutions', in J. A.
     Ankum, J. E. Spruit, F. B. J. Ankum, eds., *Satura Roberto Feenstra sexa-
     gesimun quintum annum aetatis complenti ab alumnis collegis amicis
     oblata* (Fribourg: Editions Universitaires, 1985), 571–83.
27   Stair, *Institutions of the Law of Scotland*, I.i.16.
28   Ibid., 15.
29   Ibid., 12. Note that 'as a rule' has the sense of 'as a code of regulation': see
     Alan Watson, 'The Rise of Modern Scots Law', in *La formazione storica
     del diritto moderno in Europa, Atti del Terzo Congresso Internazionale
     della Società Italiana di Storia del Diritto* (Florence: L. S. Olschki, 1977),
     III.1167–76 at 1175.
30   Walter Scott, ed., *A Collection of Scarce and Valuable Tracts, on the
     Most Interesting and Entertaining Subjects: But Chiefly Such as Relate
     to the History and Constitution of these Kingdoms. Selected from an
     Infinite Number in Print and Manuscript, in the Royal, Cotton, Sion,
     and other Public, as well as Private, Libraries, particularly that of the
     late Lord Somers*, 2nd edn (London: T. Cadell and W. Davies, 1809–15),
     XI.550.
31   See, e.g., Cairns, 'Historical Introduction', 138–9.

32   Cairns, ' "Importing our Lawyers"', 148–9.

33   On Carmichael, see, e.g., James Moore and Michael Silverthorne, 'Gershom Carmichael and the Natural Jurisprudence Tradition in Eighteenth-Century Scotland', in Istvan Hont and Michael Ignatieff, eds., *Wealth and Virtue: the Shaping of Political Economy in the Scottish Enlightenment* (Cambridge: Cambridge University Press, 1983), 73–87.

34   See generally Lord Cooper of Culross, 'The Central Courts after 1532', in G. C. H. Paton, ed., *An Introduction to Scottish Legal History* (Edinburgh: Stair Society, vol. 20, 1958), 341–9 at 342–4; N. T. Phillipson, *The Scottish Whigs and the Reform of the Court of Session 1785–1830* (Edinburgh: Stair Society, vol. 37, 1990), 43–5. On the historical development, see Hannay, *College of Justice*, 91–134.

35   Phillipson, *Scottish Whigs*, 43–6.

36   The Evidence Act, 1686, c. 30; *Acts of the Parliaments of Scotland*, eds. T. Thomson and C. Innes (Edinburgh: Record Edition, 1814–75 [hereafter APS]), VIII.599.

37   Phillipson, *Scottish Whigs*, 43–4, 56. For a flavour of the extensive written pleadings (the 'Session Papers'), see J. A. Inglis, 'Eighteenth-Century Pleading', *Juridical Review* o.s. 19 (1907–8), 42–57.

38   Inglis, 'Eighteenth-Century Pleading', 53.

39   See John W. Cairns, 'Hamesucken and the Major Premiss in the Libel, 1672–1770: Criminal Law in the Age of Enlightenment', in Robert F. Hunter, ed., *Justice and Crime: Essays in Honour of the Right Honourable the Lord Emslie, MBE, PC, LLD, FRSE* (Edinburgh: T. and T. Clark, 1993), 138–79 at 142–4.

40   *APS*, IX.365–6 (c. 6). The presentation of written argument to the criminal court is also sometimes found in the sixteenth century.

41   See J. Louthian, *Form of Process Before the Court of Justiciary in Scotland* (Edinburgh: Robert Fleming and Co. for William Hamilton, 1732), 139–84.

42   See John W. Cairns, 'Scottish Law, Scottish Lawyers and the Status of the Union', in John Robertson, ed., *A Union for Empire: Political Thought and the British Union of 1707* (Cambridge: Cambridge University Press, 1995), 243–68 at 258–9.

43   John Erskine, *An Institute of the Law of Scotland. In Four Books. In the order of Sir George Mackenzie's Institutions of that Law* (Edinburgh: John Bell, 1773).

44   On whether Hutcheson's use of Pufendorf indicates inconsistency in his thinking, see, e.g., James Moore, 'The Two Systems of Francis Hutcheson: On the Origins of the Scottish Enlightenment', in M. A. Stewart, ed., *Studies in the Philosophy of the Scottish Enlightenment*

(Oxford: Clarendon Press, 1990), 37–59; Knud Haakonssen, *Natural Law and Moral Philosophy: from Grotius to the Scottish Enlightenment* (Cambridge: Cambridge University Press, 1996), 63–85; Haakonssen, 'Natural Law and Moral Realism: the Scottish Synthesis', in Stewart, *Philosophy of the Scottish Enlightenment*, 61–85.

45 Kames first set out his moral theory in Henry Home, Lord Kames, *Essays on the Principles of Morality and Natural Religion* (Edinburgh: Printed by R. Fleming for A. Kincaid and A. Donaldson, 1751). He further developed it in *Principles of Equity*, 2nd edn (Edinburgh: Printed for A Millar, and for A. Kincaid and J. Bell, 1767) and *Sketches of the History of Man* (Edinburgh: Printed for W. Creech and for W. Strahan and T. Cadell, 1774). See generally Ian Simpson Ross, *Lord Kames and the Scotland of his Day* (Oxford: Clarendon Press, 1972).

46 From a huge literature, see, e.g., Knud Haakonssen, *The Science of a Legislator: the Natural Jurisprudence of David Hume and Adam Smith* (Cambridge: Cambridge University Press, 1981), 4–44.

47 Charles de Secondat de Montesquieu, *The Spirit of the Laws*, trans. by A. M. Cohler, B. C. Miller and H. S. Stone (Cambridge: Cambridge University Press, 1989), XVIII.8; R. L. Meek, *Social Science and the Ignoble Savage* (Cambridge: Cambridge University Press, 1976), 68–130; Peter Stein, 'The Four Stage Theory of the Development of Societies', in *The Character and Influence of the Roman Civil Law: Historical Essays* (London: Hambledon Press, 1988), 395–409.

48 Henry Home, Lord Kames, *Historical Law-Tracts* (Edinburgh: Printed for A. Millar, A. Kincaid and J. Bell, 1758). I should not be taken as arguing that Kames was the first to develop the 'four-stage' theory.

49 See, e.g., David Lieberman, *The Province of Legislation Determined: Legal Theory in Eighteenth-Century Britain* (Cambridge: Cambridge University Press, 1989), 144–75.

50 Cairns, 'Historical Introduction', 132–3; John W. Cairns, 'Ethics and the Science of Legislation: Legislators, Philosophers and Courts in Eighteenth-Century Scotland', *Jahrbuch für Recht und Ethik* 8 (2000), 159–80 at 160–1.

51 George Mackenzie, *Observations on the Acts of Parliament, Made by King James the First, King James the Second, King James the Third, King James the Fourth, King James the Fifth, Queen Mary, King James the Sixth, King Charles the First, King Charles the Second. Wherein 1. It is Observ'd, if they be in Desuetude, Abrogated, Limited, or Enlarged. 2. The Decisions relating to these Acts are mention'd. 3. Some new Doubts not yet decided, are hinted at. 4. Parallel Citations from the Civil, Canon, Feudal and Municipal Laws, and the Laws of other*

Nations, are adduc'd for clearing these Statutes (Edinburgh: Heir of Andrew Anderson, 1686), sig. A 4r.

52 See generally, Henry Home, Lord Kames, *Principles of Equity* (Edinburgh: A. Millar, A. Kincaid and J. Bell, 1760). See Lieberman, *Province of Legislation Determined*, 158–75.

53 Adam Smith, *The Theory of Moral Sentiments*, eds. D. D. Raphael and A. L. Macfie (Oxford: Clarendon Press, 1976); see generally Haakonssen, *Science of a Legislator*.

54 For the argument, see Cairns, 'Ethics and the Science of Legislation', 167–75.

55 Henry Home, Lord Kames, *Historical Law Tracts*, 4th edn (Edinburgh: Printed for T. Cadell, Bell and Bradfute, and W. Creech, 1792), [iii]

56 Henry Home, Lord Kames, *Elucidations Respecting the Common and Statute Law of Scotland* (Edinburgh: William Creech, 1777), vii–xiii.

57 John Craig, 'Account of the Life and Writings of John Millar, Esq.', prefixed to John Millar, *The Origin of the Distinction of Ranks: Or, an Inquiry into the Circumstances which give rise to Influence and Authority, in the Different Members of Society*, 4th edn (Edinburgh: W. Blackwood, 1806), xx, xl–xli.

58 Adam Smith, *Lectures on Jurisprudence*, eds. R. L. Meek, D. D. Raphael and P. G. Stein (Oxford: Clarendon Press, 1978).

59 John W. Cairns, 'Adam Smith and the Role of the Courts in Securing Justice and Liberty', in Robin Paul Malloy and J. Evensky, eds., *Adam Smith and the Philosophy of Law and Economics* (Dordrecht: Kluwer, 1994), 31–61.

60 See Gerald J. Postema, *Bentham and the Common Law Tradition* (Oxford: Clarendon Press, 1986); Lieberman, *Province of Legislation Determined*, 219–90.

61 Henry E. Strakosch, *State Absolutism and the Rule of Law: the Struggle for the Codification of Civil Law in Austria, 1753–1811* (Sydney: Sydney University Press, 1967).

62 Wieacker, *History of Private Law in Europe*, 251–5, 257–69.

63 Peter Stein, *Roman Law in European History* (Cambridge: Cambridge University Press, 1999), 110.

64 See, e.g., John W. Cairns, 'Alexander Cunningham's Proposed Edition of the Digest: an Episode in the History of the Dutch Elegant School of Roman Law', *Tijdschrift voor Rechtsgeschiedenis* 69 (2001), 81–117 (Part 1) and 307–59 (Part 11); Cairns, 'Three Unnoticed Scottish Editions of Pieter Burman's *Antiquitatum Romanarum brevis descriptio*', *The Bibliotheck* 22 (1997), 20–33.

65 Cairns, 'Historical Introduction', 149–55.

12 Sociality and socialisation

James Dunbar commented that humans are sociable long before they are rational.[1] In this chapter we shall explore the implications, both negative and positive, of that remark. The negative implications of Dunbar's remark concern the fact that certain prominent accounts of the role of reason in society must be rejected if Dunbar is correct. In particular, a major theme of writings on society and politics from the middle of the seventeenth century up to and beyond the end of the Enlightenment concerned the question whether, or to what extent, society and civic life were a product of people reasoning about what would be best for them. Thomas Hobbes, John Locke and Jean-Jacques Rousseau all wrote on this question and it was impossible for anyone else dealing with the topic to proceed as if these three had not spoken. The Scottish response to the three was in the main strongly hostile, and in the first section of this chapter their reaction will be considered. The positive implications of Dunbar's remark concern the way in which our being social affects us as individuals, and concern also the principles that produce and sustain social coherence. These implications are importantly linked in the writings of the Scots and constitute one of the most salient and characteristic features of their thought. It is to these positive implications that the remainder of the chapter will be devoted.

WAS THERE A SOCIAL CONTRACT?

The claim that humans are social before they are rational means that it is wrong to explain human social living as the product of reason, that is, of a process of calculation. Such an explanation was said by the Scots to have been made by thinkers who subscribed

243

to the doctrine that society was established by a contract accepted by people who calculated that their lives would be better in society than otherwise. It should be said, however, that mainstream versions of the contractarian doctrine dealt not with social living as such, but with civic or political living, and therefore with the establishment of government. Indeed it was central to the argument of mainstream contractarians that the pre-political condition was social. What they were centrally interested in was the *legitimacy* of government – what gave *that* individual, or group, the right or authority to command others? And the contractarian answer was that government and civil society existed not by nature but by deliberate choice. This choice, prompted by the 'inconveniences' (to use Locke's terminology) of the pre-political condition, the State of Nature, took the form of a contract whose chief term had the form: I shall lay aside my natural right to govern myself and shall obey your rule *provided* that you protect me and do not interfere with my other natural rights. This is a cost/benefit analysis that makes the role, even the existence, of government a function of an exercise of reason.

The Scots criticise this whole account on the grounds that there is no empirical warrant for the claim that there was ever a State of Nature. Adam Ferguson, for example, opens the *Essay on the History of Civil Society* with a chapter entitled 'Of the question relating to the State of Nature'. In that chapter he accuses those who talk of such a condition as deviating from the practice of the 'natural historian', who thinks the 'facts' should be collected and general tenets should be derived from 'observations and experiments'. By contrast, contractarians (he clearly has Hobbes and Rousseau in mind) resort to 'hypothesis' or 'conjecture' or 'imagination' or 'poetry'. To these Ferguson juxtaposes, respectively, 'reality', 'facts', 'reason' and 'science', and it is the latter list that 'must be admitted as the foundation of all our reasoning relative to man'.[2] We must, in other words, turn to evidence. This reveals that we have no record of any presocial state (*HCS* 6); all the evidence reveals that 'mankind are to be taken in groupes, as they always subsisted' (*HCS* 4; cf. 3, 16).

All the Scots rejected both the idea that people originally lived in a State of Nature and also the corollary, that society was brought into existence by means of a contract. Hume outlines a straightforward historical critique: that government originated in a contract is 'not justified by history or experience in any age or country of the world'.[3] And he judges the contractarian account of origins to be even less tenable when it claims that the legitimacy of current government rests on consent (*EOC* 469), since if 'these reasoners' were to examine actual practice and belief they 'would meet with nothing that in the least corresponds to their ideas' (*EOC* 470), for neither rulers nor subjects believe that their relationship is the effect of some prior pact. This is a damaging line of argument, since the very core of contractarian doctrine is that it is by some 'act of mind' (making a deliberate choice) that legitimacy is constituted. Hence the fact that any such act is 'unknown to all of them' is fatal to the theory.

Hume's refutation of contractarianism was widely followed. John Millar, for example, argues that merely obtaining some form of protection does not warrant the conclusion that this is the consequence of a promise.[4] Ferguson holds that the idea of men coming together as equals and deciding their mode of government is 'visionary and unknown in nature'.[5] Gilbert Stuart thinks there is no evidence and 'it is absurd to suppose that the original contract ever happened',[6] while Adam Smith picks up Hume's point that no contemporary obligation can stem from a past contract.[7]

It is within this rejection of the State of Nature/Original Contract that the seeds of the Scots' positive account are to be found. In the opening chapter of the *Essay*, Ferguson comments that 'all situations are equally natural'. This means, as he goes on to illustrate, that the State of Nature is 'here and it matters not whether we are understood to speak in the island of Great Britain, at the Cape of Good Hope, or the Straits of Magellan' (*HCS* 8). It equally follows that it matters not whether it is eighteenth or eighth century Britain. Since the 'natural condition' of humans is life in society the norms that bind us, for example our obligation to obey the law, must have their origin within society. It is still possible to talk of 'natural rights', as Ferguson and other Scots do, but given that we are by nature social beings these rights cannot be divorced from actual social existence.

WHY ARE WE SOCIAL?

If humans are not social as a consequence of an act of reason, what then does account for human sociality? One common account was that our sociality is instinctive or appetitive. Kames declared that it has never been called into question that man has 'an appetite for society'.[8] There was, however, a marked reluctance to push this recourse to instinct too far. To a large extent this stemmed from the desire to insist on qualitative differences between humans and animals and, of course, the possession of reason is one such difference – the fact that human sociality cannot be attributed to rational decision does not mean that humans do not reason. What is vital is not the possession of reason, nor the fact that it is purposive or calculative in its operation, but the fact that the faculty of reason takes time to develop. Whereas the infant antelope (say) is able within a few hours of birth to join and follow the herd, the newborn human baby is helpless.

In virtue of this dependence, humans require extensive nurture and Dunbar explicitly draws attention to the fact that, as a consequence, the parent/child bond is more durable than in animals (EHM 18). This durability results in family or kin ties extending beyond mere instinct, and Ferguson fastens upon this to account for the family's minor role as an explanation of sociality (PMPS 1:27). The affection that children have for their parents does not disappear, as it does in animals, once physical independence has been reached; rather, it grows closer 'as it becomes mixed with esteem and the memory of its early effects' (PMPS 1:16). The affective basis here is what is important. Children do not esteem their parents *because* they are honouring their part of a bargain or contract, the parents having already fulfilled their part. Family life, and by extension social life, is not reducible to rationalistic or instrumentalist explanations.

Ferguson makes much of this point. For him, there was more to human sociality than either 'parental affection' or an appetitive 'propensity...to mix with the herd' (HCS 16). Once some durability has been established, the independent principles of friendship and loyalty come into play. In each case they represent a sphere of human conduct that is not reducible either to animal instinct or to self-interested rational calculation. Ferguson indeed declares that the bonds formed by these principles are the strongest of all, and this is precisely because they transcend the self-centred quality of the other two. They are for that reason the most genuinely *social*. As supporting evidence he offers the observation that 'men are so far from valuing society on account of its mere external conveniencies that they are commonly most attached where those conveniencies are least frequent' (*HCS* 19). Indeed, to lay down one's life for one's friend or country is not some mental aberration, as Hobbes would have it, but is the very stuff of humans as social beings.[9]

In his argument that sociality is not reducible to the familial (a point also made by Dunbar[10]), Ferguson remarks that, as a further consequence of the durability of the child/parent relation, the instinctive attachments 'grow into habit'. This reference to habit is to a principle that plays a central role in the Scots' social theory. The very fact that humans are social creatures who require extended nurture means that they are exposed to the formative force of habit – they are, as Ferguson put it, 'withal in a very high degree susceptible of habits' (*HCS* 11, cf. *PMPS* 1:209).

Habits are repeated responses that are made possible by a stable set of circumstances. This repetitiveness leaves its mark. In a common but revealing phrase, habits become 'second nature'. As such they share some of the key features of 'first nature' or instinct. Reid quite explicitly linked them. Both are 'mechanical principles' that 'operate without will or intention'.[11] They can both in this way also be contrasted with rational action. In a straightforward sense rationality can be associated with maturity, whereas a baby's behaviour is largely instinctive (Reid prominently includes breathing, sucking and swallowing in his examples of instincts[12]). Picking up the earlier point that it is the *delayed* employment of reason that is vital, habits are especially potent in childhood; as Hume puts it, by 'operating on the tender minds of the children', they 'fashion them by degrees' for social life.[13] There is a consolidating dynamic at work here. Hume once again is instructive: 'whatever it be that forms the manners of one generation, the next must imbibe a deeper tincture of the same dye; men being more susceptible of all impressions during infancy, and retaining these impressions as long as they remain in the world'.[14] This is a crucial argument because it is central to the Scots' appreciation of the significance of the effects of sociality and their understanding of the factors underpinning social coherence, what I shall call institutional stickiness.

By stressing habit formation in childhood (what Turnbull terms 'early accustomance'[15]), the Scots are emphasising the importance of socialisation. A good example of this process in operation is provided by Hume in his positive alternative to the contractarian account of legitimation. He argues that if human generations (like silkworms) replaced themselves totally at one moment then that might give credibility to the contractarian theory, but the facts are different. Human societies are comprised of continually changing populations, so that to achieve any stability it is necessary that 'the new brood should conform themselves to the established constitution and nearly follow the path which their fathers, treading in the footsteps of theirs, had marked out to them' (*EOC* 476–7). The 'brood' conforms not as a consequence of any deliberate decision but because there is a pre-existent path. This path they follow because that is the way of their world, the one into which they have been socialised and whose institutions are correspondingly sticky.

The implications of this stickiness are that habits or customary ways of behaving, and the institutions thus constituted, not only stabilise – they constrain. Ferguson remarks that habits 'fix the manners of men' (as instinct fixes the behaviour of animals) (*PMPS* 1:232). Echoing Hume's argument about stability, Ferguson goes on to observe that without that fixity 'human life would be a scene of inextricable confusion and uncertainty' (ibid.). This fixity constrains by circumscribing the range of effective or discernible options. What might appear a 'rational' solution runs up against the 'fact' that sociality precedes rationality, so that, as Kames observed, it is 'a sort of Herculean labour to eradicate notions that from infancy have been held fundamental'.[16] These 'notions' are the socialised/habitual second nature; and 'the force of habit', as Millar felicitously terms it, is the 'great controller and governor of our actions' (*HV* IV:290). He cites, as an example, the way in which the 'power of habit', as it 'becomes more considerable as it passes from one generation to another', explains hereditary authority.[17]

Hume's discussion of chastity reinforces this point. For Hume, though not for all his fellow Scots, since women are not naturally chaste then they must be taught to be so. This teaching is nothing other than a process of socialisation: 'education takes possession of the ductile minds of the fair sex in their infancy' (*THN* 572). As he says of the related case of 'sentiments of honour', by taking root in 'tender minds' they 'acquire such firmness and solidity that they may fall little short of those principles which are most essential to our natures and the most deeply radicated in our internal constitution' (*THN* 501). It is the 'tenderness' or 'ductility' of the infant mind that makes 'custom and education' so powerful, as they inculcate 'principles of probity' and 'observance of those rules by which society is maintain'd as worthy and honourable' (*THN* 500). It is through families, and the societies within which they are embodied, that girls learn the value of chastity. This becomes so deeply 'radicated' that they will look upon extra- or pre-marital sex as conduct unbecoming a lady. They will know (will have internalised) the social consequences of the 'smallest failure', they know they will become 'cheap and vulgar', will lose 'rank', will be 'exposed to every insult'; they know, in short, that their 'character' will be 'blast[ed]'.[18] Chastity is a sticky institution; it is difficult for an individual to 'break free', and even if one does defy convention the obloquy that would follow is likely, in fact, to strengthen what has been defied.

THE EXPLANATION OF SOCIAL CHANGE

The awareness of the 'stickiness' of institutions expresses itself in various ways in the Scots' writings. A significant case in point is their explanation of social change. Since customs are creatures of time, then time, that is gradual alterations in the sentiments of people, is what changes them. In contrast to any glib confidence in 'progress' – the ever-increasing efficacy and transparency of reason – the Scots are more cautious.[19] They do believe in improvement, but it is not guaranteed and it is a gradual process.

It follows from this gradualism that it is not the case that social institutions upon being perceived as irrational can then simply be changed overnight, as it were. Institutions are 'sticky'; they are the repository of socialised norms and values. Robertson, referring to trial by combat, observes that no custom, 'how absurd soever it be', was 'ever abolished by the bare promulgation of laws and statutes'; rather, it fell into disuse with the development of 'science' and 'civility'.[20] Smith, in a well-known account, argues that the destruction of feudal power was 'gradually brought about' not by legal edict but by the 'silent and insensible operation of foreign commerce and manufactures' or, more generally, by changes in the form of 'property and manners'.[21] 'Manners', in fact, have a salience precisely because as a 'mode of behaviour' (*SHM* 1:181), as the socialised way of behaving, they are too complex for law.[22] Millar puts this principle into effect when he uses the changing lot of women to illustrate the 'natural progress' from 'rude to civilized manners' (*OR* 176), thus adding an historical dimension to Hume's discussion of chastity.

This recognition that change takes time also restricts the scope for individual, rational initiative. Much was made of this in the Scots' critique of the tradition of 'great legislators', Brama, Solon, Romulus, Lycurgus and Alfred, who were traditionally portrayed as the source of constitutions. But the role attributed to them is sociologically implausible. Millar comments that before any Legislator could have the requisite authority 'he must probably have been educated and brought up in the knowledge of those natural manners and customs which for ages perhaps have prevailed among his countrymen' (*OR* 177). Ferguson argues that if today in an age of 'extensive reflection' we 'cannot break loose from the trammels of custom' then it is very unlikely that in the times of the Legislators, when 'knowledge was less', individuals were more inclined to 'shake off the impressions of habit' (*HCS* 123).

The consequence of this 'entrammelling' is that, according to Millar, the Legislators will 'be disposed to prefer the system already established'. From the effects of this socialisation it follows that it is 'extremely probable' that they will have been 'at great pains to accommodate their regulations to the spirit of the people' and 'confined themselves to moderate improvements' rather than 'violent reformation'. Millar thinks the case of Lycurgus bears this out, because his regulations appear 'agreeable to the primitive manners of the Spartans' (*OR* 178). Alfred too fits this picture. Millar notes that his interpositions have been identified as 'the engine' to explain the origin of various English institutions (*HV* 1:271), but this is to uproot him implausibly from his social environment. Hence, for example, the institution of juries rose from the 'general situation of the Gothic nations' (ibid.) and the military institutions were not the product of some 'political projector' (*HV* 1:181); rather they stemmed 'imperceptibly' from 'the rude state of the country' (*HV* 1:179).[23]

Ferguson argues that the supposed Legislator in fact 'only acted a superior part among numbers who were disposed to the same institutions' (*HCS* 124).[24] For Ferguson the 'rise' of Roman and Spartan government came not from 'the projects of single men' but from 'the situation and genius of the people' (ibid.). Millar adopted the same line – 'the greater part of the political system' derived from the 'combined influence of the whole people' (*OR* 177). Dunbar allows, as Millar had done, that some individuals have had some impact but states that institutions are 'more justly reputed the slow result of situations than of regular design' (*EHM* 61). In his account of language, for example, he regards it as a 'fundamental error' to refer to 'great projectors' in order to explain the development of the different parts of speech (*EHM* 93).

A sociological/institutional rather than rationalist/individualist explanation is being offered here. The Scots criticise the latter as superficial and simplistic. When confronted with a particular institution or social practice the 'simplest' explanation is to attribute it to some 'previous design', that is, to attribute it to some individual's will or purpose as the cause of the institution as an effect; as Stuart observes, 'it is easy' to talk of the deep projects of princes but it is 'more difficult to mark the slow operation of events'.[25] Because individualistic explanations are simplistic they are misleading. They remove individuals from their social context, and since humans are naturally social then this removal is a distortion. From the perspective of the history of social theory this is an important conclusion: social institutions are to be explained by social causes. Stuart neatly summarises this point when he remarks that the disorders between the king and the nobles which affected the whole of Europe in the high Middle Ages are 'not to be referred entirely to the rapacity and the administration of princes. There *must be a cause more comprehensive and general* to which they [the disorders] are chiefly to be ascribed'.[26] From the earlier discussion we can identify these general causes as 'situation and genius' (Ferguson), or prevalent 'manners and customs' (Millar), or the 'slow result of situations' (Dunbar) or 'slow operation of events' (Stuart).

There is a juxtaposition here between the general (social) and the particular (rational individual), and the Scots thinkers held that of these two the former explains a much wider range of phenomena. Hume notes that from one roll of a biased die the outcome is 'chance', but from a 'great number' the bias will reveal itself as a 'determinate and known' cause.[27] Millar adopts a similar image, and aptly applies the example of a die in his assault on the 'legislator theory'. In one or two rolls the results will be random, but over time, that is, over many rolls, the results will be 'nearly equal'. The former case is like the impact of a legislator, the latter is like 'the combined influence of the whole people', which provides a more certain or 'fixed' causal explanation of a nation's 'political system' than any 'casual interposition' by a particular individual (OR 177).

As this last phrase suggests, Millar, Ferguson and the others do not deny that humans are purposive, but they nonetheless believe that individual deliberate action falls short of explanatory power when it comes to institutions. In perhaps the best-known expression of the point, Ferguson writes: 'nations stumble upon establishments which are indeed the result of human action, but not the execution of any human design' (HCS 122).[28] The insight was not his alone: Hume, for example, provides a good illustration of the point. He remarks that the first leader achieved the position because he was an effective military commander, and that in due course, through time and custom, this ad hoc position solidified into a monarchical form of government. Hume comments on this process that though it 'may appear certain and inevitable', in fact government commenced casually because it 'cannot be expected that men should beforehand be able to discover them [that is, principles of government and allegiance] or foresee their operation'.[29]

This recognition of the limitations of individual rationality and of the associated resistance, or stickiness, of institutions to rational 'quick-fixes' is only to be expected from a group of thinkers who, as social theorists, take the 'social' seriously. Human experience is experience of social life. As products of socialisation, individuals are embedded within their societies. To speak generally, the Scots plotted societies on to a temporal grid (the four-stages theory is the most famous instance of this), and then this grid was 'read across' to discern the ways in which the different institutions cohered. This is of central importance in understanding how the Scots' social theory generated a conception of society as a set of interlocked institutions and behaviours. A society of hunter gatherers will thus have little in the way of personal possessions, nothing to speak of in the form of governmental machinery, and few status distinctions except the inferiority of women, and will live in a world populated with a multiplicity of gods. These savages would also respond to this environment in a speech abounding in vivid and animated images and would likely bedaub themselves and/or indulge in self-mutilation (cf. EHM 389; SHM 11:437). They would have been socialised into accepting this conduct as normal. Millar acknowledges this clearly:

'individuals form their notions of propriety according to a general standard, and fashion their morals in conformity to the prevailing taste of the times' (HV IV:246).[30] However, as moralists the Scots do not merely accept the diversity of social experience and thus the diversity of moral beliefs was not merely accepted – they have no doubts that life in a free and civilised society is a better life than all that has gone before. The way in which they avoid inconsistency is by treating as axiomatic the uniformity and universality of human nature and then attributing to it the capacity to improve or progress (HCS 8; OR 176, etc.).

SOCIETY AND MORALITY

The point just made regarding the relation between morality and society can be illustrated with reference to Smith's moral theory. In a famous passage he likens society to a mirror.[31] The force of this comparison is that moral judgements are generated by social interaction – learning how to behave through seeing how others react to our behaviour. To give one of Smith's own examples: if I see a grief-stricken stranger and am informed that he has just learned of his father's death then I, via sympathy, approve of his grief. What makes this possible is that I have learnt from experience that such misfortune excites such sorrow (TMS I.i.3.4). The experience can only come from 'common life', from the fact that humans are social creatures. The importance and centrality of sociality is once again underwritten.

In line with the earlier argument, this now seems to imply that moral judgements are the socialised product of a particular society. Smith even seems not to exempt the principle of conscience from this process, since he declares that the authority possessed by conscience is the effect of 'habit and experience' (TMS III.3.3). The fact that it is habitual, so that 'we are scarce sensible' that we do appeal to it, means that it too is a learnt resource. However this does not mean that it, or moral judgement more generally, is a mere reflex of prevalent social norms.[32] His account of infanticide provides the concluding illustration.

While openly admitting that virtues differ between 'rude and barbarous nations' and 'civilized nations' (TMS v.2.8), Smith nonetheless believes that 'the sentiments of moral approbation and disapprobation are founded on the strongest and most vigorous passions of human nature; and though they may be somewhat warpt, cannot be entirely perverted' (*TMS* v.2.1). Infanticide is his case in point. He accounts for this by the fact that 'in the earliest period of society' it was commonplace, and the 'uniform continuance of the custom had hindered them [the practitioners] from perceiving its enormity' (*TMS* v.2.15). He does allow the practice to be 'more pardonable' in the rudest and lowest state of society, where 'extreme indigence' obtains, but the practice was inexcusable 'among the polite and civilized Athenians'. Smith is adamant that just because something is commonly done does not mean it is condonable when the practice itself is 'unjust and unreasonable' (ibid.).

What this example underlines is the fact that the thinkers of the Scottish Enlightenment combined a 'scientific' appreciation of the complexity of social life with an evaluative assessment of the relative worth of forms of social experience. On the one hand this combination makes them fully members of the Enlightenment family but, on the other, their insight into the limits of individual rational action, the stabilising yet constraining power of customs, and the stickiness of social institutions means that they never subscribed to that aspect of Enlightenment thought which could confidently envisage the conquest of dark irrationality by the irresistible force of the light of reason.

NOTES

1   J. Dunbar, *Essays on the History of Mankind in Rude and Cultivated Ages*, 2nd edn (1781; reprint, Bristol: Thoemmes Press, 1995), 16. (Hereafter inserted in text as *EHM*.) See my *Social Theory of the Scottish Enlightenment* (Edinburgh: Edinburgh University Press, 1997), 30. This paper expands the point while drawing upon the earlier discussion.

2   Adam Ferguson, *An Essay on the History of Civil Society* [1767], ed. D. Forbes (Edinburgh: Edinburgh University Press, 1966), 2. (Hereafter inserted in text as *HCS*.)

3   David Hume, 'Of the Original Contract' [1748], in E. F. Miller, ed., *Essays Moral, Political and Literary* (Indianapolis: Liberty Fund, 1987), 471. (Hereafter inserted in the text as *EOC*.)

4   John Millar, *Historical View of the English Government*, 4 vols. (London, 1812), IV:303. (Hereafter inserted in text as *HV*.)

5 Adam Ferguson, *Principles of Moral and Political Science*, 2 vols. (1792; reprint; New York: AMS Press, 1973), 1:262. (Hereafter inserted in the text as *PMPS*.)

6 Gilbert Stuart, *Historical Dissertation concerning the Antiquity of the English Constitution* (Edinburgh, 1768), 151 n. (Hereafter inserted in the text as *HDEC*.)

7 Adam Smith, *Lectures on Jurisprudence* [1762, 1766], eds. R. L. Meek, D. D. Raphael and P. G. Stein (Indianapolis: Liberty Press, 1982), v.115.

8 Henry Home, Lord Kames, *Sketches of the History of Man*, 3rd edn, 2 vols. (Edinburgh: 1774), 1:376. (Hereafter inserted in the text as *SHM*); cf. Kames, *Essays on the Principles of Morality and Natural Religion*, 3rd edn (Edinburgh: 1751), 79, 136, 139 etc. Similar assertions are made by, for example, Ferguson (*HCS* 11, 122, 182; *PMPS* 1.32); John Gregory, *Comparative View of the State and Faculties of Man with those of the Animal World* [1765], in *Works* (Edinburgh, 1788), 2, 114; George Turnbull, *The Principles of Moral Philosophy* (London, 1740), 175; and Dunbar (*EHM* 24).

9 Ferguson's thoughts on this issue are closely connected to his worries about the tendency of contemporary commercial societies to increase the prevalence of calculative behaviour. Some commentators have made much of this see, inter alia, J. Brewer, 'Adam Ferguson and the Theme of Exploitation', *British Journal of Sociology* 37 (1986), 461–78; T. Benton, 'Adam Ferguson and the Enterprise Culture', in P. Hulme and L. Jordanova, eds., *The Enlightenment and its Shadows* (London: Routledge, 1990), 103–20; J. Varty, 'Civic or Commercial? Ferguson's concept of Civil Society', in R. Fine and S. Rai, eds, *Civil Society: Democratic Perspectives* (London: Cass, 1997), 29–48.

10 Dunbar argues that even the maternal instincts were fluctuating in earlier times, *EHM* 23.

11 Thomas Reid, *Essays on the Active Powers of the Human Mind* [1788], in his *The Works of Thomas Reid, DD*, ed. Sir William Hamilton, 2 vols. (Edinburgh, 1846), 11:550A.

12 Ibid., 545.

13 David Hume, *A Treatise of Human Nature* [1739/40], ed. L. A. Selby-Bigge, 2nd edn, rev. P. H. Nidditch (Oxford: Clarendon Press, 1978), 486. (Hereafter inserted in the text as *THN*.)

14 Hume, 'Of National Characters' [1748], in *Essays*, 203.

15 Turnbull, *Principles of Moral Philosophy*, 99.

16 Henry Home, Lord Kames, *Loose Hints on Education* (Edinburgh, 1781), 282. Elsewhere Kames uses a different metaphor to the same end, 'the influence of custom in rivetting men to their local situation and manner of life', *SHM* 11:87.

17 John Millar, *The Origin of the Distinction of Ranks*, 3rd edn [1779], repr. in W. Lehmann, *John Millar of Glasgow* (Cambridge: Cambridge University Press, 1960), 250. (Hereafter inserted in the text as *OR*.)

18 Hume, *Enquiry concerning the Principles of Morals* [1751], in Hume, *Enquiries Concerning Human Understanding and Concerning the Principles of Morals*, ed. L. A. Selby-Bigge, 3rd edn, rev. P. H. Nidditch (Oxford: Clarendon Press, 1975), 238–9.

19 Cf. D. Forbes, 'Scientific Whiggism: Adam Smith and John Millar', *Cambridge Journal* 7 (1954), 643–70.

20 William Robertson, *View of Progress in Europe* [1769], in *The Works of William Robertson, DD*, ed. Dugald Stewart (London: T. Cadell, 1840), 325.

21 Adam Smith, *An Inquiry into the Nature and Causes of the Wealth of Nations* [1776], eds. R. H. Campbell and A. S. Skinner, W. B. Todd, textual editor, 2 vols. (Indianapolis: Liberty Classics, 1981), III.iv.8–10.

22 Kames, *Loose Hints on Education*, 21.

23 See also Hume who comments that as Alfred's institutions were similar to those found elsewhere then this counts against him being 'the sole author of this plan of government'; rather, 'like a wise man he contented himself with reforming, extending and executing the institutions which he found previously established', in *History of England*, 3 vols. (1786; reprint, Routledge: London, 1894), 1:50, 53.

24 Stuart cites this argument and closely follows Ferguson's terminology, *HDEC* 248.

25 Gilbert Stuart, *Observations concerning the Public Law and the Constitutional History of Scotland* (Edinburgh, 1779), 108.

26 Gilbert Stuart, *A View of Society in Europe*, 2nd edn (1792; reprint, Bristol: Thoemmes, 1995), 71 (my emphasis). Cf. Millar who argues that it was the 'improvement of arts and the consequent diffusion of knowledge' leading to dispelling superstition and 'inspiring sentiments of liberty' that 'is to be regarded as the *general cause* of the reformation', *HV* IV:434 (my emphasis).

27 Hume, 'Of the Rise and Progress of the Arts and Sciences' [1742], in *Essays*, 112.

28 See, inter alia, for comment R. Hamowy, *The Scottish Enlightenment and the Theory of Spontaneous Order* (Carbondale: Southern Illinois University Press, 1987); F. Hayek, *Studies in Philosophy, Politics and Economics* (London: Routledge, 1967), 96–105.

29 Hume, 'Of the Origin of Government', in *Essays*, 39–40.

30 See also Robertson, *History of America* [1777], in *Works*, 811.

31 Adam Smith, *Theory of Moral Sentiments* [1759], eds., D. D. Raphael and A. L. Macfie (Indianapolis: Liberty Press, 1982), III.1.3. (Hereafter inserted in the text as *TMS*.) See also Hume, *THN* 365.

32 See, inter alia, for comment D. D. Raphael, 'The Impartial Spectator', in A. S. Skinner and T. Wilson, eds., *Essays on Adam Smith* (Oxford: Clarendon Press, 1975), 83–99, 90; V. M. Hope, *Virtue by Consensus: the Moral Philosophy of Hutcheson, Hume and Adam Smith* (Oxford: Clarendon Press, 1989), 105; C. J. Berry, 'Smith and Science', in K. Haakonssen, ed., *Cambridge Companion to Smith* (Cambridge: Cambridge University Press, forthcoming).

13 Historiography

The historiography of the Scottish Enlightenment has had an un-paralleled influence on the way history has been understood in the United Kingdom, North America and throughout the erstwhile British Empire. It is to the Enlightenment that we owe the ideas of historical progress, of state development through time and, ulti-mately, the whole teleological apparatus which for many years sus-tained what was known as the school of Whig history: the analysis of the past not on its own terms, but in the light of what it could contribute to an account of progress towards the present. In the last century historiography has diversified from this model, but the tele-ological vision still exercises a hold on both the popular imagination and some areas of historical scholarship, particularly in the narrative history still dominant in media programmes and school textbooks. When, for example, some of the new British History traces the past foundations of our country 'for the sake of the present' and its contemporary anxieties over Britishness rather than 'making the past our present and attempting to see life with the eyes of another century', then in Herbert Butterfield's words, we are partaking in 'the subordination of the past to the present', and this vision was central to the Enlightenment. When in *The Whig Interpretation of History* (1931), Butterfield argued of the past that 'their generation was as valid as our generation, their issues as momentous as our issues and their day as full and vital to them as our day is to us' he was striking not only at posterity's condescension, but at issues which lay at the heart of the complex world of the historiography of David Hume (1711–76) and William Robertson (1721–93) among others.[1]

INTRODUCTION

The Enlightenment was particularly concerned with the application of reason to knowledge in a context of quantifiable improvement. In Scotland, partly because of its relative poverty, the nature
of that improvement was often material, financial or technological:
the New Town of Edinburgh as 'earthly paradise', the innovation of
John Law's dematerialised monetary economy or the steam power of
James Watt.[2] Underlying the idea of improvement lay, as a necessary
corollary, the premiss of the possibility of progressive change. The assumptions of quantifiable improvement which underpinned the Enlightenment were clearly spelt out by Adam Ferguson (1723–1816)
in his *Principles of Moral and Political Science* (1792), which argued
that 'the generation, in which there is no desire to know more or
practice better than its predecessors, will probably neither know so
much nor practice so well' and that 'to every generation the state of
arts and accommodations already in use serves but as ground work
for new inventions and successive improvement'.[3]

Change was and is the universal premiss of human affairs. But although Greek thinkers such as Thucydides had recognised this in
the study of human society, and later writers of the Renaissance had
developed it, the idea of Progress was not inherited from the classical
world, and that world was still the measure of contemporary society,
even in the late seventeenth century with its controversies between
Ancients and Moderns. The pastoral poetry of Virgil and Horace
formed part of an ideological bulwark for those who sympathised
with the landed interest against the new money of the Financial Revolution in the cities, the heartlands of the Enlightenment in Scotland
in particular.

In historiography, it was Giambattista Vico (1668–1744) who in *La
Scienza Nova* [New Science] (1725) argued that 'all nations proceed
through the same sequence of human institutions, according to the
principles of ideal eternal history'. These developed through a priest-
controlled society of gods, oracles and auspices through a heroic,
aristocratic society towards more democratic models of 'popular
commonwealths and . . . monarchies'. Vico developed Plato's ideas of
change and cyclical alteration in history into a descriptive model of
human societies.[4]

Such ideas helped to fuel one of the key intellectual drivers of the Scottish Enlightenment, that of the teleology of civility: the idea that society's material and intellectual improvement was also a development towards higher standards of culture and refinement, such 'high standards' usually being predicated on metropolitan norms of speech and culture. The Union of 1707 had put intense pressure on Scottish society, institutions, language and culture to draw closer to English models. In order to begin to succeed in British society, Scots had to conform more closely to the public standards of genteel Englishness. Some, particularly north of the Tay and among the Episcopalian nobility, remained dedicatedly patriotic towards the old Scotland, and sought to destroy the Hanoverian state by force of arms and the old way of Continental alliance: their challenge ended at Culloden in 1746, and they were marginalised by the historians of the Enlightenment, whose assessment of them still proves influential. Many abandoned traditional ways slowly and grudgingly; a few gifted individuals like Allan Ramsay (1684–1758) tried to find a place for Scottish culture in the new order. Others, particularly in central Scotland, either out of enthusiasm or *faute de mieux*, sought ways and means to accommodate themselves to English models, and made 'civility' the goal not only of their own personal ambition, but of their country's (and indeed the world's) history. As the Aberdeen professor James Beattie said in the 1770s, 'I am one of those who wish to see the English spirit and English manners prevail over the whole island: for I think the English have a generosity and openness of nature which many of us want.' With the professoriate (the backbone of the Enlightenment) endorsing such views, it was little wonder that the university curriculum in places such as Aberdeen should endorse and promote the British state and constitution.[5] The paradox of the Scottish Enlightenment was that so many autonomous ideas rose from this paradigm of conformity.

The idea of progress towards a better thought out society was arguably first developed in Britain by Englishmen. The idea of the ancient constitution of Saxon liberty found in seventeenth-century Whig thought and the idea that England was emerging from under the Norman yoke of feudalism and monarchical power to regain this liberty (a process completed in 1688), lay at the core of Whig ideology. Present in the ideas of Sir Edward Coke (1552–1634) and William Prynne (1600–69) (who argued in 1642 that kings had been elected), the idea of Saxon liberty was to be profoundly influential both on English radicalism and Scottish historiography. In England it was Henry St John, Viscount Bolingbroke (1678–1751) who appropriated it for history, although Sir Walter Raleigh (1552–1618) has been seen as 'the first Whig historian'.[6] Bolingbroke united a Tory sensibility with the Whig 'spirit of liberty, transmitted down from our Saxon ancestors' in his *Dissertation upon Parties* (1733–4), and argued that Britain was at risk of the fate of Rome.[7]

In Scotland, Thomas Blackwell (1701–57) conceived society as growing in refinement from early times, while Francis Hutcheson (1694–1746) drew history into the 'social context' of moral decision. In France, Charles, Baron Montesquieu (1689–1755) in *De l'Esprit des lois* (1748) offered 'a taxonomy of the three basic forms of government', despotism, monarchy, republic and their relation to human nature,[8] and Anne-Robert-Jacques, Baron Turgot (1727–81) in his 1750 discourse at the Sorbonne, 'On the Successive Advances of the Human Mind', clearly stated for the first time the accomplishment and expectation of progress in technology and history. Jean-Jacques Rousseau, by contrast, helped to shape the contrary view of the authenticity of the primitive. Both views were influential on Scottish thought, from James Boswell to Robertson, and Sir Walter Scott combined the two in literature.

Montesquieu anticipated Adam Smith (1723–90) and other Scottish Enlightenment writers in arguing that 'the natural effect of commerce is to lead to peace', and even identified the core problem of teleological history before it was written, saying that 'to carry back to distant centuries the ideas of the century in which one lives is of all sources of error the most fertile'. Montesquieu's identification of the 'free' nature of the Germans and England's striving for liberty were no doubt also supportive of the sociological history which followed him. But the Scottish Enlightenment historians (with the possible exception of Ferguson) may have laid an undue emphasis on this aspect of Montesquieu's work. They 'amplified and restructured the second half of *The Spirit of the Laws* so that it illustrated the development of the conditions of a modern free government. Unlike Montesquieu, they were not interested in the complex of passions, beliefs, and practices that supported other kinds of governments'.[9] Montesquieu's view of 'English liberty' was no doubt particularly congenial to those such as Hume and Robertson, who wanted to recast Scotland's past, though Turgot, whose 'On Universal History' came out in 1753, was also no doubt influential in his insistence on the progressive nature of history.[10]

THE SCOTTISH ENLIGHTENMENT

It was in Scotland that the demands of teleology of civility ensured that this approach reached its most complex pitch of development. Scotland's constitution had massively altered since 1603, possibly more than that of any other unconquered European country: the king had moved his capital, the court had left, Parliament had been abolished, restored and abolished again; heritable jurisdictions and powers of regality, the last echoes of the great Celtic mormaers, had vanished; the taxation system had completely altered, and the establishment of the church had changed five times, from Catholic to Presbyterian/Episcopalian to Episcopalian to Presbyterian to Episcopalian and back to Presbyterian again. The intellectual élite of what was still in domestic matters a separate country under its own political management had to make sense of this extraordinary turbulence: in Bolingbrokian terms, to learn the lessons of its history. David Hume, William Robertson and Adam Smith all focused on tracing 'human development through certain common stages of progress from barbarism to refinement'. To this there was a natural concomitant: the 'dismissal of much of the... past as mere barbarism and superstition'.[11]

Adam Smith provided one of the earliest models of this 'human development', arguing in 'The Four-Stage Theory of Development' in his 1762 lectures on jurisprudence, that 'there are four distinct states which mankind pass thro:– 1st, the Age of Hunters; 2ndly, the Age of Shepherds; 3dly, the Age of Agriculture; and 4thly, the Age of Commerce'. In each, society grew closer to civility.[12] A warlike aristocracy (in the Scottish Enlightenment's terms, a problem which was particularly acute in Scotland) should give way to a society pursuing personal betterment in a commercial environment. For such betterment, peace is better than war: not least because in war the ogres of traditional state, aristocratic and institutional power, can turn the clock back. Equality of opportunity, essential to the model of American society, derives from this classic Enlightenment position.[13] The view of Tom Paine (1737–1809) in the immensely influential *Common Sense* (1776), written in support of the American War of Independence, was that the best government is less government. This was consonant with Smith's views, and formed the basis of mainstream US attitudes to big government from that day forwards. Smith's model was also to be exceptionally influential in his own country, and had an immediate impact on the thought of Adam Ferguson (1723–1816), John Millar (1735–1801), Lord Kames (1696–1782) and Dugald Stewart (1753–1828).

Stewart, in his idea of 'theoretical or conjectural history', developed Smith's ideas,[14] addressing the problem of how we can conjecture historical change for which no evidence exists by examining the same stage in development for a society where the evidence does exist. Human nature, Stewart in common with many Enlightenment thinkers believed, was common everywhere and at all times, and so we can extrapolate. Conjectural history was itself a philosophical version of the stadial history of historians such as Robertson, where it is presumed that society advances through stages: Robertson provides this kind of analysis of the Native Americans, and conjectural history in Stewart's terms is implicitly present throughout Robertson's work. For the philosopher, though, the purpose of history was something more than civility: Stewart believed in the 'necessary progress and perfectibility of humanity through education and social reform'.[15]

The idea that society advances through the same stages, though not necessarily at the same rate, had a major impact on the strong Scottish contribution to early anthropology, notably in the work of Sir James Frazer (1854–1941), whose seminal *Golden Bough* (1890–1915) depended heavily on this concept, since Frazer claimed to be able to understand the religious beliefs of societies in the ancient world by studying the behaviour of nineteenth-century tribes in what was projected to be the same stage of development. The debt to Smith's and Dugald Stewart's notions of staged development and conjectural history is clear.

Henry Home, Lord Kames, was one of the early exemplars of conjectural history in his *Historical Law-Tracts* (1758), which also bear a close relationship to Bolingbroke's work,[16] and provide the beginnings of a sociology of law through the 'successive changes' they seek to chart: Kames also has the goal of underpinning beneficial mutual borrowing between English and Scots law.[17] His *Essays on*

British Antiquities (1747) had already promoted the idea of a common Britishness, and he was of one mind with Robertson (see below) in his view that 'the withering away of the feudal baronage was one of the marks of modernity'.[18] The abolition of heritable jurisdictions in 1747 could be seen as marking that transition in the Enlightenment's view: the old patriot nobility were defeated for the last time at Culloden, and modernity, Britain's gift to an ungrateful Scotland, could supervene. In what he hoped would be his crowning work, *Sketches of the History of Man* (2nd edn, 1778), Kames attempts a universal history of the 'progress toward maturity in different nations', covering man in and out of society, commerce, arts, manners and the sciences.[19]

John Millar, Professor of Law at Glasgow, who was under the patronage of Smith and subsequently Kames, and who served as tutor to Kames's son, wrote in *The Origin of the Distinction of Ranks* (1779 (first published as *Observations concerning the Distinction of Ranks in Society* (1771)) of 'differences in situation' in terms which offered the beginning of a different anthropological reading of the development of society. Millar ends the book with a discussion of the 1778 Scottish judgement against slavery, the first to state that 'the dominion assumed over this negro' was itself ipso facto 'unjust', as against previous judgements which had centred on the extent of master's rights. Millar is proud of the decision, which itself points forwards to a new state of society in a world beyond that in which he writes.[20]

HUME AND ROBERTSON

The particular role of Scotland in any generic statement of sociological history was not far from the surface. Scotland was 'the rudest, perhaps, of all European Nations' in Enlightenment eyes. Its conversion to civility must involve in part the despising of its own past, in which it had once revelled. Hume and Robertson each wrote a history which was no longer one of 'defensive patriotism', but was instead constructed 'for English readers'. Hume, who 'sought to address a new audience... who aspired to participate in polite conversation', ultimately made over £6,000 from his *History of England*, and *Charles V* alone earned Robertson £4,500 – over £400,000 at today's prices.[21]

Both Hume and Robertson sought to adapt their use of Tacitus, adopted from earlier defensive patriotism, to propound the idea of the 'personal liberty and independence' of the Germanic peoples as a whole, the 'freedom and independence' of the Huns and Alans and so on.[22] This idea, which had become popular as an underpinning to the centrality of the individual judgement in the Protestant Reformation, and which was introduced to England by Richard Rowlands/Verstegan (fl. 1565–1620),[23] was to form an almost unquestioned denominator in much of the work of Hume and Robertson. With the exception of Scotland (soon to be partially Teutonised by Enlightenment historiography) and Wales, almost every country in reformed Europe could be seen as Germanic or with a strong Germanic component: north Germany and the Baltic, Holland, Switzerland, Denmark, Norway, Sweden and England. The equation of liberty with Protestantism, in the mind of many Enlightenment figures (if not altogether that of Hume, though he regarded 'the Reformation as a constitutional event of great, though not deliberate wisdom') reinforced the basic point.[24] If the Germanic peoples had a predisposition to liberty, if liberty and equality of opportunity were necessary for commerce, and if commerce was the highest stage of human development (though the Enlightenment writers realised that it could have its own problems), then there was bound to be great virtue in the Teutonic peoples. Scotland must be Germanic to be civilised. Its discarding of its feudal nobility and 'savage' Highland/Catholic past was at the core of this process. Some Enlightenment writers even 'discovered' the struggle for Germanic liberty in Scotland's past, as for example did John Millar, who thought there had been a pre-feudal Witenagemot in Scotland, as in Anglo-Saxon England. Millar wrote of 'our Saxon forefathers' with their 'comprehensive notions of liberty', although he suggested that the 'insular situation' of Britain had done much to succour English liberty, which otherwise was not so common among primitive peoples (in his *Historical View of the English Government*, the terms 'English' and 'British' tend to slide into each other).[25] English historical models were transferred to Scotland, and Scotland's own history provincialised in a discourse where 'England represented modernity'. Robertson among others displayed an 'implied acceptance of the Anglican interpretation of the Scottish dark age', which so many of the controversialists of the Union period had struggled against.[26]

This stress on Germanicity in the work of Hume and Robertson was important. Robertson stressed German unruliness, but also stressed German 'liberty'.[27] Scotland could be seen as a nation partly Germanic (Saxon Lowlanders – though this was in part a piece of ethnic mythology) and partly Celtic (Gaelic-speaking Highlanders): it was thus constructed by Sir Walter Scott, Enlightenment historiography's greatest interpreter. Although writers such as Gilbert Stuart (1743–86) and James Macpherson (1736/8–96) linked Celtic and Saxon struggles for liberty,[28] the general trend was towards the marginalisation of Celtic Scotland as a serious contributor to history, as opposed to (as it became in the Romantic period) a comforting locale of 'old, unhappy far-off things, and battles long ago' (Wordsworth, 'The Solitary Reaper').

The perceived Germanicity of Protestantism also contributed to the paradigm whereby Highlanders/Celts were stereotyped as Catholic, which most were not. This in turn helped reinforce the mythology, sedulously fed by many of the Enlightenment writers themselves, in which Lowland Scotland was ethnically Germanic, and Highland Scotland Celtic. Thus John Pinkerton (1758–1826) divided 'ascendant Goths' from 'slavish Celts', Robert Knox (1791–1862) lectured on 'the superiority of the Anglo-Saxon race' after his medical career was damaged by his association with Burke and Hare, and George Combe (1788–1858) 'was a Teutonist who thought that "the Scotch Lowland population ... has done everything by which Scotland is distinguished"', though the view, derived from Tacitus, that the ancient Celts were themselves Germanic, complicated these positions.[29] But given this model of an ethnically divided Scotland, it could be argued that Scotland, until the Union linked its Saxons with those of England, was too divided between liberty-loving Teuton and feckless Celt to unite in the pursuit of liberty. This constructed tension in Scottish history is visible in many of Scott's novels, which contrast the settled life of the Lowland burgh with the instability of internecine private war among the clans. Just as importantly, it lay at the core of much nineteenth-century historiography.

When Hume writes, 'I am of no party, and have no bias',[30] this ringing claim of modern historiography must be understood in terms of the values which underpin it. Hume is not writing a 'party' history in the English or British sense, but he is writing teleological history:

it would be an anachronism to call it 'Whig', but this is what it became. That is not to view it crudely, for

Hume approached his subject as a moral philosopher already deeply interested in the peculiarities of human nature, the unpredictable yet decisive rule of beliefs in motivating human action...He also adopted the standpoint of a social philosopher searching (like Gibbon after him) for the secular origins of religious belief, the political effects of economic change, and the cultural basis of political stability.

Hume thought he was 'very moderate', and certainly his *History of England* (1754–62, final edn 1778) could not readily be convicted of party bias in the terms of the 1750s, though it upset many Whigs by being insufficiently partisan.[31] Hume had read Montesquieu at Turin in 1749, had subsequently corresponded with him, and shared with him the view of history as a 'continuing process'. In this sense among others, the *History* was more philosophical than partisan.[32] It was certainly nothing like Catherine Macaulay's *Whig History of England from the Revolution to the Present Time* (1778) or the magisterial Whiggism of her greater namesake and his successors in the Oxford school. Nonetheless, Hume's immensely influential work, which went through 55 editions by the early nineteenth century, helped to create the climate in which much of what followed was possible. His 'philosophical distinctions' were more balanced than T. B. Macaulay's insistence on England's consistently lofty 'view of human liberty', but Hume's historiographical model was one where the barbarities of English history were exceptional, but those of Scottish normative.[33] The constant nature of human desire, which Hume, in common with other Enlightenment thinkers, observed, nonetheless allowed of progress, and still more the elevation of norms or desirable goals. The picture is strongly teleologised: 'the diversities of British history came to matter less to Hume than his desire to bring them into focus under the perspective of a more general history of the rise of modern liberty'. A brief examination of Hume's language brings this into perspective.[34] At the beginning of Volume I of his *History*, Hume writes: 'of all the barbarous nations...the Germans seem to have been the most distinguished both by their manners and political institutions, and to have carried to the highest pitch the virtues of valour and love of liberty'(1:15). Their government 'was always extremely free' (1:160). When the

Saxons came to invade 'Britain, as they enjoyed great liberty in their own country, [they] obstinately retained that invaluable possession in their new settlement' (1:161): although the Celts had been 'free', the now 'degenerate' Britons were 'destitute of all affection to their new liberties' (1:5, 18). Despite the 'deep obscurity' of the 'uncertain traditions' of this period (1:17), Hume confidently asserts that Scotland is Germanic: 'all the lowlands, especially the east-coast... were peopled in a great measure from Germany'. To say otherwise is to descend to the 'fabulous annals... obtruded on us by the Scottish historians' (Hume, writing the *History of England*, rhetorically constructs himself as 'English' in opposition to these 'Scottish' historians). Then in true Enlightenment style, Hume presents his evidence: 'the expeditions' of the Germans to Scotland, he tells us, 'have escaped the records of history' (1:23) – thus obliquely confessing that his, too, is a 'fabulous annal', conjectured only from the linguistic evidence of his own times. In Saxon times, Hume proceeds, there are the makings of an 'ancient democracy' (1:172). He further feeds English particularism, the idea of the uniqueness of the 'island race' (Sir Henry Newbolt's phrase) by stating that before the Norman Conquest, 'this island' (Hume appears to elide England and Britain) 'was as much separated from the rest of the world in politics as well as in situation... the English... had neither enemies nor allies on the Continent' (1:297). Not Guthrum, nor Sweyn Forkbeard, nor Canute, neither the jarls of Orkney nor the kingdom of York features in Hume's view of untroubled Anglo-British insularity. John Millar also emphasised this, and yet only fifty years before, Scottish historians had been pointing out how often England had been invaded!

In this new Anglocentric history, Scotland and Ireland fare less well. The Irish, described as one people with the Scots by Robert the Bruce,[35] a people whose soldiers had been found in Scottish armies as recently as Culloden in 1746, are in Hume's words 'from the beginning of time... buried in the most profound barbarism and ignorance (1:339)... savage and untractable'(1:345): so bad were they, that the 'inroads' of Viking 'barbarism' 'tended rather to improve the Irish' (1:340). They are only now becoming 'a useful conquest to the English nation' (1:345). Although Hume does acknowledge English injustice in Ireland (11:159), he sees this in part as 'joining the ardour of revenge' to the 'as yet untamed barbarity' of the Irish, whom the English settlers have let down by going native themselves (1:344–5; III:311). Emphasis on Irish 'sloth and barbarism' is a feature of Hume's work, while the Scots are 'more uncultivated and uncivilized' (than the English), while Scots Highlanders are 'most disorderly and least civilized'. In dealing with Scotland's attacks on England, Hume has a tendency to attach disapprobatory adjectives: hence the 'barbarous devastation' of David I, and the 'horrible depradations', 'wantonly' war and 'great devastations' of William the Lion contrast with the simple 'ravage' and 'burn' of English activity in Scotland and the lack of violence and injustice by which Henry II is specifically characterised as against William (1:285, 354, 355, 358; III:145). Hume notes the propensity to fanaticism in the Scots and Irish,[36] and though he condemns the Popish Plot, seems to see it as ultimately atypical of English society. Fanaticism is the normative property of fanatical countries, but an aberration in tolerant ones, even if it reaches the same or higher levels.[37]

Hume's *History* pushes gently but repeatedly in this direction: he could be sympathetic to James VI and Charles I, and could express reservations about the British Constitution, but his view of the 'Glorious' Revolution and the years that followed place him 'on the side of the Walpolean Whigs'.[38] As Hume advised Boswell on 28 October 1774, Boswell 'should write the history of the Union' so that he 'might with great justice to my countrymen please the English by my account of our advantages by the Union'. Even in 'ill feudal times', Hume inaccurately observed to Boswell, 'we never gained one battle but Bannockburn' and 'our great improvements are much owing to the Union'. This latter may in large part be true, but it is one side of a *parti pris*. Boswell also observed Hume's bias in a conversation on 6 March 1775, when Hume told him that the Highlanders were 'continually concerned to keep themselves from starving or being hanged', and made a simple opposition between starving, thieving, credulous primitives and the civil English, who 'would not be so ready to support such a story' as Ossian. Hume's virtues as a historian should be observed from outwith his own paradigm, for by no means all of his contemporaries shared such views.[39]

William Robertson (1721–93) was perhaps influenced by native Scottish intellectual traditions to a greater degree than Hume. There are 'traces of...classical republican vocabulary which reveal Robertson's disquiet' at aspects of the history of Scotland.[40]

Robertson was also influenced by Montesquieu and François-Marie Arouet de Voltaire (1694–1778). Robertson was certainly at the core of the Scottish establishment, Principal of Edinburgh University from 1762 and Moderator of the General Assembly in 1766. As a historian his methodology was more careful than Hume's, who could be casual about sources and did not update his scholarship for subsequent editions of his *History*. Robertson, by contrast, although he did not travel nor check a wide geographical range of archives, 'prided himself on his exact documentation, and published original material in supplementary volumes'.[41]

Robertson's *History of Scotland* (1759) 'exemplified and promoted the idea of Scotland as a place of learning, polite culture, and religious and political moderation', a country in other words much changed from what it had been, and for the better. Nonetheless, Robertson could still allow 'some emotional allegiance to the enduring virtues of Scottish culture, such as its martial spirit of independence and self-reliance'. The key word here is 'emotional': the limits of Robertson's consent to the traditional values of Scottish nationality were those set by sentiment and nostalgia. In particular, in his portrayal of Queen Mary 'as a sentimental heroine rather than as a fully responsible political agent...Robertson laid the ground for the subsequent reinvention of Jacobitism, by Walter Scott and others, as an aesthetic attitude only'.[42] Robertson certainly begins his *History of Scotland* with a claim which almost seems to negate the point of writing such a history at all, and which has arguably had a profound influence on the subsequent status of Scotland's national history: 'Nations, as well as men, arrive at maturity by degrees, and the events which happened during their infancy or early youth, cannot be recollected, and deserve not to be remembered.' In the construction of the teleology of civility, the 'maturity' of Scotland is that it is Scotland no longer, but part of Britain. Hence anything that is particularly Scottish belongs to a youth, which one may recall with sentiment, but which cannot be revisited: and this well describes the state of much popular history in Scotland since Robertson and Hume wrote. Britain could evolve into civility; Scotland could not as a separate entity. How could this be shown? By stressing Scottish barbarism as normative. Small wonder that in his preface to the 1827 edition of Robertson's *History*, Dugald Stewart noted that 'such is the effect of that provincial situation to which Scotland is now reduced, that the transactions of former ages are apt to convey to ourselves exaggerated conceptions of barbarism'.[43]

With regard to Scotland, Robertson in Book 1 stresses its barbaric chieftains, 'the fierce and mutinous spirit of the nobles', men 'of unpolished manners, surrounded with vassals bold and licentious', a nation clearly, as were the Jacobites in Hanoverian propaganda, both sexually disordered and lawlessly belligerent. Robertson follows the same broad path as Smith in finding the growth of civility in a move away from the power of feudal aristocratic heroism towards commerce and peace, with its implicit (at least for the middle class) equality of opportunity: 'as the nobles were deprived of power, the people acquired liberty' (Robertson 11:247). Robertson also endorses what became a very marked feature of Scottish historiography: in order to demonstrate Scotland's inability to reach civility on its own as a nation, he emphasises what he chooses to portray as the almost incurably disorderly nature of the Scottish aristocracy. The landscape, want of great cities, history of warfare and clannishness were all features which were seen by Robertson as rendering the Scottish nobility especially mutinous. Scotland as a nation was stuck in retrograde feudalism because 'among the great and independent nobility of Scotland, a monarch could possess little authority' (1:235). Thus, James V could not deliver the beginnings of peace and commerce, as Henry VIII could:

His [Henry's] rapaciousness, his profusion, and even his tyranny, by depressing the ancient nobility, and by adding new property and power to the commons, laid or strengthened the foundations of the English liberty. His other passions contributed no less towards the downfal of Popery, and the establishment of religious freedom in the nation. (Robertson, *History of Scotland*, 1:97)

This passage evidences another feature of Robertson's *History*: because England/Britain is progressing towards civility, even the rapacity, tyranny and war of the past serve the ends of progress; but in Scotland, they hinder it irretrievably. Thus Henry's tyranny is providential, while kings of Scots were doomed to failure, whatever they did: 'Never was any race of monarchs so unfortunate as the Scottish' (Robertson 1:27). Indeed, despite his status as a Presbyterian minister, Robertson questions whether the Scottish Reformation itself can be 'part of an authentic history of liberty'.[44] Scottish history, doomed to disappointment in its quest for progress on its own terms, is cast by the teleological historian as unlucky and unfortunate. It is a problem with only one solution:

The union having incorporated the two nations, and rendered them one people...the Scots...were at once put in possession of privileges more valuable than those which their ancestors had formerly enjoyed; and every obstruction that had retarded their pursuit, or prevented their acquisition of literary fame, was totally removed. (Robertson, *History of Scotland*, 11:254)

In other words, Scottish history can only be properly written when it is over. Robertson's rhetoric is telling: he writes of 'the two nations' becoming 'one people', but the manner in which he does so clearly indicates the predication of teleology of civility: that Scotland gains from the normative and superior civilised values of England. Robertson 'argued that the post-Union Anglicisation of Scottish life and institutions had been a major contribution to Scotland's civil liberty'.[45] The dramatic finale to Scotland's struggle against the inevitable was the Jacobite Rising of 1745, a view further developed by later historians, who described the Scottish Jacobites as engaged in 'a fantasia of misrule...in defiance of Parliament and the laws' (G. M. Trevelyan (1952)), as 'a savage Highland horde' (Charles Chevenix Trench (1973)) or 'as savage and as desperately courageous as Sioux or Pawnees' (Justin McCarthy (1890)).[46]

Robertson's *The History of the Reign of the Emperor Charles V* (1769) and still more his *History of America* (1777) break new ground. In the former work, he provides a tour-de-force 'View of the Progress of Society in Europe', and the replacement of the feudal system by rising commercial cities: an anticipation of Marx or Braudel. Robertson's Tacitean inheritance clearly shows through in his description of 'the dominion of the Romans', which 'like that of all great Empires, degraded and debased the human species' (*Charles V*, 3). Those whom the Romans 'denominated barbarians...were nonetheless brave and independent. These defended their ancient possessions with obstinate valour' (1). This is a historiography which complicates Robertson's view of the Scottish situation, for it is surely Scotland's history that is speaking here, through the language of Calgacus from Tacitus' *Agricola*. The old school of 'defensive patriotism', visible as early as the Declaration of Arbroath, makes a reappearance where empire is at issue, for it was deeply ingrained in the Scottish historiographical tradition that empire was a bad thing. In the Preface to his *History of America*, Robertson states that he will avoid modern history in view of the War of Independence: 'in whatever manner this unhappy contest may terminate, a new order of things must arise in North America, and its affairs will assume another aspect'. Cautious as this is, it sounds as if the status quo is not an option, and, when in 1796 Robertson's son published a fragmentary third volume on the early colonial administration of Virginia and New England from his father's posthumous papers, it offers the occasional reflection on the restrictive nature of colonial government, and the lack of rights the Americans had in Virginia.[47] Yet the temptations of teleology could prove too strong, and commentators have again detected Robertson placing history's losers in a prejudiced light. In the *History of America*, Bruce Lenman notes a 'sustained prejudice against Amerindian and creole', one not inevitable at the time, as Edmund Burke, who wrote to Robertson that he had 'hardly done justice to the savage character', exemplifies in this comment and in his public speeches.[48]

FERGUSON AND OTHER THINKERS

Other writers had a stronger sense of the mixed blessings of progress than Robertson. Gilbert Stuart saw a greater mixture of 'wisdom and accident' underlying human history, and was more sympathetic to traditional Scottish accounts of popular sovereignty; he also believed that Robertson was narrow and simplistic as a writer, undervaluing 'legal and military inquiry'.[49] James Burnett, Lord Monboddo (1714–99) continued to challenge the notion of teleological change itself, inheriting ideas of decline from classical times mixed with a Providentialism which relates him more closely to his English than to his Scottish contemporaries. Nonetheless, the author of *Of the Origin and Progress of Language* (1773–92) and *Antient Metaphysics* (1779–99) believed that civil society was necessary to contribute to the recuperation of humanity.[50]

Monboddo came from a Jacobite background in the north-east of Scotland,[51] and perhaps this coloured not only his views but those of Adam Ferguson, the only major Enlightenment figure to come from the Gaidhealtachd, the Gaelic-speaking part of Scotland. In his Montesquieu-influenced *Essay on the History of Civil Society* (1767),

Ferguson combines the idea of progress with the idea of different features of people in different societies, all seen through the sensibility of a man who clearly saw both losses and gains in historical change. The primitive, according to Ferguson, is not merely 'rude', but has its strengths, the strengths that Rousseau and Boswell would elsewhere identify as those of the noble savage or epic hero: 'freedom of mind', 'a delicious freedom from care . . . where no rules of behaviour are prescribed, but the simple dictates of the heart' with 'that vigour of spirit' which 'qualifies men . . . to lay the basis of domestic liberty as well as to maintain against foreign enemies their national independence and freedom'.[52] Ferguson, in keeping with the values of an older patriot historiography sees a tension between material and moral advance; unlike other Enlightenment thinkers, he also sees 'highly developed societies' as 'in near and clear danger of retreating into barbarian despotism' (*Essay*, xx).

Nonetheless, society does advance, and change is requisite: 'not only the individual advances from infancy to manhood, but the species itself from rudeness to civilization' (*Essay*, xxi, 7, 17). The idea of the infancy of entire peoples, found also in Robertson, can be clearly traced in later thinkers: it occurs, for example, in John Stuart Mill's *On Liberty* (1859), which withholds liberty of action from 'children, or . . . those backward states of society in which the race itself may be considered in its nonage'.[53] The teleology of civility had become embedded in Victorian liberalism: it also became systemically embedded in the Positivism of Auguste Comte (1798–1857) and his successors.

If Scotland is not the specific exemplar in the *Essay*, it is close to the surface. Ferguson provides an almost utilitarian explanation for the Union, stating that 'the sense of a common danger' causes nations to unite 'more firmly together' (*Essay*, 26), and arguing that this situation has been particularly prevalent in modern times, with a tendency to move away from small nations visible in 'modern Europe':

Where a number of states are contiguous, they should be near an equality . . . When the kingdoms of Spain were united, when the great fiefs of France were annexed to the Crown, it was no longer expedient for the nations of Great Britain to continue disjointed. (Ferguson, *Essay*, xxi, 61)

This 'enlargement' also helps to control rude nations, though Ferguson, perhaps influenced by the tradition of patriot historiography, strongly warns against 'the ruinous progress of empire' and cautions that the 'admiration of boundless dominion is a ruinous error' (*Essay*, 61–2) – interesting sentiments in the wake of the prolonged and expensive Seven Years' War (1756–63). More immediately, Ferguson is endorsing the Enlightenment view that one of the key benefits of the Union is its eventual success in terminating the civil war of the seventeenth century: but he does so in terms which do not establish it as a simple move from barbarism to civility, but one which was 'expedient', 'useful' to the parties concerned (*Essay*, 26, 61, 104–5). In short, *An Essay on the History of Civil Society* pursues a view of human and social development which is both sensitive to the past and the processes of political history, and arguably provides a less clear-cut contrast between the 'primitive' and the present than do some other Enlightenment writings. If Ferguson has learnt from Montesquieu, he at least nods towards Rousseau. In this breadth of approach, it can be argued that it is Ferguson, among the first rank of Enlightenment thinkers, who most clearly points beyond the teleology of civility towards 'total history', towards the inclusivity and breadth which more modern practitioners of the discipline believe they seek. In his emphasis on the 'Influence of Climate and Situation' (*Essay*, 106), Ferguson, building on earlier models, almost anticipates Fernand Braudel's *longue durée*; in the sophistication and many-layered nature of his sociological history, he provides an extraordinarily rich sense both of the gains and losses of change, and of the provisionality of progress itself.[54]

CONCLUSION

The historiography of the Scottish Enlightenment remains of profound interest partly because it has shaped our own. If Ferguson provides a model arguably more suitable to Continental theory and the sophisticated historiographies of our own day, both Hume and Robertson provided a powerful impetus for the rise of British empirical history. Their achievement was enormous, so great in its legacy that commentators on their work can still stand in the shadow of their paradigm. It is, however, important to interrogate it, not merely comment upon it, for its effect on Scottish history, as Colin Kidd and others have shown, has been partial and dismissive. Robertson's internal narrative tone varies more than Hume's, and he is thus, as a historian though not as a philosopher, more sophisticated; but it is perhaps Ferguson who, of this great trio, is most sensitive to the demands of historical change not as a moral imperative or a deterministic broadening of liberty, but as a matter of sociological shift and political decision.

NOTES

1   Herbert Butterfield, *The Whig Interpretation of History* (London: Bell, 1931), 16–17.
2   A. J. Youngson, *The Making of Classical Edinburgh* (1966; reprint, Edinburgh: Edinburgh University Press, 1988), xiv; Antoin Murphy, *John Law* (Oxford: Clarendon Press, 1997).
3   Isaac Kramnick, ed., *The Portable Enlightenment Reader* (New York and London: Penguin, 1995), 381–2.
4   Giambattista Vico, *New Science*, trans. David Marsh, intr. Anthony Grafton, 3rd edn (London: Penguin, 1999), 440; Kramnick, *Portable Enlightenment Reader*, 351.
5   Paul Wood, *The Aberdeen Enlightenment: the Arts Curriculum in the Eighteenth Century* (Aberdeen: Aberdeen University Press, 1993), 129, 162.
6   John Kenyon, *The History Men* (London: Weidenfeld and Nicolson, 1983), 18, 20, 39.
7   Henry St John Bolingbroke, *Political Writings*, ed. David Armitage (Cambridge: Cambridge University Press, 1997), xv.
8   Colin Kidd, *Subverting Scotland's Past* (Cambridge: Cambridge University Press, 1993), 113; Karen O'Brien, *Narratives of Enlightenment* (Cambridge: Cambridge University Press, 1997), 41.
9   Charles-Louis de Secondat de Montesquieu, *The Spirit of the Laws*, trans. and eds. Anne M. Cohler, Basia Carolyn Miller and Harold Samuel Stone (Cambridge: Cambridge University Press, 1989), xxvi, 167, 338, 636.
10 David Wootton, 'David Hume, "the historian"', in David Fate Norton, ed., *The Cambridge Companion to Hume* (1993; reprint, Cambridge: Cambridge University Press, 1998), 281–312 (293, 295).
11 John Cannon, ed., *The Blackwell Dictionary of Historians* (Oxford: Blackwell, 1988), 201 (Hume), 354 (Robertson).
12 Adam Smith, *Lectures on Jurisprudence*, eds. R. L. Meek, D. D. Raphael and P. G. Stein, (1978; reprint, Indianapolis: Liberty Classics, 1982), 14; David Spadefora, *The Idea of Progress in Eighteenth-Century Britain* (New Haven and London: Yale University Press, 1990), 271.
13 Kramnick, *Portable Enlightenment Reader*, xvii–xviii.

14 Dugald Stewart, *The Collected Works of Dugald Stewart*, ed. Sir William Hamilton (1854–8; reprint, intro. Knud Haakonssen, Bristol: Thoemmes, 1994), 1:384; x:34; Alexander Broadie, ed., *The Scottish Enlightenment: an Anthology* (Edinburgh: Canongate, 1997), 669–74.

15 Stewart, *Collected Works*, 1:xiii; O'Brien, *Narratives of Enlightenment*, 133, 157.

16 James E. Reibman, 'Kames's Historical Law-Tracts and the Historiography of the Scottish Enlightenment', in Jennifer J. Carter and Joan H. Pittock, eds., *Aberdeen and the Enlightenment* (Aberdeen: Aberdeen University Press, 1987), 61–8 (61–2).

17 Henry Home, Lord Kames, *Historical Law-Tracts*, 3rd edn (Edinburgh: T. Cadell, J. Bell and W. Creech, 1776), xii, 111; Alexander Fraser Tytler, *Memoirs of the Life and Writings of the Honourable Henry Home of Kames*, 2 vols. (1807; reprint, intro. John Valdimir Price, London: Routledge/Thoemmes, 1993), 1:215.

18 Kidd, *Subverting Scotland's Past*, 120–1, 176.

19 Henry Home, Lord Kames, *Sketches of the History of Man*, 2nd edn, 4 vols. (1778; reprint, intro. John Valdimir Price, London: Routledge/Thoemmes, 1993), 1.84.

20 John Millar, *The Origin of the Distinction of Ranks* (1779; reprint, ed. John Valdimir Price, Bristol: Thoemmes, 1990), 2, 295–6.

21 Wootton, 'David Hume', 281–5, 299; Alexander du Toit's recent unpublished PhD thesis on William Robertson (Queen Mary College, London, 2000) makes much of this issue; cf. also Kenyon, *The History Men*, 50, 57; O'Brien, *Narratives of Enlightenment*, 106, 129.

22 William Robertson, *History of the Reign of Charles V*, 4 vols. (Chiswick, 1824), 1.14.

23 Murray G. H. Pittock, *Celtic Identity and the British Image* (Manchester: Manchester University Press, 1999), 55–6.

24 O'Brien, *Narratives of Enlightenment*, 87.

25 John Millar, *An Historical View of the English Government* (London: A. Strahan, T. Cadell and J. Murray, 1787), 5, 41, 555–6.

26 Kidd, *Subverting Scotland's Past*, 137, 196, 210.

27 Robertson, *Charles V*, 1.250; see also 1.197–9, 1.249–52.

28 Kidd, *Subverting Scotland's Past*, 233, 239–41.

29 Colin Kidd, 'Sentiment, Race and Revival: Scottish Identities in the Aftermath of Enlightenment', in Laurence Brockliss and David Eastwood, eds., *A Union of Multiple Identities: the British Isles c. 1750–c. 1850* (Manchester: Manchester University Press, 1997), 110–26 (117–18); Pittock, *Celtic Identity*, 56.

30 David Hume, *The History of England*, 6 vols. (1778; reprint, Indianapolis: Liberty Fund, 1983), 1.XIII.

31 Karen O'Brien, 'Historical Writing', in D. Womersley, ed., *A Companion to Literature from Milton to Blake* (Oxford: Blackwell, 2000), 522–35 (527–8).

32 Kenyon, *History Men*, 41.

33 Nicholas Phillipson, *Hume* (London: Weidenfeld and Nicolson, 1989), 137–9.

34 Cannon, *Blackwell Dictionary of Historians*, 201; O'Brien, *Narratives of Enlightenment*, 57.

35 Cf. G. W. S. Barrow, *Robert Bruce* (London: Eyre and Spottiswoode, 1965), 434–5 and subsequent editions from Edinburgh University Press.

36 O'Brien, *Narratives of Enlightenment*, 73.

37 For the peculiar nature of this mindset, see my *Inventing and Resisting Britain* (Basingstoke: Macmillan, 1997), ch. 1.

38 Kenyon, *History Men*, 42, 46, 48.

39 Charles Ryskamp and F. A. Pottle, eds., *Boswell: the Ominous Years, 1774–1776* (New York: McGraw-Hill; London: William Heinemann, 1963), 29–30, 73.

40 O'Brien, *Narratives of Enlightenment*, 106; Nicholas Phillipson, 'Providence and Progress: an Introduction to the Historical Thought of William Robertson', in Stewart J. Brown, ed., *William Robertson and the Expansion of Empire* (Cambridge: Cambridge University Press, 1997), 55–73, 56.

41 Kenyon, *History Men*, 57, 61, 64.

42 O'Brien, 'Historical Writing', 530–1.

43 William Robertson, *The History of Scotland*, intro. Dugald Stewart, 2 vols. (London: Jones and Co., 1827), i.xviii, 1.

44 Kidd, *Subverting Scotland's Past*, 193.

45 Ibid.

46 Murray G. H. Pittock, *The Myth of the Jacobite Clans* (1995; reprint, Edinburgh: Edinburgh University Press, 1999), 10–11.

47 William Robertson, *The History of America*, 3 vols. (London: Strahan, Cadell, Balfour, 1777–96), I.v, III.90–1.

48 Bruce P. Lenman, 'From Savage to Scot via the French and the Spaniards: Principal Robertson's Spanish Sources', 196–209, in Brown, *William Robertson*, 204, 205.

49 Gilbert Stuart, *A View of Society in Europe, in its Progress from Rudeness to Refinement* (1792; reprint, intro. William Zachs, Bristol: Thoemmes Press, 1995), viiii; William Zachs, *Without Regard to Good Manners: a Biography of Gilbert Stuart 1743–1786* (Edinburgh: Edinburgh University Press, 1992), 102, 138.

50 David Spadefora, *The Idea of Progress in Eighteenth-Century Britain* (New Haven and London: Yale University Press, 1990), 254, 317–18.

51 Cf. the exchange between Samuel Johnson and Monboddo's son, dis-
    cussed by me in 'Johnson and Scotland', in Jonathan Clark and Howard
    Erskine-Hill, eds., *Samuel Johnson in Historical Context* (Basingstoke:
    Palgrave, 2002), 184–96. Monboddo's father fought for James VIII at
    Sheriffmuir in 1715.

52 Adam Ferguson, *An Essay on the History of Civil Society*, ed. Fania Oz-
    Salzberger (Cambridge: Cambridge University Press, 1995), xx, 94, 105.

53 John Stuart Mill, *Utilitarianism*, ed. Mary Warnock (1962; reprint,
    London: Fontana, 1977), 135–6.

54 Kenyon, *History Men*, 58.

14 Art and aesthetic theory

Philosophers of the Scottish Enlightenment did not invent aesthetics, the philosophical study of beauty, the sublime, and related categories, but they did make a highly significant contribution to it. The two most important writers in the field were Francis Hutcheson[1] and David Hume,[2] though others, such as George Turnbull, George Campbell, Alexander Gerard, Allan Ramsay (the painter), Henry Home (Lord Kames), Adam Smith, Thomas Reid, Hugh Blair and Archibald Alison,[3] were significant writers on the subject. Indeed, the sheer number of truly inventive works on aesthetics was a distinctive feature of the Enlightenment in Scotland. In section one I offer some critical reflections on Hutcheson's work, paying particular attention to the role that the doctrine of the association of ideas plays in his thinking. Hume's work on aesthetics owes a great deal to Hutcheson's though he reaches different conclusions. Section two explores Hume's conclusions regarding the existence and identification of the standard of taste. In the writings of the two men moral and aesthetic categories are often combined. A particularly interesting exercise in the combination of these categories is to be found in the writings of George Turnbull,[4] regent at Marischal College, Aberdeen between 1721 and 1727, and section three contains a discussion of his contribution to this field. In the final section I consider the views of George Turnbull and his pupil George Campbell on truth in the arts. Aesthetic theory in the Scottish Enlightenment is a field filled with a rich variety of good things, and in this chapter I shall cover only a small area of this field and shall attend to only a very few of the thinkers who made a significant contribution.

HUTCHESON ON AESTHETIC JUDGEMENT

Hutcheson raises questions about the nature of beauty and about the means by which we know whether a given object is beautiful. The influence of Lord Shaftesbury is clearly discernible in his replies,[5] though Hutcheson undoubtedly takes matters a good deal further. And the influence of Locke is yet deeper since Hutcheson took from him his entire epistemological framework, including the theory of ideas, the doctrine of association of ideas and the idea of the mind's reflective awareness of its own operations. As regards the means by which we are aware of the beauty of things, Hutcheson affirms that we sense beauty not with any of the five external senses, but with our aesthetic sense, also called an 'internal sense'. Hutcheson uses 'sense' as a technical term referring to a 'Determination of our Minds to receive Ideas independently on our Will, and to have Perceptions of Pleasure and Pain'.[6] My visual sensing is an immediate and natural effect of my opening my eyes. It is not a consequence of an act of will, even though I can will to redirect attention from the natural object of vision without redirecting my eyes. Two elements are in play here, the immediacy of the visual experience and the fact that the will is not engaged – the act of perception is achieved by natural means only.

It is Hutcheson's contention that in his sense of 'sense' we have an aesthetic sense. He discusses the following sequence. First the operation of the external senses upon an object produces in us an idea of the object, and then our internal or aesthetic sense operates on that external sensory idea, producing in us, immediately and unbidden, the idea of the object's beauty.[7] Associated with that latter idea, and perhaps one part or even all of it, is the pleasure that we take in the thing. We *enjoy* beautiful things, and our enjoyment is not merely incidental to our aesthetic sensing, for we are told: 'it plainly appears that some objects are *immediately* the occasions of this pleasure of beauty, and that we have senses fitted for perceiving it'.[8] This passage might imply that Hutcheson identifies beauty with the pleasure that wells up in us when we perceive objects that we judge beautiful, but it is hardly firm evidence that he makes this identification, as opposed to holding that the pleasure and the sense of beauty are distinct things which are bound to each other by a natural necessity.

In either case Hutcheson appears to hold that beauty is in the beholder rather than in the thing beheld. For he tells us that beauty is an idea,[9] and ideas are certainly in the mind: 'the word *beauty* is taken for *the idea raised in us*, and a *sense* of beauty for *our power of receiving this idea'*. Given the distinction between primary qualities (such as figure and number, which our ideas are said to resemble) and secondary qualities (such as colour and taste, which our ideas are said not to resemble) we are bound to wonder whether the idea of beauty is of a primary or secondary quality. Unfortunately Hutcheson seems to imply that it is almost, but not quite, both:

The ideas of beauty and harmony, being excited upon our perception of some primary quality, and having relation to figure and time, may indeed have a nearer resemblance to objects than these sensations [namely of cold, hot, sweet, bitter], which seem not so much any pictures of objects as modifications of the perceiving mind; and yet, were there no mind with a sense of beauty to contemplate objects, I see not how they could be called beautiful.[10]

It remains a matter for debate whether a clear answer is to be extracted from Hutcheson concerning the nature of the relation between pleasure, the idea of beauty and the distinction between primary and secondary qualities.[11]

As regards the features, or elements, of a thing that cause us to see it as beautiful and to take pleasure in it, Hutcheson affirms: 'The figures which excite in us the ideas of beauty seem to be those in which there is *uniformity amidst variety.*'[12] The underlying insight appears to be that if a work has too much uniformity it is simply dull or boring, and if too much variety it is a jumble, a confused mixture. It is therefore only an object perceived to occupy the intermediate position that gives rise to a sense of beauty. Hutcheson's examples, such as the aesthetic superiority of a square over an equilateral triangle and of a pentagon over a square,[13] now strike us as bizarre and certainly do not help his case; but the point that excessive uniformity is boring and operates against aesthetic merit, and that a mere jumble, excessive diversity, is no more attractive, has something to be said in its favour, though there is room to wonder whether the doctrine that beautiful objects display uniformity amidst variety can in the end escape the charge of vacuity.

It should be added that Hutcheson's account of beauty in terms of uniformity amidst variety is not the whole part of his story, since he makes a distinction between absolute and comparative beauty, and it is only beauty of the absolute kind that is analysed in terms of uniformity amidst variety. Comparative beauty, 'that which we perceive in objects commonly considered as *imitations* or *resemblances* of something else',[14] is the beauty that a painting or statue may have when considered as a representation of something else, an original, where the imitation is being judged as an imitation and independently of the beauty of the original. A painting may be beautiful, in the comparative sense, even if the original is ugly; though, as Hutcheson adds, the beauty of a painting may be more 'abundant' if it is a fine imitation of an absolutely beautiful original.[15]

I shall examine one aspect of Hutcheson's account of our judgements of absolute beauty by considering how to deal with what appears to be a serious problem with it. The problem is this: there is surely little room for dispute over whether or not an object displays uniformity amidst variety, from which it would seem to follow that there is little disagreement amongst us in our judgements about whether given objects are beautiful. In addition, granted that there are degrees of beauty, and that 'variety increases the beauty in equal uniformity' and '[t]he greater uniformity increases the beauty amidst equal variety',[16] there must surely be general agreement about how beautiful something is. We can all observe the uniformity and the variety displayed by things. Yet in fact there is a good deal of disagreement both about whether something is at all beautiful, and about the level of beauty of beautiful things.

Hutcheson's solution starts from the fact that whether or not we find something beautiful depends not only on whether we perceive uniformity amidst variety in the thing, but also on the associations that the thing arouses in our mind. If an object that we had found beautiful comes to be associated in our mind with something disagreeable this will affect our aesthetic response; we might even find the thing ugly. Two of Hutcheson's examples will suffice. One concerns wines to which men acquire an aversion after they have taken them in an emetic preparation: 'we are conscious that the idea is altered from what it was when that wine was agreeable, by the conjunction of the ideas of loathing and sickness of the stomach'.[17] Secondly, Hutcheson refers to a face which is in itself beautiful but which has something about it that prompts us to think its owner morally bad, in consequence of which judgement we do not find the face attractive.[18] Later we might discover that the person was in fact morally exemplary, in which case, thinks Hutcheson, our aesthetic judgement of the person's face will correct itself – thus providing evidence that the association of ideas had distorted our aesthetic judgement. And our aesthetic response can also be affected in the opposite direction. It is this mechanism of association that Hutcheson invokes to explain the fact of disagreements over aesthetic matters.

This doctrine is not free of problems. Hutcheson affirms: 'But there appears no ground to believe such a diversity in human minds, as that the same simple idea or perception should give pleasure to one and pain to another, or to the same person at different times, not to say that it seems a contradiction that the same simple idea should do so.'[19] It is, however, difficult, perhaps impossible, to give an empirical disproof of this claim, since if two people do in fact disagree about the aesthetic merit of an object, it is always open to Hutcheson to say that the object produces different associations in the two spectators. This may be a way of saying that Hutcheson's position is empirically vacuous – that he has so described what occurs that nothing can count as evidence against his claim.

Since Hutcheson believes that our disposition to form associations in respect of aesthetic properties is a cause of error in our aesthetic judgements, it is reasonable that he should conclude, as he does, that one route to the truth on aesthetic matters is to locate the accidental associations and, so to say, to factor them out of the judgemental process. We hear very little from him about associations that are helpful to that process, and much about those that are the opposite.

There is an interesting question as to why Hutcheson has so little to say in favour of associations in respect of our aesthetic judgements, especially given his acknowledgement that some of our associations of ideas are natural and do not lead to error. For in that case why does he not explore the associations that do not impede sound aesthetic judgement and can readily be seen to support and enhance it? Our knowledge and experience concerning the history of the various art forms determine the quality of our aesthetic judgements, and indeed make the difference between our having something worth saying on these topics and our uttering inanities. A person unacquainted with the western tradition of musical composition can have nothing worthwhile to say about Bartok's string quartets. Informed judgement on such a matter requires an ability to bring to bear an immense collection of associated ideas that are integral to the western compositional tradition. Not to have this background set of ideas is to leave you listening to Bartok as you might listen to a speech in a language you do not know.

In this point concerning the importance of association for informed aesthetic judgement there is no suggestion that aesthetic sensibility is reducible to the disposition to associate, though later in the century Archibald Alison and Dugald Stewart held precisely this view, for we might still agree with Hutcheson's claim that our sense of beauty is natural to us and that we are therefore capable of passing aesthetic judgements antecedent to any associated ideas that might be factored into the judgement. But if we are to make aesthetic judgements that are not worthless we need a battery of associated ideas. Since Hutcheson created an opening for such development by distinguishing between accidental and non-accidental association his failure to develop this line is the more puzzling.

HUME AND THE STANDARD OF TASTE

I turn now to the idea of a 'standard of taste' and shall explore it in the company of Hume.[20] I shall first consider whether such a standard exists, and shall then probe the question of what it is (if it exists). Hutcheson is not however left far behind; as we shall see, Hume wrote in his shadow.

There are arguments for the claim that there is a standard of taste, and others, equally strong, for the claim that there is not. Supporting the former claim is the general belief that not everyone's opinion is as good as everyone else's; we each think that we are right on many matters of taste and that those who disagree with us are wrong. And since they are wrong we dispute with them in an effort to draw them to the truth. Surely we would neither think them wrong nor be disposed to put them right unless we had in mind a standard that our judgements measure up to, and that the judgements of our opponents do not.

Supporting the claim that there is not a standard of taste is the very fact just noted, that there is so much dispute on matters of taste, for if there is a standard to which we all appeal, why is there so much disagreement? The situation therefore is curious; opposite conclusions are being plausibly drawn from the same premiss. At the start of his essay 'Of the standard of taste', Hume emphasises the fact of disagreement. Our acquaintances disagree on matters of taste: 'But those, who can enlarge their view to contemplate distant nations and remote ages, are still more surprized at the great inconsistence and contrariety.'[21] Hume here brings his empirical method to bear. The evidence regarding the existence of a standard of taste is the stronger the more the search for evidence is extended to distant places and distant times; and the broader perspective adopted by Hume leads him to the conclusion that disagreement in taste is widespread. Hence if there is a standard of taste it is unlikely to apply across great spans of space or of time.

It should be said therefore that Hume believes there to be a sort of standard of taste, and bases this belief on the consideration with which I started, the fact that we think that we are right in our judgements of taste and that therefore people who disagree with us are wrong. This is an empirical fact about us and of course the empiricist Hume, attempting 'to introduce the experimental method of reasoning into moral subjects',[22] respects this empirical fact. He therefore affirms: 'It is natural for us to seek a Standard of Taste; a rule, by which the various sentiments of men may be reconciled; at least, a decision, afforded, confirming one sentiment, and condemning another.'[23] Of course, the fact that it is natural for us to seek a standard does not imply that a universally valid standard is anywhere to be found. The standard that Hume identifies is of parochial rather than universal validity.

Hume holds that in relation to any work of art some aesthetic responses are demonstrably more appropriate or fitting than others – 'demonstrably' given the role of argument in discussions on the aesthetic merits of works of arts. In the arguments we produce we seek to demonstrate the propriety, indeed the reasonableness, of our judgements. If you judge a painting beautiful and another person judges to the contrary, you can defend your position by pointing out things about the painting that the other might have missed, such as the fact that the colouring is proper to the subject, that there are well-chosen contrasts, and that one part of the painting is a nicely judged counterpoint to another part. With such observations, and therefore by rational means, you can induce the other to revise his judgement of the painting. If you succeed, this surely implies that he has decided that his previous judgement failed to measure up to a standard on which you both agree. What standard?

Hume's assertion, 'Reason is, and ought only to be the slave of the passions, and can never pretend to any other office than to serve and obey them',[24] was deployed in the course of a discussion of moral judgements, judgements which are 'more properly felt than judged of'. But Hume believed reason to be the slave of the passions in almost every aspect of our experience, and certainly in our aesthetic experience. In our judgements of taste it is our feelings, sentiments or passions that are in the driving seat. Nevertheless we believe a rational defence of our aesthetic judgements to be a proper response to criticism.

Hume was prepared to mount such a defence on behalf of the claims that John Bunyan is inferior to Joseph Addison, and that John Ogilby, a seventeenth-century verse translator of Homer and Virgil, is inferior to Milton: 'Though there may be found persons, who give the preference to the former authors; no one pays attention to such taste; and we pronounce without scruple the sentiment of these pretended critics to be absurd and ridiculous.'[25] Light is cast on Hume's own literary values by the fact that he thinks it absurd and ridiculous to say that Bunyan is better than Addison, but here I shall attend instead to his reference to 'these pretended critics'. Their 'absurd and ridiculous' literary claims are proof of the hollowness of their claim to be critics, for a good critic would be able to demonstrate the superiority of Addison over Bunyan. We therefore need to identify some good critics; for if we are not confident about an aesthetic judgement that we have passed we can evaluate it by seeing whether it measures up to the judgement of a good critic. But how are we to recognise a good critic? This question is at the heart of Hume's aesthetic theory, for in effect his doctrine is that the judgement of the good critic gives us the standard of taste. Hume therefore enumerates the qualities of the good critic.

There are rules, learned through experience, regarding the kinds of thing that give aesthetic pleasure. The rules are 'general observations, concerning what has been universally found to please in all countries and in all ages',[26] and though Hume does not enumerate the rules, it may be supposed that he has in mind the sorts of features of works of art that were invoked earlier, such as the fact that

the colouring is proper to the subject, that there are well-chosen contrasts and that different parts of the painting are in nicely judged
counterpoint. There is however no suggestion in this that works
which accord with the rules will always please us. It is the finer, not
the grosser emotions that are engaged in our adequate response to the
beauties of a work of art, and a person in an unsuitable frame of mind
will not judge well. He will not be duly receptive to the subtleties,
the delicately balanced relationships, the finely judged distinctions,
in the work of art. Delicacy of sentiment, the first quality of a good
critic, is excluded by strong emotion. In clarification of his concept
of delicacy of sentiment Hume invokes an incident in *Don Quixote*
when two brothers tasted wine in a hogshead; one said it tasted of
iron and the other said it tasted of leather. The bystanders scoffed,
but when the hogshead was drained an iron key on a leather thong
was found at the bottom.[27]

The second quality of the good critic is his long practice in the
exercise of his critical powers. He has considerable experience of
works of the relevant kind, and by such experience has learned what
to look out for. In addition he frequently gives close attention to
an individual work and, if there is more to be seen in it, then each
time he will see something more. The third quality of the good critic
is this, that he is experienced in making comparisons with other,
related kinds of works of art. Without such experience the critic
might well give undue weight to superficial or frivolous features
of the work being judged. Fourthly, the good critic is unprejudiced
in his judgement. If the poet is a dear friend of the critic, then the
latter must somehow distance himself from this relationship as a
prerequisite to a fair judgement of the poem. In this sense, the good
critic is an 'impartial spectator'. If the critic fails in this, 'his taste
evidently departs from the true standard; and of consequence loses
all credit and authority'.[28] Fifthly, and finally, the critic must have
'good sense' if he is to judge the fittingness of works of art in relation
to their end. For example, in assessing a rhetorical performance the
critic's good sense should tell him that he should take into account
the nature of the audience for whom the performance was originally
intended. Thus Hume sums up the character of the good critic in
these terms: 'Strong sense, united to delicate sentiment, improved
by practice, perfected by comparison, and cleared of all prejudice, can
alone entitle critics to this valuable character; and the joint verdict

of such, wherever they are to be found, is the true standard of taste and beauty.'[29]

This position is not however without its difficulties. In particular it has been suggested that Hume's argument in support of the standard of taste is circular.[30] He enumerates the virtues of a good critic, since his aim is to identify the standard of taste with the verdict of people who have those virtues. Yet he arrives at the list of virtues by noticing that it is people with those virtues who make sound judgements of taste. Apparently, therefore, criteria for soundness of judgement must precede Hume's criteria for the qualities of a good critic, though he appears to be arguing that we reach the criteria of soundness of judgement via the criteria for good critics. We need to know therefore whether Hume bases the idea of sound aesthetic judgement on the idea of the good critic, or the idea of the good critic on the idea of sound aesthetic judgement, or (and this is the circle) both.

I believe that if there is a circle here it is not of the vicious variety. Let us agree with Hume that if a work of art is good then good critics will approve of it and that if good critics jointly approve of a work of art then it is a good work of art, and let us also accept Hume's list of the five qualities that characterise a good critic: 'Strong sense, united to delicate sentiment, improved by practice, perfected by comparison, and cleared of all prejudice'. Of these five, all but the second plainly concern matters of fact, for it is a question of fact whether a person has good sense, a record of practice, has experience of many types of example and is free of prejudice.

What of the question whether someone has delicacy of sentiment? Hume's reply is that this also is a question of fact. Those who have delicacy of sentiment have the greatest sensitivity to the qualities in works of art that make the works good ones. The qualities in question are determined by empirical means. They are the qualities that have consistently pleased through the ages, qualities to be found in, say, the Homeric poems or Virgil's *Aeneid*. A person with delicacy of sentiment will tend to be pleased by these qualities even if they are present in a work in only a small amount, or present with other, louder, more attention-seeking qualities.

Evidently, therefore, Hume's account of the standard of taste presupposes that the most famous, lasting and esteemed works really are good, and he regards the standard as a means to settling disputes over other cases. In short, Hume presupposes that certain works are good, those that have pleased through the ages; and he holds that a newer work can reliably be supposed to be good if the good critics all pass that judgement on it. Evidently therefore the charge of circularity is based on a misinterpretation of Hume's objectives in the essay on the standard of taste.[31]

TURNBULL'S *TREATISE ON ANCIENT PAINTING*

The relation between art and morality was a major topic in the Scottish Enlightenment, and I shall open up the topic here with the help of George Turnbull, whose chief work on art, *A Treatise on Ancient Painting*, was written expressly for those about to set out on the Grand Tour.[32] Turnbull had two main objectives.

First, the best answer to the question: 'Why go on the Grand Tour?', is 'education'; a tourist should learn to appreciate objects of high cultural value. Turnbull's first objective therefore was to enumerate and discuss the works of the painters of ancient Greece and Rome. The tourist, armed with Turnbull's book, would thus learn what to look at, and also what to look out for in those works in order to get a due sense of their quality.

Turnbull's second objective was the promotion of moral, and particularly civic, virtue among the élite of Scottish civic life. The idea of attaining that objective by writing on ancient painting might seem strange to us; but we need to attend to Turnbull's arguments, and therefore should note that he believed there to be two sorts of object of human enquiry. First there are truths, 'that is, real Connexions in Nature or Facts', and secondly there are the various ways in which we can be brought to understand the truths or feel them. These ways are linguistic, in a broad sense of the term 'linguistic', because among the languages Turnbull lists as a means of bringing us to grasp the truth are oratory, poetry, all the arts of design, painting and sculpture. Next he articulates a principle: 'And therefore if right Education ought to teach and instruct in Truths, and in the various good Methods or Arts of conveying Truths into the Mind; no sooner is one led to the Discovery of any truth, than he ought to be employed in comparing and examining several different ways by which it may be unfolded, proved, embellished, and enforced by Oratory, Poetry, or Painting.'[33] Among the truths that Turnbull has in mind are those concerning morality: 'But one Point aimed at in this Treatise is to shew how mean, insipid and trifling the fine Arts are when they are quite alienated from their better and nobler, genuine Purposes, which, as well as those of their Sister Poetry, are truly philosophical and moral: that is, to convey in an agreeable manner into the Mind the Knowledge of Men and Things; or to instruct us in Morality, Virtue, and human Nature.'[34]

Turnbull believed ancient paintings to be a priceless resource for eighteenth-century Scottish society on account of their portrayal of morality, virtue and human nature. The ancient painters found their own way of representing the virtues so forcefully, in such attractive colours, that the paintings were, in Turnbull's view, a powerful argument for adopting the corresponding lifestyle. We can of course appreciate beauties in a painting while yet giving no thought to the moral significance of what is portrayed, but that would be to miss the rhetorical significance of the painting. Rhetoric is the art of persuasion by speech, and since Turnbull believes that painting is a kind of language, and believes also that a painting can persuade us of a moral truth, he is committed to the view that a painting can be a piece of rhetoric, a persuasive argument on behalf of virtue. He hoped that by a proper education in painting, young Scots on the Grand Tour would hear the rhetoric of ancient painting and be persuaded of the merits of such classical virtues as dignity and humanity, courage and magnanimity, temperance and justice. To be persuaded of such things is more than merely intellectual assent; it is an assent of feeling, and those persuaded will therefore be motivated to embody those virtues in their lives.

ART AND TRUTH

Turnbull writes about nature as seen by the artist, who is turned outward to what is aesthetically pleasing and turned inward to an idea of a composition which, even if not found in nature, is natural and is aesthetically pleasing:

... what superior Pleasures one must have, who hath an Eye formed by comparing Landscapes [i.e. landscape paintings] with Nature, in the contemplation of Nature itself in his Morning or Evening Walks, to one who is not at all conversant in Painting... he will feel a vast Pleasure in observing and chusing picturesque Skies, Scenes, and other Appearances, that would be really beautiful in Pictures. He will delight in observing what is really worthy of being painted; what Circumstances a good Genius would take hold of; what Parts he would leave out, and what he would add, and for what Reasons.[35]

There are two kinds of object here, one the actual scene spread out before the spectator, and the other a mental composition, a concept of what is physically before the spectator except for changes he has mentally made to it. The latter exercise is of interest to Turnbull, for the ability to conceive things which do not exist in nature but are congruent with nature is an ability of the creative imagination. The painter can paint the landscape that is before him, yet alter the relative sizes of the fields, or make the hills seem closer, or bathe the whole in a different light. But the changes must be within bounds. Even if the painting is not exactly faithful to the landscape, it must be credible; a scene like the one he paints must be possible in nature. Otherwise the aesthetic value of the painting will be diminished.

This concept of nature, which includes what can occur naturally even though it does not in fact do so, allows Turnbull to develop the idea of painting and poetry as more philosophical than history is. For history is constrained to a faithful representation of what actually happened, and therefore eschews the amplitude of vision characteristic of painters and poets, who can deal directly with universal features of experience. On the other hand, a painter *explores* human nature; he imagines people in a variety of naturally possible situations, and considers the ways in which in those situations they might express their humanity. Thus, the painter, within the bounds of the naturally possible, can explore the gamut of emotions. As Turnbull affirms: 'the imitative Arts become Magnifiers in the moral way, by means of chusing those Circumstances which are properest to exhibit the Workings and Consequences of Affections, in the strongest Light that may be, or to render them most striking and conspicuous. All is Nature that is represented, if it be agreeable to Nature.'[36] Since painting functions as a magnifying glass to the moral dimension of our lives Turnbull can regard the study of painting as part of moral education; and since he finds in ancient painting so many examples of appropriate portrayals of virtue and vice, that is, virtue portrayed in a good light and vice in a bad, he sees the study of ancient painting as a beneficial educative force.

It may be noted that Turnbull's doctrine on the relation between painting and the possible is no less applicable to the arts of language than to painting, as his student George Campbell knew. Campbell discusses uses of speech, and the different ways in which we evaluate the truth of what is said.[37] Truth is not to be sought in poetry or in fictional writings as it is in history, for history aims to report events that actually occurred, whereas novels do not and in general neither do poems. Yet novels, works of fiction, articulate truths, and must do so if they are to be acceptable even as works of fiction. This idea is explored by Campbell:

Nay, even in those performances where truth, in regard to the individual facts related, is neither sought nor expected, as in some sorts of poetry, and in romance, truth still is an object to the mind, the general truths regarding character, manners, and incidents. When these are preserved, the piece may justly be denominated true, considered as a picture of life; though false, considered as a narrative of particular events. And even these untrue events may be counterfeits of truth, and bear its image; for in cases wherein the proposed end can be rendered consistent with unbelief, it cannot be rendered compatible with incredibility. Thus, in order to satisfy the mind, in most cases, truth, and in every case, what bears the semblance of truth, must be presented to it.[38]

It is necessary to distinguish between being believed and being credible, and between being disbelieved and being incredible. If we do not believe that an episode in a novel could have happened, the episode will not satisfy us. Since the work is fictional we do not insist that it contain nothing but the truth, but the story must not exceed the bounds of possibility. Similarly a fictional character must be credible – the character sketch will not satisfy us unless we think that even if no such person, one precisely answering to the description in the novel, ever lived, there could have been such a person. The reason the portrayal of such possibilities is sufficient to satisfy us is that we humans are naturally truth-seeking creatures, and fiction at a certain level of abstraction contains truths, perhaps not individual or singular truths, whether about *this* event or *this* person, but at any rate universal truths. When Campbell speaks about statements that have a semblance of truth, he has in mind truth of the universal sort, which is important for us in countless contexts where it is a message of universal validity that we are seeking to convey. Great fictional characters, Ulysses, Hamlet, Don Quixote, are great partly because they are archetypal. They embody in a supreme way a quality which we all embody or for which we all by nature strive, and in that sense they are not fictional. If anything they are even larger than life. That is why we find great works of fiction so satisfying. To call the characters 'fictitious' is to miss their point. The novelist must aim for universal truth, though not for truth at a level at which the historian aims.

Campbell's remarks point to a whole theory of literature. But they are no less applicable to painting, and are foreshadowed in Turnbull's *Treatise*. Painting is an immensely powerful resource for moral education because a painting can speak at a universal level about fundamental moral truths, such as the immeasurable value of justice, temperance, mercy and humility, and it can convey the contemptible nature of moral vice, the cruel, lecherous, cowardly dispositions that form the corrupt soul. A painting conveys a moral message, not merely by representing virtuous or vicious acts, but by representing them in such a way that the painting persuades us of the truth of moral universals. Hume opens his first *Enquiry* with a description of two kinds of 'moral philosopher'. What he says of one kind is particularly apposite here:

As virtue, of all objects, is allowed to be the most valuable, this species of philosophers paint her in the most amiable colours; borrowing all helps from poetry and eloquence, and treating their subject in an easy and obvious manner, and such as is best fitted to please the imagination, and engage the affections ... They make us *feel* the difference between vice and virtue; they excite and regulate our sentiments; and so they can but bend our hearts to the love of probity and true honour, they think, that they have fully attained the end of all their labours.[39]

In this sense of moral philosophy, the paintings to which Turnbull directs the attention of those going on the Grand Tour are works of moral philosophy, and it is precisely therein that their chief value resides.

Behind Turnbull's doctrine there lies a large agenda. His hope was that Scottish Grand Tourists, most of whom came from the upper rungs of society, would return to Scotland eager to exercise power in the name of civic virtue and would therefore help to ensure that Scottish society proceeded along the path of sound morality. From this perspective Turnbull's *Treatise on Ancient Painting* must be classed as a contribution to the general programme of improvement that characterised the Scottish Enlightenment from its earliest days.

NOTES

1   See especially *An Inquiry Concerning Beauty, Order, Harmony, Design* (hereinafter *Inquiry*), the first treatise in *An Inquiry into the Original of our Ideas of Beauty and Virtue*, 1st edn, 1725. The 4th edn, of the first treatise, the last edition published in Hutcheson's lifetime, appeared in 1738. There is a modern edition prepared by Peter Kivy (The Hague: Nijhoff, 1973), a volume which also contains Hutcheson's other main work on aesthetics, *Reflections upon Laughter*.

2   See especially 'Of the Standard of Taste' (hereinafter *ST*) and 'Of the Delicacy of Taste and Passion', in David Hume, *Essays Moral, Political and Literary*, ed. Eugene F. Miller, rev. edn (Indianapolis: Liberty Fund, 1987), 226–49 and 1–8 respectively.

3   George Turnbull, *A Treatise on Ancient Painting* (London, 1740); Allan Ramsay, *A Dialogue on Taste*, 1755, republished in Ramsay, *The Investigator*, 2nd edn (London, 1762); George Campbell, *The Philosophy of Rhetoric*, 2 vols. (London, 1776); Alexander Gerard, *An Essay on Taste* (London, 1759); Henry Home, Lord Kames, *Elements of Criticism*, 3 vols. (Edinburgh, 1762); 5th edn, 2 vols. (Edinburgh, 1774); Adam Smith, 'Of the Nature of that Imitation which takes Place in what are called the Imitative Arts', in Adam Smith, *Essays on Philosophical Subjects*, eds. W. P. D.Wightman, J. C. Bryce and I. S. Ross (Indianapolis: Liberty Fund, 1982), 176–213; Thomas Reid, 'Essay VIII – Of Taste', in *Essays on the Intellectual Powers*, text edited by Derek Brookes, annotations by Derek Brookes and Knud Haakonssen, introduction by Knud Haakonssen (Edinburgh: Edinburgh University Press, 2002); Hugh Blair, *Lectures on Rhetoric and Belles Lettres*, 2 vols. (London, 1783); and Archibald Alison, *Essays on the Nature and Principles of Taste* (Edinburgh, 1790).

4   See especially *A Treatise on Ancient Painting*.

5   Anthony Ashley Cooper, 3rd Earl of Shaftesbury, *Characteristics of Men, Manners, Opinions, Times*, ed. Lawrence Klein (Cambridge: Cambridge University Press, 1999), esp. 62–7, 318–27.

6   Francis Hutcheson, *An Essay on the Nature and Conduct of the Passions*, 3rd edn (London, 1742), 4. There is a modern edition of the 1728 (1st) edn, introduced and annotated by Andrew Ward (Manchester: Clinamen Press, 1999).

7   It is probably because of this sequence that in later editions of the *Inquiry* Hutcheson calls the internal sense a 'subsequent' or 'reflex' sense.

8   *Inquiry*, 37.

9   That beauty is an idea does not imply that Hutcheson does not identify beauty with pleasure, since for Hutcheson, writing under the influence of Locke, pleasure is a kind of idea. See Dabney Townsend, 'Lockean Aesthetics', *Journal of Aesthetics and Art Criticism* 49 (1991), 349–61, and a critical response by Peter Kivy, in 'Hutcheson's Idea of Beauty: Simple or Complex?', *Journal of Aesthetics and Art Criticism* 50 (1992), 243–5.

10 *Inquiry*, 39.

11 The best full-length discussion of these matters is in Peter Kivy, *The Seventh Sense: a Study of Hutcheson's Aesthetics and its Influence in Eighteenth-Century Britain* (New York: Franklin, 1976); see also George Dickie, *The Century of Taste: the Philosophical Odyssey of Taste in the Eighteenth Century* (Oxford: Oxford University Press, 1996).

12 *Inquiry*, 40, 47, 54.

13 Ibid., 40.

14 Ibid., 40; cf. 54–8.

15 Ibid., 55.

16 Ibid., 40.

17 Ibid., 32.

18 Ibid., 75.

19 Ibid., 33.

20 *ST*, 226–49. It has generated a substantial literature. See Peter Kivy, 'Hume's Standard of Taste: Breaking the Circle', *British Journal of Aesthetics* 7 (1967), 57–66; Noel Carroll, 'Hume's Standard of Taste', *Journal of Aesthetics and Art Criticism* 43 (1984), 181–94; S. Sverdlik, 'Hume's Key and Aesthetic Rationality', *Journal of Aesthetics and Art Criticism* 45 (1986), 69–76; N. Zangwill, 'Hume, Taste, and Teleology', *Philosophical Papers* 23 (1994), 1–18; James Shelley, 'Hume's Double Standard of Taste', *Journal of Aesthetics and Art Criticism* 52 (1994), 437–45; Jonathan Friday, 'Hume's Sceptical Standard of Taste', *Journal of the History of Philosophy* 36 (1998), 545–66.

21 *ST*, 227.

22 Subtitle of *A Treatise of Human Nature*.

23 *ST*, 229.

24 David Hume, *A Treatise of Human Nature*, ed. L. A. Selby-Bigge, 2nd edn, rev. P. H. Nidditch (Oxford: Clarendon Press, 1978), 415.

25 *ST*, 231.

26 Ibid.

27 Miguel de Cervantes, *Don Quixote*, pt. 2, ch. 13.

28 *ST*, 240.

29 *ST*, 241.

30 There are similar versions of this line of criticism by Kivy, 'Hume's Standard of Taste', 57–66; and Zangwill, 'Hume, Taste, and Teleology', 1–18.

31 Jonathan Friday and Gary Kemp have helped me to understand Hume's *Standard of Taste*. I thank them.

32 For helpful discussion of Turnbull's aesthetic theory see Carol Gibson-Wood, 'Painting as Philosophy: George Turnbull's *Treatise on Ancient Painting*', in Jennifer J. Carter and Joan H. Pittock, eds., *Aberdeen and the Enlightenment* (Aberdeen: Aberdeen University Press, 1987), 189–98.

33 Turnbull, *Treatise*, ix.

34 Ibid., xv.

35 Ibid., 146.

36 Ibid., 147.

37 For discussion of Campbell on language see A. Broadie, 'George Campbell, Thomas Reid, and Universals of Language', in Paul Wood, ed., *The Scottish Enlightenment: Essays in Reinterpretation* (Rochester: Rochester University Press, 2000), 351–71.

38 Campbell, *Philosophy of Rhetoric*, bk 1, ch. 4.

39 *Enquiry Concerning Human Understanding*, in David Hume, *Enquiries Concerning Human Understanding and Concerning the Principles of Morals*, ed. L. A. Selby-Bigge, 3rd edn, rev. P. H. Nidditch (Oxford: Clarendon Press, 1975), 5–6.

15   The impact on Europe

THE BROAD PICTURE

Hippolyte Taine relates the following story: on an autumn morning in 1811, Pierre-Paul Royer-Collard, newly appointed professor of philosophy at the Sorbonne, is strolling along the banks of the Seine, thinking over the content of his teaching. He is dissatisfied with the philosophy of Condillac and his followers, the *Idéologues*, which seems to him too sceptical and materialistic. He happens to pass a bookshop where a title catches his eye: *Recherches sur l'entendement humain d'après les principes du sens commun, par le docteur Thomas Reid* (the first translation, published in 1768, of Reid's *Inquiry into the Human Mind on the Principles of Common Sense*). He opens the book, reads a few pages and his mind is filled with light. Taine concludes: 'He had just bought and founded the new French philosophy.'[1] Among Royer-Collard's first students was Victor Cousin, dedicatee of Sir William Hamilton's *The Works of Thomas Reid*.

This anecdote might be too nice to be true – in fact, Thomas Reid was already known to the French – but we can draw a lesson from it. When we study the impact or influence of one nation upon another, of one philosophical tradition upon another, we cannot ignore the various accidents and circumstances which intervene in the causal connections of a sequence of events. We have to consider the role played by translations (and the ability of the translator), the reception given by philosophical or literary journals, the import of the message in such and such intellectual contexts, the position of people, the pliability of doctrines, the ability of a philosopher to assimilate a new idea or a new way of ideas, and so on.

298

It is a fact that Scottish philosophy exercised an ascendancy over Continental Europe from about 1760 to about 1840; mainly over Germany and France, later on over the rest of Europe, mixed up with the Continental Enlightenment. But there is no official beginning or ending to this. And what do we mean by Scottish philosophy? Shall we exclude Hume, whose scepticism met with most resistance, or Adam Smith, whose *Wealth of Nations* is commonly separated, by scholars, from his *Theory of Moral Sentiments*? Shall we restrict our study to the threesome of Thomas Reid, James Beattie and James Oswald? And let us compare France and Germany in 1760: in Germany the philosophy of Christian Wolff was faltering, though still holding on in a few universities, and there was a kind of philosophical void which would not be filled until Immanuel Kant's *Critique of Pure Reason* in 1781. In France Etienne Bonnot de Condillac, an inventive disciple of John Locke, offered a reliable and influential doctrine; the *Encyclopédie* of Diderot and d'Alembert, in spite of its diversity and weaknesses, was a great success and was becoming known all around Europe, and though perhaps it contained no new doctrines, it certainly conveyed a new sense of philosophy. Montesquieu was a sage, Voltaire a master and Jean-Jacques Rousseau a paradoxical but admired writer. But by the start of the nineteenth century the Kantian philosophy was dominant in Germany and spreading across Europe; young and brilliant philosophers, Fichte, Schelling and then Hegel, were questioning the master. At the same time, in France, Condillac's nephews, the *Idéologues*, had won and lost the political and ideological war; they seemed too sensationalist and analytical for the new sort of feelings which were excited by the Napoleonic adventure or fostered by the royalist reaction. Thus, if it is unquestionably true that Scottish philosophy made an impact during this period, it is also true that it meant different things at different times and in different places, that it permeated various trends of intellectual life or systematic traditions, and that it contributed to philosophical movements which might themselves compete with one another.

THE MATERIAL EVIDENCE

Some of the best-known authors, such as Diderot, Hamann, Jacobi and Cousin, could read English, but others, such as Kant, could not.

Nor could many of the reading public.Translations therefore were needed, and several of them, though by no means all, were very good. Not all of those that were good would meet our contemporary standards, since they were more faithful to the authorial intentions than to the words; besides, the same collected works could have several translators. Texts in these translations are not always presented in exactly the same order as in the original.

Some of the translators deserve special mention. The most noteworthy is Christian Garve, who was very influential in the diffusion of Scottish philosophy. He translated Lord Kames's *Elements of Criticism*, with J. N. Meinhard, in 1763–6, Ferguson's *Institutes of Moral Philosophy* in 1772, and Adam Smith's *Wealth of Nations* in 1794–6. To these translations he added prefaces and explanatory footnotes which occasionally amount to a true commentary, and dispersed throughout his own works he gives many exegeses of the Scots' writings.[2]

The first influential translations were those of Hume's collected works. Translations from Hutcheson appeared at almost the same time, but were scattered, and had a more diffuse, if powerful, impact mainly in Germany. Hutcheson's *Inquiry into the Original of our Ideas of Beauty and Virtue*, his first book, was translated into French in 1749, but not into German until 1762. A translation of Hutcheson's *A System of Moral Philosophy* was made in 1756 by young Gotthold Lessing himself, and it attracted a wide readership. One might be surprised that the Scottish influence entered the Continent by means of the collected works of Hume after the successful *Political Discourses*, but it should be remembered that these collected works contained only the *Essays* and the *Enquiries* written in the style of 'easy philosophy', and that the *Treatise of Human Nature* was not translated into German until 1790–2, nor into French until 1878! The translations of the successive volumes of the *History of Great Britain* appeared quickly both in France (from 1760) and in Germany (from 1763), and Hume was soon known as one of the best historians of his time.

After the 1750s a new period began which lasted till 1800. A striking feature of this period was the notable success of Scottish philosophers in Germany: more than forty titles were translated into German between 1760 and 1800, and the delay between publication in Britain and translation in Germany became shorter and shorter.

By contrast, French production was much more modest, amounting to approximately one third of German translation and publication.

If we turn to the details, the landscape is varied. Unexpectedly, Reid is not prominent. It is true that the *Essays on the Intellectual Powers of Man* and the *Essays on the Active Powers of Man* were not published until 1785 and 1788 respectively, rather late in the period which we are considering. But although the *Inquiry into the Human Mind* had real success in Britain and was soon translated into French (1768), it did not appear in German until 1782, and we have to wait for Théodore Jouffroy's translation of the *Œuvres complètes* of Thomas Reid to offer full access to Reid's philosophy in France.[3] This fact is all the more remarkable when we compare the rather modest reception of Reid with the very great success of James Beattie. Beattie's *Essay on the Nature and Immutability of Truth* (1770) was not translated into French, but C. Reidinger published a German version as early as 1772. The role played by this German translation was very important, since it provided access to Reid's *Inquiry* and to Hume's *Treatise*; German translations of Beattie's other works also appeared regularly. But Beattie does not seem to have been much read in France, and the first (and only) French translation of his *Elements of Moral Science* was not published until 1840.

The good fortune of Beattie abroad is related to another note-worthy fact: the numerous translations into German and French of books concerning literary criticism. Alexander Gerard's *Essay on Taste* (1759) appeared in both French and German in 1766.[4] Lord Kames's *Essays on the Principles of Morality and Natural Religion* (1751) and his *Elements of Criticism* (1762) soon appeared in German. A German translation of George Campbell's *Philosophy of Rhetoric* appeared in 1791, and of Hugh Blair's *Lectures on Rhetoric and Belles Lettres* (1783) in 1785-9. The latter work appeared in French in 1797.[5] Only Adam Ferguson could match Kames's success. His *Essay on the History of Civil Society* (1767) and the *Institutes of Moral Philosophy* (1769) were quickly translated into German and French, although translations of his *Principles of Moral and Political Science* (1792) took longer. The general picture is of public interest in rhetoric and belles lettres going in step with philosophical studies of human nature.

This popular reception was greatly helped by the many literary journals and philosophical reviews which were read at that time. We can chart their influence by comparing the number and the length of reviews after the publication of a title in English and after its German or French translation. A very short review, sometimes with a lapidary comment, is first given to inform the readers of new publications in a foreign language, in the spirit of the Republic of Letters. Then, either because some interest is aroused or because one person or institution takes the initiative, the translation is made and news of the book is spread wide, often by the same journals.[6]

Lastly, special mention must be made of the reception of Adam Smith's works. The *Theory of Moral Sentiments* (1759) was immediately popular, not only in Britain but also in France and Germany. French translations appeared in 1764, 1774 and 1798. The first German translation appeared in 1770, followed by a second in 1791–5 which included the revisions of the sixth English edition. The *Wealth of Nations* (1776) had the same instantaneous success, but very soon had an independent life, the severance of economics from moral philosophy being under way. Garve's translation (Breslau, 1794–6), the second German translation, achieved widespread recognition and was re-edited several times. In France there were also translations by Blavet, Roucher and, especially, Germain Garnier.

After 1800, the number of new translations falls drastically. Blair's *Lectures on Rhetoric* are an exception,[7] as is the aforementioned *Œuvres complètes de Thomas Reid* by Jouffroy. Historical works by Hume or Millar were still of interest: Hume's *History* was newly translated by G. Timaeus at Lüneburg (1806–7) and in France by J. B. Després (Paris, 1819–22) and M. Langlois (1829–32), while a Spanish translation was made by Don Eugenio de Ochoa (Barcelona, 1842–45).

The same decline can be observed among the Scottish philosophers of the following generations. Dugald Stewart was almost ignored in Germany, though he was undoubtedly popular in France. He had visited France in the first years of the Revolution and was in constant correspondence with people on both sides of the political divide; and later on, after the Restoration, he established relations with younger people, especially Victor Cousin. Most of Stewart's works were translated. Sir William Hamilton fared less well, for though he too was a correspondent of Victor Cousin, only some fragments of his writings were made available in French. Scottish philosophy had become a matter of scholarly discussion, and had vanished from the field of public reading and conversation.

THE RECEPTION OF HUME AND REID

When *le bon David* (or *Saint David*) arrived in France in 1763, his reputation had preceded his person and everybody wanted to see him. His fame had spread well beyond the circle of *les philosophes*. He was invited to Parisian *salons* and was surprised and delighted by the welcome he received. His reception can be explained in several ways. Although his essay 'On Miracles' and, later, *The Natural History of Religion* alarmed the orthodox party which ranked him among the *philosophes*, and his *Œuvres philosophiques* were regularly condemned,[8] his works were widely read and he was welcome in the best political circles, where he could meet people who were very close to the heart of royal power. Scandalous as he might appear on matters of religion, he was appreciated for the shrewdness and sagacious moderation of his moral, political and economic essays. 'Mr Hume is small minded when he attacks religion; but he deserves to be listened to, when he talks politics, morals, history, and all that concerns taste and letters. On these topics, he should be taken as one of the leading writers of this century.'[9] Indeed, he was in tune with *l'air du temps* which both the *philosophes* and their learned adversaries breathed. The other side of this situation was that, although Hume could attend a banquet given by the Encyclopedist Baron d'Holbach, Hume's name appears only a few times in the *Encyclopédie* (whose first volume, it is true, appeared in 1751), even if occasional allusions are made to his political and historical writings. One can go through the complete works of Diderot without finding any explicit mention of a philosophical argument borrowed from the *Enquiries* or the *Essays*.[10] The notable exception, and it concerns religion, is Président de Brosses, who, in his *Culte des dieux fétiches* (*Cult of the Fetish Gods*) (1760), reproduced the content of Hume's *Natural History of Religion* in the third part of his book and justified his borrowing in a later correspondence with the Scottish philosopher.[11] Anyone searching for a discussion of Hume's doctrine of causation would find only Friedrich Grimm's rather negative comment on the *Enquiry*, praising the sections on miracles and on providence but warning his reader against the preceding essays:

'You will not be very satisfied with the first eight essays of the first volume. Mr Hume is wordy here; He turns over the same idea, again and again.'[12] As a philosopher, even for the *philosophes*, Hume was what he was in his own country: a sceptical metaphysician; but as a man of taste and learning, he could be honoured and applauded.[13]

Until 1800 this philosophy of taste provided the general framework for the reception of Scottish authors in France, at least on the surface, and it perhaps explains the apparent lack of success of Reid's *Inquiry*. The book's whole polemical aspect was ignored for three reasons. First, Hume's *Treatise* was known to very few, so Reid's anti-Humean polemic did not serve a widely perceived need. Secondly, Hume's scepticism appeared excessive to people who were not in the habit of discussing either their own certainties or, generally speaking, the possibility of an experimental science of man, so that Reid's critique seemed useless. Thirdly, Reid's claim against the theory of ideas could not get much purchase on French minds, which were Cartesian at bottom, Lockean on the surface. Of course, there were parallels to be drawn between Condillac's *Traité des sensations* (1754) and Reid's *Inquiry* (1764). But quite apart from the lapse of time which separated the two books, there was also a difference of philosophical spirit. The genealogy of Condillac's 'operations of the mind' is more consonant with Hume's arguments (apart from his scepticism) than with Reid's, and Reid's opportunity for a rendezvous with the French was missed.

Nevertheless, that rendezvous would happen. Let us leap forward to the first years of the nineteenth century. In December 1802 Maine de Biran's second *Mémoire sur l'habitude* appeared in bookshops. In the marginal notes of his own copy, Maine de Biran makes a few well-informed references to Hume, Reid and Smith; the same thing can be observed in his *Mémoire sur la décomposition de la pensée* (1805). In 1815, Maine de Biran wrote the *Comparaison des trois points de vue de Reid, Condillac et Tracy sur l'idée d'existence et le jugement d'extériorité* (*A Comparison of the Three Points of View of Reid, Condillac and Tracy on the Idea of Existence and the Judgement of Exteriority*), giving a summary of various remarks in a note on *La Philosophie de Reid au sujet de la vue* (The Philosophy of Reid on the Subject of Sight), and describing Reid as 'a profound and highly judicious writer' whose philosophy is 'a good, solid starting point'. Reid was at the centre of the polemics conducted between Maine de Biran and Ampère on the essence of perception and the relationship between touch and sight. We can see from this that the philosophical context had changed, that Beattie was now forgotten, and that Reid and Hume, and Reid especially, were known for their own merits and would henceforth play a part in the epistemological debate on such topics as sensation, perception and causation.

SCOTTISH PHILOSOPHY AND THE IDÉOLOGUES

In 1802 Maine de Biran became known to the *Idéologues*, heirs of Condillac, who were in most cases steady and moderate supporters of the ideals of the French Revolution and who played an influential role, during the Directoire and Bonaparte's Consulat, in the establishment of intellectual foundations for the new systems of teaching and of law. The original impact of the Scottish philosophers had been mainly in the fields of aesthetics and moral philosophy; now political events required that a new sense of sociability come into being, especially after the convulsions of the Terror and the dramatic upheavals of the civil war and the European wars. This must partly account for Smith's success at that time. Sophie de Grouchy, Marquise de Condorcet added *Huit lettres sur la sympathie* (*Eight letters on sympathy*) to her new translation of *The Theory of Moral Sentiments* and *Considerations concerning the First Formation of Languages*, a work that was much cited and discussed. Pierre Prévost, who in his youth had attended the Berlin Academy and who later became professor at the University of Geneva, met the *Idéologues* while he was translating Smith's *Essays on Philosophical Subjects* (1795).

Commentators began to introduce the translated texts into contemporary debates. For instance, Madame de Condorcet underlines the importance of sympathy in social relationships, but reproaches Smith for entertaining the idea of moral sense and for taking insufficient account of physical factors. And Georges Cabanis comments in these terms:

These [sympathetic] tendencies are, then, really what is understood by moral sympathy, a celebrated principle in the writings of the Scottish philosophers. One of them, Hutcheson, had recognised its great power to produce sentiments, and another, Smith, made an analysis which, though full of sagacity, was incomplete because he was unable to bring it into accord with physical laws.[14]

This question of moral and physical law is related to the *Idéologues'* more general attempt to develop a new psychology and linguistics, for the purposes of their lectures at the Ecole Normale and elsewhere. Condillac had bequeathed the doctrine of transformed sensation, as expounded in *Le Traité des sensations* (1754). But he was not a materialist; and if he later appeared to be so, this is because he was seen through the lens of some of the *Idéologues* who had an interest in medical topics. Reid's *Inquiry* was therefore of interest on account of its descriptions of the various operations of the mind, descriptions which matched those given by Condillac. In addition, Reid's commitment to experiment was well received. Nevertheless, he was criticised on two counts: his concept of common sense and the kind of idealist consequence to which this concept condemned any philosophical enquiry into the principles of human nature.

Among the people who played a part in bringing the Scottish philosophy to bear in this new philosophical atmosphere were the aforementioned Pierre Prévost, as well as François Thurot and Baron Degérando. Thurot is an interesting figure, since on the one hand he had studied Reid (as we can see from his *De l'Entendement humain* [*On Human Understanding*] (Paris, 1830)) and translated several works by Dugald Stewart, but on the other hand he tried, in accordance with Condillac's teaching, to emphasise the strong connection between linguistics and psychology. Degérando is less closely tied to Condillac and contests the idea of a transformed sensation, since in his view, each operation of the mind must be taken as being original and described as such. But Degérando is chiefly known for his considerable *Histoire comparée des systèmes de philosophie* (Paris, 1804), written (supposedly) in accordance with Bacon's experimental method. The book is divided into two parts: the first expounds the different systems of philosophy, while in the second the different systems are compared in the light of their answer to what is posited as the fundamental philosophical question: the origin and formation of human knowledge. In this *tableau historique*, the Scottish school (that is, the Reidian school) takes its place alongside the French school (Condillac and the *Idéologues*) and the German school. Reid 'attacked the very foundations of Hume's reasoning; he brought to light the long-lasting mistake of philosophers, who assumed that there must be something intermediate between the act of thought and the object of thought, and he looked, in the mind itself, for a more immediate and secret relationship (between the thought and its object)'.[15] Degérando is not a passive historian; he offers a critical evaluation of Reid's performance.

This book is of interest because it shows us, in outline, a profound change that was taking place. Its review of philosophical systems, understood as natural history but with the purpose of illustrating and promoting the onward march of the human spirit, is to inform the reader in an inductive way of the answer to the problem of the origin and formation of human knowledge. This problem, formulated in France by Condillac, reiterated more urgently by the *Idéologues*, and for some time thereafter considered the most important question of philosophy, is dealt with in a *tableau*, and the French tradition (traceable back to Descartes) is compared with other traditions, English, Scottish and German, in a way that is rather eclectic, but adds up to a general historical schema. Hume's scepticism is pronounced to be the outcome of the errors of preceding philosophies; this scepticism, however, cannot be accepted and philosophy must resolve its internal problems. Two answers are offered: the Scottish one, which continues to use the experimental method but is compelled to acknowledge the priority of the most fundamental principles of the human mind, and the Kantian one, whose source is in the Leibnitzian tradition, and which posits a priori principles but limits knowledge to the realm of possible experience. Each answer is a real advance, but they are unable to prove their claims. In Reid, the first principles are based upon an overly naturalistic account of the human constitution and in Kant, they are still unable fully to triumph over scepticism. The next generation of French philosophers propose a new and metaphysical solution, *le spiritualisme*, in order to resolve this. But, before telling this story, we must come back to what was going on in Germany before the publication of Kant's *Critique of Pure Reason* in 1781.

SCOTTISH PHILOSOPHY IN GERMANY

We have seen that Scottish thought had a wide readership in Germany after 1760, although not quite as extensive as in France. In both countries there was intense interest in moral, historical and aesthetic issues, but in Germany, the breakdown of metaphysics, following a decline of Wolffianism (Christian Wolff's revised version of the philosophy of his teacher Leibniz), led to a perceived need for a new approach. Scottish philosophy was a welcome means of combating scepticism, the new and dangerous consequence of the loss of metaphysics. Of course, the fight against scepticism was not a new one, the pernicious consequences of scepticism for morals and religion having already been thoroughly aired. But from now on the worm was inside the fruit. Hume was questioning a principle which is essential to human knowledge and there was no longer a reliable metaphysical answer.

The French translation of Hume's collected works appeared in 1758–60, a few years after the German one (1754–6), and was undertaken by J. B. Mérian at the behest of Pierre Louis Maupertuis and Jean Henri Formey, president and permanent secretary of the Prussian academy. Formey's introduction to the first volume[16] reminds the reader of the purpose of the undertaking: to check and control sceptical arguments. But this statement was ambiguous, because Maupertuis and Formey were themselves arguing sceptically against the dogmatism of Wolffians and French materialists, since scepticism also meant free enquiry. It should be noted that Mérian, though at first a mere translator, later presented to the Prussian Academy (in 1793) a very shrewd paper, 'Le Phénoménalisme de Hume', in which he discussed Hume's doctrine of empirical elements, inductive method, causation and substance. This suggests that with the passage of time Hume's texts, including the *Treatise*, could and did have a deep impact.

This ambivalence in the reception of Hume is a striking feature of the whole period. He could be regarded as the model of a genuinely popular philosopher, whose style was admired and whose essays were paradigms of civil and polite philosophy. He was also the sceptic to be fought against, and it is likely that the incredible success of Beattie is partly explained by the possibility that his violent critique of the *Treatise* satisfied a felt need for certainty. For more thoughtful philosophers, though, Beattie's attacks were no answer to Hume's tough questions about causality, and the Germans were more receptive than the French to this epistemological pressure. In one sense, therefore, Hume can be seen as part of the Scottish Enlightenment, but in another sense he stands alone by comparison with Reid, Beattie and the other common sense philosophers.

Reid's *Inquiry* and the books of Beattie and Oswald were reviewed almost immediately,[17] and their defence of common sense against abstruse systems was generally applauded. But there were still problems. The claim that we perceive objects directly and immediately, that is, without any mediating representation, ran counter to a long idealistic tradition, and many who espoused the anti-sceptical cause were not ready to give up on representationalism. Secondly, the question of how to identify first principles was made more urgent by the uncritical way in which Beattie and Oswald, acting in the name of common sense, produced more and more such principles. Many philosophers were not satisfied by this appeal to common sense, and insisted on a rational investigation of the credentials of the alleged first principles. Thirdly, there are two kinds of rationalism, the a posteriori or experimental kind and the a priori or metaphysical kind, and the fatal tendency in the common sense school to separate internal sense and reason from each other emphasised the shortcomings of Reid's experimental method. Scottish philosophy, therefore, prompted more questions than it provided solutions in the form of philosophical tenets.

Of course, suggestive philosophical texts could be interpreted in several ways, some of them mutually antagonistic. Manfred Kuehn[18] distinguishes five main groups. The first one, the 'Berlin Enlightenment', is the best known, since it includes Gotthold Lessing, Moses Mendelssohn, Johann Georg Sulzer and Johann August Eberhard; it still belonged to the declining tradition, and tried to open new avenues for Wolffian philosophy; for instance with Mendelssohn's attempts to show that all the judgements of 'good sense' can be reduced to reason, and even moral judgements can be analysed into rational and distinctly expressed principles. The second group, the Göttingen philosophers, Johann Feder and Christian Meiners, are not as distinguished, but their profile is interesting. Wavering between Wolffian dogmatism and scepticism, they considered themselves to be moderate sceptics; and, in comparing philosophical systems, they drifted in a rather eclectic spirit towards a common sense position, for they held it to be necessary to defend the first principles which are essential to morals. The third group, which included Dietrich Tiedemann, Karl Franz von Irwing, Christian Lossius and Ernst Platner, moved the empiricism that they had in common with the Göttingers towards physiological explanations, being convinced that

sensation and its corporeal root were the key to a scientific understanding of human nature; but they did not go so far as to present
themselves as materialists, like Claude-Adrien Helvétius, Julian
Offray de La Mettrie or Baron Paul Henri d'Holbach. The fourth
group, still on the side of Enlightenment, consists of philosophers of
consequence such as Christian Garve, Johann Heinrich Lambert and
Johann Nicolaus Tetens. These were the German philosophers most
influenced by the Scots. This group also includes the pre-critical
Kant. All of them were very alive to the difficulty of combining
British empiricism with German rationalism, even if Tetens in his
*Uber die allgemeine speculativische Philosophie (On General Spec-
ulative Philosophy)* (1775) and *Philosophische Versuche über die
menschliche Natur und ihre Entwicklung (Philosophical Investigations on Human Nature and its Development)* (1776–7) tried
to reconcile speculative philosophy and common sense. In the view
of this group the main shortcoming of the Scots was their inability
to solve the question of objective existence. The last group is made
up of the so-called 'counter-enlighteners', who were close to the
literary movement of *Sturm und Drang* (storm and stress) in the
seventies, and who rejected the idea of a rational foundation of
knowledge. In their partial critique of the German Enlightenment,
these philosophers – Johann Georg Hamann, Johann Gottfried
Herder and Friedrich Heinrich Jacobi – found Scottish sources very
helpful, as is apparent in Jacobi's *David Hume über den Glauben,
oder Idealismus und Realismus (David Hume on Belief, or Idealism
and Realism)* (1787).

The publication of Kant's *Critique of Pure Reason* in 1781
was a considerable event, even if it did not disarm all opposition.
Henceforth there would be a before and an after, a fact which makes
it all the more difficult to assess the impact of Scottish philosophy on Kant's philosophy. This question is much disputed because
it closely affects our understanding of the evolution of Kant's critical philosophy. 'Hume was not understood by anybody. It is pos-
itively painful to see how utterly his adversaries, Reid, Oswald,
Beattie and lastly Priestley, missed the point of the problem.' This
well-known comment from the introduction to his *Prolegomena
zu einer jeden künftigen Metaphysik (Prolegomena to all Future
Metaphysics)* (1783) offers us a valuable insight into Kant's critique
of Scottish philosophy. It points up the sharp opposition between

Humean scepticism and common sense, and it points to the weakness Kant observed in Reid and his followers, namely their inability to give a rational justification for their list of first principles. That comment acknowledges Kant's formal debt to Hume, and particularly to Hume's attack on causation, and it indicates the Scottish failure to find a general solution to the problem of knowledge (a solution which Kant develops in the Transcendental Analytic in the *Critique of Pure Reason*).

THE TEACHING OF SCOTTISH PHILOSOPHY IN FRANCE

Back in France, from 1811 onward, Scottish philosophy was not only read, cited and discussed – it was taught in universities. In his 1811–12 lectures, Paul Royer-Collard taught the anti-systematic method of the Scots, which extrapolates from facts to causes and accepts the plurality of primary principles; he commented on Reid's *Inquiry*, and concentrated on the existence of the external world, insisting along with Maine de Biran and against Condillac that sensation and perception should be sharply distinguished. In 1815, Victor Cousin was appointed to Royer-Collard's chair, and in 1819–20 he devoted twelve lectures to Scottish philosophy. These lectures, published in 1829 under the title *Philosophie écossaise (Scottish Philosophy)*, analyse the main works from Hutcheson to Ferguson (but do not include Hume). Jouffroy, Cousin's disciple, taught Scottish principles and values at the Ecole Normale, where future teachers were schooled, and when this school closed, he continued to teach at home. As early as 1816, at the beginning of the Restoration (the return of the Bourbon Monarchy in post-Napoleonic France), it was suggested that Scottish philosophy should be taught in schools, since it had managed to join free enquiry with the essential values of human life, and that this would counter the pernicious influence of the *Idéologues* while a new French philosophy, for a new era, came into being. Further political upheavals prevented the accomplishment of this project. But after the July Revolution, Victor Cousin, who was appointed *conseiller* of the University, had a new programme drawn up (by Laromiguière and Jouffroy) for schools, which was promulgated in 1832,[19] and in this programme the spirit of Scottish philosophy was intermingled with a more French tradition.

Scottish philosophy, especially Reid's, is often seen as parallel to Kantian philosophy, and this conjunction is apparent not just in the eclecticism of thinkers such as Cousin. Let us consider the general outline given by Hyppolite Taine in his *Les Philosophies classiques du XIXème siècle*. During the first half of the nineteenth century French philosophy is dominated by the opposition between *la philosophie positiviste* of Bichat, Lavoisier, Geoffroy Saint-Hilaire, Cuvier, and later on by Auguste Comte, and *la philosophie spiritualiste*. The former is the true heir to Condillac's philosophy (and, in a way, to Hume's); its methods require an analysis of the ideas in the mind, a critique of language, and a theoretical system, using signs for expressing ideas. There is no knowledge of general facts, other than abstract knowledge that arises from the phenomena. Science does not know the inner principles of things or events, and causation is only a correlation between facts or series of facts. These facts can be physical or spiritual, and there is no difficulty in linking a spiritual fact to a physical one. Against such a doctrine, which is epistemologically sceptical and metaphysically materialist (or supposedly so), the main claim of spiritualism is that the force and the activity of the mind cannot be obliterated and must be acknowledged as a first principle of which we are intimately conscious. Positivism is philosophically disastrous: it is unable to give a just account of the activity of knowledge and it encourages the abandonment of moral duties, since it affirms that the mind is passive. Here Reid and Kant are useful. Both of them acknowledged the value of the activity of the mind, Reid by laying down the first principles of common sense, Kant by building up the system of categories and principles. In opposition to a philosophy mainly concerned with objects or phenomena, they reinforced the need for a subjective philosophy, where the act of the subject is the foundation of the determination of the object. And they never lost sight of the practical ends of philosophy. They can thus be considered reliable guides for the foundation of a new psychology.

We must, however, go beyond Reid and Kant. Reid is unclear on common sense and on method. On common sense he is satisfied with taking first principles as being inscribed in the human constitution, which is something he leaves undefined. On method, he remains committed to the experimental method; and for this reason, Cousin, sensitive to the Scot's practice of describing discoveries made by introspection, does not hesitate to assign him Descartes as an ancestor and make him an ardent supporter of the reflexive (or reflective) method. Kant is systematic, but with the doctrine of the Transcendental Deduction he is still committed to a kind of phenomenalist scepticism, since principles of the faculty of understanding must be connected with empirical data, the science of things in themselves being regarded as impossible. But it must be said in his defence that he did not entertain such a scepticism in moral matters. The challenge for spiritualist philosophy was to strive to provide a rational foundation to the first principles of the mind in such a way as to ascertain the reality of human knowledge: in a word, to provide psychology with a metaphysical basis. This development, which becomes more and more evident in Cousin's philosophy, is taken further by Jouffroy. Scottish philosophy includes, to its credit, the defence of the idea of science against both speculative metaphysics and excessive analysis. On one side, it restricted the field of philosophy to the study of mental phenomena and restricted its methodology to observation and induction (which were easily justified as first steps of the reflexive method); on the other side, it sought to identify the conditions for the possibility of knowledge of objects. But the Scottish philosophers did not exactly realise their aims, because they claimed that questions concerning the mind cannot have a satisfactory answer, though they did not go so far as to declare, as Kant did, that these questions should be rejected.

According to Jouffroy, the whole story can be read in the following way: the starting point was Hume's scepticism, which destroyed not only the old metaphysics but also the dogmatism of the French materialists and encyclopedists. But the human mind cannot remain in a sceptical state indefinitely, which is why Reid tried to restore certainty by a new approach which restricted the scope of philosophical enquiry. Then came Kant in Germany who rationally justified, but critically and unduly limited, our claim to knowledge. But from now on the new French philosophy, starting with Maine de Biran and Royer-Collard, would realise the aim of a new ontology.

In his essay *The Rise and Progress of the Arts and Sciences*, Hume affirms: 'Nothing requires greater nicety, in our enquiries concerning human affairs, than to distinguish exactly what is owing to *chance*, and what proceeds from *causes*; nor is there any subject, in which an author is more liable to deceive himself by false subtleties and refinements.'[20] The warning is a good one, but how is the balance to be struck? It is a matter of reason, but also of taste, i.e. of sense. This precious ambiguity may be the best legacy of Scottish philosophy to the history of philosophy.

NOTES

1   Hippolyte Taine, *Les Philosophies classiques*, 3ème édition (Paris, 1868), 21–2.

2   Among the well-documented studies of the German reception of Scottish philosophy, see Günter Gawlick and Lothar Kreimendahl, *Hume in der deutschen Aufklärung* (Stuttgart-Bad Canstatt: Frommann-Holzboog, 1987); Manfred Kuehn, *Scottish Common Sense in Germany, 1768–1800* (Kingston and Montreal: McGill-Queen's University Press, 1987); and Norbert Waszek, *The Scottish Enlightenment and Hegel's Account of 'Civil Society'* (Dordrecht: Kluwer, 1988).

3   Readers in Britain also had to wait some time for a complete edition of the works of Thomas Reid. The edition by G. N. Wright appeared in 1843, and the standard edition, by Sir William Hamilton, appeared in 1846.

4   His *Essay on Genius* (1774) was translated by Christian Garve in 1775.

5   An Italian translation appeared in 1801–2, by Francesco Soave (Genoa, 3 vols.).

6   On this aspect of the reception, see (for Hume), Gawlick and Kreimendahl, *Hume in der deutschen Aufklärung*, ch. 3; and (for other philosophers) Waszek, *Scottish Enlightenment*, appendix 1.

7   In Germany, by J. Eiselen (Donauöschingen, 1820); there were many new editions and translations in France: 1808, 1821, 1830, 1845.

8   No review of the *Œuvres philosophiques* appeared in the *Mémoires de Trévoux*, the Jesuit journal and the most formidable adversary of *l'Encyclopédie*. This journal announced the publication of *The History of Great Britain*, in January and February 1759. Longer comments were provided on the Hume/Rousseau dispute in 1766 and 1767.

9   *Bibliothèque des sciences et des beaux-arts* (La Haye, 1763), 550; quoted from the well-informed essay by Laurence L. Bongie, 'Hume, "Philosophe" and Philosopher in Eighteenth-century France', *French Studies* 15 (1961), 213–27. This judgement is confirmed in the preface by the anonymous translator of the *Pensées philosophiques, morales, critiques, littéraires et politiques de M Hume* (London, 1767). This digest is all the more curious as it offers a summary of the doctrine of indirect passions which can be found in book two of the *Treatise*.

10 In contrast, in a letter written to the marquise du Deffand in 1764, Voltaire says that he likes Hume's philosophy even more than his historical works.

11 De Brosses could read English. His attention had been drawn by Diderot to Hume's *Natural History of Religion*. On this remarkable story, see M. David, 'Le président de Brosses, historien des religions et philosophe', in Jean-Claude Garreta, ed., *Charles de Brosses, 1777–1977: Actes du Colloque*, Biblioteca del Viaggio in Italia, 2 (Geneva: Slatkine, 1981).

12 F.-M. Grimm, *Correspondance littéraire et philosophique et critique de Grimm et de Diderot*, 16 vols. (Paris, 1829–31), XVI.114–15, 15 janvier 1759.

13 L. Bongie, 'Hume', justly insists upon the fact that for the *philosophes*, as for Condillac, the true philosopher was Locke, the author of *An Essay Concerning Human Understanding*.

14 P. J. G. Cabanis, *Rapports du physique et du moral de l'homme* (1844; reprint, Geneva: Slatkine Reprints, 1980), quoted by J. P. Cotten, in his extremely well-documented essay 'La philosophie écossaise en France avant Victor Cousin, Victor Cousin avant sa rencontre avec les Ecossais', *Victor Cousin, les Idéologues et les Ecossais* (Paris: Presses de l'Ecole Normale Supérieure, 1985), 99–157, note 37.

15 Quoted by Cotten, 'La philosophie écossaise en France', 115.

16 A large part of this introduction is a French translation of John Leland's refutation of Hume in *A View of the Principal Deistical Writers* (1754) which had been published in German in 1755 (for more details, see J. C. Laursen and R. H. Popkin, 'Hume in the Prussian Academy', *Hume Studies* 23 (1997), 153–91).

17 See Kuehn, *Scottish Common Sense in Germany*, 52.

18 Ibid., 40.

19 For more details, see E. Boutroux, 'De l'influence de la philosophie écossaise sur la philosophie française', *Etudes d'histoire de la philosophie* (Paris, 1897), Alcan, 413–43.

20 Hume, *Essays Moral, Political and Literary*, ed. Eugene F. Miller (Indianapolis: Liberty Fund, 1985), 111.

16 The impact on America: Scottish philosophy and the American founding

Over the past half century or so, there has been an outpouring of literature on the many ways in which Scottish thinkers influenced America in the period of the founding.[1] For social and cultural historians, this literature has meant a deeper understanding of the 'outlying provinces' of the British Empire; for historians of ideas, it has meant a better understanding of the reception of Scottish thought in its time; and for political theorists, it has inspired a reinterpretation of the political vision represented by the founding of the American republic.

As a political philosopher, I am primarily interested in this last project. The Scottish influence has been used to counter an earlier picture of the founders, according to which they were putting into practice the natural-rights theories, and concomitant radical individualism, to be found in Hobbes and Locke. So the debate between the Scottish and the Hobbesian–Lockean view of the founders is part of a larger controversy over whether the political philosophy expressed in the American Declaration of Independence and Constitution is primarily a 'liberal' or a 'civic republican' one. Like most scholars who attend to the role of the Scots, I agree that the Hobbes–Locke picture, still very common in schools and popular literature, is badly misleading. But I do not think the distinction between, especially, Locke's political philosophy and the political vision to be found among the Scots is quite as sharp as it has been taken to be. This is but one instance, moreover, of a general tendency of the literature on the Scots and America to draw distinctions that are too sharp. It is also something of an error to speak of 'Scottish views', in a comprehensive way: there were many important intellectuals in eighteenth-century Scotland, who disagreed vehemently with one another on many things.

Accordingly, this chapter will be devoted to the relations between certain specific Scottish thinkers and certain specific American ones, and to a set of philosophical distinctions, suggested by these relationships, that I think need more careful consideration. After a quick overview of the history of intellectual exchange between Scotland and America, I will make forays into three aspects of that exchange. These forays are intended to present, by way of example, both some of the respects in which attention to the Scots can help illuminate American thinking, and some of the difficulties in the way of saying exactly what role the Scottish influence played.

A large number of people moved from Scotland to America on the eve of the Revolution, including several who participated prominently in the Revolution. John Witherspoon, who began his career as a leading Scottish cleric, emigrated to America to become president of the College of New Jersey (later called 'Princeton'), and was a signer of both the Declaration of Independence and the Articles of Confederation. His countryman James Wilson signed both the Declaration and the Constitution, helped shape the debates at the 1787 Constitutional Convention, served on the first Supreme Court, and gave the first set of lectures on American law. Another immigrant from Scotland, Francis Alison, became the first Rector of the College of Philadelphia in 1752, and his compatriot William Smith was made its first provost.

Other names to conjure with were not Scottish themselves but were students of Scots. Jefferson had a Scottish teacher as a boy, and regarded his conversations at William and Mary college with William Small, an emigré from Aberdeen, as having first opened him up to 'the expansion of science, and...the system of things in which we are placed'.[2] Madison was a pupil at the boarding school of Donald Robertson, a Scot who had studied at Aberdeen and Edinburgh,[3] and then went to study under Witherspoon, as did many other future American leaders.[4] John Marshall, the first Chief Justice, was educated by a Scots deacon named James Thompson and by Archibald Campbell, who also taught James Monroe.[5] Benjamin Rush, another signer of the Declaration, a participant in the ratification debates, and an important early promoter of education in

America, attended medical school in Edinburgh, where he persuaded Witherspoon to come to America. Benjamin Franklin became acquainted with both David Hume and Adam Smith during his stay in Britain, and may have discussed early drafts of *The Wealth of Nations* with the latter.

Intellectual historians have drawn on this overall context to help underwrite specific claims for the importance of Hutcheson to Jefferson, of Hume to Madison, and of Reid to several eighteenth-century leaders of American education.[6] The first two of these claims, but not the last, are controversial. I shall revisit the Hutcheson–Jefferson and the Hume–Madison theses, more to expand them in various ways than to rebut them, and turn subsequently to Reid's influence.

HUTCHESON VS LOCKE: SOCIABILITY AND RIGHTS

In 1978, Gary Wills published *Inventing America*, his book on the Scottish roots of Jefferson's thought, which simultaneously received widespread acclaim in the non-academic world and a series of harsh scholarly reviews.[7] Some of the criticism was unfair, but the critics did pick up on an issue with important ramifications for both the history and the philosophical significance of the American founding. That issue can be put historically by asking whether Locke's *Second Treatise*[8] was really as unimportant to the Declaration of Independence as Wills suggests, and it can be put philosophically by asking whether Jefferson's conception of politics really centres around Hutchesonian sociability, as Wills would have it, or is centrally concerned, as more traditional accounts have held, with protecting Lockean individual rights.

Wills clearly overstates his case for the importance of Hutcheson vis-à-vis Locke. Two passages in the Declaration resemble Locke so closely that Jefferson, were he presenting the document as a scholarly paper today, could be convicted of plagiarism:

1 all experience hath shewn that mankind are more disposed to suffer while evils are sufferable than to right themselves by abolishing the forms to which they are accustomed. (Jefferson)
    till the mischief be grown general . . . the people who are more disposed to suffer than right themselves by resistance are not apt to stir. (Locke)[9]

2 But when a long train of abuses and usurpations...pursuing invariably
the same object, evinces a design to reduce them under absolute despotism it is their right, it is their duty to throw off such government, and to
provide new guards for their future security. (Jefferson)
But if a long train of abuses, prevarications, and artifices, all tending
the same way, make the design visible to the people,...it is not to be
wondered that they should then rouse themselves and endeavour to put
the rule into such hands which may secure to them the ends for which
government was at first erected. (Locke)[10]

Wills acknowledges these 'verbal echoes', but dismisses them as
'good Blackstone doctrine, shared by all whigs and voiced in earlier documents of the Congress – nothing distinctively Lockean'.[11]
This is implausible: there are no such echoes either in Blackstone
himself or in the earlier Congressional documents Wills cites.
Elsewhere Wills tries to graft the passages on to Hutcheson rather
than Locke,[12] but again there are no similarities of language between
the passages and his quotations from Hutcheson. However fond
Jefferson might generally have been of Hutcheson, here he is quoting
Locke.

And for good reason. There was something Jefferson could find
in Locke of great importance to his purposes that he was unlikely
to find elsewhere. Wills presents the Declaration too much as a
statement of philosophical principles. Only the first two preliminary
paragraphs are devoted to such principles, and they, as Jefferson famously said, are supposed to be stating 'the common sense' of the
subject – the accepted, standard view of the purposes of government
and the right of resistance to governments that do not fulfil their
purposes. The rest of the document takes up the much more difficult, much more controversial question of whether the situation in
the American colonies, at the time of writing, properly fitted the description of a case in which resistance is justified. The Declaration is
a legal brief, more than a philosophical statement, laying out the evidence for the claim that what the King and Parliament were doing to
the colonists amounted to the kind of illegitimate governance that
warranted revolution. And this claim was a difficult, controversial
one precisely because there had been no overwhelming imposition of
tyrannical rule, comparable to the excesses of a Nero or Caligula, or
even a Cromwell, that any eighteenth-century thinker could recognise as a perversion of government. What had occurred instead – just

as had occurred, according to Locke at least, in Britain in the 1680s –
was 'a long train' of laws and policies that offended against freedom
or defied the people's will. Jefferson's central argument is that this
series of relatively small betrayals of political legitimacy, when
taken as a whole, added up to evidence that complete tyranny was
on its way:

> The history of the present king of Great Britain is a history of unremitting
> injuries and usurpations, among which appears no solitary fact to contradict
> the uniform tenor of the rest but all have in direct object the establishment
> of an absolute tyranny over these states.[13]

The Declaration continues, famously: 'To prove this let facts be submitted to a candid world', and the rest of the document is devoted
to proving 'this'. But 'this' – the claim that the arrival of absolute
tyranny could be foreseen from small insults to freedom, along with
the implicit claim that rebellion can be justified before tyranny fully
arrives – is something Jefferson could find only in Locke, not in
Hutcheson. Locke had lived through similar times, and had justified
a similarly pre-emptive rebellion.

Having said this against Wills, I still find his case for the importance of Hutcheson to Jefferson more convincing than the views of
his critics. On the few occasions when Jefferson wrote on fundamental questions of moral philosophy, he seems clearly to have identified his views with Hutcheson's moral-sense doctrine rather than
with the views of Hobbes and Locke, Clarke and Wollaston, or indeed
either of the two other major moral-sense philosophers, Hume and
Smith.[14] And there is good reason to believe that Jefferson first came
to these views very early, in the 1760s or '70s.[15] So it is perfectly
reasonable to see Hutcheson's influence behind the appeals to sentiment that Jefferson put into his draft of the Declaration, and it makes
excellent sense to say, as Wills does, that Jefferson had intended, in
a passage omitted by Congress, to rest a fundamental argument for
independence on the damage Britain had inflicted on the community of sentiments between her people and the colonists. More generally, Jefferson seems throughout his life to have wanted America
to have institutions nurturing fellow-feeling, and, like Hutcheson, to
have seen the achievement of virtue as more or less independent of
intellectual accomplishments. Hence his strong egalitarianism, his
abiding trust in the common people.

What mars both Wills's case and the criticisms of Wills is a failure to recognise the extent to which Hutcheson was himself indebted to Locke's political philosophy. Daniel Walker Howe rightly says that 'the Scots always honored Locke and considered themselves to be working within his tradition'.[16] Hutcheson, Hume and Smith all begin from Locke, if only to disagree with him, when they discuss property, the state of nature, the functions of government and the right to resistance. All three, moreover, accept Locke's conclusion, as against Hobbes, that resistance to government is sometimes legitimate, although Hume rejects Locke's reasoning to that conclusion and offers his own alternative.[17] And all three accept the general conception of government to be found in Locke, according to which the primary function of government is to protect certain conditions for individual liberty, rather than to represent, or lead people towards, any thick conception of religious or moral virtue. Despite their emphasis on sociability, they are all thus rightly thought of as primarily having a liberal, rather than a Christian or civic republican, conception of politics.

Hume is the furthest from Locke of the three, referring to Locke's accounts of property and the state of nature mostly in order to attack or ridicule them. Hutcheson is, by far, the closest to Locke. Unlike his successors, Hutcheson believes in the reality of the state of nature and in a contractual account of political legitimacy.[18] One excellent chapter of the *System* is devoted to defending Locke's version of the state of nature against Hobbes's, although on a moral-sense basis alien to Locke's thinking.[19] Hutcheson also affirms the importance of rights, although, again, he provides a new basis for them.[20] The *Inquiry*, *Compendium* and *System* all contain detailed lists of natural rights, which articulate the general notion that Hutcheson, followed by Smith, calls 'natural liberty'. And Hutcheson famously defends the right of resistance to government in passages that several scholars have argued had a direct impact on the American founders.[21]

But of course, as I have said, Hutcheson tends to recast Locke in his own terms. That means, for instance, that the state of nature becomes no longer a state of 'absolute solitude' – that Hutcheson, like Hume and Smith, regards as impossible – and that the law of that state ('natural law') has roots in our sentiments rather than in our reason. 'Natural rights' become a projection of our care for one another: we grant each other certain absolute protections because it would be cruel or callous of us not to. But this derivation does not make individual rights any less important for Hutcheson than they were for Locke. Others were to come along, in the utilitarian tradition especially, who would take the idea that good political action reflects care for other people to imply that 'absolute rights' are a ridiculous idea: why focus on one person's rights if that makes it difficult to promote the well-being of many other people? Hutcheson did not say anything like this. He maintained, rather, a vocabulary of 'perfect' and 'imperfect' rights in which the perfect ones could be used as trump cards against casual appeals to 'public interest'.[22] He did believe that we should each do our best to extend our benevolence to the entire human species, but he also had great respect for the degree to which human life is fundamentally an individual affair. Rights and obligations are grounded, he says, in 'some tendency either to the general happiness, *or to that of individuals consistently with the general good, which must result from the happiness of individuals*',[23] and he elaborates the nature and importance of this individual happiness in thoughtful detail. Our 'sense of natural liberty is so strong', he says, 'and the loss of it so deeply resented by human nature', that it is generally much worse to override that sense than to put up with the imprudent, inefficient and amoral conduct that may come of allowing people to act on it.[24] Hutcheson criticises religious coercion on this ground, insisting that we all need to come to our own 'opinions about the Deity, religion, and virtue', even if that means many people will arrive at false opinions.[25] He also uses the importance of our sense of natural liberty to defend private property. We have within us 'a strong desire of acting according to our own inclinations, and to gratify our own affections, whether selfish, or generous' and it is 'morally evil' to obstruct designs based on this desire, unless those designs are themselves directed against the liberty or happiness of other people.[26] On this basis, Hutcheson considers it far better for people to acquire property on their own than for magistrates to attempt to distribute property or for property to be communally owned, as in the schemes of Plato and Sir Thomas More. About these latter Hutcheson notes, following Aristotle, that they would 'exclude...much of the loveliest offices of life, of liberality and beneficence, and grateful returns; leaving men scarce any room for exercising them in the distribution of their goods'.[27]

Far from being a natural extension of our sociability, communal ownership would offend against beneficence.

So a moral philosophy based on our concern for other human beings, in what today we might call our 'connectedness' as opposed to our individualism, was in Hutcheson's hands quite compatible with a concern precisely for the individuality so important to each human being, and therefore with a respect for individual rights. To trace Jefferson's thought to Hutcheson, then, does not necessarily make the former a 'communitarian' as opposed to a 'liberal', in today's political terms. Jefferson follows Hutcheson in combining a strong commitment to rights – in the opening of the Declaration and, later, in his correspondence with Madison about the Constitution – with his appeals to sentiment. The modern dichotomy between 'liberal' and 'communitarian' does not illuminate much about Hutcheson and Jefferson; they both, for one thing, recognise the importance of protecting individual rights to the maintenance of community itself. Imposed community is not true community, does not grow out of the natural human inclination to care for other people, and certainly does not meet the end of true community, which results, as Hutcheson says, from 'the happiness of individuals'. This careful balance between a recognition of the deep ways in which human beings are and want to be enmeshed in relationships with others and a recognition that, for all the importance of these social bonds, we all in the end live out individual lives, is a characteristic mark of Scottish thinking that Hutcheson passed down to his successors. Hume came dangerously close, when he discussed personal identity in the *Treatise*, to dissolving individuality into a social construct, but even he did not pursue this thought in his moral writings, and Smith and Kames emphatically reiterated that individuals take moral priority over the society they constitute, even if those individuals are at the same time heavily shaped by their society. Kames, perhaps, best put the view that all four shared: 'Man by his nature is fitted for society and society by its conveniences is fitted for man. The perfection of human society consists in that just degree of union among the individuals, which to each reserves freedom and independency.'[28]

Unsurprisingly, Jefferson entered this passage into his Commonplace Book.[29] It represents beautifully both the extent and the limits of Jefferson's commitment to a socialised conception of humanity – a conception that can certainly be called 'Scottish' but can be even better characterised as what resulted from the peculiar Scottish embrace of Locke. Wills is both right and wrong. Jefferson, with his belief in the moral sense and tendency to trust 'the Heart' over 'the Head',[30] is deeply Hutchesonian, but he is equally Hutchesonian in the prominent place he gives to 'inalienable rights'. One does not need to choose between Locke and Hutcheson; sociability and rights can go together.

SMITH VS HUME – OVERCOMING FACTION

In a famous article, Douglas Adair argued for the influence of Hume on Madison's Tenth *Federalist* Paper.[31] Adair's thesis has been challenged in recent years,[32] but while he may have exaggerated the extent of Hume's influence, the verbal parallels he cites make it hard to doubt that he was, at least in general, right. One thing that should always have struck readers as a bit perplexing, however, both in Adair's original piece and in the many scholarly works that have relied upon it, is why an investigation of Madison's reliance on Hume was never extended to Smith.[33] Hume and Smith have such similar views, on so many topics in moral, political and economic philosophy, that the extension seems a natural one.

Adair's argument eventually faces a problem, moreover, to which Smith would have given him a solution. That problem is the fact that central to Madison's paper is an extended analysis of competing economic interests in a nation – 'a landed interest, a manufacturing interest, a mercantile interest, a moneyed interest, ... [which] divide [civilised nations] into different classes actuated by different sentiments and views' – for which there is no parallel in Hume. There is, however, a close parallel in Smith's *Wealth of Nations*: at the end of Book 1, where Smith explains how 'every civilized society' naturally divides into 'three great orders' – 'those who live by rent, ... those who live by wages, and ... those who live by profit' – and how the contribution each of these orders makes to public deliberations will be shaped by their economic interests.[34] Furthermore, one example Madison gives of the sort of thing over which competing economic interests might divide could have come straight out of Smith: 'Shall domestic manufactures be encouraged, and in what degree, by restrictions on foreign manufactures?' Adair, oddly, treats all this as if it were completely new with Madison, an original addition to what the American had found in Hume: '[Madison] had his own ideas about the importance of economic forces'.[35] But if Hume is a plausible source for Madison's defence of large republics, *Wealth of Nations* is a yet more plausible source for Madison's economic views.

A deeper connection to Smith, however, comes at the heart of Madison's most famous argument. In a large republic, Madison says, the very fact that there will be more 'distinct parties and interests' means that none of those parties and interests can be as dangerous as they would be in a small republic. The greater the number of factions, the more difficult it will be for a majority to form around any 'common motive', and the more difficult it will be for groups to communicate among themselves, and to coordinate their actions. This will be particularly difficult, moreover, if the purpose they are pursuing is a dishonourable one, one that involves 'invading the rights of other citizens', since 'where there is a consciousness of unjust or dishonorable purposes, communication is always checked by distrust'.[36] The multiplicity of factions thus makes each faction less dangerous than it would otherwise be.

But this is just an extension of the argument Smith offers in *Wealth of Nations* for the advantages of a multiplicity of religious sects. Against Hume, who had defended the establishment of a church on the grounds that members of an established clergy tend to be lazier, hence less fanatic, in the promotion of their beliefs than the clergy of small sects, Smith argues that a world in which small sects proliferated would be one in which their very conflict with one another would reduce the danger each presented. The 'zeal' of each fanatic religious teacher could not do much damage where society 'is divided into two or three hundred, or perhaps...as many thousand small sects', and would probably in the long run be replaced with 'candour and moderation', since each teacher would have to compete for disciples with so many others:

The teachers of each little sect, finding themselves almost alone, would be obliged to respect those of almost every other sect, and the concessions which they would mutually find it both convenient and agreeable to make to one another, might in time...reduce the doctrine of the greater part of them to that pure and rational religion...such as wise men have in all ages of the world wished to see established.[37]

A multiplicity of sects makes it difficult for any religious group to become large enough to threaten the whole society, and puts pressure on each group to use honourable and decent means, about which they can communicate openly. The competition for believers will thus bring about better results for society than any government establishment of religion would have done. When governments refrain from putting their powers at the disposal of any religion, an invisible hand guides the free market of competing religious sects to promote the public good.

Not only does the structure of this argument closely resemble Madison's argument about political factions, but there is reason to believe that Madison alludes directly to Smith. In the penultimate paragraph of *Federalist* x (¶ 22),[38] he says the following: 'a religious sect, may degenerate into a political faction in a part of the Confederacy; but the variety of sects dispersed over the entire face of it, must secure the national Councils against any danger from that source'. And he argues similarly, in *Federalist* LI: 'In a free government, the security for civil rights must be the same as that for religious rights. It consists in the one case in the multiplicity of interests, and in the other, in the multiplicity of sects' (¶ 10).[39] In the second case it is clear, and it may be implicit in the first, that religious sects are less an example of factions than a comparison to them. The point in LI is that some protection of freedom, known to follow from the multiplicity of religious sects, can be brought to bear on the comparable case in which political 'sects' compete with one another. What protection is that? The one Smith had analysed so nicely in his argument for religious disestablishment.

Now the point of Smith's invisible-hand accounts of social phenomena is that individuals generally promote the public good whether or not they intend to do so. This point is supposed to hold regardless of whether the individual's own interest is furthered, harmed or left alone by his or her actions: individuals will promote the public good even when they thereby defeat their own interests. The reason for this is nothing mysterious – it is just that society structures both the means available for any individual to attain his ends and his very conception of those ends. The opening chapters of *Wealth of Nations* show that opportunities for an individual to 'better' himself are normally made possible by the needs of his society, and chapters i.iii and iii.i–iii of *The Theory of Moral Sentiments*[40] make clear that the notion an individual has of what will count as 'bettering' himself normally arises out of the influences upon him of his friends and neighbours. There is therefore an asymmetry between an individual's good and the society's: even when social forces lead us to a false conception of our ends, what we do to pursue these illusory goods will benefit the society that has misled us. Thus while Smith uses the phrase 'invisible hand' in *Wealth of Nations* for a case in which the individual's interest and the public good are jointly benefited, the passage in which that phrase appears in *Theory of Moral Sentiments* describes a case in which agents contribute to the public good without advancing their own good, and the famous account of the decline of feudalism in Book iii of *Wealth of Nations* presents us with agents who foolishly destroy their own favourite good (power over their vassals) but thereby promote a good for society as a whole.

Smith's analysis of what happens to religious sects when left alone by government follows this last pattern. Each sect will quickly fail to achieve its self-set end – the promotion of a fanatical and rigid doctrine when faced by similarly fanatical sects with different doctrines. Instead they will all have to show respect for one another and 'reduce' their doctrines to 'pure and rational religion'. This is a good for society, but it is an abandonment of what the sects took to be their own good. Competition makes them all less successful in 'selling' their fanatical product: which is, in this case, a good thing for everybody. In one sense the logic of the market is thus exactly inverted – competition slows down, rather than stimulates, the 'sales' of the relevant product – but in another sense the logic of the two cases is the same: competition results in a good for society.

And just this logic underlies Madison's analysis of factions. In their mutual conflict, all factions become weaker, and less capable of achieving what they regard as their good. But this very decline is good for society, and it is brought about by deeply entrenched facts about human beings and their societies: the fact that people generally want to be addressed in truthful, decent terms, rather than with the accent of passion and prejudice; the fact that the emotions driving fanaticism tend to overcome people only for short periods of time, and are discouraged in normal social intercourse; and the fact that people have economic and other interests that connect them, across groups, to practically everybody else in their society, and therefore in the long run do not want to be committed to a group that defines itself against other people. Like Smith, Madison sees factions as growing out of the social nature of human beings and as likely, therefore, to be tempered by the very social forces that make them possible. Like Smith, he is also willing to trust these social forces to do that job where, as will usually be the case, 'enlightened statesmen' to reconcile 'clashing interests' cannot be found.[41] And like Smith, he sees the liberty that thus gives rein to 'interest' as compatible with a republic concerned, for the most part, to foster virtue.

REID VS HUME – COMMON SENSE AND CONSERVATISM

The Declaration of Independence and the Constitution are two of the three pillars of the American founding; the American academy is the third. Breaking free from Britain and setting up a viable political structure were two essential tasks for the new republic, but its founders believed firmly that these acts would not succeed unless Americans were also educated to think like republicans. We need 'to convert men into republican machines', Benjamin Rush notoriously said,[42] and while the word 'machine' may make us wince today, it remains widely accepted that democratic political institutions require an education for democratic citizenship.

But if it is reasonable to suggest Scottish influence on the Declaration of Independence and the Constitution, the Scottish impact on the structure and content of the American university is indubitable. William Smith, the first provost of the College of Philadelphia, and Francis Alison, its first Rector, were both Scots, the first from Aberdeen, and the second a student at both Edinburgh and Glasgow. Smith drew up the first systematic curriculum in America, stressing modern rather than classical knowledge, as the Scots did, and using Hutcheson as the basis for the upper-level ethics classes. Alison knew Hutcheson in Britain and remained in touch with him after coming to America; he may also have influenced his friend Ezra Stiles, the president of Yale, to incorporate Hutcheson into the Yale curriculum.[43] Jonathan Edwards, whose own works were widely read in philosophy courses and who served as a senior tutor at Yale and, briefly, as the president of the College of New Jersey, developed a sophisticated philosophical argument to show that Hutcheson's moral system required Christian conversion.[44] John Witherspoon satirised Hutcheson in Scotland, but when he came to America his moral lectures incorporated Hutcheson's moral sense theory, as well as the ideas of other Scots. This immersion in Scottish thought continued after the Revolution, moreover, with the arguments of Thomas Reid, in particular, being used to shore up a generally conservative attitude towards matters of faith and virtue. Samuel Stanhope Smith, Witherspoon's successor at Princeton, saw in Reid a way 'to show the compatibility between good science and true religion'; Benjamin Rush found Reid's follower Beattie useful for the same reason.[45]

It is thus with good reason that Lundberg and May say that 'the Scottish moralists [were]...used in America for conservative purposes'.[46] But they seem insufficiently struck by the oddity of this fact. In their own context, the Scots were quite radical. Hutcheson was accused of heresy, Hume, Smith and Kames were all suspected of being atheists, and Reid was a political utopian who supported the French Revolution enthusiastically until 1792. How did these people turn into bulwarks of conservatism in the United States?

Well, in the first place, it is not entirely true that they did. As Douglas Sloan points out, Stanhope Smith was accused of heresy, Rush developed for himself a peculiar combination of 'New Side' Calvinism and Scottish scientific, moral and political thought, and both Alison and Witherspoon used Hutcheson to support the right of resistance to oppressive rulers.[47] But on the whole it seems that the leaders of the American academy looked to Scottish texts while either ignoring or toning down the Scots' more radical doctrines, especially as regards religion. Edwards, Witherspoon and Alison all managed to minimise the optimism in Hutcheson that clashed with the doctrine of original sin. And Reid was already well suited for the project of reconciling Enlightenment thought with Christian faith. I want in this concluding section to explore a little the uses of Reid, who was by far the most important Scot to the American university from the late eighteenth century onwards, and who was employed, above all, to refute the doctrines of his fellow Scot, David Hume.

It is important to be clear about exactly how Reid was used against Hume. Shannon Stimson argues persuasively that James Wilson drew a radically democratic approach to politics and jurisprudence out of Reid, and suggests that Reid helped undermine Humean elitism. But Stimson overstates Reid's differences with Hume. She attributes to Hume the belief that 'the vast majority of our moral rules...must be supplied by long chains of reasoning and demonstration' and says that he therefore 'placed the claim to moral knowledge well out of the reach of common men, who must rely on others to extrapolate for them'.[48] This misrepresents Hume's moral philosophy, however, with its great stress on the superiority of feeling to reason in morality, and constant appeal to how we view things in 'common life'. And the passage Stimson uses to support her claim in fact says nothing about either moral rules or the need for common people to rely on others for moral guidance.[49]

Stimson thus misreads Hume, but her misreading reflects a deep problem about how exactly to contrast Hume and Reid. After all, Hume's affirmation of our 'common life' beliefs, at the end of Book I of the *Treatise*, looks a lot like something Reid might say, as does his attack on excessive philosophical abstraction, there and throughout his writings. Reid, on the other hand, tends more to reject than to refute Hume's philosophical scepticism, to acknowledge that the principles of common sense cannot be philosophically defended but then to embrace common sense in defiance of philosophy. Insofar as philosophy has not the power to dispel the clouds of scepticism, he says, 'I despise Philosophy, and renounce its guidance: let my soul dwell with Common Sense'.[50]

But now it becomes hard to tell Hume and Reid apart. As the nineteenth-century Edinburgh philosopher Thomas Brown remarked:

'Yes', Reid bawled out, 'We must believe in an external world'; but added in a whisper, 'We can give no reason for our belief.' Hume cries out, 'We can give no reason for such a notion'; but whispers, 'I own we cannot get rid of it.'[51]

Of course, this is a bit too crude. Reid had an intriguing argument for free will, against Hume's determinism,[52] and buttressed his rejection of Hume's scepticism with a diagnosis of the 'way of ideas' that he considered, rightly, to underlie the Humean position. Hume, on the other hand, believed that we can at least momentarily suspend the beliefs of common life, that philosophy, therefore, need not be entirely 'root[ed in] the principles of Common Sense', as Reid was to maintain,[53] and that our common beliefs do not in any case form a coherent, systematic body. These are important philosophical differences. But do they make a difference in practice? For Hume, philosophical scepticism can be conjoined with a full-bodied acceptance of the beliefs we employ in the course of 'common life', and indeed philosophical scepticism is supposed to help underwrite the claim that our common-life beliefs are the best foundation we can have for science (including, importantly, the science of history), for ordinary moral practice, and for politics. Famously, Hume stresses the importance of 'opinion' – ordinary people's beliefs – to the resolution of all moral and political questions.[54] He was certainly more élitist than Reid in many ways, and he was more sceptical of the superiority of republics to monarchies. But in principle, and often in practice as well, it is almost as easy to draw on Hume as on Reid to ground the importance of ordinary people's views that impresses Stimson.

Where Hume's scepticism is supposed to have practical effects, and where Hume differs sharply from Reid, is in the matter of religion. In the *Treatise*, the first *Enquiry*, and the *Dialogues Concerning Natural Religion*, Hume tries to use the sceptical results he has achieved to debunk the metaphysical basis on which belief in God had long rested. Whether the position he ultimately prefers is better described as atheism or agnosticism, or even some minimal sort of deism, is a controversial question that we need not consider here, but he clearly thought that philosophical thought should lead one at least to treat religious affirmations sceptically, to shy away from firm, 'enthusiastic' religious convictions. By contrast, Reid seems to have believed that religious convictions could be readily derived from the principles of common sense,[55] and he was certainly used in this way by the religious believers who dominated higher education in early America.[56] Again, we need to be careful about how 'conservative' this use of Reid was – Stanhope Smith was accused, with some reason, of being an Arminian in his Reidian insistence on the importance of free will[57] – but at a minimum, Reid seems to have become a tool for silencing, rather than responding to, the sorts of sceptical doubts about the foundations of religion that Hume had so forcefully raised.

I would locate the 'conservatism' of the American use of Reid above all in this silencing of certain doubts. Knud Haakonssen has rightly emphasised the way in which Reid's philosophy represents an abandonment of the fallibilist attitude that characterised earlier Scottish thought.[58] Hutcheson, Hume and Smith represent a model of intellectual enquiry in which disagreement and questioning are welcome, exploration of new and possibly mistaken ideas is encouraged, and a tentative tone dominates throughout. Reid's diatribes against 'philosophy' and proclamations of the unquestionable reliability of common sense, cleverly argued although they may themselves be, send readers in the opposite direction, towards a position from which many investigations will appear as foolish or worse.

This stance may or may not be present in Reid himself. In America, it had indigenous roots and Reid's philosophy may merely have provided an excuse for it to flourish. As we have noted, American teachers like Alison, Witherspoon and Stanhope Smith tended to play down radical elements in all the philosophies they considered, especially if those radical tendencies posed any threat to conventional religious belief. They also favoured a university system teaching 'useful' subjects, and pursuing scholarly research in science and technology, rather than one fostering intellectual controversy.[59]

It was in fact to be a long time before the United States became known for vigorous intellectual debate on religious or philosophical questions. Hume's writings on these issues helped to inspire an explosion of intellectual activity in Germany, from the middle of the eighteenth century onwards. Nothing similar happened in America before the middle of the nineteenth century at the earliest, with the writings of the Transcendentalists, and American universities were not really to flourish until an influx of European refugees breathed life into them in the 1930s. The relative torpor of the American academy, as regards religious and philosophical matters, must have come as a disappointment to some of the founders. Jefferson urged on his correspondents a sceptical, naturalistic orientation towards religion throughout his life, and predicted that Unitarianism, which he took to be the truly rational form of Christianity, would 'become the general religion of the United States' within a generation.[60] For him, at least, the American Revolution was supposed to open up intellectual worlds as well as political and social ones. To some extent, Witherspoon, Stanhope Smith and

Rush presumably agreed with this, at least in principle. Why else would they re-make college curricula to emphasise contemporary thought? What else could Rush have meant when he expressed the hope that Philadelphia would become the Edinburgh of the United States? But if they really wanted the United States to have as lively a world of intellectual discourse as eighteenth-century Scotland, they should probably have nurtured a much livelier debate over the foundations of religion and morality. And that means they should probably have given more attention to Hume and less to Reid. The use of Reid against Hume seems symptomatic of a wider unwillingness – characteristic of America for much of its history – to let intellectuals severely challenge, let alone override, conventional beliefs.

I am ending, of course, on a highly speculative note. What we can more confidently draw from our reflections on Reid vs Hume is a reluctance to speak of 'the' Scottish impact on America. One irony about the impact of the Scottish Enlightenment on America is that one great Scottish figure was used to combat what was regarded as the corrosive influence of another great Scot. Given the wonderful feistiness of the Scottish Enlightenment, however, this is really not surprising. It should serve as a reminder, rather, of the fact that the Scottish Enlightenment was made up of people with different beliefs on many subjects, all arguing vigorously with one another. The Scots did tend to share some general views – on the sociability of human nature, on the importance of history to moral philosophy and social science, on the dignity and intelligence of ordinary people – that were of great importance to their followers in America and elsewhere. But their internal debates matter as much as what they agreed on, and indeed one of their great legacies was the model of an intellectual community made up of people who could learn from one another, and remain friends, amid vehement disagreement. Instead of speaking of 'the' Scottish impact on America, therefore, we might better rest satisfied with the conclusion of Daniel Walker Howe: '[t]he Scots spread a rich intellectual table', he says, 'from which the Americans could pick and choose and feast'.[61]

NOTES

1   The literature seems to have been launched by two things: a symposium in the 1954 *William and Mary Quarterly* – see especially John

Clive and Bernard Bailyn, 'England's Cultural Provinces: Scotland and America', *William and Mary Quarterly*, 3rd ser., 11 (1954), 200–13, and Caroline Robbins, ' "When it is that Colonies may turn Independent": An Analysis of the Environment and Politics of Francis Hutcheson (1694–1746)', *William and Mary Quarterly*, 3rd ser. 11 (1954), 214–51; and a highly influential 1957 article by Douglas Adair, ' "That Politics may be Reduced to a Science": David Hume, James Madison and the Tenth *Federalist*', *Huntingdon Library Quarterly* 20 (1957), 343–60. For some of the books and articles since then, see Roy Branson, 'James Madison and the Scottish Enlightenment', *Journal of the History of Ideas* 40 (1979), 235–50; Samuel Fleischacker, 'Adam Smith's Reception among the American Founders', *William and Mary Quarterly*, 3rd ser., 59 (2002), 897–924; Knud Haakonssen, *Natural Law and Moral Philosophy* (Cambridge: Cambridge University Press, 1996), ch. 10; Daniel Walker Howe, 'Why the Scottish Enlightenment was Useful to the Framers of the American Constitution', *Comparative Studies in Society and History* 31 (1989), 572–87; David Fate Norton, 'Francis Hutcheson in America', *Studies on Voltaire and the Eighteenth Century* 154 (1976), 1547–68; Richard B. Sher and Jeffrey R. Smitten, eds., *Scotland and America in the Age of the Enlightenment* (Edinburgh: Edinburgh University Press, 1990); Douglas Sloan, *The Scottish Enlightenment and the American College Ideal* (New York: Teachers College Press, Columbia University, 1971); Gary Wills, *Inventing America* (New York: Vintage Press, 1978); Wills, *Explaining America* (Garden City, NY: Doubleday, 1981). The introduction to Sher and Smitten gives a helpful overview of the literature.

2   Thomas Jefferson, *The Life and Selected Letters of Thomas Jefferson*, eds. A. Koch and W. Peden (New York: Random House, 1993), 8.

3   Bernard Bailyn, ed., *The Debate on the Constitution*, 2 vols. (New York: Library of America, 1993), 1.1022.

4   Among others: a vice-president, 21 US senators, 29 members of the House, and three Supreme Court justices (Wills, *Explaining America*, 18).

5   Bailyn, *Constitution*, 1.1025.

6   Wills, *Inventing America*; Adair, 'That Politics may be Reduced to a Science'; and Shannon Stimson, ' "A Jury of the Country": Common Sense Philosophy and the Jurisprudence of James Wilson', in Sher and Smitten, *Scotland and America*.

7   See especially Ronald Hamowy, 'Jefferson and the Scottish Enlightenment', *William and Mary Quarterly*, 3rd ser., 36 (1979), 503–23.

8   See John Locke, *Two Treatises of Government*, ed. Peter Laslett, student edn (Cambridge: Cambridge University Press, 1988).

9 Ibid., sect. 230.

10 Ibid., sect. 225.

11 Wills, *Inventing America*, 172–3.

12 Ibid., 239.

13 Jefferson's draft of the Declaration, in Jefferson, *Life and Letters*, 24.

14 In his 1814 letter to Thomas Law, Jefferson dismisses Wollaston in a way that both Hutcheson and Hume do, rejects egoistic foundations for morality in the same way that Hutcheson and Smith do, but then goes on to proclaim that 'self-love is no part of morality', that self-love is indeed 'the sole antagonist of virtue'. Only Hutcheson holds that view; Hume and Smith both agree with Hutcheson that morality is not founded in self-love, but believe there is nonetheless a legitimate place for self-love in morality. Jefferson goes on to say that once selfishness is eliminated or subdued, 'virtue', which here means concern for others, will simply flow forth from us: exactly this view can be found also in Francis Hutcheson, *Inquiry into the Original of our Ideas of Beauty and Virtue*, 4th edn (London: D. Midwinter, 1738), VII.ii.

15 Jefferson writes, in a 1771 letter to Robert Skipwith: 'When any original act of charity or of gratitude . . . is presented either to our sight or to our imagination, we are deeply impressed with its beauty and feel a strong desire in ourselves of doing charitable and grateful acts also.' Everything in this sentence, from the reference to 'original acts' of virtue, through the emphasis on the particular virtues of charity and gratitude, to the notion of moral 'beauty' and the suggestion that moral approval and moral motivation go together, is classic Hutchesonian doctrine.

16 Howe, 'Why the Scottish Enlightenment was Useful', 579.

17 David Hume, *A Treatise of Human Nature*, ed. L. A. Selby-Bigge, 2nd edn, rev. P. H. Nidditch (Oxford: Clarendon Press, 1978), 549–53.

18 Francis Hutcheson, *A System of Moral Philosophy*, 2 vols. (London: A. Millar, 1755), 1.283.

19 Ibid., II.IV.

20 Hutcheson, *Inquiry*, 182; Hutcheson, *System*, 1.306–19, 324–8.

21 Robbins, 'When it is that Colonies may turn Independent', 214–17, 245–6; and Sloan, *American College Ideal*, 93–4, 139.

22 He allows that 'great publick interest' might require some restrictions on natural liberty (Hutcheson, *System*, 1.295), but here and elsewhere the word 'great' or 'important' is an important qualifier (e.g. ibid., 1.320).

23 Ibid., 1.284; my emphasis.

24 Ibid., 294.

25 Ibid., 295–6.

26 Ibid., 318, 320.

27 Ibid., 322–3.

28 Henry Home, Lord Kames, *Historical Law-Tracts*, 2 vols. (Edinburgh: A. Millar, 1768), 1.124.

29 Thomas Jefferson, *The Commonplace Book of Thomas Jefferson*, ed. Gilbert Chinard (Baltimore, MD: Johns Hopkins, 1926), 107–8. James Wilson also incorporated this passage into his law lectures, see his *The Works of James Wilson*, ed. Robert Green McCloskey, 2 vols. (Cambridge: Belknap Press of Harvard University Press, 1967), 1.233.

30 See Wills's discussion of Jefferson's 1786 letter to Maria Cosway, in Wills, *Inventing America*, 275–80.

31 Adair, 'That Politics may be Reduced to a Science'.

32 See Lance Banning, *The Sacred Fire of Liberty: James Madison and the Founding of the Federal Republic* (Ithaca, NY: Cornell University Press, 1995), 467, n. 35, and the literature cited therein.

33 I discuss Smith's influence on Madison, and on a number of the other founders, in Fleischacker, 'Adam Smith's Reception'.

34 Adam Smith, *An Inquiry into the the Nature and Causes of the Wealth of Nations*, eds. R. H. Campbell, A. S. Skinner and W. B. Todd, 2 vols. (Oxford: Clarendon Press, 1976), 1.265–7. Henceforth *WN*.

35 Adair, 'That Politics may be Reduced to a Science', 359.

36 All quotations in this paragraph from *Federalist* x, ¶ 20, see Bailyn, *Debate on the Constitution*, 410.

37 *WN*, II.793.

38 In Bailyn, *Debate on the Constitution*.

39 Ibid.

40 Adam Smith, *The Theory of Moral Sentiments*, eds. D. D. Raphael and A. L. Macfie (Oxford: Clarendon Press, 1976). Henceforth *TMS*.

41 *Federalist* x, ¶ 9, in Bailyn, *Debate on the Constitution*.

42 Benjamin Rush, 'Of the Mode of Education Proper in a Republic', in Rush, *Essays: Literary, Moral and Philosophical*, ed. M. Meranze (Schenectady, NY: Union College Press, 1988), 9. See also this entire essay.

43 See Robbins, 'When it is that Colonies may turn Independent', 219.

44 Sloan, *American College Ideal*, 99–101.

45 Ibid., 219, n. 135.

46 David Lundberg and Henry F. May, 'The Enlightened Reader in America', *American Quarterly* 28 (1976), 262–71.

47 Sloan, *American College Ideal*, 93–4, 139, 164–9, 196–8.

48 Stimson, 'A Jury of the Country', 197.

49 David Hume, *Enquiries Concerning Human Understanding and Concerning the Principles of Morals*, ed. L. A. Selby-Bigge, 3rd edn, rev. P. H. Nidditch (Oxford: Clarendon Press, 1975), 173.

50 Reid, *An Inquiry into the Human Mind on the Principles of Common Sense*, ed. D. R. Brookes (Edinburgh: Edinburgh University Press, 1997), 19.

51 Quoted in Stewart R. Sutherland, 'The Presbyterian Inheritance of Hume and Reid', in R. H. Campbell and A. S. Skinner, eds., *The Origins and Nature of the Scottish Enlightenment* (Edinburgh: John Donald, 1982), 132.

52 Haakonssen, *Natural Law*, 188–91.

53 'Philosophy...has no other root but the principles of Common Sense; it grows out of them, and draws its nourishment from them', see Reid, *Inquiry*, 19.

54 Hume, 'Of the Original Contract', in David Hume, *Political Essays*, ed. Knud Haakonssen (Cambridge: Cambridge University Press, 1994), 200.

55 Thomas Reid, *Essays on the Intellectual Powers of Man*, eds. D. R. Brookes and K. Haakonssen (Edinburgh: Edinburgh University Press, 2002), 509.

56 Sloan, *American College Ideal*, 163.

57 Ibid., 166.

58 Haakonssen, *Natural Law*, 84–5, 180–1.

59 'Witherspoon's exaltation of utility provided a favorable climate for the sciences and the professions. At the same time, his readiness to dismiss hard intellectual problems and his distaste for specialized knowledge may have discouraged creative scholarship' (Sloan, *American College Ideal*, 130–1). Both Rush and Stanhope Smith seem to have followed him in this regard.

60 Letter to James Smith, 8 December 1822.

61 Howe, 'Why the Scottish Enlightenment was Useful', 580.

17 The nineteenth-century aftermath

It is a striking fact that while Scottish philosophy of the eighteenth century is studied to the point of being a major academic industry, Scottish philosophy in the nineteenth century is not only neglected but virtually unknown. Hume, Reid and Hutcheson are names familiar to almost all philosophers; Hamilton, Ferrier and Bain to hardly any. Evidence for this sharp contrast between eighteenth- and nineteenth-century Scottish philosophy lies in this startling statistic: the *Philosopher's Index* currently lists over 4,000 publications relating to the first three names, fewer than 40 relating to the next three.

Why should this be the case? Why should one period of Scottish philosophy be so perennially interesting and intensively studied and that which followed it have fallen so completely into oblivion? In this chapter I aim to offer a partial answer to this question, an answer couched in terms of the story of Scottish philosophy itself. The nineteenth century, I shall argue, saw the unravelling of the great philosophical project that had animated the eighteenth.

It might be thought that even the statement of this contention presupposes that there is some important unity between these eighteenth- and nineteenth-century authors, something that entitles us to classify them under the common term 'Scottish philosophy' – as opposed to the more pedestrian label 'philosophy in Scotland'. This distinction is important because if the subject is really 'philosophy in Scotland' there is no reason to suppose that one period must share any special affinity with any other. In the eighteenth century the University of Edinburgh was pre-eminent in medical teaching and research; in the nineteenth it was less so. But these are just phases in the history of medicine in Scotland, not a grand narrative of the rise and fall of something called 'Scottish medicine'. In short, there is only any special interest in the puzzle I have alluded to if there is or was something properly called Scottish philosophy. And the question is: is there?

One good reason for supposing so is that the expression 'Scottish philosophy' is very familiar. By contrast, the expression 'Belgian philosophy' (say) is effectively unknown, even though there are ancient universities teaching philosophy in Belgium no less than in Scotland. At first sight, of course, the mere existence of the expression 'Scottish philosophy' does not appear to show very much; equally familiar are the expressions German philosophy, British philosophy, American philosophy and so on. On closer inspection, however, these counterparts in other places are not quite as they seem. It is in fact more accurate, and more usual, to speak of German *idealism*, British *empiricism* and American *pragmatism*. What these expressions do is to associate geographical areas with distinctive schools or doctrines, rather than with philosophy itself. In this respect the expression 'Scottish philosophy' is different.

These linguistic facts may be taken to imply that there is more to Scottish philosophy than philosophy in Scotland. They are not conclusive, of course, or even very weighty. This is especially true of the second since it is widely supposed that 'Scottish philosophy' *is* the name of a school, viz the Enlightenment 'School of Common Sense'. Now it is worth observing that the identification of 'Scottish philosophy' with 'common sense' is not one that the eighteenth-century philosophers themselves made. Indeed, it was not in the eighteenth but the nineteenth century that something called 'Scottish philosophy' came to self-consciousness. As evidence of this it may be noted that the three major books which expressly take Scottish philosophy as their title and their subject are by nineteenth-century authors. These are J. F. Ferrier's *Scottish Philosophy, the Old and the New* (1856), Andrew Seth Pringle-Pattison's *The Scottish Philosophy* (1885), and far better known than either of these, James McCosh's *The Scottish Philosophy* (1875). A further important work which was self-consciously concerned with its subject – George Davie's *The Democratic Intellect* (1961) – came rather later, but it too had as its principal concern the philosophy of the nineteenth century, within the wider context of Scottish university education.

'Scottish philosophy' then, is a largely post-Enlightenment conception. But if self-consciousness is indeed the mark of nineteenth-century Scottish philosophy, there are grounds for thinking that it arose not so much from self-confidence as from uncertainty, uncertainty as to what could and could not count as Scottish philosophy and whether it still existed. McCosh's book is subtitled *From Hutcheson to Hamilton*.[1] Since Hamilton had been dead for about twenty years by the time it was published, this suggests, if it does not strictly imply, that Scottish philosophy had had its day by the mid-nineteenth century. Whether or not McCosh thought this, there is other reason to give the suggestion serious consideration. In the mid-1880s Pringle-Pattison writes as follows:

The thread of national tradition, it is tolerably well known, has been but loosely held of late by many of our best Scottish students of philosophy. It will hardly be denied that the philosophical productions of the younger generation of our University men are more strongly impressed with a German than with a native stamp.[2]

The suggestion here that the demise, or at least decline, of Scottish philosophy was a result of the philosophers of the four ancient universities abandoning native philosophy in favour of German idealism is a theme repeated by others. Indeed, it is to this charge that Ferrier is responding in *Scottish Philosophy, the Old and the New*.[3] In the contest for the Chair of Moral Philosophy at Edinburgh (then still in the gift of the Town Council) Ferrier was accused by the Free Church party of departing from 'the Scottish philosophy' in favour of some sort of Hegelianism, an accusation to which he replied with some feeling:

It has been asserted, that my philosophy is of Germanic origin and complexion. A broader fabrication than that never dropped from human lips or dribbled from the point of a pen. My philosophy is Scottish to the very core; it is national in every fibre and articulation of its frame.[4]

This charge, that Scottish philosophy was simply abandoned by philosophers in Scotland in favour of some version of German idealism, has gained some currency. Yet in so far as the attention of philosophers in Scotland did indeed turn elsewhere this, as we shall see, had less to do with academic *ennui* and more to do with the nature of Scottish philosophy itself, its place in the universities and in public life.

Pringle-Pattison is himself an interesting case in point. On graduating from the University of Edinburgh, he went to study in Germany, drawn in part by the sense that it was there that the most stimulating and original philosophy was being pursued. Yet when he returned and became Professor of Logic and Metaphysics at St Andrews and then successor to Campbell Fraser in the Chair of Logic and Metaphysics at Edinburgh, he did so with a consciousness of continuing a tradition, a consciousness made explicit in his Inaugural Lecture at Edinburgh, *The Present Position of the Philosophical Sciences* (1891). In short, Pringle-Pattison's intellectual history shows that there was more to the demise of Scottish philosophy than mere boredom with Scottish authors, or admiration for fresher German philosophical ideas.

But whether Scottish philosophy died or was abandoned is a secondary question to what it *was*. In the world at large there is no doubt that Hume is the one name identified universally with philosophy in Scotland. Even Reid and Hutcheson are minor figures in comparison. Yet in the early nineteenth century the dominant figure was not Hume but Reid, and McCosh numbers Hume as only one among forty-seven identifiable figures in the school. More striking yet, Reid was regarded as an *opponent* of Hume, and a defender of the essentials of the Scottish school against him. It might seem odd to say so, given contemporary perceptions, but there is reason to hold that Scotland's most famous philosopher is not properly regarded as an exponent of Scottish philosophy at all. At best, the naturalism Hume shares with the Scottish school is at war with the empiricism he inherits from Locke.[5]

However this may be, it is certainly the case that Hume was regarded by his Scottish contemporaries (Beattie is a notable instance) as someone whose philosophical opinions it was of the greatest importance to refute. The known and advertised opposition which Hume provoked among the philosophers collectively known as the School of Common Sense was endorsed by Dugald Stewart and Sir William Hamilton, who thus self-consciously perpetuated it into the next century. In perpetuating it, however, they made the central tenets of the school more explicit. McCosh picks out three in particular. First, there was the method of observation – a careful account of how the mind actually works, in terms both of its animating principles and its universal characteristics. Second, there was the emphasis on the importance of self-consciousness both as an instrument and a subject of this observation. Importantly, this is not a matter of introspection. 'The operation of introspection', McCosh remarks, 'is felt to be irksome if continued for any length of time, and will certainly be abandoned when thought is rapid and feeling is intense...He who would obtain an adequate and comprehensive view of our complex mental nature must not be satisfied with occasional glances at the working of his own soul: he must take a survey of the thoughts and feelings of others...from the acts of mankind generally...from universal language as the expression of human cogitation and sentiment; and from the commerce we hold with our fellow men'.[6] Thirdly, the aim of such a survey is to arrive at principles that are 'prior to and independent of experience'.

It is worth noting that these three tenets of 'the Scottish philosophy' are all methodological principles, not doctrines. There are *also* doctrines that might be taken to be foundational – libertarianism, direct realism, even theism.[7] But to make these essential features of the Scottish school has the disadvantage of determining Hume's place outside it by definitional fiat. Since it is evidently important for present purposes not to prejudge the place of Hume in the tradition, it is best to focus upon these methodological principles, rather than substantive philosophical doctrines, as the distinguishing marks of Scottish philosophy.

This brief account of the matter allows us, I think, to make some headway with this question: if there is such a thing as Scottish philosophy, when was its heyday? The answer I think is plain. It was *not* the eighteenth but the early nineteenth century, when Stewart and Hamilton taught at Edinburgh and dominated the intellectual culture of the times. Stewart may not have been among the most penetrating or original of philosophers, but unquestionably he loomed large in the intellectual life of the nation.[8] Hamilton has suffered from John Stuart Mill's *Examination* of his philosophy which has, ever since, cast him in a poor light (though I imagine that few read more than its title nowadays). The pompous character of Hamilton's style, a pomposity manifest in the extensive footnotes to his edition of Reid's *Collected Works*, has served to promote Mill's estimate. But we ought to acknowledge that Hamilton was hugely influential in his day, and impressed many of those who went on to teach philosophy in Scotland with his intellectual accomplishments. It is probably correct to say that the times vastly overestimated Hamilton. As evidence we may note that Hamilton was included in the series of *Philosophical Classics*, edited by William Knight, Professor of Moral Philosophy at St Andrews, and thus bizarrely ranked alongside Descartes, Berkeley, Locke, Kant and Hegel. Something of the same overestimation is to be found in the inclusion of Ferrier in the *Famous Scots* series. Far from being famous, who, apart from a few enthusiasts, has even heard of Ferrier now?

With hindsight, this estimation of Hamilton and Ferrier does seem excessive, and hints at a parochialism in nineteenth-century Scottish philosophy's self-understanding. Even so, the Blackwood's volume on Hamilton authored by John Veitch,[9] Professor of Logic and Rhetoric at Glasgow, is not without interest. Though it is not my purpose here to rescue Hamilton's reputation, it is important to observe that the nineteenth century had a quite different perception of Scottish philosophy than that which now prevails. In particular, as I have already noted, Hume was regarded as the renegade. Veitch's volume, however, reserves its wrath not for Hume but for Mill, and from this there is, as it seems to me, something to be learned. Notably, Veitch praises Hamilton (to the skies one might say) for broadening the horizons of Scottish philosophy, for pushing it beyond the narrower confines of common sense, and in particular for bringing to wider attention the importance of Kant.

Now this is somewhat odd. If, as has been supposed, the demise of Scottish philosophy arose from eyes turned admiringly to Germany, the rot began not with Ferrier but with Hamilton (whose personal library, now at the University of Glasgow, includes a large number of philosophical works in German, copiously annotated). Yet how could this be? Veitch is eloquent in his identification of Hamilton as the greatest exponent of Scottish philosophy, the true inheritor of Reid, to the publication of whose collected works he (Hamilton) devoted enormous, if not entirely well spent, effort. McCosh, who is not unquestionably admiring of Hamilton, nonetheless makes him the final repository of its distinctive character. And Ferrier, while rebutting the charge of alien influences, claims the right to be the inheritor of, though not restricted by, the programme of Reid and Hamilton.

The heart of this issue about the nature of Scottish philosophy, in my view, is the question of psychology. There is first this point. Ferrier shares with the school of Reid and Hamilton an almost unspoken assumption that the question of mind and world lies at the heart of philosophy. In this they all differ from the alternative conception of moral philosophy as social enquiry that is to be found in Ferguson, parts of Hume, and above all Adam Smith. Second, Ferrier's thought, no less than that of his predecessors, can be seen to proceed (broadly) in accordance with the three methodological principles marked out by McCosh. But it is in the deployment of these same principles that the division emerges. As philosophy in Scotland developed over the course of the nineteenth century, two possibilities, both of them in accord with these methods, became more evident. Ferrier's fame rested upon an earlier series of essays on *The Philosophy of Consciousness*. In these essays he took his stand on the contention that consciousness implies the impossibility of a naturalistic science of mind, and in a later essay robustly defends a version of Berkeleyan idealism. 'Among all philosophers ancient or modern, we are acquainted with none who presents fewer vulnerable points than Bishop Berkeley. His language it is true, has sometimes the appearance of paradox; but there is nothing paradoxical in his thoughts, and time has proved the adamantine solidity of his principles.'[10] But the point to stress is that Ferrier builds his defence of this claim on the basis of the observation of fact – a modified introspection which we might call phenomenology,[11] together with some appeal to the universal characteristics of human thought and language of the sort noted by McCosh.

A quite different outcome is to be found in another major figure in the nineteenth-century Scottish philosophical establishment – Alexander Bain, Regius Professor of Logic at the University of Aberdeen from 1860 to 1880. In the set of essays, *Dissertations on Leading Philosophical Topics*,[12] many of which were published in the journal *Mind* that he was instrumental in founding, Bain takes Reid and Hamilton as his starting point and, broadly, follows the same methods. But he pushes them in a much more strongly empirical direction. The most interesting of his *Dissertations*, in this connection, is entitled 'Associationist Controversies' and at the heart of these controversies we can find the differentiation of philosophy and psychology to which I have just referred:

We are, at the moment, in the midst of a conflict of views as to the priority of Metaphysics and Psychology. If indeed the two are closely identified as some suppose, there is no conflict; there is in fact, but one study. If, on the other hand, there are two subjects, each ought to be carried on apart for a certain length, before they can either confirm or weaken each other. I believe that in strictness, a disinterested Psychology should come first in order, and that, after going on a little way in amassing the facts, it should revise its fundamental assumptions . . . I do not see any mode of attaining a correct Metaphysics until Psychology has at least made some way upon a provisional Metaphysics.[13]

Bain is a practitioner of the science of mind no less than Reid or Hume. His claim to attention in the present context, as this quotation reveals, is that he drew a distinction between psychology and metaphysics, and gave priority to the former. That is to say, Bain, like Ferrier, adopted the methods of Scottish philosophy, but in contrast to Ferrier, he did so in ways that removed it from metaphysical questions and pressed the science of mind in the direction of empirical psychology.

Bain was one of the principal exponents and defenders of associationism. Associationism is the application of empirical observation to the relation between ideas and experiences. What it seeks is observed regularities, in the hope of formulating psychological laws that will enable us to order the contents of mind. Two such principles – Contiguity and Similarity – were widely accepted, and identified by Bain as being employed by Reid and Hamilton. A third – Contrast – was more disputable, and in this essay Bain is principally concerned with the nature and identifiable independence of principles such as these. However, for my purposes his arguments are interesting chiefly for the light they throw on the development of Scottish philosophy in this period. One point in particular seems to me illuminating.

In the dispute between Reid and Hume with respect to the operations of the mind there is a fundamental point of difference. Reid is trying, in the main, to establish basic principles of the mind's operation which will vindicate its rationality, and hence avoid the depths of scepticism into which Hume's account forces it. Whereas Hume declares that 'reason is nothing but a wonderful and unintelligible instinct in our souls, which carries us along a certain train of ideas . . . [and that this] habit is nothing but one of the principles of nature, and derives all its force from that origin',[14] Reid's purpose is precisely to show that the basic operations of the mind are those of intelligibility. Elsewhere I have explored this important difference,[15] but here I want to observe that Bain is, in this respect, of Hume's persuasion. This is revealed not merely in his striking deployment of decidedly Humean terminology when, for instance, he contrasts the perception and the memory of a thing in terms of 'vividness'.[16] It is even more evident when he asserts: 'The flow of representations in dreaming and madness offers the best field of observation for the study of associations as such'.[17]

What this remark reveals is that Bain is interested first in establishing empirical laws with respect to the contents of the human mind. The reason that he thinks dreaming and madness are the best places to start is precisely because he sees that the pursuit of rational principles, that is to say, philosophically coherent principles, is likely to distort our observation by inclining us to see rational connections rather than empirical associations, or as he puts it 'associations as such'. In this respect he is employing Hume's rather than Reid's conception of human nature. Certainly he reserves judgement on the final outcome of these investigations with respect to philosophy, arguing only for the priority of psychology over metaphysics and not, as Hume may be said to do, for the elimination of the second by the first. But so far as the science of mind that had been such a marked feature of Scottish philosophy goes, Bain clear-sightedly pursues its empirical ambitions.

Ferrier, by contrast, goes in the other direction. Noting that 'the inert and lifeless character of modern philosophy is ultimately attributable to her having degenerated into a physical science',[18] he roundly condemns the resulting 'picture of man' as 'a wretched association machine, through which ideas pass linked only by laws over which the machine has no control'.[19] Ferrier derives his alternative to the 'wretched association machine' from the contention that 'Consciousness is philosophy nascent; philosophy is consciousness in full bloom and blow. The difference between them is only one of degree, and not one of kind; and thus all conscious men are to a certain extent philosophers, although they may not know it'[20] and in this last remark we detect his continuation of a familiar theme in the School of Common Sense.

For Ferrier the empirical laws of association that Bain seeks are not 'truths in philosophy'. No one can be called a philosopher who merely knows and says that in dreaming or madness this mental representation tends to be associated with that. The philosopher aspires, rather, to make sense of experience, and the whole point about the experience of the dreamer or the madman is that no sense is to be made of it. Accordingly, while Ferrier's important and influential essays are entitled 'The Philosophy of Consciousness', his major work is unambiguously *The Institutes of Metaphysics.*

If what I have been arguing is correct, nineteenth-century Scottish philosophy saw a parting of the ways within the tradition that had come down to it from the eighteenth. In his illuminating study *Scottish Philosophy*, importantly subtitled *A Comparison of the Scottish and German Answers to Hume*, Pringle-Pattison, as it seems to me, identifies the sources of this potential fracture in Reid himself.

The Scottish and German answers to Hume turn out to be largely those of Reid and Kant. Pringle-Pattison is sympathetic to Reid and critical, but in the end more admiring, of Kant, and this for one reason in particular:

Though Kant's style is involved, his terminology cumbrous, and his works abounding in repetitions, yet he mingles no extraneous and strictly indifferent matter with his argument. In each of his great works there is the sense of a unity of aim which the repetitions only serve to make more prominent. On the other hand, Reid's properly philosophical positions are imbedded in a mass of irrelevant psychological matter of fact, which obscures their bearing and impairs their force.[21]

Ferrier, if I have understood the matter correctly, saw and discarded the extraneous psychological matter, whereas Bain identified in it, and warmed to, the first stirrings of a truly scientific psychology. From this we may conclude that the demise of Scottish philosophy which the nineteenth century witnessed lay not in the contingent and cavalier abandonment of an inherited tradition by those who saw and were enamoured of continental novelties, but in the nature of that tradition itself. As the works of its principal author reveal, it had within it a fatal ambiguity.

This is not the whole of the story, however. Pringle-Pattison offers us an interesting explanation of the difference he detects in the otherwise very similar philosophies of Reid and Kant. This lies in the respective social position philosophy enjoyed. It is here, I think, that we find the answer to another important question: what makes Scottish philosophy Scottish?

Kant and Reid were both university professors, but their method of working was different. Reid's books, especially his later 'Essays', are in the main his lectures prepared for publication; and they are marked therefore by a greater diffuseness and by a more popular character than we have a right to expect in a written treatise. Kant, on the other hand, appears to have made a rigid distinction between his work as a university teacher, and his work as a regenerator of philosophy. The latter was addressed not to students and to general readers, but to teachers and to a learned public. If, as we are told, not actually written down with the care which a *magnum opus* might be supposed to demand, no labour has been spared in working out the plan and phraseology of the 'Critique' with a precision worthy of its destination. Reid wrote no *magnum opus* in the sense in which Kant wrote several. He had no learned class to whom he could have appealed, if he had written with the elaborate technicality of Kant. His works were addressed to the reading portion of his countrymen generally – to his old students, in great part, and the ministers of religion, into whose ranks many of them had doubtless passed. The *Fachmann*, or specialist, has hitherto not flourished amongst us.[22]

Pringle-Pattison overstates the case a little; there were German philosophers who wrote for a general audience. Nevertheless, it is worth remembering that in the eighteenth century and for most of the nineteenth, professional philosophers in Scotland numbered fewer than a dozen. Moreover, their intellectual activities were limited to the 'lower' Faculty of Arts. The role of philosophy was circumscribed to the teaching of two classes in the course of four years, and postgraduate degrees in philosophy were unknown. This was a result of two factors: the maintenance in Scotland, unlike most other places, of the medieval curriculum and the existence of a university 'system' – four universities with a common and coordinated pattern of study. The declared and recognised purpose of philosophy, in short, was to play its part in the formation of what George Davie famously designated *The Democratic Intellect*. That is to say, the public role of philosophy was not to push back the frontiers of knowledge, to engage in the cutting edge of research as we would now say, but to contribute to the education of the minds that would populate the professions.

This is not to say that there was no engagement in original enquiry; who could deny that Reid's was an original mind? Indeed the move from the system of Regents to that of Professors (Reid was Regent in Aberdeen but Professor in Glasgow) signalled a move towards specialisation. But for all that, the place of philosophers in higher education was that of social educators. Accordingly, the conception of philosophy within which they worked was primarily one suited to this purpose. It is this that allows us, in my view, to speak not merely of philosophy in Scotland, but of Scottish philosophy, and the weaknesses that Pringle-Pattison detects in Reid, if weaknesses they be, are a result of this.

In consequence, the explanation of the demise of Scottish philosophy over the course of the nineteenth century lies in large part in the reform of the universities which Davie, not altogether accurately, charts. And the move on the part of Scottish philosophers, on the one hand to Germanic metaphysics and on the other to scientific psychology, reflects this. Pringle-Pattison (whose own philosophical endeavours would repay much further enquiry) stands at this watershed. It is no accident, I think, that over the period in which he occupied the Chair of Logic and Metaphysics at Edinburgh the curriculum underwent significant change, opening the way to a different role for philosophy. For his part, in the end he stood out for the Scottish tradition, though he did so in terms of doctrine rather than method. It is this that marks him out, for all his admiration of Kant, as a philosopher still in the Scottish tradition – and possibly the last.

NOTES

1   James McCosh, *The Scottish Philosophy, Biographical, Expository, Critical, from Hutcheson to Hamilton* (1875: reprint, Bristol: Thoemmes, 1990).

2   A. S. Pringle-Pattison, *Scottish Philosophy: a Comparison of the Scottish and German Answers to Hume* (Edinburgh: Blackwood, 1885), 1–2.

3   James F. Ferrier, *Scottish Philosophy, the Old and the New* (Edinburgh: Sutherland and Knox, 1856).

4   Ibid., 12.

5   For a recent and illuminating defence of this claim see H. O. Mounce, *Hume's Naturalism* (London: Routledge, 1999).

6   McCosh, *Scottish Philosophy*, 5–6.

7   In *Why Scottish Philosophy Matters* (Edinburgh: Saltire Society, 2000), Alexander Broadie finds the origin of an abiding subscription to libertarianism and direct realism in the medievals, notably Scotus and Mair.

8   This is strikingly revealed by remarks about Stewart in *Memorials of his Time* (Edinburgh: Black, 1856) by Henry Cockburn, the eminent lawyer, and even more so perhaps, in Catherine Carswell's celebrated *Life of Robert Burns* (Edinburgh: Canongate, 1990).

9   John Veitch, *Hamilton* (Edinburgh: Blackwood, 1882).

10 Ferrier, James F. *Philosophical Remains*, in *Philosophical Works of James Frederick Ferrier*, eds. A. Grant and E. L. Lushington, 3 vols. (1875; reprint, intro. John Haldane, Bristol: Thoemmes Press, 2000), II.291.

11 In describing it thus we may be pointing to a greater continuity with Reid than Ferrier acknowledged. On this see Paul Gorner, 'The Phenomenology of Thomas Reid', *Journal of European Philosophy* (forthcoming).

12 Alexander Bain, *Dissertations on Leading Philosophical Topics* (1903; reprint, Bristol: Thoemmes, 1990).

13 Ibid., 38.

14 David Hume, *A Treatise of Human Nature*, ed. L. A. Selby-Bigge, 2nd edn. rev. P. H. Nidditch (Oxford: Clarendon Press, 1978), 179.

15 Gordon Graham, 'Morality and Feeling in the Scottish Enlightenment', *Philosophy* 76 (2001), 271–82.

16 Bain, *Dissertations*, 42.

17 Ibid., 45.

18 Ferrier, *Philosophical Works*, II.191.

19 Ibid., 196.

20 Ibid., 197.

21 Pringle-Pattison, *Scottish Philosophy*, 127.

22 Ibid., 128.

SELECT BIBLIOGRAPHY

PRIMARY SOURCES

Beattie, James. *An Essay on the Nature and Immutability of Truth, in Opposition to Sophistry and Scepticism.* 1770. Reprint, intro. Roger J. Robinson, Bristol: Thoemmes Press, 1999

Campbell, George. *The Philosophy of Rhetoric.* 2 vols. London, 1776

Carmichael, Gershom. *Natural Rights in Scottish Philosophy on the Threshold of the Enlightenment: the Writings of Gershom Carmichael.* Eds. James Moore and Michael Silverthorne. Indianapolis: Liberty Press, 2002

Dunbar, James. *Essays on the History of Mankind in Rude and Cultivated Ages.* 2nd edn. 1781. Reprint, intro. C. J. Berry, Bristol: Thoemmes Press, 1995

Ferguson, Adam. *Institutes of Moral Philosophy.* Edinburgh, 1769

Ferguson, Adam. *Principles of Moral and Political Science.* 2 vols. 1792. Reprint, Hildesheim: Olms, 1995

Ferguson, Adam. *An Essay on the History of Civil Society.* Ed. Fania Oz-Salzberger. Cambridge: Cambridge University Press, 1995

Fletcher, Andrew. *Political Works.* Ed. John Robertson. Cambridge: Cambridge University Press, 1997

Home, Henry (Lord Kames). *Sketches of the History of Man.* 4 vols. 1774. Reprint, intro. John Valdimir Price, London: Routledge/Thoemmes Press, 1993

Home, Henry (Lord Kames). *Historical Law-Tracts.* 3rd edn. Edinburgh: T. Cadell, J. Bell and W. Creech, 1776

Home, Henry (Lord Kames). *Essays on the Principles of Morality and Natural Religion.* 3rd edn. 1779. Reprint, intro. John Valdimir Price, London: Routledge/Thoemmes Press, 1993

Hume, David. *The Letters of David Hume.* Ed. J. Y. T. Greig. 2 vols. Oxford: Clarendon Press, 1932

Hume, David. *Enquiries Concerning Human Understanding and Concerning the Principles of Morals*. Ed. L. A. Selby-Bigge. 3rd edn. Rev. P. H. Nidditch. Oxford: Clarendon Press, 1975

Hume, David. *A Treatise of Human Nature*. Ed. L. A. Selby-Bigge. 2nd edn. Rev. P. H. Nidditch. Oxford: Clarendon Press, 1978

Hume, David. *A Treatise of Human Nature*. Ed. David Fate Norton and Mary Norton. Oxford: Oxford University Press, 2000

Hume, David. *Essays Moral, Political and Literary*. Ed. Eugene F. Miller. Rev. edn. Indianapolis: Liberty Fund, 1985

Hume, David. *Principal Writings on Religion including 'Dialogues Concerning Natural Religion' and 'The Natural History of Religion'*. Ed. J. C. A. Gaskin. Oxford: Oxford University Press, 1993

Hume, David. *Political Essays*. Ed. Knud Haakonssen. Cambridge: Cambridge University Press, 1994

Hutcheson, Francis. *A System of Moral Philosophy*. 2 vols. London: A. Millar, 1755

Hutcheson, Francis. *Collected Works of Francis Hutcheson*. Facsimile editions prepared by Bernhard Fabian. 7 vols. Hildesheim: Olms, 1969–90

Hutcheson, Francis. *An Inquiry Concerning Beauty, Order, Harmony, Design*. 4th edn. Ed. P. Kivy. The Hague: Nijhoff, 1973

Hutcheson, Francis. *On Human Nature, Reflections on our Common Systems of Morality, On the Social Nature of Man*. Ed. Thomas Mautner. Cambridge: Cambridge University Press, 1993

Hutcheson, Francis. *On the Nature and Conduct of the Passions*. 1728. Reprint, ed. Aaron Garrett, Indianapolis: Liberty Press, 2002

Hutton, James. *Theory of the Earth with Proofs and Illustrations*. Edinburgh, 1795

Maclaurin, Colin. *An Account of Sir Isaac Newton's Philosophical Discoveries*. London: A. Miller et al., 1748

Millar, John. *The Origin of the Distinction of Ranks*. Reprinted in William C. Lehmann, *John Millar of Glasgow*. Cambridge: Cambridge University Press, 1960, 173–332

Reid, Thomas. *Practical Ethics*. Ed. Knud Haakonssen. Princeton: Princeton University Press, 1990

Reid, Thomas. *Thomas Reid on the Animate Creation*. Ed. Paul Wood. Edinburgh: Edinburgh University Press, 1995

Reid, Thomas. *An Inquiry into the Human Mind on the Principles of Common Sense*. Ed. D. R. Brookes. Edinburgh: Edinburgh University Press, 1997

Reid, Thomas. *The Works of Thomas Reid, D. D.* Ed. Sir William Hamilton. 6th edn. 2 vols. 1863. Reprint, Bristol: Thoemmes, 1999. It includes *Inquiry into the Human Mind on the Principles of Common Sense*, 1.93–211;

Essays on the Intellectual Powers of Man, I.213–508; *Essays on the Active Powers of the Human Mind*, II.509–679

Reid, Thomas. *Essays on the Intellectual Powers of Man*. Eds. Derek R. Brookes and Knud Haakonssen. Edinburgh: Edinburgh University Press, 2002

Sinclair, Sir John, ed. *The Statistical Account of Scotland*. 20 vols. 1791–9. Reprint, eds. Donald Withrington and Ian R. Grant, East Ardsley: EP Publishing, 1973–83

Smith, Adam. *An Inquiry into the Nature and Causes of the Wealth of Nations*. Eds. R. H. Campbell and A. S. Skinner; textual editor W. B. Todd. 2 vols. Oxford: Clarendon Press, 1976; Indianapolis: Liberty Classics, 1981

Smith, Adam. *Essays on Philosophical Subjects*. Eds. W. P. D.Wightman and J. C. Bryce. Oxford: Clarendon Press, 1980; Indianapolis: Liberty Classics, 1982

Smith, Adam. *Lectures on Jurisprudence*. Eds. R. L. Meek, D. D. Raphael and P. G. Stein. Oxford: Clarendon Press, 1978; Indianapolis: Liberty Classics, 1982

Smith, Adam. *The Theory of Moral Sentiments*. Eds. D. D. Raphael and A. L. Macfie. Oxford: Clarendon Press, 1976; Indianapolis: Liberty Fund, 1984

Smith, Adam. *The Theory of Moral Sentiments*. Ed. Knud Haakonssen. Cambridge: Cambridge University Press, 2002

Steuart, Sir James. *The Principles of Political Oeconomy*. Ed. Andrew S. Skinner. 2 vols. Edinburgh: Oliver and Boyd, 1966

Steuart, Sir James. *The Principles of Political Oeconomy*. Eds. A. S. Skinner, Noboru Kobayashi and Hiroshi Mizuta. London: Pickering and Chatto, 1998

Stewart, Dugald. *The Collected Works of Dugald Stewart*. Ed. Sir William Hamilton. 1854–60. Reprint, intro. Knud Haakonssen, Bristol: Thoemmes, 1994

Turnbull, George. *The Principles of Moral and Christian Philosophy*. 2 vols. 1740. Reprint, ed. A. Broadie, Indianapolis: Liberty Fund. Forthcoming

Turnbull, George. *A Treatise on Ancient Painting*. 1740. Reprint, without plates, Munich: W. Fink, 1971

SECONDARY WORKS

Allan, David. *Virtue, Learning and the Scottish Enlightenment*. Edinburgh: Edinburgh University Press, 1993

Baier, Annette. *A Progress of Sentiments: Reflections on Hume's Treatise*. Cambridge: Harvard University Press, 1991

Bain, Alexander. *Dissertations on Leading Philosophical Topics*. 1903. Reprint, Bristol: Thoemmes Press, 1990

Berry, Christopher J. *Social Theory of the Scottish Enlightenment.* Edinburgh: Edinburgh University Press, 1997

Brady, F., *James Boswell: the Later Years, 1769–1795.* New York: McGraw-Hill; London: Heinemann, 1984

Broadie, Alexander., ed. *The Scottish Enlightenment: an Anthology.* Edinburgh: Canongate Press, 1997

Broadie, Alexander. *The Scottish Enlightenment: the Historical Age of the Historical Nation.* Edinburgh: Birlinn, 2001

Brown, Stewart J., ed. *William Robertson and the Expansion of Empire.* Cambridge: Cambridge University Press, 1997

Bryson, Gladys. *Man and Society: the Scottish Inquiry of the Eighteenth Century.* Princeton: Princeton University Press, 1945

Bury, J. B. *The Idea of Progress: an Inquiry into its Growth and Progress.* 1920. Reprint, New York: Dover, 1955

Cairns, John W. 'Ethics and the Science of Legislation: Legislators, Philosophers and Courts in Eighteenth-Century Scotland'. *Jahrbuch für Recht und Ethik* 8 (2000), 159–80

Cairns, John W. 'Historical Introduction'. In *A History of Scots Private Law*, eds. Kenneth Reid and Reinhard Zimmermann. Vol. 1. Oxford: Oxford University Press, 2000, 14–184

Campbell, R. H. and Andrew S. Skinner, eds. *The Origins and Nature of the Scottish Enlightenment.* Edinburgh: John Donald, 1982

Carter, J. J. and J. H. Pittock, eds. *Aberdeen and the Enlightenment.* Aberdeen: Aberdeen University Press, 1987

Clow, Archibald, and Nan L. Clow. *The Chemical Revolution: a Contribution to Social Technology.* London: Batchworth Press, 1952

Cuneo, Terence and René van Woudenberg, eds. *The Cambridge Companion to Thomas Reid.* Cambridge: Cambridge University Press. Forthcoming

Davie, George E. *The Democratic Intellect: Scotland and her Universities in the Nineteenth Century.* Paperback edn Edinburgh: Edinburgh University Press, 1981

Davie, George E. *The Scottish Enlightenment and Other Essays.* Edinburgh: Polygon, 1991

Davie, George E. *A Passion for Ideas.* Essays on the Scottish Enlightenment, vol. 2. Edinburgh: Polygon, 1994

Doig, A. et al., eds. *William Cullen and the Eighteenth-Century Medical World.* Edinburgh: Royal College of Physicians of Edinburgh, 1993

Dwyer, John. *The Age of the Passions: an Interpretation of Adam Smith and Scottish Enlightenment Culture.* East Linton: Tuckwell Press, 1998

Dwyer, John and Richard B. Sher, eds. *Sociability and Society in Eighteenth-Century Scotland.* Edinburgh: Mercat Press, 1993. First published as a special issue of *Eighteenth-Century Life* n.s. 15, nos. 1–2 (1991)

Emerson, Roger L. *Professors, Patronage and Politics: the Aberdeen Universities in the Eighteenth Century*. Aberdeen: Aberdeen University Press, 1992

Ferrier, James F. *Scottish Philosophy, the Old and the New*. Edinburgh: Sutherland and Knox, 1856

Ferrier, James F. *Philosophical Remains*. In *Philosophical Works of James Frederick Ferrier*. Eds. A. Grant and E. L. Lushington. 3 vols. 1875. Reprint, intro. John Haldane, Bristol: Thoemmes Press, 2000

Fleming, J. *Robert Adam and His Circle*. Cambridge: Harvard University Press, 1962

Flynn, Philip, ed. *Enlightened Scotland*. Edinburgh: Scottish Academic Press, 1992

Forbes, Duncan. *Hume's Philosophical Politics*. Cambridge: Cambridge University Press, 1975

Forbes, Duncan. 'Scientific Whiggism: Adam Smith and John Millar'. *Cambridge Journal* 7 (1954), 643–70

French, R. K. *Robert Whytt, the Soul and Medicine*. London: Wellcome Institute of the History of Medicine, 1969

Gaskin, J. C. A. *Hume's Philosophy of Religion*. 2nd edn. London: Macmillan Press, 1988

Gibson, A. J. S. and Smout, T. C. *Prices, Food and Wages in Scotland, 1550–1780*. Cambridge: Cambridge University Press, 1995

Griswold, Charles L. *Adam Smith and the Virtues of Enlightenment*. Cambridge: Cambridge University Press, 1999

Haakonssen, Knud. *The Science of a Legislator: the Natural Jurisprudence of David Hume and Adam Smith*. Cambridge: Cambridge University Press, 1981

Haakonssen, Knud. *Natural Law and Moral Philosophy: from Grotius to the Scottish Enlightenment*. Cambridge: Cambridge University Press, 1996

Haakonssen, Knud., ed. *The Cambridge Companion to Adam Smith*. Cambridge: Cambridge University Press. Forthcoming

Hamowy, Ronald. 'Jefferson and the Scottish Enlightenment'. *William and Mary Quarterly*, 3rd ser., 36 (1979), 503–23

Hamowy, Ronald. *The Scottish Enlightenment and the Theory of Spontaneous Order*. Carbondale, IL: Southern Illinois University Press, 1987

Hont, Istvan and Michael Ignatieff, eds. *Wealth and Virtue: the Shaping of Political Economy in the Scottish Enlightenment*. Cambridge: Cambridge University Press, 1983

Hook, Andrew and Richard B. Sher, eds. *The Glasgow Enlightenment*. East Linton: Tuckwell Press, 1995

Hope, Vincent M. *Virtue by Consensus: the Moral Philosophy of Hutcheson, Hume and Adam Smith*. Oxford: Clarendon Press, 1989

Howe, Daniel Walker. 'Why the Scottish Enlightenment was Useful to the Framers of the American Constitution'. *Comparative Studies in Society and History* 31 (1989), 572–87

Jenkinson, Jacqueline. *Scottish Medical Societies, 1731–1939: their History and Records*. Edinburgh: Edinburgh University Press, 1993

Kenyon, John. *The History Men*. London: Weidenfeld and Nicolson, 1983

Kidd, Colin. *Subverting Scotland's Past: Scottish Whig Historians and the Creation of an Anglo-British Identity, 1689–c. 1830*. Cambridge: Cambridge University Press, 1993

Kramnick, Isaac, ed. *The Portable Enlightenment Reader*. London: Penguin, 1995

Kuehn, Manfred. *Scottish Common Sense in Germany, 1768–1800: a Contribution to the History of Critical Philosophy*. Kingston and Montreal: McGill-Queen's University Press, 1987

Lehmann, William C. *John Millar of Glasgow, 1735–1801*. Cambridge: Cambridge University Press, 1960

Lehrer, Keith. *Thomas Reid*. London: Routledge, 1989

McCosh, James. *The Scottish Philosophy, Biographical, Expository, Critical, from Hutcheson to Hamilton*. 1875. Reprint, Bristol: Thoemmes, 1990

McIntyre, Jane. 'Hume: Second Newton of the Moral Sciences'. *Hume Studies* 20 (1994), 3–18

Macmillan, Duncan. *Painting in Scotland: the Golden Age*. Oxford: Phaidon Press, 1986

Malloy, Robin Paul and J. Evensky, eds. *Adam Smith and the Philosophy of Law and Economics*. Dordrecht: Kluwer, 1994

Mitchison, R. and L. Leneman. *Sexuality and Social Control: Scotland, 1660–1780*. Oxford: Blackwell, 1989

Mounce, H. O. *Hume's Naturalism*. London: Routledge, 1999

Norton, David Fate. 'Francis Hutcheson in America'. *Studies on Voltaire and the Eighteenth Century* 154 (1976), 1547–68

Norton, David Fate. *David Hume: Common-Sense Moralist, Sceptical Metaphysician*. Princeton: Princeton University Press, 1982

Norton, David Fate., ed. *The Cambridge Companion to Hume*. Cambridge: Cambridge University Press, 1993

O'Brien, Karen. *Narratives of Enlightenment: Cosmopolitan History from Voltaire to Gibbon*. Cambridge: Cambridge University Press, 1997

Oz-Salzberger, Fania. *Translating the Enlightenment: Scottish Civic Discourse in Eighteenth-Century Germany*. Oxford: Clarendon Press, 1995

Phillipson, Nicholas. 'Culture and Society in the Eighteenth-Century Province: the Case of Edinburgh and the Scottish Enlightenment'. In *The University in Society*, ed. Lawrence Stone. Vol. 2. Princeton: Princeton University Press, 1974, 407–48

Phillipson, Nicholas. 'The Scottish Enlightenment'. In *The Enlightenment in National Context*, eds. Roy Porter and Mikulas Teich. Cambridge: Cambridge University Press, 1981, 19–40

Phillipson, Nicholas. *Hume*. London: Weidenfeld and Nicolson, 1989

Pocock, J. G. A. *Virtue, Commerce and History: Essays on Political Thought and History, Chiefly in the Eighteenth Century*. Cambridge: Cambridge University Press, 1985

Pottle, F. A. *James Boswell: the Early Years, 1740–1760*. New York: McGraw-Hill, 1966

Pringle-Pattison, Andrew Seth. *Scottish Philosophy: a Comparison of the Scottish and German Answers to Hume*. Edinburgh: Blackwood, 1885

Pringle-Pattison, Andrew Seth. *The Present Position of the Philosophical Sciences: an Inaugural Lecture*. Edinburgh, 1891

Riley, P. W. J. *The Union of England and Scotland: a Study in Anglo-Scottish Politics of the Eighteenth Century*. Manchester: Manchester University Press, 1978

Riley, P. W. J. *King William and the Scottish Politicians*. Edinburgh: John Donald, 1979

Robertson, John. *The Scottish Enlightenment and the Militia Issue*. Edinburgh: John Donald, 1985

Robertson, John. 'The Scottish Enlightenment'. *Rivista Storica Italiana* 108 (1996), 792–829

Robertson, John, ed. *A Union for Empire: Political Thought and the British Union of 1707*. Cambridge: Cambridge University Press, 1995

Rosner, Lisa. *Medical Education in the Age of Improvement: Edinburgh Students and Apprentices, 1760–1826*. Edinburgh: Edinburgh University Press, 1991

Ross, Ian Simpson. *Lord Kames and the Scotland of his Day*. Oxford: Clarendon Press, 1972

Ross, Ian Simpson. *The Life of Adam Smith*. Oxford: Clarendon Press, 1995

Schneider, Louis, ed. *Scottish Moralists on Human Nature and Society*. Chicago: University of Chicago Press, 1967

Scott, William R. *Francis Hutcheson: his Life, Teaching and Position in the History of Philosophy*. Cambridge: Cambridge University Press, 1900

Sher, Richard B. *Church and University in the Scottish Enlightenment: the Moderate Literati of Edinburgh*. Edinburgh: Edinburgh University Press; Princeton: Princeton University Press, 1985

Sher, Richard B. and Jeffrey Smitten, eds. *Scotland and America in the Age of the Enlightenment*. Edinburgh: Edinburgh University Press, 1990

Simpson, A. D. C., ed. *Joseph Black, 1728–1799: a Commemorative Symposium*. Edinburgh: Royal Scottish Museum, 1982

Skinner, Andrew S. *A System of Social Science: Papers Relating to Adam Smith*. 2nd edn. Oxford: Oxford University Press, 1996

Skinner, Andrew S. and T. Wilson, eds. *Essays on Adam Smith*. Oxford: Clarendon Press, 1975

Sloan, Douglas. *The Scottish Enlightenment and the American College Ideal*. New York: Teachers College Press, Columbia University, 1971

Smout, T. C. *A History of the Scottish People, 1560–1830*. 2nd edn. London: Collins, 1970

Spadefora, David. *The Idea of Progress in Eighteenth-Century Britain*. New Haven and London: Yale University Press, 1990

Stewart, M. A., ed. *Studies in the Philosophy of the Scottish Enlightenment*. Oxford: Clarendon Press, 1990

Stewart, M. A. and John P. Wright, eds. *Hume and Hume's Connexions*. Edinburgh: Edinburgh University Press, 1994

Suderman, Jeffrey. *Orthodoxy and Enlightenment*. Montreal: McGill-Queen's University Press, 2001

Trevor-Roper, Hugh. 'The Scottish Enlightenment'. *Studies on Voltaire and the Eighteenth Century* 58 (1967), 1635–58

Veitch, John. *Hamilton*. Edinburgh: Blackwood, 1882

White, Morton. *The Philosophy of the American Revolution*. Oxford: Oxford University Press, 1978

Whyte, I. D. and K. Whyte. *The Changing Scottish Landscape, 1500–1800*. London: Routledge, 1991

Wills, Gary. *Inventing America*. New York: Vintage, 1978

Wills, Gary. *Explaining America*. Garden City, NY : Doubleday, 1981

Withers, Charles W. J. *Geography, Science and National Identity: Scotland since 1520*. Cambridge: Cambridge University Press, 2001

Withers, Charles W. J. and Paul Wood, eds. *Science and Medicine in the Scottish Enlightenment*. East Linton: Tuckwell Press, 2002

Wolterstorff, Nicholas. *Thomas Reid and the Story of Epistemology*. Cambridge: Cambridge University Press, 2001

Wood, Paul B. *The Aberdeen Enlightenment: the Arts Curriculum in the Eighteenth Century*. Aberdeen: Aberdeen University Press, 1993

Wood, Paul B., ed. *The Scottish Enlightenment: Essays in Reinterpretation*. Rochester: Rochester University Press, 2000

Young, Jeffrey T. *Economics as a Moral Science: the Political Economy of Adam Smith*. Cheltenham: Edward Elgar, 1997

Youngson, A. J. *The Making of Classical Edinburgh*. Edinburgh: Edinburgh University Press, 1966

INDEX

SE = SCOTTISH ENLIGHTENMENT

Aberdeen, 5, 21-2
  its clerical literati, 48
  its Musical Society, 22
Abernethy, John, 40
Academy of St Luke, 20
Adair, Douglas, 324, 334
Adair, John 98
Adam, William, 16
aesthetic sense, 281
Aikenhead, Thomas, 14, 34, 55
Alembert, Jean le Rond d', 299
Alexander, William, 87
Alison, Archibald, 280, 285
Alison, Francis, 317, 328, 329
American Revolution, 22
Ampère, André Marie, 304
Anderson, George, 49
Anderson, John, 23, 109
animal rights, 84, 85
Argathelians, 14, 27
Argyll, 2nd Duke of, see John Campbell
Argyll, 3rd Duke of, see Archibald
  Campbell
Arminians, Dutch, 15
Articles of Confederation, 317
associationism
  Bain on, 345
  Ferrier on, 346-7
Atholl, Marquis of, 16
attributes, God's communicable and
  incommunicable, 38

Bacon, Sir Francis, 102
Baier, Annette, 134

Bain, Alexander, 338, 344-5
Balfour Robert, 97
Ballantyne, John, 51
Barbeyrac, Jean, 83, 84, 230
Barfoot, Michael, 114
Baxter, Andrew, 41, 55
Bayle, Pierre, 17
Beattie, James, 21, 22, 51, 54, 58, 88,
  208, 260, 309, 329
  his success in Europe, 301
beauty, comparative, 283
Beccaria, Giovanni Battista, 23
Bell, John, 18
benevolence, 137, 209, 210
Bentham, Jeremy, 234
Bentley, Richard, 104
Berkeley, Bishop George, 21, 56, 102, 127
Berry, Christopher, 3, 90
Bichat, Marie François Xavier, 312
Biran, Maine de, 304, 311, 313
Black, Joseph, 4, 16, 106, 109
Blackwell Jr, Thomas, 21, 261
Blair, Hugh, 280, 301
Blaug, Mark, 199
Blount, Charles, 34
Board of Trustees for Arts, Fisheries and
  Manufactures, 20
Bodin, Jean, 225
Bolingbroke, Viscount, 261
Boscovich, Roger Joseph, 105
Boswell, James, 261
Bower, Thomas, 21, 114
Boyle, Robert, 96, 103
Bradley, James, 105

359

Broadie, Alexander, 4, 78, 277, 297, 349
Brosse, Charles de, 303
Brown, Thomas, 119, 330
Brown, William Laurence, 51, 54
Bruce, James, 18
Buffon, Georges Louis Leclerc de, 22, 23,
  80, 87, 108
Burke, Edmund, 273
Burnet, Gilbert
  his relations with Hutcheson, 140
  his relations with Reid, 152
Burnet, Thomas, 108
Burnett, James (Lord Monboddo), 81-2,
  87, 88, 104, 273
Bute, 3rd Earl of, 16
Butler, Bishop Joseph, 139, 141, 147
Butterfield, Herbert, 258

Cabanis, Georges, 305
Cairns, John, 6, 236, 237, 240
Caledonian Mercury, 20
Calvinism, 32-53
Campbell, Archibald, 3rd Duke of
  Argyll, 12, 14, 15, 16
  his role in SE, 16
Campbell, Archibald (teacher of James
  Monroe), 317
Campbell, Archibald (theologian), 36
Campbell, George, 16, 21, 22, 50, 53,
  280, 301
  on truth in fiction, 293-4
Campbell, John, 2nd Duke of Argyll, 16
Campbell Fraser, Alexander, 341
Cantor, Geoffrey, 115
Carmichael, Gershom, 37, 38, 56, 214,
  215, 228
Carribean, 18
Carolina, North and South, 18
Catholics, toleration of, 15
causal reasoning 121
Chamley, Paul, 185
Charlevoix, Pierre-François de, 83
Cheyne, George, 39, 106
Christianity, natural science and, 104
Christie, John, 94
Cicero, 139, 150
civic virtue, 81
Clarke, John, 139
Clarke, Samuel, 36, 37, 49, 52, 56, 107,
  140, 141, 147, 209

Cleanthes, a protagonist in Hume's
  Dialogues, 39, 46
Coke, Sir Edward, 260
Colden, Cadwallader, 18
Combe, George, 266
common sense philosophy, 6, 127-9,
  341
comparative history, 81
Comte, Auguste, 274, 312
Condillac, Etienne Bonnot de, 23, 298,
  299, 304, 306
Condorcet, Sophie de Grouchy,
  marquise de, 305
conjectural history, 79-80, 263
Cook, George, 54
Cooper, Anthony Ashley (3rd Earl of
  Shaftesbury), 21, 83, 91, 136, 209,
  231, 281
Copland, Patrick, 22
Coppock, J. T., 25
Corss(e), James 96
counter-enlighteners, 310
Cousin, Victor, 298, 299, 302, 311,
  312
Craig, Thomas, 224-6
Cromarty, Earl of, 16
Cudworth, Ralph, 49, 209
Cullen, William, 4, 16, 54, 106, 107
Culloden, 260
Cumberland, Richard, 209
Cuvier, Georges Chrétien Léopold
  Dagobert, Baron, 312

Dalrymple, James, Viscount Stair, 226,
  227-8
Darien, 11
Davie, George E., 114, 339, 348
Declaration of Independence, American,
  316, 317, 318
Degérando, Joseph Marie, Baron, 306
deism, 33
Delaware, 18
Demea, protagonist in Hume's
  Dialogues, 36
demographic pressures, 10
Descarte, René, 37, 38, 117, 119
Dick, Thomas, 56
Diderot, Denys, 299
Ditton, Humphrey, 100
Douglass, William, 18

Drummond, George, Provost of Edinburgh, 100
Dudgeon, William, 35, 55, 56
Dunbar, James, 22, 88, 243, 246, 251
Dundas, Henry, 14, 16

Eberhard, Johann August, 309
Edinburgh, 5, 10, 19, 20, 96, 97, 99, 100, 228, 340
Edinburgh Assembly, 20
Edinburgh Medical Essays, 20
Edinburgh Medical School, 20
Edinburgh New Town, 259
education, motivation for, 11
Edwards, Jonathan, 328, 329
Elphinstone, William, 224
Emerson, Roger, 4, 27, 91, 94, 110, 111, 113
Encyclopaedia Britannica, 53, 87
Encyclopédie, 185
Episcopalians, Scottish, 13, 14, 21, 32
Erskine, Charles, 16
Erskine, John, 231
evangelicals, 14
evil, problem of, 37

Faculty of Advocates, 222
Feder, Johann, 309
Ferguson, Adam, 16, 81, 86, 88, 168–9, 174, 244, 245, 246–7, 250, 251, 252, 259, 263, 300, 301
    on the being and attributes of God, 51
    his concept of politics, 162–3
    on conjectural history, 80
    as historian, 273–5
    on institutional stability, 248
Ferguson, William, 25
Ferrier, James F., 338, 339, 343, 345, 346–7
Finlayson, James, 54
first-person perspective, 64
Fleischacker, Samuel, 6, 334
Fletcher of Saltoun, Andrew, 12, 16, 158, 159, 160, 165, 166
Forbes, Duncan, 104, 174
Fordyce, David, 208
Formey, Jean Henri, 308
Franklin, Benjamin, 177, 318
Frazer, John, 34, 55
Frazer, Sir James, 263

freedom, Reid's concept of, 75
French Revolution, 22
Fry, Michael, 28

Gaelic, 10, 13
Garnett, Thomas, 110
Garrett, Aaron, 3, 91, 92
Garve, Christian, 300, 302, 310
General Assembly of the Kirk, 34, 58
Geoffroy Saint-Hilaire, Etienne, 312
Gerard, Alexander, 50, 51, 280, 301
Gibbon, Edward, 79, 90
Gibson-Wood, Carol, 297
Glanvill, Joseph, 96
Glasgow, 5, 10, 19, 21, 22–4, 96, 99, 100, 233, 343
    its two Enlightenments, 23
    its Physic Garden, 100
Gleig, George, 53
God
    the being and attributes of, 32–54
    his necessity, 58
Gordon's Mill Farming Club, 22
Gorner, Paul, 350
Graham, Gordon, 6, 350
Grand Tour, 18, 290–1, 294–5
Gregory I, James, 96
Gregory of Kinnaird, David, 96
Gregory, James, 22
Gregory, John, 81, 84
Grotius, Hugo, 6, 169, 227, 235
Guerrini, Anita, 112

Haakonssen, Knud, 6, 91, 219, 220, 332
Hales, Stephen, 106
Halket, James, 97
Halley, Edmund, 100, 112
Halyburton, Thomas, 33–5, 40, 42, 55
Hamann, Johann Georg, 299, 310
Hamilton, Alexander, 172, 190
Hamilton, Robert, 22
Hamilton, Sir William, 298, 302, 338, 341
    his personal library, 343
Hamowy, Ronald, 334
Harrington, James, 165
Hay, George, 21
Helvétius, Claude-Adrien, 310
Herbert, Edward, 34
Herder, Johann Gottfried, 310

Hill, George, 24
history, philosophical significance of
    study of, 63
Hobbes, Thomas, 136, 208, 243, 247
Holbach, Paul Henri Thyry, Baron d',
    303, 310
Holland, 17
Home, Henry (Lord Kames), 15, 16, 20,
    49, 50, 58, 81, 87, 93, 104, 208, 214,
    231, 232, 233, 245, 248, 263, 280,
    300, 301
  on human liberty, 49
  on the perfection of human society,
    323
  on racial diversity, 88
Home, John, 16
Hont, Istvan, 183
Hope, Thomas Charles, 109
Houston, Joseph, 57
Houston, R. A., 26
Howe, Daniel Walker, 321, 333
Hume, David, 17, 21, 22, 24, 79, 84, 92,
    104, 107, 127, 159, 160-2, 170, 171,
    206, 215, 231, 247-8, 252, 258, 266,
    280, 300, 308, 318
  on animals, 84
  the attempt to excommunicate him,
    58
  his attitude to religion in the *History
    of England*, 47
  Bain's relation to, 346
  on chastity, 248-9
  his critique of belief in miracles, 42-6
  the difference between his *Treatise*
    and the first *Inquiry*, 125
  his economics, 179-85
  on feeling of freedom, 64
  on history, 265-9
  on impressions and ideas, 66
  on indirect passions, 142
  on memory, 6
  on national character, 88
  on the natural history of religion, 47
  his naturalism, 84
  on nature and artifice, 210-11
  on non-white races, 88
  his philosophical use of history, 63, 67
  his philosophy of common life, 45
  principles of association of ideas, 67
  his reception in France, 303-4

  on religion, 31-59
  his scepticism with regard to reason
    and the senses, 45
  his scientific study of mind, 62-70
  on social contract, 244
  on the standard of taste, 285-90
  his support for the Moderate Party, 48
  on sympathy, 143
  on utility and morality, 141-6
  on women, 85-6
Hutcheson, Francis,, 83, 144, 147, 160,
    206, 207, 209, 214, 220, 231, 261,
    266, 280, 318
  on aesthetic judgment, 281-5
  on animal rights, 84
  on association of ideas, 68, 283-5
  as beneficiary of patronage, 16
  his debt to Locke, 321-3
  his moral algebra, 138
  on moral sense, 136-41, 209, 215
  on natural justice, 209-10
  on perfect and imperfect rights, 322
  prototype of SE, 3
  his 'public sense', 139
  on resistance to government, 321
  as theologian, 38, 56
  on the theological significance of
    beauty, 39
  on three kinds of good, 137
Hutchinson, John, 104
Hutchison, Terence, 201
Hutton, James, 16, 109
  his religious belief, 109

Idéologues, 299, 305-7
ideas
  association of, 67-70
  theory of, 66
Introspection, evidence based on, 64
invisible hand, 326-7
Irvine, William, 106
Irwing, Karl Franz von, 309
Islay, Lord, *see* Campbell, Archibald

Jacobi, Friedrich Heinrich, 299, 310
Jacobites, 13, 21, 272
Jacobitism, 167
James VII, 13, 19, 111
Jefferson, Thomas, 177, 317, 318, 320,
    323, 332, 335

Johnson, David, 29
Jones, William, 100
Jouffroy, Théodore, 301, 311, 313
justice, 144
    its artificiality, 144
    the precision of, 213
    theory of, 205–18
Justinian, 233

Kames, Lord, see Home, Henry
Kant, Immanuel, 55, 118, 299, 307,
    310–11, 313
Kemp Smith, Norman, 119
Kennet, Basil, 230
Kidd, Colin, 275, 276
King (Shepherd), Christine M., 111
King's College, Aberdeen, 19, 61, 99, 100
Kirk, the, 14
Kivy, Peter, 296
Klemme, Heiner, 5
Knight, William, 343
Knox, Robert, 266, 280
Kuehn, Manfred, 309

Lambert, Johann Heinrich, 310
Lafitau, Joseph-François, 80, 81, 83
La Mettrie, Jules Offray de, 310
Latitudinarians, English, 15
Lavoisier, Antoine Laurent, 108, 312
Law, John, 12, 259
Le Clerc, Jean, 34
legitimacy of government, 244
Leibniz, Gottfried Wilhelm, 107, 209
Lenman, Bruce, 27
Lessing, Gotthold, 300, 309
Liddell, Duncan, 99
light, theories of, 106
Linnaeus, Carl, 22
Literary Society of Glasgow, 5, 23
literati, 4
Locke, John, 34, 37, 40, 43, 103, 107,
    117, 127, 136, 243, 244, 281, 299,
    318–19
Logan, John, 88
Lossius, Christian, 309
Lounger, The, influential periodical, 17
Lundberg, David, 329

Macaulay, Catherine, 267
Macfie, A. L., 178

MacIntyre, Alasdair, 218
Mackaile, Matthew, 108
Mackenzie, Sir George, 226, 232
MacLaurin, Colin, 21, 39, 56, 101–2,
    103, 104, 105, 178
    on the theological significance of
    science, 61
Macpherson, James, 266
Machiavelli, 165
    Hume's criticism of, 166
Madison, James, 172, 177, 317, 318, 323
Malebranche, Nicolas, 139
Malherbe, Michel, 6
Mandeville, Bernard, 83, 91, 141, 145,
    169, 198, 209
Marischal, Earl, 16
Marischal College, Aberdeen, 19, 38, 61,
    68, 99, 100, 101
Marshall, John (Chief Justice of
    America), 317
Marshall, John (director of Glasgow
    Physic Garden), 100
Martin, Martin, 98
Maupertuis, Pierre Louis, 308
May, Henry F., 329
McCosh, James, 339, 340, 341
Medical Society (Edinburgh), 20
Meek, R. L., 193
Meiners, Christian, 309
Meinhard, J. N., 300
Melvill, Thomas, 105
Mendelssohn, Moses, 309
Mérian, J. B., 308
Mill, John Stuart, 274, 342
Millar, John, 80, 81, 82, 86, 171, 217,
    233, 245, 248, 249, 250, 251, 252,
    263, 264, 265
Mirabeau, Victor Riqueti, Marquis de,
    190
miracles, 41–6
Mirror, The, influential periodical, 17
Moderate Party of the Kirk, 48
Monboddo, see Burnett, James
Monroe, James, 317
Montesquieu, Charles Louis de
    Secondat de, 79, 81, 83, 170–2, 178,
    191, 232, 261, 267, 299
Montrose, marquis of, 16
Moore, James, 91, 218, 220
Moray, Sir Robert, 96

More, Henry, 209
Murray, Patrick, 97
Musical Society (Edinburgh), 20

natural signs, three kinds of, 129
nature, 126
New England, 18
New Jersey, College of, 329
Newton, Sir Isaac, 17, 100, 101, 105,
    112, 178, 206
  his law of gravity, 67
  his *regulae philosophandi*, 63
Newtonianism, 106-7
Noodt, Gerard, 227
'North Britons', 14, 15
Norton, David Fate, 133, 218, 334

O'Brien, Karen, 276
Oswald, James, 51, 208, 309
Oswald, John, 91
Oz-Salzberger, Fania, 3

Paine, Tom, 262
Paley, William, 51
Park, Mungo, 18
Paterson, William, 12
patronage, 15-17
personal identity, 124
Perth, 24
Philadelphia, College of, 317, 328
Phillipson, Nicholas, 94, 110, 278
Philo, a protagonist in Hume's
    Dialogues, 46
Philosophical Society of Edinburgh, 20
philosophy
  relation between psychology and,
    344
  social role of, 348
Physiocrats, 6
Pinkerton, John, 266, 280
Pitcairne, Archibald, 35, 97, 106
Pittock, Murray, 3
Platner, Ernst, 309
Plato, 259
Playfair, John, 105, 108
Pocock, J. G. A., 158, 159
Port-Royal *Logic*, 40, 43
Prévost, Pierre, 305, 306
primary qualities, 120
Princeton University, 24, 317, 329

Pringle-Pattison, Andrew Seth, 339, 340,
    341
  on the Scottish and German answers
    to Hume, 347-9
professorial chairs 19
Prynne, William, 260
Pufendorf, Samuel, 6, 83, 84, 169, 208,
    214, 227, 228, 235

Quesnay, François, 192

racial theory, 87, 92
Raleigh, Sir Walter, 261
Ramsay, Allan (father), 260
Ramsay, Allan (son), 16, 280
Ramsay, Andrew Michael, 41
Rankenian Club, 21
reason and passion, combat between, 143
reflection, power of, 65
regenting, 19
Reid, Thomas, 21, 22, 50, 56, 85, 104,
    106, 107, 118, 208, 214, 220, 247,
    280, 306, 308, 318, 329
  on active power , 75-6, 127-9
  his common sense philosophy, 127
  differences between Hume and, 132,
    330-1, 345
  on distinction between matter and
    mind, 71
  on duty, 150-2
  on faculties of mind, 74
  on habits, 74
  on what mind is, 70
  his naturalism different from Hume's,
    131
  on Newton's *regulae*, 63
  on perceptual acts, 73
  on philosophical significance of
    language, 71
  on pneumatology, 61
  on power, 74-5
  on principles of common sense, 128
  his reception in France, 304
  on relative knowledge, 70
  on religious belief, 331
  on signs of design, 51
  on suggestion, 129
Reidinger, C., 301
Republic of Letters, 5, 17, 24
revelation, rational support for, 40

rhetoric, 291, 301
Robertson, Donald, 317
Robertson, John
  his definition of SE, 3, 7, 94
Robertson, Principal William, 15, 16, 81,
    88, 171, 249, 258, 261, 263, 265,
    269-73
  on conjectural history, 80
  his *History of Scotland*, 270-2
  on Scottish Reformation, 271
Robinson, Bryan, 106
Robison, John, 100, 105
Rotwein, E., 180
Rousseau, Jean Jacques, 23, 79, 80, 82,
    83, 84, 87, 172, 243, 261, 275, 299
Roxburghe, Duke of, 16
Royal Bank of Scotland, 20
Royal College of Physicians of
  Edinburgh, 97, 111
Royal Infirmary, 20
Royal Society of Edinburgh, 20, 102,
  107, 109
Royal Society of London, 48, 96, 101, 103
  its influence on theology, 36
Royer-Collard, Pierre Paul, 298, 311, 313
Rush, Benjamin, 317, 328, 329

Say, J. B., 186
scepticism, 117
  four kinds of, 117-18
  Humean, 118
  nature's cure for, 127-9
Schulthess, Daniel, 134
Schumpeter, J. A., 191, 193
Scotland
  geography of 9
  population of 10
Scots Law, history of, 223-6
'Scottish Enlightenment', coinage of the
  phrase, 3
Scott, Sir Walter, 261, 266
Scott, William Robert, 3, 7
secondary qualities, 120, 137
Select Society, 5
sensus divinitatis, 33
sentimentalism, 152
Shaftesbury, *see* Cooper, Anthony
  Ashley
Shepherd, Christine M. *see* King,
  Christine M.

Sher, Richard B., 4, 7, 90, 94
Sibbald, Sir Robert, 11, 12, 95, 97-8
Simon, Richard, 17
Simson, Robert, 100, 105
Simson, John, Glasgow Professor of
  Divinity, 14, 34, 36, 56
Sinclair, George, 95-7, 100
Sinclair, Robert, 100
Skene, David, 22
Skene, Sir John, 226
Skinner, Andrew S., 3, 6
slavery, 181, 264
Sloan, Douglas, 329, 334
Small, William, 317
Smart, Alastair, 29
Smellie, William, 81, 87, 108
Smith, Adam, 5, 16, 54, 79, 82, 86, 92,
    170, 206, 233, 245, 249, 280, 300,
    318
  on artificiality of morality, 211-13
  his concept of sympathy, 147-50
  his economics, 191-200
  his influence on Madison, 324-8
  his lectures on jurisprudence, 234
  his moral theory, 253-4
  on multiplicity of religious sects, 325
  his reception in Europe, 302
  on rights, 215-16
  his stadial theory, 217, 262
Smith, William, 317, 328
Smout, T. C., 25
social change, 249-53
social contract, 243-5
  Hume on, 244
society, stadial theory of, 82
Spinoza, Benedictus, 41
St Andrews, 19, 24, 33, 99, 100, 341
Stair, Viscount, *see* Dalrymple, James
Stanhope Smith, Samuel, 329, 331
state of nature, 244
Stein, Peter, 235
Steuart, Sir James, 24, 191
  his economic thought, 185-91
  his stadial theory, 185
Stewart, Dugald, 22, 51, 52, 206, 214,
    263, 270, 285, 306, 341
  on conjectural history, 79
  on memory and attention, 72-4
Stewart, John, 113
Stewart, M. A., 4, 76

Stewart, Matthew, 100, 105
Stiles, Ezra, 328
Stillingfleet, Edward, 40
Stimson, Shannon, 330
Stirling, James, 103, 105
Strathclyde, University of, 24, 110
Stuart, Gilbert, 80, 245, 251, 266, 273
Sulzer, Johann Georg, 309
Supreme Court, 317
Sutherland, James, 97
sympathy
  Hume on, 143, 145
  Smith on, 147–50
syntax, philosophical significance of, 71

Tableau économique, 192
Tacitus, 80, 81, 265
Taine, Hippolyte, 298, 312
teleological explanation, 207
testimony, 42–4, 50, 121
Tetens, Johann Nicolaus, 310
third-person perspective, 64
Thompson, James, 317
Thurot, François, 306
Tiedemann, Dietrich, 309
Toland, John, 21
Toulmin, George Hoggart, 108
Townshend, Charles, 192
translations of Scottish writings,
  300–3
Traill, William, 100
Trembley, Abraham, 108
Trevor-Roper, Hugh (Lord Dacre), his
  definition of SE, 3, 7, 94
Tucker, Josiah, 184
Turco, Luigi, 3
Turgot, Anne-Robert-Jacques, 172, 192,
  261, 262
Turnbull, George, 21, 35, 38, 40, 55, 61,
  131, 208, 280
  on association of ideas, 68–9
  his Principles of Moral and Christian
    Philosophy, 76
  on the scientific study of the human
    mind, 62, 107
  his Treatise on Ancient Painting,
    290–1
  on truth in art, 291–2
Tweeddale, Marquis of, 16

uniformity amidst variety, 282
Union with England, 13, 235, 260

Veitch, John, 343
Vico, Giambattista, 259
Viner, Jacob, 200
virtue, 205
Vitriarius, Ph. R., 227
Voltaire, Jean François Marie Arouet de ,
  23, 299

Wallace, George, his anti-slavery stance,
  88
Wallace, Robert, 35
Walpole, Robert, 15
Watson, Robert, 24
Watt, James, 4, 259
Wealth of Nations, 5, 324–7
Westminster Confession, 32
Whatley, Christopher A., 26
Whichcote, Benjamin, 209
Whig history, 258
Whytt, Robert, 106
Wieacker, Franz, 234
Wilkie, William, 16
will, 38, 67, 75
Wills, Gary, 318–20
William and Mary, 13
William and Mary College, 317
Wilson, Alexander, 16, 105
Wilson, James, 317, 330
Wilson, Patrick, 106
Winch, Donald, 178
Wise Club, 5, 22
Wishart the elder, William, 35
Wishart the younger, William, 35
Withers, Charles W. J., 111
Witherspoon, John, 24, 52, 172, 317,
  318, 329
Wodrow, Robert, 98
Wolff, Christian, 209, 235, 299, 308
Wollaston, William, 49, 140, 209,
  335
Wood, Paul, 4, 7, 29, 90, 111

Yale University, 328
Young, Jeffrey, 197

Zeiler, Franz von, 234